PHENOMENOLOGY AND
DECONSTRUCTION

Phenomenology and Deconstruction

VOLUME THREE · *Breakdown in Communication*

Robert Denoon Cumming

CHICAGO & LONDON · *The University of Chicago Press*

ROBERT DENOON CUMMING is the Frederick J. Woodbridge Professor emeritus of philosophy at Columbia University. He is the author of *Human Nature and History, Starting Point: An Introduction to the Dialectic of Existence,* and *Phenomenology and Deconstruction,* volumes 1 and 2, all published by the University of Chicago Press.

The University of Chicago Press, Chicago 60637
The University of Chicago Press, Ltd., London

© 2001 by The University of Chicago
All rights reserved. Published 2001
Printed in the United States of America
10 09 08 07 06 05 04 03 02 01   5 4 3 2 1

ISBN (cloth): 0-226-12370-7
ISBN (paper): 0-226-12371-5

Library of Congress Cataloging-in-Publication Data
(Revised for vol. 2)

Cumming, Robert Denoon, 1916–
    Phenomenology and deconstruction.

    Includes bibliographical references and index.
    Contents: v. 1. The dream is over—v. 2. Method and imagination.
    1. Phenomenology—History.   I. Title.
B829.2.C85   1991   142'.7'.09   91-12696
ISBN 0-226-12366-9 (v. 1)
ISBN 0-226-12367-7 (v. 1, pbk)

♾ The paper used in this publication meets the minimum requirements of the American National Standard for Information Sciences—Permanence of Paper for Printed Library Materials, ANSI Z39.48-1992.

FOR ANN

Amicus Plato, magis amica veritas.

CONTENTS

INTRODUCTION: 1. The Two Traditions   3
DIFFICULTIES IN   2. Disciples   11
COMMUNICATION   3. Fellow Workers   17
                    4. The Work of the Other   27

PROCEDURES   5. The Shift in Subject   43
                    6. The Shift in Method   54
                    7. The Retrieval   64
                    8. The Translation   70

DECONSTRUCTION   9. Destruktion   87
                    10. The Edge   93
                    11. The Boundary   100

THE SIGN   12. The Ambiguity   109
                    13. The Indicative Sign   120
                    14. The Indicator   128

RELATIONAL   15. The Context   137
ANALYSIS   16. Der Weg Der Abhebung   148
                    17. Umgang   154
                    18. Ausgang   164

BEING-IN   19. Concept Construction   175
                    20. Aufgehen In   189
                    21. Psychologism   196
                    22. The Theory of Knowledge   204

COMMUNICATION

23. *Language   217*
24. *The Monologue   225*
25. *The Public Reckoning   234*

Conclusion: The End of Philosophy   247
Notes   259
Works Cited   287
Index   295

Citations from *Ideas I* are to section numbers, since there are two English translations. Citations from *Being and Time* are to the German pagination, which is found in the margin of the two English translations. The italics throughout are retained from the original texts except when I indicate they are mine.

Translations from the French, German, and Greek are usually my own.

INTRODUCTION · # DIFFICULTIES IN COMMUNICATION

Husserl and Heidegger (1921)

The Two Traditions

*The Anglo-American journals . . . were
completely silent.*—Husserl

Introductions

"Ponderous," "involved," "diffuse," "opaque"
—these are epithets Edmund Husserl culled
from a review of his *Logical Investigations,*
while complaining that it was the only review
that had covered both of its two volumes.
Even "professional philosophers," he comments, had appraised the work as "repulsive."
He sought some consolation in dismissing
them as "complacent."[1]

This repulsive work was to become one
of the most propulsive works in twentieth-
century philosophy. It ushered in the century;
the first volume was published in 1900 and
the second in 1901. In the jargon of historians, it "founded" phenomenology, which
eventually came to dominate Continental
philosophy longer than any other philosophical movement in the past century. Thus a
French philosopher can announce, more or
less as a matter of course, "Phenomenology
takes on, in our century, the role of philosophy itself."[2]

When I dealt, in my first volume on the
history of phenomenology, with Sartre's conversion to phenomenology or, in my second
volume, with his relation to Husserl, I was
dealing with phenomenology when it was on
its way to dominance. I was skipping over the
earlier difficulties which Husserl himself had
encountered, which are illustrated by the epithets he culled. In this chapter I intend to recognize certain of these difficulties before I go

on in the second chapter to link my interpretation of phenomenology in this third volume, in which I deal with Husserl and Heidegger's relation to him, to my interpretation in the preceding volumes.

The epithets were culled by Husserl in an introduction to the second edition (1913) of the *Logical Investigations*. This introduction he did not publish. Husserl had published an introduction to the first volume of the *Logical Investigations*—itself a prolegomena—and an introduction to the second volume. To the foreword for the first edition, he added in 1913 a second foreword for the second edition. In this second foreword he presented the *Logical Investigations* as an attempt to "introduce the reader to the nature of genuinely phenomenological . . . work."[3]

He also presented *Ideas I* (1913), with the subtitle *A General Introduction to a Pure Phenomenology*, but he was unable to follow it up with *Ideas II*, as he had planned. His next publication was the *Cartesian Meditations: An Introduction to Phenomenology*. These were lectures at the Sorbonne that were published in a French translation (1933), and Husserl eventually gave up his attempt to rework the lectures for publication in German. He began *The Crisis of European Sciences*, which was once again called *An Introduction to Phenomenological Philosophy*. He was unable to finish it. I would accordingly take introductions as almost the characteristic genre of Husserl's philosophy. This can be taken in conjunction with what we shall see he describes as his "inability to finish" and his remaining a "miserable beginner."

In order to begin explaining this "inability to finish," I would go back to the beginning of this history of multiplying introductions. The first volume of the *Logical Investigations* was introductory in that it was composed of *Prolegomena*. Husserl began the preface to this volume by admitting that he had run into difficulties: "The *Logical Investigations*, whose publication begins with these *Prolegomena*, have arisen out of unavoidable problems which have continually hindered and finally interrupted [*unterbrochen*] the progress of my efforts, over many years, at achieving a philosophical clarification of pure mathematics." Here he had encountered "remarkable difficulties."[4] But he never returned to pure mathematics. Phenomenology thus began with Husserl as an interruption—an interruption which was never finished. He was detained by difficulties he encountered in philosophy itself.

Few philosophers have been as aware as Husserl of encountering difficulties that interrupted his progress. The accumulation of "difficulties" he sometimes segregated and provided with the heading *Schwierigkeiten*, so that they too, like his introductions, might be said almost to have become a characteristic philosophical genre for him.

Any philosophy worth understanding is difficult to understand, and to understand it is to understand why it has to be difficult. In Husserl's case I shall eventually show why the difficulties he encountered were of a sort that he tried to cope with by writing introduction after introduction.

Communication

My present concern, however, is still with my own approach. To explain it, I would latch onto a distinction that Husserl draws with respect to difficulties. Having completed his *Prolegomena*, he begins the second volume of the *Logical Investigations* with an introduction that includes a section headed "The Difficulties of Pure Phenomenological Analysis." After indicating the "extraordinary difficulties" of this analysis itself, he distinguishes as a "further difficulty" that of *communicating its results to others.*[5] Thus, on the one hand, there are the difficulties the philosopher himself encounters in working out his philosophy; on the other hand, there are the difficulties he encounters in getting others to understand it. While I shall later try to sketch in the difficulties of phenomenological analysis itself, I do not propose to offer still another introduction to it. A difference between what Husserl repeatedly attempted in the way of introductions and what I am attempting is that the "further difficulty" in communication remained in his appraisal merely marginal, but it is the difficulty which I, in contrast, would bring to the fore. I have accordingly begun my introduction with the epithets he culls from reviews—as evidence of this difficulty.

I am not concerned yet to explain why Husserl regards this difficulty in communication as merely marginal. I am concerned now only to sample further obvious evidence of this difficulty.

Even in Germany, as late as 1909–10, when Heidegger began his academic studies at Freiburg University, the *Logical Investigations* were, he later recalled, "obviously of little interest to the students," for the library copy he had out "could easily be renewed again and again."[6]

In Husserl's unpublished introduction to the second edition, the difficulty in securing understanding is dramatized by his finding that "misinterpretations" were as pervasive in the favorable as in the unfavorable reviews.[7] Much of the later history of phenomenology would be regarded by Husserl as a misunderstanding of phenomenology, even by those who favored it—most notoriously Heidegger.

I pause in my account of Husserl's difficulty in securing understanding in Germany in order to take a larger view. Some English-speaking philosophers are already jittery over the announcement I have cited that "phenomenology takes, in our century, the role of philosophy itself." They are shrugging the statement off as parochially Continental and thus a rank failure to understand what has been going on in this century ever since philosophy got on the right track in England. After all, we all know that it is analytic philosophy which has taken on the role of philosophy itself.

Having allowed them their shrug, I would continue to envisage the situation from Husserl's own perspective at the time. One of his comments on the reception of the *Logical Investigations* is that "The Anglo-American journals were completely silent."[8] What also can hardly be overlooked is how long it took for him to secure much understanding in Anglo-America. Today, it is fairly fashionable to proclaim, "There are just philosophical problems: not Anglo-American problems, on the one hand, and Continental problems on the other."[9] These are admirable sentiments, though they may betray some flagging in our native philosophical vigor. Richard Rorty likewise argues that "the difference" between Anglo-American "analytic" philosophy and Continental philosophy "is relatively unimportant."[10]

I am skeptical. But in any case the historian should not simply lean on a recent outcome; he should shoulder responsibility for bringing back to our attention how things were when they were happening—*wie es wirklich war*. The difference did for a long time seem insurmountable. This breakdown in communication between "the two traditions" (as they have often been called) is all the more striking because it took place at the time phenomenology was emerging, before its eventual triumph, not only on the continent of Europe but also over most of the world—aside from Anglo-America.

Further historical perspective may be helpful. Before World War I, a German pilgrimage still launched an American graduate student in philosophy—but Husserl was not on the route. When a future Harvard professor, William Ernest Hocking, was in Germany on a Harvard traveling fellowship, he lingered in Göttingen to study with Husserl, but he received a letter of stern warning from the chairman of the Harvard department that it "did not grant fellowships in order that students might seclude themselves in provincial universities."[11] He moved on obediently to Berlin. If he had stayed on at Göttingen under Husserl's tutelage, some understanding of phenomenology might have been propagated at Harvard, though of course if he had stayed on, Harvard would not have welcomed him back to a teaching position.

Neither Harvard nor any other American university would welcome back a later recipient of Harvard's postdoctorate traveling fellowship, Dorian Cairns. Presumably his mistake was seeking out Husserl's tutelage. Later I shall consider Cairns's difficulties in getting a job.

Common Sense

Before I continue with Husserl, let me anticipate the similar difficulty in securing understanding experienced by his successor, Heidegger. (I shall soon be more concerned with Heidegger's case than with Husserl's, for how Heidegger is to be understood is much more controversial.) Heidegger emphasizes the philosophical character of the difficulty by insisting that his is "not the lament of someone who is misunderstood, but rather indicates the insurmountable difficulty of understanding." Even when he might have been buoyed by the fame that the publication of *Being and Time* was bringing him, he cited Rilke: "Fame is ultimately only the sum of the misunderstandings which cluster around a new name."[12]

For the present, I would get by with a not-too-complicated illustration of his difficulty. From 1918 to 1969 Heidegger carried on a warm correspondence with Elisabeth Blochmann—107 letters. From the beginning, he reported rather regularly on his work, sent her publications, and on occasion a typescript of something not yet published.

After all those years, during which he apparently counted on her understanding, she wrote her last letter in 1969, in which she acknowledged receipt of his last lecture course and comments:

> I admit I am rather perplexed regarding the *Question of Thinking*. I cannot follow it step by step. It is altogether too alien to my simple *common sense*. That I must tell you at once, dear Martin, even if it disillusions you, for it involves my reluctance [*Scheu*] regarding the prospect of further personal discussions.... My way of seeing things in life . . . is so remote from your philosophical vision.[13]

We do not know how disillusioned Heidegger was by this letter, for she never mailed it, but sent instead "a shortened version," which has apparently not survived. There she was unlikely to have been so frank, since she had never been before.

I have singled out an unmailed letter as an illustration of a breakdown in communication. Blochmann was not a philosopher. But in Volume 4 we shall find Karl Jaspers putting his unmailed letters to Heidegger in the same file as the letters he did mail, and we shall have to determine their bearing on the problem of his communicating with Heidegger.

What justifies citing her letter now is Blochmann's explanation that his lecture course was "altogether too alien to my simple *common sense*." She has resorted to English. Indeed her "common sense" may not have been all that "simple," for she further explains how "my way of seeing things in life" has been "conditioned . . . strongly by Oxford." Thus her inability to understand Heidegger may have become more insurmountable due to her exposure to "Oxford philosophy"—as "analytic philosophy" was becoming labeled in the thirties. Perhaps I should have explained that Blochmann had lost her job in Germany in 1933 because she was half-Jewish and that she had relocated herself at Oxford with some assistance from the then Nazi rector of Freiburg University, Heidegger. I don't know if he anticipated how disastrously Oxford might influence her "way of seeing things."

Translation

I return to Husserl in order to present the most obvious evidence of the actual difficulty his phenomenology encountered in securing an understanding in Anglo-America: the length of time it took for his *Logical Investigations* to be translated into English. (This historical fact should of course be taken in conjunction with the declining proficiency in German of American philosophers after World War I.) Consider what happened to a translator of the *Logical Investigations*. Or perhaps I should identify Walter Pitkin instead as a would-be translator, for when he failed to make an arrangement for publishing his translation of the *Logical Investigations,* he went looking for some other German philosopher to translate. Such had been the tyranny of German philosophy over America that he apparently felt it was necessary to become a translator in order to launch his own career in America. But it was too late in history to make such a deal, and he could only redeem himself when, as a philosophy instructor at Columbia, he wrote a best-seller, *Life Begins at Forty* (1932). By forty, he had put Germany as well as Husserl behind him.

In his autobiography Pitkin tells the story of his inability to publish his translation in America. He reports how William James, "much to Husserl's lasting grief, had advised one of the great Eastern publishing houses against accepting [the] . . . translation of the *Logical Investigations* on the grounds that 'Nobody in America would be interested in a new and strange German work on logic.'"[14] If the report is a concoction, as has been suggested, perhaps it ought to be true. At any rate, now that the divergence between the two traditions was apparent, what was out of date was what Pitkin reports was Husserl's "lasting grief," for his expectation belonged to a bygone age. In particular the work of Husserl's senior colleague, Carl Stumpf, to whom the *Investigations* were dedicated, had received the attention of William James. The friendly relation and intellectual affinity between Stumpf and James illustrate how close American and German philosophy were before World War I and Husserl.[15]

The newness and strangeness of that "work on logic" is evident in the fact that the *Investigations* had to wait so long for an English translation to be published—nearly seventy years. The translator himself, J. N. Findlay, was not entirely in tune with philosophy in England, for by birth he was a "colonial"—as they then could be called.

It is true that an English translation of Husserl's *Ideas I* was published in 1931 by another "colonial," W. R. Boyce Gibson, but this is questionable evidence, for the translation demonstrated how little the translator understood. Husserl himself came to recognize that the translation, "instead of being a bridge to an understanding of my philosophy will prove to be a wall against such understanding."[16]

That translation was the product of Boyce Gibson's stay in Freiburg in 1928. During the young man's first visit, Husserl obviously wanted to establish some rapport. He recalled how well received he had been when he gave four lectures in London in 1926. But it should be pointed out that the reason for inviting him to London seems to have been less any general interest in the little that was known about his philosophy than concern to put the Great War behind them on the part of an older generation who still remembered what the two countries had earlier shared philosophically. His lectures instead demonstrated that he and his hosts no longer shared what some of them may have assumed they would find they still shared. There is no evidence that the lectures had any impact at all on his English audience.[17]

In an entry in his Freiburg diary, Boyce Gibson reports Husserl's mentioning a student of his, Christopher Verney Salmon, "a most gifted Englishman," who had "written a thesis on Hume as the founder of phenomenology, or some such title." This thesis was about to be published in German, and Husserl thought that "it should introduce Phenomenology in a very pleasant suggestive way to English readers."[18] There is no evidence that it ever performed this function, and it was never translated into English.

Salmon also was the translator of the only work of Husserl's besides *Ideas I* to be published in English before the late fifties—the article on phenomenology for the *Encyclopaedia Britannica*.[19] The excessive length of what Husserl himself had written was an extenuating circumstance, but the butchery of Salmon's translation makes it clear that he, like Boyce Gibson, did not understand Husserl. The article was another "wall."

Refugees

When Nazism drove Jewish philosophers from the Continent to England and America, their arrival lent impetus to new developments in philosophy. But the phenomenologists did not make it big, unlike several representatives of other philosophical movements—notably the logical positivists.

Husserl did get an invitation from the University of Southern California. The inviting letter extolled "the philosophical and climatic merits" of the locale,[20] but it apparently left Husserl cold. One reason he held back was his inability to negotiate a position as his assistant for Dorian Cairns, whom he regarded as his most competent American expositor. Husserl had had assistants in Germany, and he must have thought Cairns would be indispensable to him in presenting his philosophy to an American audience.

Probably he also wanted to help Cairns get a job. I have mentioned that Cairns, like Hocking, had gone to Germany on a Harvard traveling fellowship. But quite aside from the difficulty of securing employment during the Depression, his single-minded dedication to Husserl did not advance his career. Eventually he did secure a position at Rockford College, which he held until 1950. Then he made it to the New School for Social Research, where the standards of philosophical competence were, at that time, more Continental than American. There he authored the first adequate translation of Husserl into English.

To make a story which could be longer short, although refugees from Europe were to be found in all of the prestigious American universities, none of them were phenomenologists. And I might well not be telling this story at all if phenomenology had not triumphed in Europe after World War II. Delay in recognizing a significant undertaking in any field (in art or literature as well as philosophy) can be a tantalizing time-warp to the historian.[21] Of course, observing such delays in the history of philosophy is unlikely to shake any philosopher's complacency. Philosophers are usually confident that they know where it's at when they take as consequential what prevails in philosophy at some present moment. Only a generation or two later does it sometimes seem that prevalence was not the final evidence.

TWO

Disciples

*I become depressed by the fact that my better
students, instead of finishing what I have started
. . . time and time again prefer to go their own
way.—Husserl*

Access

The influence of refugee phenomenologists
who arrived in the United States and England,
as I have explained, was not widespread in
the thirties and the forties. Phenomenology
first gained wider recognition in versions
propounded by French disciples of Husserl
and Heidegger. A long time passed before
the *Logical Investigations,* the work with
which Husserl "founded" phenomenology,
was translated into English, but certain French
phenomenological writings did not have to
wait so long. Although the *Logical Investigations* (1900–1901) had to wait until 1970,
Jean-Paul Sartre's *Being and Nothingness*
(1943) was translated in 1956, and Merleau-
Ponty's *Phenomenology of Perception* (1945)
was translated in 1962.

Chronology in the history of philosophy,
as elsewhere in history, is not entirely arbitrary, and the chronology of these translations suggests a rough *ordo cognoscendi* in
the Anglo-American understanding of phenomenology. Access routes to understanding
are a feature not unique to the history of philosophy; they are so inescapably a feature of
human experience that novelists are often at
pains to devise them, as I pointed out in my
first volume. Thus Henry James confesses
that he is "addicted to seeing through." He
repudiates "the mere muffled majesty of . . .
'authorship'" in favor of a "preference for
dealing with my subject matter, for 'seeing my

story,' through the opportunity and sensibility of . . . some person who contributes . . . a certain amount of criticism and interpretation of it." We are thus provided with this "person's access to it."[1]

In the second volume I considered *L'imaginaire* as the phenomenological work Sartre wrote as a self-styled "disciple" of Husserl. But Sartre did not claim that his access to Husserl was direct—at least not initially. He admitted, "I came to Husserl *via* Lévinas.[2] The dissertation Lévinas had written on Husserl was the only exposition that Sartre could lay his hands on when he first heard of phenomenology. In this dissertation Lévinas himself was convinced as an expositor that "the influence of a thought on important disciples permits without doubt . . . a more accurate assessment than would the laborious study of a conscientious commentator." Accordingly, instead of offering laborious commentary, Lévinas turns "in particular to Martin Heidegger, whose influence on the dissertation will often be recognizable."[3]

However, in the same year (1933) that Sartre was reading Lévinas, Husserl replied to an American, E. Parl Welch, who had written him reporting that he was a "thoroughgoing convert to your movement." In his reply Husserl is pleased that his "efforts in philosophy arouse interest even in America." But he warns that there is "no alternative to studying my own . . . very difficult writings."[4] It will become clear later, when I refer to a lecture Husserl had given in 1931, that Husserl may be warning Welch against relying on Heidegger in particular. But Husserl's "no alternative" would also eliminate other ostensible disciples, such as Sartre and Lévinas.

Prevailing Trends

Husserl's warning poses a problem for us. I have spoken of an *ordo cognoscendi*, the sequence in which phenomenology first came to be understood—to a considerable extent in terms of Sartre's and Merleau-Ponty's versions. Even if this understanding later came to be dismissed as a misunderstanding of Husserl, I shall eventually claim there are certain methodological issues posed by Sartre's and Merleau-Ponty's versions that still deserve attention. But the present problem is that Husserl's "no alternative" is in effect the denial of the feasibility of the access routes on which I have approached him in previous volumes. The philosophical justification for his denial is that he regards the evidence for his phenomenology as immediately accessible. This justification I shall consider later. But I am anticipating now that it is the criterion of immediate accessibility which renders marginal the difficulties of communication which I propose to bring to the fore.

This immediate accessibility of the evidence enables Husserl to "push aside" the history of philosophy in favor of "starting some place of my own."[5] Yet consider the kind of history Husserl himself does envisage in the *Introduction* (1913):

> A preface or an introductory chapter [to the *Logical Investigations*] ought to have prepared the reader historically . . . and ought to have warned him of all of the misinterpretations which were prompted by the prevailing trends of thought. In this way the understanding of the uniqueness [*Eigentümlichkeit*] of the thoughts communicated and, hence, of their proper effect [*Wirkung*] would surely have been promoted.[6]

The historian of philosophy may well be concerned to do justice to the "uniqueness" of some philosopher's "thoughts" but not usually in the strong sense Husserl would have his emerge as opposed to "the prevailing trends," which are to be taken into account simply as prompting the "misinterpretations" which had in effect deprived his "thoughts" of their "uniqueness."

Husserl never wrote this historical introduction and did not even publish the *Introduction* with this statement regarding a historical introduction. If I have nonetheless cited it, it is to suggest that when his "thoughts" did become themselves "prevailing trends" in Sartre, Merleau-Ponty, and others, he might well have regarded these as improper effects.

Your Fate

These "prevailing trends" I have dealt with in my two preceding volumes. I am not proposing now any final adjudication as between "prevailing trends" and the "uniqueness" of a philosopher's "thoughts." My continuing focus on Husserl's relation to other philosophers is not warranted solely by my bringing the problem of communication to the fore, or by the broader recognition that the historian of philosophy cannot avoid the relations between philosophers. I would press for a more concrete consideration. No one begins thinking philosophically entirely on his own; he is subject in some measure to influences bequeathed by preceding philosophies and so is entering into relations of some sort with other philosophies, however informally, and however rudimentary his own philosophy may be. If relations are this inescapable, it seems worthwhile to examine instances when the relations between philosophies are not rudimentary but fully articulated.

This claim of mine can be decorated with a Latin tag: *Tua res agitur*— "Your own fate is at stake here."[7] This tag I borrow from Husserl. He is making the claim that he is philosophizing on your behalf. (How this claim is to be reconciled with starting out on one's own I shall deal with later.) The quite different claim I am making is that your fate is less likely to be at stake in any single philosophy, as Husserl proposed it was in his, than in the relations between philosophies.

My claim might seem even more plausible if it had been couched in the broader terms of intellectual influences. But intellectual influences are often almost unmanageable. The advantage of philosophies is that their succession is not just a flow of influences. Any influence on a succeeding philosophy is caught up in the formulation of that philosophy and, in becoming subject to its sway, is no longer impetuously an influence but can be tracked down in terms of the structure of that philosophy. It does not just slip out of the control of one philosophy and then dangle loosely between it and another philosophy.

Of course a philosophy cannot, as a matter of history, exercise final control over what its own influence will become. It is an illusion of Husserl's that he might have written a history which would have helped his philosophy outmaneuver the "misinterpretations" that he felt had plagued it. What I would emphasize now is that I have selected the phenomenological movement for attention not simply because it was to become dominant on the Continent, but because it poses in a remarkable fashion the problems of the relation between two philosophies. Many, perhaps most, philosophical movements are identifiable with their founders—Platonism, Aristotelianism, Thomism, Kantianism, Hegelianism, and so forth. What is remarkable about the phenomenological movement is the extent to which it became enmeshed in the relation between Husserl and a second philosopher. In the instance of rationalism one would want to take Spinoza as well as Descartes into account; in the instance of empiricism, Hume as well as Locke; but those instances lack the philosophical intimacy which initially held between Husserl and Heidegger. To deal with how pragmatism got under way is to deal with the relations between Peirce, James, and Dewey, but here again there is not the same philosophical intimacy as that which held initially between Husserl and Heidegger, to whom Husserl used to say, "You and I are phenomenology."[8]

The Miserable Beginner

What must be added now is an explanation as to why a philosopher who was committed to "starting out some place on my own" was also concerned to recruit disciples. In a letter Husserl wrote in 1904, from which I have already quoted, he lamented, "How I would like to live on the heights, for this is what all my thinking craves for. But shall I ever work my

way upwards, if only for a little, so that I can gain something of a free dis-
tant view? I am now forty-five years old, and I am still a miserable beginner."[9] That period of struggle culminated in *Ideas I* (1913).

Then the war came and was distracting. In a 1915 letter Husserl
waxed eloquent on the "magnificent stream of national will [which] floods
through everyone of us," on the "marvelous heroism" of the German sol-
diers, who "rush on with ringing song," on how they "have gone out to
fight this war . . . as a truly sacred war, and to offer themselves with full
heart as a sacrifice for the fatherland."[10] His younger son died at the head
of his column at Verdun; his older son was wounded twice.

Later Husserl admitted that he even "lost track of some of what was
already started in *Ideas I*," and he attributed "this retrogression to the effect of the war on him, or rather the effect of Germany's defeat," so that
"he was able . . . to work only on isolated problems, not on the larger aspects of phenomenology."[11]

When he did manage to work on some scale, he still had to concede, in
a letter written in 1922, "I could almost curse my inability to finish, and so
belatedly. Only now and only partially am I able to rework the universal
systematic thoughts which my detailed investigations require."[12]

The London lectures that same year provided an opportunity for
scope, as well as for seeking a wider audience. On returning to Germany,
he tried to expand these lectures into a general introduction to phenomenology, which he gave in the form of lectures in Freiburg in 1923–24. He
was enjoying a rebirth of confidence. But he put further revisions to one
side when he received an invitation to lecture at the Sorbonne in 1929, and
went to work on the *Cartesian Meditations*. After his return from Paris, he
undertook to recast these lectures in an expanded and more systematic
form for the German version. In a letter to Ingarden in 1930 he explains
that he does not want to "postpone the German version of the *Cartesian
Meditations*. For it will be the major work of my life. . . . At least for *me* [it
will be] a conclusion and ultimate clarity, which I can answer for and with
which I can die in peace."[13] Though he scheduled this work for publication, he abandoned it too, as I noted earlier. Apparently his revisions were
not yielding a conclusion and ultimate clarity.

Prompted by invitations to lecture in Vienna and Prague in 1935,
Husserl embarked on *The Crisis of European Sciences*. This last undertaking, I have noted, was also left unfinished when Husserl died in 1938.

Time had run out for Husserl even before his death. This German,
whose patriotism may have sounded invincible to us, was still a Jew, even
though thoroughly assimilated, having been baptized a Lutheran and
married as a Lutheran. I have already mentioned Emmanuel Lévinas, a
Baltic Jew living in France. He recalls how Husserl's wife always referred

to a Jew in the third person. On one occasion she had been to Strasbourg on a shopping expedition and was enthusiastic about a store where she had made an important purchase. "The people there," she reported, "though Jews, are very trustworthy [*zuverlässig*]." Lévinas was visibly upset. Husserl soothed, "Let it pass, Monsieur Lévinas, I myself come from a family which owned a business, and . . ." [14] He broke off the sentence. Apparently he could not think of anything more that could be said.

Finishing

During the last decade of his life Husserl began to resign himself to not being able to finish what he had started, but he still hoped his disciples would. When Boyce Gibson began in 1928 his English translation of *Ideas I,* Husserl undertook some revisions, which were not completed or incorporated, but he did add a preface in which he characterized himself as a "beginner," as he had a quarter of a century before, although he was more specific as to what he had accomplished:

> The encompassing horizon for the work of a phenomenological philosophy has unfolded according to what may be called its main geographical structures, and the essential layers of the problems and the methods of approach fitted to them have been clarified. The author sees spread out ahead of him the open space of a true philosophy in its infinity, the Promised Land, which he himself will not live to see brought into cultivation. . . . The author would hope that those who come after will take over and carry steadily further what he has begun. [15]

The transition from "essential layers"—from the geographical (or even geological) idiom to the more superficial agricultural idiom—dramatized Husserl's conviction that what he had accomplished was fundamental.

Yet there were moments when Husserl himself had lost hope. In 1935 he made his famous announcement, "Philosophy as rigorous science . . . the dream is over." [16] The announcement has sometimes been interpreted as a failure of confidence in his own phenomenology. But it is rather (as I suggested in my first volume, for which I adopted the title *The Dream is Over*) a failure of confidence in the readiness of others—"those who come after"—to continue the phenomenological undertaking as Husserl had conceived it. He had to admit, "I become depressed by the fact that my better students, instead of finishing what I have started . . . time and time again prefer to go their own way." [17] This is the juncture at which I want to determine more precisely what Husserl's expectations of his disciples were, in order to deal with his frustrations over his relation to Heidegger.

Fellow Workers

A generation of resolute fellow-workers . . .
would suffice to settle fully the most important
questions. —Husserl

The Team

Look back from Husserl's later depressed mood to the hope he had entertained at the beginning of the past century, when he launched his phenomenology with the *Logical Investigations*. I cite the conclusion of the introductory section on "The Difficulties of Pure Phenomenological Research":

> However great are the difficulties standing in the way of a pure phenomenology in general, . . . they are by no means of a character that can let the attempt to overcome them appear hopeless. . . . A generation of resolute fellow-workers, conscious of their goal, and dedicated to the great undertaking, would (I risk the judgment) suffice to settle fully the most important questions in the field, those having to do with its fundamental structure. Here we have a sphere of discoveries which are *attainable* and fundamental to the possibility of a *scientific* philosophy.

Only one consideration dampens his optimism:

> Such discoveries, I grant you, have nothing dazzling about them; they lack any immediately discernible usefulness in practice or in the satisfaction of higher emotional needs; they lack too any imposing apparatus of experimental methodology through which

experimental psychology has gained so much credit, along with an ample supply of fellow-workers.[1]

One portion of the "dazzle" can be pinned down now—the reference to experimental psychology. Having envisaged the possibility of a philosophy which would be scientific, Husserl cannot keep from ironizing over the ease in recruiting fellow workers enjoyed by the scientific laboratory of Wilhelm Wundt, the so-called founder of experimental psychology, who was an implacable antagonist of Husserl.

Husserl's conception of "fellow workers" does not embody a sweeping commitment to the profession of philosophy or to his peers in the field. They were not working at phenomenology as he conceived it. When he mentions fellow workers, he has in mind primarily younger disciples. "What he wanted," one of them later recalled (Jean Héring, whom Husserl acknowledged as having helped with reading the proofs of the second edition of the *Investigations*) "was to form a limited group of disciples which was well-trained, and which would work as a team in complete conformity with his method and on a program which he had outlined."[2]

There were, however, problems in maintaining conformity. Among those Husserl warned the American Welch against was Héring. In effect Héring was not deterred by Husserl's cautioning against premature attempts to satisfy "higher emotional needs." He had hastened on to problems in the phenomenology of religion, which should have waited, according to Husserl, until after the foundations of phenomenology were properly laid.

Welch himself had apparently been careful, in reporting to Husserl in 1933 his conversion to phenomenology, not to explain that the book he was writing was merely a dissertation and that it was on Max Scheler's phenomenology of religion. Welch may have heard that Husserl had Scheler as well as Heidegger in mind when, two years before, in 1931, in a public lecture in Berlin, Husserl attacked a "new kind of anthropology which is very influential at present and has even affected the so-called phenomenological movement."[3]

The Reductions

In order to clarify how Husserl's method would ensure this complete conformity and thereby dispose of the difficulties in communication, so that they could remain merely marginal for him, let me offer a merely preliminary sketch of certain component procedures. One of these is the "eidetic reduction" (initially labeled by Husserl "ideation" or "ideative abstraction," but I shall employ his later terminology), by which the phenomenologist arrives at "intuitions"—insights into essences. (Later we shall observe his reasons for discarding the German *Wesen* and replacing it with the Greek term *eidos*). The distinctive character of "essences" I shall bring out more definitely in Chapter 11 with the contrast Husserl would maintain between his eidetic procedure for obtaining generality and the inductive generalizations of experimental psychology.

For the present I offer only some indication as to what Husserl meant by an "essence." The geometer does not arrive at the essential structure of a triangle by generalizing from the three wobbly lines he draws on the blackboard when he is undertaking a geometrical proof. Phenomenology is in this respect an "eidetic science" affiliated to geometry. It too seeks insights into structures which are essential. That they are essential is demonstrated by their invariance, which emerges from the "free variation" carried out by an eidetic reduction. Particular examples of the structure are varied: "In perception, something is perceived; in imagination, something imagined; . . . in desire, desired; and so on." In the course of varying these examples, I become conscious of what remains invariant—that consciousness is essentially "consciousness *of* something."[4] In other words, any act of consciousness (whether perceptive or imaginative, and so forth) is seen to be structured by its essential reference to an object. This is seen as soon as this reference emerges as identical, as over against the differences between perception, imagination, and so forth. The recognition of the essential structure, "consciousness *of* something," is intuitive in the sense that it emerges, during the variation, as knowledge which is immediately given, whether the example is perceptual or imaginative. This eidetic analysis can be pursued further in order to determine what is essential to an act of consciousness when it is perceptual or imaginative, and so forth.

Another procedure which ensures "complete conformity," and thereby disposes of any difficulties in communication, is an elaborate operation. I mention only the feature which is crucial with respect to the problem of communication. Much as the eidetic reduction eliminates as irrelevant to an essential structure of experience the differences between particular experiences, so an accomplishment of the phenomenological reduction is its elimination as irrelevant the differences between the particular persons having these experiences—the differences, say, between the flourish with which one individual may draw the lines of his triangle on a blackboard and the lines drawn gingerly by another individual, which may betray his timidity. Such personal characteristics are as irrelevant as the blackboard itself is to geometry. Phenomenology deals with experiences (perceptual, imaginative, emotional, and so forth), but it does not deal with experiences as "the . . . experiences of empirical persons," and "knows nothing . . . of my experiences or those of others."[5] The experiences phenomenology deals with are to be assigned instead to a "transcendental ego" as distinguished from an "empirical ego."

The most obvious effect of the two reductions is the distinction achieved between Husserl's phenomenology and the merely introspective phenomenology which he discounted as "picture-book phenomenology,"[6] and in which he suspected too many members of the so-called "phenomenological movement" indulged.

That Husserl expected his fellow workers to work, as Héring recalls, "in complete conformity with his method" was not, at least not in principle (since he would eliminate personal characteristics as irrelevant to phenomenology), the sign of a domineering, authoritarian personality. The conformity to be secured by the reductions has to do with more than Husserl's relation to fellow workers; it involved his commitment to invariance, indeed to the assimilation of the structure of experience to a geometrical model. Thus my undertaking to deal with him in terms of his relations to other philosophers would itself be irrelevant to Husserl. He would not endorse my transferring his Latin tag *tua res agitur* from its application to his philosophy itself to the relation between philosophies.

Given that conformity was to be secured by relying on the reductions, there was a certain irony in Husserl's having launched in 1913 a collaborative *Jahrbuch* for phenomenological research. His own contribution, *Ideas I*, included the first published formulation of the phenomenological reduction. This procedure proved for many—perhaps most—of his followers a stumbling block to collaboration. Thus instead of enlisting a generation of fellow workers who would succeed in settling fully the most important questions in phenomenology, the phenomenological movement was put in a certain jeopardy by *Ideas I*. This was perhaps the most important issue when Husserl eventually distanced himself from what we have heard him refer to with disdain as "the phenomenological movement."

Assistants

I have already alluded to World War I. Its external difficulties impeded Husserl's retention and recruitment of disciples as fellow workers. Most of his students left for military service, some of them to be killed. The occupant of the chair in philosophy at Freiburg decided it was dangerously close to the French border and left for Heidelberg. Husserl was thus able to move on from Göttingen to Freiburg. But there he was unable to rebuild his team. The trouble was in part the strength of tradition at Freiburg—in particular neo-Kantianism. But one compensation went with Husserl's elevation to a chair: he acquired a research assistant.

Further evidence as to how Husserl envisaged phenomenology as requiring fellow workers was his reliance on his successive research assistants. What he expected of them only became well known when, after
World War II, the Husserl archives at Leuven were opened; they included
course lectures, but were mainly "research manuscripts," where Husserl
was thinking to himself. As such they were unpublishable. They illustrated
how Husserl endlessly struggled with "difficulties" in "supplements" and
"annexes." They also illustrated the sort of task for which he needed assistants—a special kind of *Ausarbeitung* ("working up") of manuscripts
to prepare them for publication.

The first of Husserl's assistants, Edith Stein, was eloquent about the
unflagging editorial work Husserl expected of an assistant: she anticipated
that when she married, her husband would have to be recruited and eventually her children. But she finally came to recognize that her editorial
work would not bear fruit in any publications by Husserl.[7] She resigned
her position, converted to Catholicism, and became a nun. Jewish, she
died in Auschwitz and became a saint. Whatever her other merits, her de-
votion to Husserl and his manuscripts was little short of miraculous.

Stein's work has not always been appreciated. When phenomenology
had become predominantly francophone (French and Belgian), Henri
Dussort examined the manuscripts on *The Internal Consciousness of
Time*, which had been "worked up" by Stein, and was shocked to discover
that the material "had been profoundly altered by disciples whom the
master had made responsible for its publication, so as to distort his
thought completely."[8]

Roman Ingarden leaped to Stein's defense by explaining how Husserl
utilized his assistants. He did plan to read the final *Ausarbeitung* an assistant had prepared. But if he actually did so, he was usually dissatisfied. He
often became "bored." If his interest was reawakened, rather than rework
the old material, he would put it to one side and start all over again: "A
new pile of manuscripts would be produced." The exhausted assistant
would then be back at square one, since these new manuscripts were in no
condition to be published.[9]

Dussort does not ask, and Ingarden does not explain, how Husserl
could have come to allow manuscripts so altered to be published. I suspect
Husserl may have confidently assumed that anyone who worked (in
Héring's phrase) "in complete conformity with his method," and who was
also aided by what he had himself already got down on paper, could be expected to arrive at insights which would be essentially identical with those
he had originally obtained.

Husserl's dissatisfaction, his boredom, and the reawakening of his interest as he started all over again—were these merely temperamental, personal quirks? His starting all over again might also manifest the misgiving

Husserl would feel when he encountered his researches in the guise of their "results." These he preferred to go behind in order to "reactivate" the original experiences, which would be immediately given once he started all over again.

This explanation requires further clarification. In his defense of Stein, Ingarden alludes to "a certain diffidence [on Husserl's part] when confronted with the prospect of publication" (*eine gewisse Scheu vor der Publikation*).[10] This diffidence was perhaps not entirely a personal hang-up. Preoccupied as he was in his research manuscripts with the struggle to arrive at experiences which would be immediately given, the prospect of publication could not compete. Thus I would attach a certain methodological significance to the seemingly innocuous distinction Husserl draws in the section, "The Difficulties of Pure Phenomenological Analysis." Only when Husserl has indicated how this analysis itself is to be carried out does he acknowledge, as a further and separate difficulty, "*communicating its results to others*."[11]

Husserl's difficulties are assessed in a more colloquial fashion by Stein in 1926—on the eve of the publication in 1927 of *Being and Time,* which Husserl would soon find devastating. In 1926 he could still hope, as he had in 1913, that his thoughts would attain their "proper effect." In 1926 Stein returned briefly to Freiburg, visited Husserl, and reported as follows in a letter to another former student, Ingarden:

> The master brought me up to date regarding his progress in recent years. And in fact everything has come together in a grand unity, all the isolated investigations which I knew about earlier fit together within this unity. However—and now we reach what is really tragic about the situation—while this whole certainly is living in him, yet I doubt if he will ever get it down on paper, let alone publish it, and he simply has no student who works in conformity with his aims. When he retires, he will presumably propose Heidegger as his successor, and Heidegger is going his own way.[12]

When Stein comments, "let alone publish it," she is commenting on what Ingarden will characterize as Husserl's *eine gewisse Scheu vor der Publikation.*

The Successor

"Heidegger is going his own way" is a casual comment. Stein does not anticipate the philosophical significance that "going along a way" is to acquire in Heidegger or how it could be opposed to Husserl's commitment, as the title of his programmatic work put it, to *Philosophy as Rigorous*

Science. Husserl is likewise casual when he applies the idiom to students who "instead of finishing what I have started, . . . prefer to go their own way," and adds, "So too Heidegger."[13] Although Husserl here speaks of Heidegger along with former students, Heidegger had never officially been one of his students. As late as 1925, however, Heidegger still refers to himself in a lecture as a "disciple" of Husserl's.[14]

After the publication of *Being and Time* in 1927, Husserl sought Heidegger's criticisms on a draft of an article, "Phenomenology," for the *Encyclopaedia Britannica.* He then enlisted Heidegger as a collaborator. Heidegger responded with detailed comments and with proposed insertions. After much negotiation, Husserl decided he just could not incorporate what Heidegger was proposing. Thus their collaboration produced a breakdown in communication.[15]

Husserl had earlier approached Heidegger regarding the editing of the *Internal Consciousness of Time* manuscripts, which Stein had "worked up." Presumably Husserl felt that exposure to his manuscripts, especially on a topic which was crucial to Heidegger himself, might promote Heidegger's understanding of phenomenology. But Heidegger's own presumption of their irrelevance was implicit in his begging off until he had *Being and Time* ready for publication. When in 1928 he did take on the manuscripts, he further demonstrated their irrelevance by not bothering with any additional *Ausarbeitung* beyond Stein's. Husserl was also disappointed in Heidegger's perfunctory preface.[16] Thus this episode added up to another breakdown in communication. Years later their irrelevance became explicit in Heidegger's contribution to the memorial marking the thirtieth anniversary of Husserl's death. He concluded his contribution by explaining that *Being and Time* "proceeded in a direction which always remained alien to the investigations of Husserl on the inner consciousness of time."[17]

When, even before Husserl retired, his better students were deserting him for Heidegger, Husserl sometimes consoled himself with the thought that some of them might yet build a "bridge" between him and Heidegger.[18] At other times he could only lament that Heidegger "carries all the young away with him." Eventually he stigmatizes Heidegger as a "seducer" and insinuates that Heidegger "studies his public and caters [*berücksichtigt*] to them in his writings."[19]

Husserl's misgivings, with his first cursory reading of *Being and Time,* were consolidated by Heidegger's inaugural address in 1929, "What Is Metaphysics?" with which he took over Husserl's chair. When retirement provided Husserl with the leisure for a careful reading of *Being and Time,* he vented his indignation in the margins of his copy. Later I shall sample the issues he raised.

This summary history of the relation between Husserl and Heidegger is merely preparatory for my attempt in this volume to deal with the philosophical relation as illustrated by *Being and Time* and by Husserl's marginal comments.[20]

Work

Two fundamental issues I can anticipate now because Husserl does not seem to have been sensitive to them, so that their illustration does not have to wait on further exposition. Whereas Husserl recruited followers as fellow workers, Heidegger declared (in the 1935 summer course that intervened between Husserl's May *Crisis* lecture in Vienna and his November *Crisis* lectures in Prague) that philosophy was not an undertaking for which followers could be recruited: "When we hear of a following [*Gefolgshaft*] . . . philosophical questioning is misunderstood."[21]

The second issue is also a matter of how philosophy is to be understood. At the beginning I cited Husserl's defense of reissuing the *Logical Investigations* in 1913, despite his having come to regard them as superseded by *Ideas I.* I neglected the italics with which he still recommended the *Investigations* as an attempt to "introduce the reader to the nature of genuinely phenomenological . . . *work.*"[22]

Heidegger similarly emphasizes work. Confronted with the misunderstanding of *Being and Time,* he protested, "To see what is accomplished [*das Positive*] here, one must have first of all put in the effort of actual work."[23] Visiting Karl Jaspers, Heidegger asked, "When do you work?"[24] Jaspers reports the question, which he may have interpreted only as an allusion to the amount of time he spent at his desk, given his rather relaxed lifestyle. If so, his interpretation itself is too relaxed. If he had read with more care the "Comments on Jaspers's *Psychology of World Views,*" which Heidegger sent him in 1921, he might have suspected something more aggressive might be in question. There Heidegger stressed that the "philosophical shortcoming" in "Jaspers's work" was "with respect to actually coming to grips and getting down to [*im Hinblick auf ein eigentliches Zugreifen und Losgehen auf*] problems."[25]

To this challenge, we can oppose Jaspers's own claim, although it was made without any reference to Heidegger: "Contemplation and 'laziness' are the sources of all good ideas."[26] Issues between Heidegger and Jaspers I am not pursuing now. I cited Jaspers only to show how, in contrast, Heidegger and Husserl were both committed to philosophy as "work."

This, however, brings me to the contrast between them. When Heidegger characterizes his own undertaking in *Being and Time* as the "working out [*Ausarbeitung*] of the question of being,"[27] the "work" in question was very different from the *Ausarbeitung* which Husserl delegated to assistants. Neither Husserl nor Heidegger confront directly the differences between their conceptions of *Ausarbeitung*. I mention these differences now as suggesting how fundamentally different was their understanding of the "work" of philosophy itself. *Ausarbeitung* carries no reference in Heidegger to publication, but determining the distinctive force of the *aus* in Heidegger must wait upon my examining later the procedures on which he relies as different from Husserl's.

So far I have largely restricted my attention to Husserl. We have seen that the *Ausarbeitung* which he delegated to research assistants (and, in the instance of the *Internal Consciousness of Time*, to Heidegger) was the revision needed to ready manuscripts for publication. A quite different procedure of revision was characteristic of the kind of "work" that philosophy itself, as phenomenological analysis, was for Husserl: *Umarbeitung*, a "working over again."

This revisionary character of phenomenology is illustrated by Husserl's recurrent starting out again—as we have seen he did when he put his revision of an assistant's revision aside, or when he embarks on still another "introduction" to phenomenology. His dissatisfaction with even the revised version of the *Logical Investigations* and later with *Ideas I* as the work which had superseded it, is not just a psychological hang-up any more than his *gewisse Scheu vor der Publikation*. What is involved in both instances is Husserl's methodological commitment to *reactivating* experiences as they are immediately given. This is a commitment which we shall better understand when we eventually take into more specific account how he proposed to overcome with the reductions the specific difficulties which impede gaining access to the immediately given.

These will explain Husserl's general emphasis that phenomenology is "difficult work." Indeed, he insisted it entails "a lot of grubby work [*schmützige Arbeit*]."[28] Unless the reader is prepared to get down himself to the nitty-gritty of the "work" Husserl was undertaking, there isn't much point in reading him.

To understand any philosophy worth understanding (I asserted at the beginning of this volume on behalf of my exposition) is to understand why it has to be difficult to understand—that is, why it cannot be summarized, encapsulated, labeled in a fashion which would exorcise the devil in its details.

I shall later explain the differences between Husserl's and Heidegger's conceptions of "work" in terms of their different conceptions of "difficulty." For the present I would only deliver what I take to be Husserl's own dismay regarding difficulties:

At some point, after prolonged efforts, the clarity we have yearned for seems in the offing. We think that the most superb results are so

close that we need only reach out. . . . And now only a final step remains. We are about to take it, and begin with a self-conscious
"therefore," and then we suddenly discover a point that is obscure
[but] that continues to loom larger. It grows to a monstrous size,
swallowing up all our arguments. . . . The corpses come back to life;
they leer; they snicker. The work and struggle start all over again.[29]

Starting all over again is what phenomenology is for Husserl as revisionary work—as *Umarbeitung*.

FOUR

The Work of the Other

Husserl became at one and the same time the distance between us and the basis of our friendship. —Sartre

The Idiom

My interest in the differences between Husserl's and Heidegger's conception of a "difficulty," and thus in the different procedures each relies on when at work on difficulties, is in the way these differences led to a breakdown in communication—perhaps the most notorious such breakdown between philosophers in this century.[1]

This breakdown is the climax which is the justification for my exposition of the relation between Husserl and Heidegger. But I have admitted that reaching this climax will entail "grubby work." So I would stand back now and contemplate larger issues, as I did when I urged that in the relation between philosophers, *tua res agitur.*

What solicits initial attention is the idiom itself, "breakdown in communication," for it has become flattened in our time into a cliché. Nothing is more banal in literature (and hence in life) than a "breakdown in communication." The idiom is so loosely used that it can be stretched to cover an unmanageable variety of instances of misunderstanding. I cannot pretend that the idiom is readily salvageable for the specific purpose of assessing philosophical misunderstandings until I have carried out my exposition.

Just as I exploited Henry James's preference for "seeing through" as an initial approximation to how one philosopher comes to understand another philosopher via an intermediary, so I would exploit James's remarkable delineation of how he had to cope with the misunderstandings of his philosopher brother:

> I mean to try to produce some uncanny form of thing, in fiction, that will gratify you as brother—but let me say, dear William, that I shall be greatly humiliated if you do like it, and thereby lump it, in your affection, with things of the current age that I have heard you express admiration for and that I would sooner descend to a dishonoured grave than have written. Still, I *will* write you your book, on that two-and-two-make-four system on which all the awful truck that surrounds us is produced, and *then* descend to my dishonoured grave. . . . But I'm always sorry when I hear of your reading anything of mine, and always hope you won't—you seem to be constitutionally unable to "enjoy" it, and so condemned to look at it from a point of view remotely alien to mine in writing it, and to the conditions out of which, *as* mine, it has inevitably sprung—so that all the intentions that have been its main reason for being (with *me*) appear never to have reached you at all.[2]

I am not sure Henry did really "mean to try"; I suspect he may only have wanted to communicate to his brother regarding the breakdown in communication itself. That suits my purpose.

In citing James, I am not proposing to dress up a cliché. I would rather exploit James's flourishing—undeterred by its delicacies—in order to point out some of the requirements that should be taken into account, if the idiom is to be applied philosophically.

Ideally a proper breakdown in communication presupposes an attempt to communicate—really meaning to try. Thus the breakdown with which I began, between Continental and Anglo-American philosophy, was perhaps not, by and large, a proper breakdown. For instance, the lectures Husserl gave in England can hardly pass muster as an attempt to communicate, since he did not bother to take into account any of the philosophical convictions widespread among his audience. At the same time, most of his audience seem to have been less interested in being communicated with than in repairing war damage symbolically—as I have already suggested.

Also incompatible with a proper breakdown is what might be called "consignment"—such as Henry's lumping dear William's taste in fiction together "with things of the current age"—"all the awful truck that surrounds us." Husserl similarly once consigned Heidegger when in the early twenties he discounted him with the observation, "The war and ensuing difficulties drive men into mysticism."[3] Husserl was thereby regarding

Heidegger as philosophically irrelevant, inasmuch as the "difficulties" to which Husserl alluded were not of the sort he had designed phenomenology to resolve.

A hope I entertain in citing James is that no reader would be so consignable to the current age as to suppose that a proper breakdown can be got around with a psychological explanation—in the case of the two brothers, sibling rivalry, or any other awful truck. Such a psychological explanation would be as unworthy an insult to the author of the *Principles of Psychology* as it would be to the author of the late novels, in which breakdowns in communication are pivotal.

A further requirement I would suggest for a proper breakdown is a certain depth to the differences—as is exhibited by James's raising such considerations as "constitutionally unable," "remotely alien," and "inevitably sprung." With Husserl and Heidegger, the depth of their differences involves genuine philosophical issues.

Breaking Off

Philosophical communication can break down in different ways, and philosophical issues are not always in evidence. An instance can be cited from Heidegger's early career of a notorious breakdown in communication. A student's transcript reports that the "Methodological Introduction" to his course, "Introduction to the Phenomenology of Religion," was "broken off on November 30, 1920." When Heidegger began again, he commented on the break:

> Philosophy, as I conceive it, is in difficulty [*Schwierigkeit*]. The student in other lecture courses is guaranteed something from the start: in art history he can look at pictures; in other courses his costs are covered because he is being prepared for an examination. In philosophy it is different, and that I cannot alter because I have not invented philosophy. But I still want to rescue myself from this calamity and break off these very abstract considerations, and without any further consideration of approaches and method, take a definite, concrete phenomenon as my starting point [*Ausgang*]. This I do on the assumption that you will misunderstand the entire treatment from beginning to end.[4]

Heidegger's lecture course then became, "Phenomenological Explication of Concrete Religious Phenomena in Conjunction with Paul's Letters."

The breaking off was apparently due to the students' general complaints to the dean over the lack of religious relevance in the course.[5] Their complaints were apparently no more specific than that, and we can usually be sure that whenever the intervention of a dean is involved, philosophical issues are not much in evidence. Thus the episode is worth recalling, not just because it provides a harbinger of Heidegger's comment that I have cited from forty years later regarding the "almost insurmountable difficulty of understanding," but also because it illustrates a breakdown in communication to which philosophers may well be prone when confronted with philistines, but which is of too clumsy a sort to be philosophically worth lingering over.

In contrast, the breakdown in communication between Husserl and Heidegger is not a simple but a multiple fracture. I shall expose several different "breaks" as taking place at different junctures in their respective philosophies. In dealing with these "breaks," an advantage of the idiom "breakdown" is that it can refer to an analysis by which a "structure" is exposed. I shall not be satisfied with sorting out specific issues, but shall attempt to analyze these as betraying more fundamental differences in structure between Heidegger's and Husserl's philosophies.

It is true that taking a "breakdown" in this sense of an analysis exposing a structure has not gone unchallenged. The *O.E.D.* has seen fit to immortalize a repudiation of such usage: "The latest threat to clarity is the use of 'breakdown' to mean 'analysis.'"[6] This threat is presumably compounded when the analysis is—as it will be here—the breakdown of a breakdown. Yet I persist with the compound by way of suggesting that the breakdown in communication itself exposes the issues that need to be picked out.

Confrontation

To "breakdown" there is an alternative idiom to which I shall sometimes resort: "confrontation." Its interest for my purposes is its ambiguity, since it can be employed in a negative or a positive sense. It can imply that there has been no attempt at understanding and communication. Let me mention an illustration of its negative usage. Jacques Derrida is pertinent to my present undertaking, since he has been an important interpreter of both Husserl and Heidegger. He would also be the most prominent philosopher of his generation in France if he were willing to be labeled a philosopher. Michel Foucault (who would have been the most prominent philosopher of the preceding generation in France if he had not preferred to be regarded as a historian) reportedly denounced Derrida's writing as "terrorist obscurantism"—its obscurity being designed to enable him to respond to any criticism with, "You have misunderstood me, you are stupid."[7] Such a denunciation may well suggest that Derrida was hopelessly "confrontational."

"Confrontation" can, however, also be used in a positive sense. When the requisite attempt at understanding has not been made, we can impute that a "confrontation never quite takes place."[8] I am citing John Searle's imputation regarding Derrida's misunderstanding of John Austin. It is then up to an expositor to intervene and eke out the confrontation, so that it does at last take place. This Searle proposes to accomplish by rectifying Derrida's misunderstanding of Austin. But this of course led to a confrontation instead between Derrida and Searle, which the latter may have taken as another illustration of how insurmountable is the breakdown in communication between Continental and Anglo-American philosophy. At any rate, Searle rebuffed any prospect of further communication with Derrida.[9]

It is worth recognizing here, before going further, that the confrontation that never quite takes place has been a rather regular occurrence in the history of philosophy. Aristotle often lined up the opinions of his predecessors before he undertook to treat some problem of his own. Historians have had little trouble demonstrating how Aristotle's interpretation of these opinions was dictated by how he proposed to treat the problem in his own philosophy. They have often demonstrated more particularly that Aristotle's references to Plato (or to Platonists) failed to do justice to Plato's philosophy. But Plato's philosophy is not easily rescued from Aristotle's interpretation. Indeed, would Plato have entered the history of philosophy as primarily the proponent of a "theory of ideas," had it not been for Aristotle's refutation of this theory? I mention their confrontation, because Boyce Gibson, the translator of Husserl's *Ideas* and a visitor to Freiburg in the twenties, was probably reporting a standard appraisal there when he tossed off, "Husserl is the Plato to Heidegger's Aristotle."[10]

The history of philosophy provides many instances when we could argue that communication has broken down in the sense that the successor, however accredited he may be, gives an account of a predecessor which is riddled with misunderstandings. Does Kant give an adequate account of the philosopher who awakened him from his dogmatic slumbers? Does Fichte provide an adequate account of Kant's philosophy? Does Marx or Kierkegaard, of Hegel's? Philosophers are supposedly dedicated to understanding—but how frequently the successor misunderstands a previous philosopher. Indeed, such misunderstandings are a justification that can be alleged for the history of philosophy: the historian is to intervene with his interpretation of what is at issue. But an adequate theory of interpretation—an adequate hermeneutics as a theory of philosophical understanding—should take into account philosophers' misunderstandings of other philosophers.

The contemporary and past instances I have cited may suggest that "breakdowns in communication" or "confrontations" (in the negative sense) are congenital in philosophy. But what happened between Heidegger and Husserl merits particular attention. On the one hand, the initial philosophical solidarity, which Husserl kept emphasizing to Heidegger in the twenties ("You and I are phenomenology"), has not often held when the successor has already reached maturity as a major philosopher. On the other hand, predecessors of some repute have even less often still been around and had Husserl's opportunity to be outraged by the misunderstandings of a successor with Heidegger's repute. Among the instances of famous philosophers I have just plucked from history, no account is available from a predecessor comparable to Husserl's.

One of Husserl's disabused comments on Heidegger was entirely traditional. At some point when he was exhibiting his sense of outrage by entering his protests, his question marks, his exclamation marks, in the margins of his copy of *Being and Time,* he must have interrupted his reading in order to turn back to the title page and enter the conventional tag, *Amicus Plato, magis amica veritas.* This tag had derived from Aristotle's distinction in his *Ethics* between his personal relation to Plato and his misgivings regarding Platonic philosophy. I paraphrase, "Personally I'm a friend of Plato's, but philosophically the truth is the friend who matters."[11]

This rough paraphrase is designed to make explicit the traditional distinction, which I have already mentioned Heidegger as well as Husserl would draw, between the philosophical and the personal. Thus, in a *Der Spiegel* interview (an interview with the leading German newsweekly in which Heidegger defended himself against various imputations), he distinguishes the "substantive" (that is, philosophical) issues between himself and Husserl from their later personal break. But this distinction between the philosophical and the personal is itself a philosophical distinction, and it can be challenged philosophically. I shall exhibit in Volume 4 this challenge as made by Jaspers, who had a longer and more personal relation to Heidegger than did any other prominent philosopher of their generation.

The Other

There is something about Aristotle's comment which Husserl may not have noticed; it is usually overlooked. Although Aristotle is frequently critical of Platonists in different works, he does not bother to draw elsewhere the distinction which will become in Husserl a distinction between the philosophical and the personal. Aristotle draws it in an *Ethics,* because he commends friendship there as itself an ethical relation.

Ethical issues surface with respect to the philosophical relations between philosophers when Derrida speaks of "the ethics of discussion." He is rebuking those "who excuse themselves from attentively reading and listening to the other."[12] If an Aristotle shows his hand by making his comment in an *Ethics*, Derrida introduces a different ethical emphasis with his reference to "the other." This reference acquires momentous relevance in Derrida's own philosophy. Here we can take into account a debt to Lévinas, whom we have already encountered as a student of Husserl's. I reintroduce him briefly now, for he played a role in the understanding of both Heidegger and Husserl in France.

Sartre, who was initially the most influential French mediator, never pretended to have gained his initial understanding of Husserl directly. I have already cited his admission, "I came to Husserl *via* Lévinas."[13] Later Lévinas played a different role by arguing against Husserl on behalf of a phenomenology in which the otherness of the other was recognized as fundamental. He was critical too of Heidegger's analysis of "being-with," inasmuch as the preposition *with* failed to convey the fundamental relation to the other.

I shall not probe Lévinas's or Derrida's criticisms of Husserl and Heidegger. I would beg off with Maurice Blanchot's generalization that "the relation with the other" is "as it were a new starting point for philosophy and a leap which it and we ourselves are exhorted to carry out."[14] If it is indeed "a new starting point" and "a leap," I cannot pretend to do justice to it here, since my concern is earlier—with Husserl and Heidegger.

I have nonetheless a motive for citing Blanchot's generalization: it is Derrida's citation from Blanchot, who is himself interpreting Lévinas, and this piling up suggests how pervasive a preoccupation "the relation with the other" has become in French philosophy. I take note of this pervasive preoccupation as a possible recommendation for my own approach: if "the relation with the other" deserves acknowledgment in general as philosophically decisive, why should not the relation of one philosopher's philosophy to another philosopher's philosophy be sought out, even in an instance when "the relation with the other" was not acknowledged as decisive by the philosophers themselves. It is not so acknowledged by Husserl and Heidegger, as it is by Lévinas, Blanchot, and Derrida.

Let me secure a more specific link. In Lévinas "the relation with the Other [*Autrui*] as interlocutor . . . is prior to all ontology. It is the ultimate relation in being."[15] Here "interlocutor" conveys no implication that any distinctively philosophical locution is in question. The priority Lévinas is asserting does not privilege philosophical discussion over any other human activity. But my own claim is only that if the relation with the other "as interlocutor" is "ultimate," philosophically speaking, then the relation between philosophies deserves consideration.

A Startling Deviation

Let me relocate my undertaking in relation to Heidegger's, since it is with his philosophy that I shall be primarily concerned. I select as pertinent here, by virtue of its generality, his lecture, "What Is Philosophy?" As so often, the translation does not do justice to Heidegger's German, *Was is das—die Philosophie?* Titles become for him a crux, as I shall recognize in Volume 4. In this instance the moment of hesitancy in the German title receives what I take to be a certain elucidation in the lecture itself. There he cites Plato:

> This is especially the passion of a philosopher, to be astonished. Indeed there is no other controlling starting point wherefrom [*archē / beherrschendes Woher*] for philosophy than this.[16]

I would set alongside this citation one in which Sartre assesses his relation to another philosopher, Merleau-Ponty:

> By himself, each of us was too easily convinced he had understood what phenomenology was; . . . Each of us understood, as a startling deviation from his own work, the alien, sometimes hostile work of the other. Husserl became at one and the same time the distance between us and the basis of our friendship.[17]

I have already stressed how the issues in my four volumes on phenomenology have to do with how phenomenology is understood in different phenomenologies.[18] Thus, continual restatement of the issues is in order along with the recasting of previous comparison between phenomenologies.

In the present volume I shall eventually be concerned to pick out as "controlling," not a "starting point," a "wherefrom," for determining what philosophy is in general—Greek astonishment, according to Heidegger—but a specific juncture at which there is "a startling deviation" on Heidegger's part from Husserl's starting point. Heidegger's analysis of signs in *Being and Time,* I shall recognize, is "a startling deviation" from the analysis of signs which had been Husserl's starting point in the first of his *Logical Investigations.*

Heidegger was not himself startled at this juncture, even though he must have been aware of his deviation. His astonishment is different in character; he never was startled by his relation to another philosopher. I am therefore bringing Sartre and Merleau-Ponty back temporarily in order to advance my own analysis. Some issues as to the relations between philosophers are raised in a much more readily ascertainable fashion by Sartre's account of the relation between his phenomenology and Merleau-Ponty's. Husserl and Heidegger may both stress that philosophy is "work" and entertain different conceptions of this "work," but neither concedes the relevance Sartre concedes in his memorial essay to "the work of the other."

Let me recast for present purposes my previous presentation of the relation between Sartre and Merleau-Ponty. Observe first how "the work of the other" is interpreted by Sartre as "alien, sometimes hostile." Even though Merleau-Ponty was not around to respond to the memorial essay, he had earlier criticized Sartre's philosophy as "too exclusively antithetical." The "distance" between them which Sartre emphasizes is something Merleau-Ponty would be reluctant to accept when he deals generally in his own philosophy with the relation to the other, for Merleau-Ponty's emphasis is instead on how "I borrow myself from the other." Hence he views Sartre as misinterpreting the relation to the other as mutually exclusive; he ascribes to Sartre the conviction that "between the other or myself one must choose."[19] Merleau-Ponty would have found an illustration of this conviction in the general explanation (at the beginning of Sartre's memorial essay) of how Sartre has lost friends: "They were they; I was myself."[20] So brusque an antithesis is incompatible with my borrowing myself from the other—as the individual does in Merleau-Ponty. The other is "there for us, doubtless not with the frontal evidence of a thing, but installed athwart [à travers de] our thinking."[21]

Deriving from Merleau-Ponty's own philosophy is the continual effort he made in his own writings to arrive at some understanding with Sartre, even though Sartre made no similar effort himself to overcome the "distance" between them in his own writings. Jean Hyppolite knew them both well, but when he stresses in his memorial essay Merleau-Ponty's "living dialogue, never interrupted, with Sartre,"[22] he neglects to add that there is no evidence of a comparable dialogue going on from Sartre's side. Here again I would move from their personal relation to the level of generality each reaches in his philosophy. Merleau-Ponty appeals in his philosophy to the general "experience of dialogue"—when "we are for each other collaborators in a perfect reciprocity."[23] No such general experience of collaboration, no such perfection of reciprocity, is ever proclaimed by Sartre. Instead "the work of the other" retains its otherness.

The Breakdown

My point, I repeat, is that the breakdown in communication between them extends even to how the breakdown itself is to be interpreted. We shall see that this is true also of the breakdown between Heidegger and Husserl. It is true as well of the breakdowns between Heidegger and Jaspers and between Heidegger and Sartre, as we shall see in Volume 4.

The idiom "breakdown" has itself an appropriateness in Sartre's interpretation of what had taken place between them that it does not have in Merleau-Ponty's interpretation. According to Sartre, it was an abrupt "breaking away" (*arrachement*). Sartre visualizes Merleau-Ponty as well as himself reaching this juncture by engaging in *le travail de rupture*. But Sartre also has to admit that

> Merleau, smiling, took care not to rupture anything and not to let anything break loose; the placid dandyism of his caution . . . should have achieved completion in a philosophy of the continuous.[24]

Sartre's proclivity to vehement rupture achieves completion rather in a philosophy of the discontinuous, in which relations tend to become (at least this is Merleau-Ponty's interpretation) "too exclusively antithetical."[25] Thus Sartre characterizes what happened between them in a fashion Merleau-Ponty (still "smiling") would have repudiated: "Each of us was thrown to the opposite extreme of the other."[26]

Merleau-Ponty may make a brief concession to the Hegelian struggle in Sartre between the individual and the other. "With the *cogito*" in Sartre, Merleau-Ponty argues, "begins that struggle between consciousnesses, each of which . . . seeks the death of the other." But what Sartre would interpret as an illustration of Merleau-Ponty's conciliatory placidity soon takes over when Merleau-Ponty in effect circumvents Sartre's interpretation: "For the struggle to begin, and for each consciousness to be capable of suspecting the alien presences which it negates, there must necessarily be some common ground."[27] In other words, there cannot be, strictly speaking, a final breakdown in communication in Merleau-Ponty's philosophy.

Merleau-Ponty also alludes to the devastating place of "the look" in Sartre's interpretation of the struggle: "The objectification of each by the other's look is felt as unbearable"; but after this concession to Sartre, he adds, "only because it takes the place of a possible communication. The refusal to communicate is *still a mode of communication*."[28] Again there cannot be, strictly speaking, a final breakdown in communication in Merleau-Ponty.

In order to get at the philosophical differences at issue in the breakdown of communication between Husserl and Heidegger, I proceed more circumspectly and more slowly than I have with Sartre and Merleau-Ponty, for the differences between Husserl and Heidegger do not coalesce around the issue of the relation between the individual and the other. Instead a distinction between the philosophical and the personal prevails.

Focus

There are further complications. Not only is the relation between Husserl and Heidegger differently interpreted by each of them (as is the relation between Sartre and Merleau-Ponty by each of them), but it also incurs different interpretations in later philosophies. One reason I have recalled Sartre and Merleau-Ponty is the extent to which each managed in his own phenomenology, during the forties and the fifties, to reconcile Husserl and Heidegger. But given the intent of my present focus on the relation between individual philosophers, it is important to recognize that such a relationship is not something established once and for all during the history of philosophy, but is as subject to the vagaries of interpretation as are individual philosophies themselves.

I have already mentioned that the waning of the vogue of Sartre and Merleau-Ponty contributed to the lessening of philosophical interest in the relation between Husserl and Heidegger. Increasingly in the sixties the scholarly tendency was to interpret each of them separately. In 1970 the first noteworthy anthologies of interpretations of Heidegger appeared.[29] Of the thirty-two essays presented, only one was an attempt to deal with Heidegger's relation to Husserl. (That essay, by Gérard Granel, I shall glance at in my next chapter.) Derrida represents the increasing tendency to treat them separately. He offered interpretations of Husserl in 1962 and 1967 in which references to Heidegger were minimal, and an interpretation of Heidegger in 1968 in which there was no mention of Husserl.[30]

A third period, however, must be demarcated, during which irresistible new evidence became available as to the relation between Heidegger and Husserl. At the end of his career, in 1975, Heidegger gave a final seminar ("the Zähringen seminar") concerned largely with his early relation to Husserl. Interest in their early relation was further reinforced when it received more detailed illustration with the publication in 1979 of the *Prolegomena*—a lecture course which Heidegger had given in 1925. The "Main Part" of that work was promptly recognized as an "early version" or "draft" of *Being and Time* (1927), but it was preceded by a "Preparatory Part," which was primarily an exposition of Husserl. Additional evidence as to his earlier relation to Husserl became available as other early lecture courses were published.

Although I shall make supplementary use of earlier lecture courses (as well as of the Zähringen seminar and late essays of Heidegger's), what I shall try to bring into focus is the relation of Heidegger to Husserl in *Being and Time,* where we can watch Heidegger break away from the relation to Husserl that still held as recently as two years before in the *Prolegomena,* in which Heidegger had presented himself as "a disciple in relation to Husserl."[31]

Being and Time deserves close attention because Heidegger worked particularly hard on it. It was the one stretch in his life when he neglected to shave. Such concentrated work was demanded not only by the uncertainty then of his career prospects, but also (I shall emphasize) by his conception of the "difficulties" to be "worked out" in phenomenology. In Chapter 19 I shall examine his own emphasis on how "difficult" he found "concept construction" in *Being and Time* and his explanation of this difficulty as due to "the *Umständlichkeit* of these constructions."[32] I shall pick up again my interpretation of the sense in which philosophy was "work" (*Ausarbeitung*) for Heidegger by exploring the implications of *Umständlichkeit* (a "minuteness of detail" which suggests that the construction is "labored"). I shall then examine in particular those concepts of his which illustrate respects in which his work can be regarded as expended in breaking away from Husserl.

There is an inescapable limitation to my exposition. An expositor who would bring into focus a philosopher's relation to another philosopher can hardly at the same time do justice to the so-called internal development of either of their philosophies, or even determine the sense in which the ascription of an "internal development" is warranted in the case of either philosophy. Thus I shall refer to Heidegger's earlier and later writings, when the references are notably helpful in clarifying his relation to Husserl in *Being and Time,* but I shall not attempt to expand these references into the developmental account which historians ordinarily crave.

The *Prolegomena,* however, I cannot overlook as the work in which Heidegger still viewed himself as "a disciple" of Husserl. But when he employed the *Prolegomena* as a "draft" for *Being and Time,* he discarded the "Preparatory Part" with its exposition and criticism of Husserl. He is thereby breaking away in *Being and Time* from Husserl in a more general fashion than the specific breaks in *Being and Time.* Because of their specificity, these will be my first concern, but I shall attempt in Chapters 21 and 22 a comparison between *Being and Time* and the *Prolegomena.*

There was a final break with Husserl which I cannot entirely overlook. References to Husserl disappeared from Heidegger's writings in the thirties. We may anticipate that Heidegger no longer accorded Husserl the relevance he had earlier enjoyed. Heidegger further demonstrated Husserl's irrelevance by his indifference to the lectures which composed Husserl's *The Crisis of European Sciences* (1935). This last work of Husserl's would have to be taken into account by any scholar concerned with the internal development of Husserl's phenomenology. A scholarly interpreter of *The Crisis* may also allege, "It is impossible to overlook the fact that in this last treatise Husserl finally gave his reply to his pupil and challenger Heidegger."[33] But Husserl himself seems to have found it possible to overlook this fact; at least he never mentioned Heidegger by name in *The Crisis*. If this last work was implicitly a reply to Heidegger, it was one to which Heidegger himself never replied in turn. In short, neither would acknowledge the other—not even as an adversary. How could a breakdown in communication be more complete?

"With regard to the relation of my thought to Husserl's," Heidegger himself has warned, "some gross errors have cropped up which can only be removed by careful philological work."[34] I shall not pause to ask what has happened in this instance to Heidegger's reputed scorn of careful philological work. I shall simply undertake the work he suggests is needed.[35]

ONE · PROCEDURES

The Shift in Subject

*Heidegger cannot succeed . . . in sharing with his
master the question of the relation between their
respective thoughts.*—Gérard Granel

The Principle

What is initially enticing about Heidegger's
relation to Husserl is Heidegger's explicit acknowledgment, which I have already cited,
that *Being and Time* "would not have been
possible, if the foundation had not been laid
by Edmund Husserl."[1] Such an acknowledgment is rather unusual, for a major philosopher usually reserves the laying of a
foundation to himself.

If we could take this acknowledgment at
its face value, it would then seem most puzzling that Heidegger does not cite a single
sentence from Husserl anywhere in *Being and
Time.* How can Heidegger proceed without
any indication as to the foundation which
had been laid for this work? Let me throw in
a contrast: Sartre's debt to Husserl takes the
form in *L'imaginaire* of Sartre's translating
numerous passages from Husserl. These he
can often be regarded as incorporating in his
own phenomenology. They enabled me to
deal in my *Method and Imagination* (Volume
2 of this work) with Sartre's relation to
Husserl. Indeed they enabled me to go behind
this relation, as Sartre himself interpreted it,
and to determine what the relation actually
was—in particular, the junctures at which
Sartre parted company with Husserl but
without usually being aware of so doing.

In the case of *Being and Time* there has to
be some explanation as to why Heidegger
does not cite Husserl. The explanation seems

most likely to be Heidegger's calculation that it was just not prudent to exhibit in a published work philosophical differences from Husserl. Out of a desire to spare Husserl's feelings? Out of a desire to avoid any risks to a smooth transition into the chair from which Husserl would soon be retiring?

Some such explanation is plausible. What is not thereby explained are the philosophical differences which Heidegger is reluctant to avow publically, but which remain implicit. Indeed, Husserl himself suspects, in many of the comments he enters in the margins of his copy of *Being and Time,* that Heidegger is attacking him.

Even if there is a plausible explanation as to Heidegger's reticence in *Being and Time,* a broadly philosophical explanation is also feasible, although it may seem ironic that Heidegger would have been in debt to Husserl for it. It is the principle to which Husserl himself adhered in philosophy, and which Heidegger took over from him, of proceeding directly "to the things themselves" and not allowing the opinions of previous philosophers to intervene. Husserl had explained this procedure: "Formulated explicitly, the philosophical epochē . . . entails our completely abstaining from any judgment regarding the *doctrinal content of any previous philosophy.*"[2]

For my part, I do not find the principle viable, as could be inferred from my not proceeding myself, in this volume as in previous volumes, directly "to the things themselves," but proposing instead to reach judgments regarding the relations between philosophies. I am cherishing here an irony of my own: what I shall repudiate in the long run is the principle which Heidegger took over from Husserl's philosophy. The principle, we shall also see, takes on quite different implications in Heidegger from those it had in Husserl. But the differences cannot be adjudicated by appealing to the principle itself.

Before we can reach this conclusion and decide what is to be made of it, we must patiently put up with "grubby work."

Ambiguities

Since Heidegger's acknowledgment is explicit, whereas his later attacks, which Husserl detected in *Being and Time,* are merely implicit, the first step is to look for clues in the acknowledgment itself as to how Heidegger envisages their relation. I now cite the acknowledgment in its setting:

> The following investigation would not have been possible, if the foundation had not been laid by Edmund Husserl, with whose *Logical Investigations* phenomenology reached its breakthrough. Our [Heidegger's] explanation of the preliminary concept of phenome-

nology has shown that what is essential in it does not lie in being actual as a "movement." Higher than actuality is possibility. The understanding of phenomenology lies uniquely in grasping it as possibility.

Unfortunately the clues here are riddled with ambiguities, partly because the acknowledgment is couched in terms which Heidegger shares with Husserl. Tracking these clues is a matter of trying to pin these ambiguities down in a fashion Heidegger himself was not inviting. Indeed, they may suggest his intention of avoiding a confrontation with Husserl. In this Heidegger was to an extent successful, since Husserl was not initially suspicious when he undertook his first cursory reading of *Being and Time*.

One ambiguity in the acknowledgment is that "breakthrough" is a different appraisal from "laying a foundation," so that both are not readily applicable to the same work. In fact, they would be applied to different works by Husserl himself. He had characterized the *Logical Investigations* (in his introduction to the second edition) as having been "for me a breakthrough work, and thus not an end but a start."[3] The inference to be drawn is that it is, as "a breakthrough work," now being superseded by another work—that is, by *Ideas I*, which was published the same year as this second edition of the *Investigations* and which Husserl clearly regards as foundational.

When Heidegger in his acknowledgment borrows the appraisal "breakthrough" (though without mentioning it had been Husserl's), the appraisal still refers, as it did in Husserl, to the *Logical Investigations*. But since Heidegger does not mention *Ideas I, Being and Time* can itself become instead the "investigation" which Heidegger has just indicated Husserl's *Investigations* have made "possible." Indeed, since he has transcribed the appraisal "breakthrough" from Husserl, its implication in Husserl might accompany the transfer—"thus not an end but a start."

Once we begin reading Husserl into Heidegger, another ambiguity emerges. Heidegger downgrades "phenomenology" as a 'movement.'" Is its founder Husserl included? Perhaps not. I have already mentioned that Husserl himself was given to disavowing "the phenomenological movement." Thus, from Heidegger's reference in quotation marks to the "'movement,'" we cannot infer that he is necessarily disavowing Husserl's phenomenology. Husserl himself apparently took the reference to the "movement" as if he were being quoted. At least there is no protest here in the margin of his copy of *Being and Time*—not even a question mark or exclamation mark, to which he frequently resorts elsewhere when he is suspicious or outraged.

Still another ambiguity is Heidegger's sweeping exaltation of "possibility" over "actuality." This may seem to enable Heidegger to exalt *Being and Time* unambiguously as the ensuing "investigation" that Husserl's *Investigations* had made "possible," over the actual *Investigations* themselves. Yet at the same time Heidegger could again seem to be only quoting Husserl, who asserts in *Ideas I,* "The old ontological doctrine, that knowledge of 'possibilities' must take precedence over knowledge of actualities is, in my opinion, insofar as it is correctly understood, . . . a great truth."[4]

If Heidegger is taking over this distinction of Husserl's, there is another unresolved ambiguity. The "precedence" as "correctly understood" by Husserl is the outcome of the shift, which he carries out with the eidetic reduction, from the empirical level (for instance, particular examples of an act of consciousness) to the level of of "essences," at which the structure of any act of consciousness is identified as "intentional." Husserl's phenomenology itself, as "eidetic" (a science of "essences"), is "methodologically foundational" (Husserl explains in *Ideas I*) in a fashion which is comparable to the sense in which the "mathematical disciplines (for instance, geometry . . .) are foundational for physics [which only exemplifies relations which are mathematically possible]."[5]

This affiliation of phenomenology with geometry is regularly criticized by Heidegger in his lectures earlier in the twenties. But the ambiguity introduced by his taking over Husserl's distinction between "possibilities" and "actualities" can only be dealt with when the procedure is determined which he himself employs in lieu of the eidetic reduction. I am encouraged to anticipate this problem now because the acknowledgment of his debt to Husserl occurs in the section of *Being and Time* entitled "The Phenomenological Method of Investigation." Indeed, in this section Heidegger has already identified "phenomenology" itself as "*a concept of method.*"[6] Yet I cannot go on directly to a comparison of their conceptions of phenomenological method, since no mention appears in this section (or elsewhere in *Being and Time*) of the eidetic reduction.

The Lurch

What Heidegger does avow in this section is the procedural principle which, I have mentioned, he takes over from Husserl—that of proceeding directly "to the things themselves."[7] This principle poses a problem of translation. I have just translated *Sachen* by "things," but this is the cognate for the German *Dinge,* which usually refers to "things" which occupy real space. *Sachen* need not do so, and the "things" which are crucial to Husserl do not—they are "essences," which are the ideal "possibilities" that he reaches with the eidetic reduction. In an attempt to minimize the hazard of the translation "things," I shall sometimes resort to the alternative of Heidegger's later usage when the commitment becomes for him "to the subject [*Sache*] itself."[8] He never comments on this revision of Husserl and even reads it back into Husserl. Since it is Heidegger's later usage, I do not pause now to explain why he came to prefer the singular to the plural.

My own general presumption is that there is no comprehensive adjustment to be envisaged of the relation between "the subject" and the procedures that compose a method for treating it; the adjustment is a matter of how the respective requirements of subject and method are met in the elaboration of a particular philosophy.[9]

In *Being and Time* Heidegger could be said to have already proceeded directly "to the subject itself." The first chapter of his introduction is entitled "The Necessity, Structure, and Priority of the Question of Being," whereas he does not arrive at the topic, "The Phenomenological Method of Investigation," until the next to the last section of his introduction. Moreover, in this section Heidegger might himself be said to begin by recognizing the sense in which he has already in effect proceeded directly to his subject: "With the preliminary characterization of the thematic subject [*Gegenstand*] of our investigation (the being of beings, or the meaning of being as such), we seem to have thereby already indicated its method."[10] Accordingly, I glance first at this subject in order to determine its bearing on the relation between Heidegger and Husserl.

What I characterize generally as a shift in *subject* usually takes place with a successor, even when he is considerably indebted to the previous philosopher. The illustration I provided in Volume 2 was Sartre's annexing in *L'imaginaire* the "imaginary" to the subject of "perception" as a subject Husserl had already treated.[11]

The relation between Heidegger and Husserl in *Being and Time* has almost always been interpreted as a shift in subject: Heidegger transforms phenomenology, which in Husserl is an eidetic analysis of meanings, into an ontology by posing the question of the meaning of being. Thus Sartre apparently thought of himself as following in Heidegger's wake when he chose for *Being and Nothingness* the subtitle, *An Essay in Phenomenological Ontology*. Sartre's "synthesis" (Sartre's term for his handling of the relation between Husserl and Heidegger)[12] is a facile reconciliation, whereas Heidegger's transformation is so abrupt as to amount to a "lurch" (*Ruck*), an idiom I borrow from a contemporary German review of *Being and Time*.[13]

Although there is undoubtedly a lurching shift in subject in *Being and Time*, it cannot adequately be characterized as a shift from phenomenology to ontology, inasmuch as Husserl himself elaborates an ontology in *Ideas I* and elsewhere.

The Blur

Other expositors have recognized that what I am characterizing as a lurch is so drastic a shift as to render Heidegger's relation to Husserl hard to get at. Thus Granel observes, "*Being and Time,* aside from occasional assertive moments whose *brusquerie étoufée* ['suppressed brusqueness'] itself creates problems, is swamped in a kind of *flou* [the "blur," the "fuzziness," of something which is "out of focus"] with respect to what had to do with its relation to Husserl's phenomenology."[14]

Granel's idiom is an appropriate rendering of the effects of such ambiguities as I have been considering. But we should also observe, when Granel comes up against the "blur," the "fuzziness," how hesitant he is in handling the relation between Heidegger and Husserl. Hence his diffident title, "Remarks on the Relation between *Being and Time* and Husserl's Phenomenology," and his characterization of these remarks as "meager."[15] This diffidence of Granel's in 1970 is in sharp contrast with the cavalier confidence displayed earlier by Sartre and Merleau-Ponty when they dealt with the relation between Heidegger and Husserl.

Granel's diffidence also illustrates the extreme difficulty of bringing into focus the relation to Husserl which is "out of focus" in Heidegger himself. The difficulty is further manifested by a certain incongruity in Granel's interpretation of Heidegger. He is a sympathetic expositor of Heidegger, and when Heidegger is engaged in the elaboration of his own philosophy, Granel does not accuse him of such a failing as "fuzziness."

We encounter a similar incongruity in another competent scholar's interpretation of Husserl. Denise Souche-Dagues got a look at the marginal comments Husserl entered in his copy of *Being and Time* before they were published in full, and she appraises Husserl's interpretation as "illustrating . . . what, seen from Heidegger's side, must be considered crude misinterpretation, lacking . . . in any generosity." But this crude misinterpretation, she adds, "dominates [Husserl's] entire reading of *Being and Time*."[16] Souche-Dagues would credit Husserl with subtlety (as Granel would credit Heidegger) in elaborating his own separate philosophy. But this talent seems strangely lacking as soon as he becomes guilty of "crude misinterpretation" when it comes to his relation to Heidegger. The fuzziness of Heidegger's interpretation and the crudity of Husserl's would seem alike to betray the difficulty these two philosophers had in coping with their relation, as compared with other philosophical problems. A heavy burden then is put on the expositor of *Being and Time,* for he must intervene and discern the confrontation that never quite takes place (I retain Searle's phrasing) between the two philosophers themselves.

I return to Granel's explanation of their relation in terms of what I characterize as a shift in *subject.* He explains that the question of being is not, and cannot be, for Husserl, a question. Consequently anyone [sc. Heidegger] who poses this question, and who only poses other questions in its terms or under its domination, speaks a language which cannot be understood or translated in Husserl's fashion; that is why, too, Heidegger cannot succeed . . . in sharing with his mentor the question of the relation between their respective thoughts.[17]

This inability of Heidegger to share this question presumably explains the brusqueness as well as the fuzziness which Granel finds characteristic of Heidegger's treatment of the relation.

The interpretation of Heidegger's relation to Husserl has itself a history, which I have been respecting. As I indicated with the rough periodization in my last chapter, it was after Granel's article that Heidegger's Zähringen seminar came as a revelation. I have held back on it because no scholar engaged in the exposition of *Being and Time* had anticipated what Heidegger revealed.

Beaufret could have had Granel's article in mind when he formulated the question for the seminar, "To what extent can it be said that there is not in Husserl a question of being?" This negative formulation reproduced what seemed Heidegger's own conviction. He had himself referred, in the first section of *Being and Time,* to the "negligent omission" (*Versäumnis*) of this question by philosophers. In the seminar, Heidegger does not quarrel with Beaufret's negative formulation (indeed, he may have solicited it), but he explains how Husserl, in his analysis of categorial intuition in the *Logical Investigations,* "grazes slightly [*effleure*] the question of being. . . . I had finally the foundation."[18] Heidegger no longer says, as he had said in *Being and Time,* that it was Husserl who had "laid the foundation." In fact "grazing slightly" is a very different operation from laying a foundation. Thus Heidegger's retrospective comment in the seminar does not render any less blurred his relation to Husserl as presented in *Being and Time.*

The Idiom

I turn to another idiom which Granel offers with his assertion that when Heidegger raises the question of the meaning of being, he "speaks a language which cannot be understood or translated in Husserl's fashion." This use of the idiom of "translation" raises another question, which I would characterize as that of philosophical translation. This is a procedure, according to Richard Rorty, which can help us to understand what we mean by "understanding" a philosophy:

There is indeed a sense in which we can understand what a philosopher says in his own terms before relating his thought to ours, but . . . this minimal sort of understanding is like being able to exchange courtesies in a foreign tongue without being able to translate what one is saying into our native language. . . . Translation is necessary if "understanding" is to mean something more than engaging in rituals of which we do not see the point.[19]

I am not sure if we should privilege in this fashion our understanding of a philosopher in our own terms over the attempt to understand him in his own terms; after all his philosophy is his own "native language."

I am, however, dealing with a less easily negotiable matter: the understanding one philosopher has of another. One reason I am bringing the question of (philosophical) translation to the fore is that Husserl does so when he employs the idiom himself in his first sweeping appraisal (in the margin of his copy of *Being and Time*) of the relation between his own philosophy and Heidegger's:

H[eidegger] transposes or transfers the clarification which is . . . phenomenology of all regions of being and of the universal, of the total region 'world,' into the anthropological. The entire problematic [in *Being and Time*] is a translation [*Übertragung*] of my own problematic.[20]

The relevance of this marginal comment can be more readily appreciated if we glance back at a marginal comment two pages earlier: "That would be a reproduction of my own theory [*Lehre*]."

"That" refers to a claim of Heidegger's regarding "all ontology," which I shall soon quote. What I would draw attention to now is only the promptness with which Husserl envisages the prospect of assessing in terms of his own theory a claim of Heidegger's. This promptness is not just personal arrogance. I have already explained how identity of meaning is secured in Husserl's philosophy by the eidetic reduction. The problem for his philosophy is that we have to "keep our meanings *unshakably identical*" (my italics). There is "a continuing need for caution and for frequent reexamination to see whether what was fixed in the earlier context [the meaning originally secured for a concept by an eidetic reduction] is actually employed in the identical sense." The danger is that "unnoticed ambiguities may allow other concepts to slip subsequently underneath our words."[21] The meanings arrived at reductively should be kept identical each time they are used. Thus "reconfirmation," "reactivation," is necessary—the carrying out "all over again" of an eidetic reduction.

Trans-lation

When Husserl regards phenomenology as an eidetic science comparable to geometry, he assumes that geometry is "identically the same in the 'original language' of Euclid and in all its 'translations' [into other languages besides Euclid's Greek]."[22] Thus he further assumes that phenomenology should remain "identically the same," when it enlists the services of any other philosopher. This assumption is implicit in his training his students as a "team."

Here we can begin to recognize the implications that the idiom of "translation" has for him. On the one hand, Husserl tends to evaluate *Being and Time* not as the work of another philosopher but in terms of his own philosophy: "The entire problematic is a translation of my own problematic. To the ego corresponds the Dasein, etc." The "etc." implies that Husserl could come up with a list of further correspondences between his original "problematic" and Heidegger's "translation." The sweep of "entire" suggests that the only philosophy that comes into focus for Husserl as he reads *Being and Time* is his own, reproducible in the same sense that geometry is "identically the same . . . in all its 'translations' [into different languages from Euclid's Greek]." On the other hand, there is an ambiguity in his employment of the term *translation*. Husserl is not employing the more usual word for "translation," *Übersetzung*. He employs instead *Übertragung*, perhaps in order to bring to our attention the etymology of *trans-lation,* so that he can more definitely stigmatize Heidegger's ambiguous relation to him, whereby Heidegger does not simply *reproduce* Husserl's philosophy but "transposes or transfers" (*transponiert oder transversiert*) it "into the anthropological."

This etymologizing of *Übertragung* is unusual on Husserl's part. As Derrida points out (though without any reference to the comment of Husserl's that we are examining), Husserl "almost never resorts to etymological variations."[23] Tolerating variations would ordinarily be inconsistent with his eidetic reduction as a procedure for securing identity of meaning. Husserl here indulges for once in an etymology for the very special purpose of conveying how perverse a mistranslation is Heidegger's trans-lation, as a transposition or transference. The perversity, Husserl claims elsewhere, is that his phenomenology has been interpreted "backward from the level" which was its "entire meaning to overcome."[24] The twist to his claim brings out the perversity he would attribute to Heidegger.

The "entire" here, whereby his phenomenology would seem to have entirely lost its meaning, presumes his other claim of "entire," whereby Heidegger's "entire problematic" was "a translation of my own." But the issue for Husserl is not simply a matter of the identity of meaning achievable by his eidetic reduction; the etymology kicks in when he recognizes that Heidegger's "transference" or "transposition" reverses the shift in *level,* which Husserl had himself carried out with the phenomenological reduction, from the empirical to the transcendental. (The phenomenological reduction is a procedure of Husserl's I shall consider later.) The result in Heidegger's case (Husserl goes on from the "etc." I previously quoted to assert) is that "the whole becomes profoundly unclear and loses its value as a philosophy." In other words phenomenology has reverted to the level of an empirical science—anthropology.

"It must be said" (and it is Souche-Dagues, whom I have already quoted, who says it) "that Husserl carries out the inverse 'transposition' of that for which he reproaches Heidegger." It is at this juncture that she accordingly complains that Husserl's interpretation must be regarded, when viewed from Heidegger's side, as a "crude misinterpretation, lacking —one feels—in any generosity." And at this juncture as well she further concludes that this crude misinterpretation "dominates [Husserl's] entire reading of *Being and Time*," and claims that "the confusions committed [by Husserl] on the text [of *Being and Time*] are so crude that one asks oneself if they are not deliberate insults."[25]

I have been explaining instead how Husserl is trammeled in his reading of *Being and Time* by his commitment to a conception of the meaning of "meaning" that involves maintaining identity in meaning. Heidegger, in contrast, tolerates ambiguities—at least we have seen that he does when he is acknowledging his debt to Husserl. I admit the ambiguities of his acknowledgment to Husserl are not very interesting, so that we are ready to acquiesce in the explanation that he only wants to avoid a confrontation with Husserl. More interesting are the ambiguities which we shall later watch Heidegger wield in elaborating his own philosophy.

Perversion

In reaching his marginal appraisal of *Being and Time* as a "trans-lation," Husserl seems to have been still brooding over Heidegger's italicized claim which he had read two pages earlier:

> *All ontology, no matter how rich and coherent a system of categories it has at its disposal, remains fundamentally blind and a perversion [Verkehrung] in the aim which is most its own, if it has not first adequately clarified the meaning [Sinn] of being and conceived this clarification as its fundamental task.*[26]

This allegation of perversity could have caught Husserl's attention because it foists on "all ontology" Heidegger's own preoccupation with "the meaning of being."

Husserl's prompt reaction to Heidegger's claim, which I began quoting earlier, is, "That would be a reproduction of my own theory, if 'clarified' meant [*besagt*] clarified in . . . phenomenological fashion." But there is no longer any "if" two pages further on, when Husserl reaches the verdict, "The whole becomes profoundly unclear and loses its value as philosophy." Later, when I have exposed Heidegger's competing criterion, I shall come back to Husserl's criterion of clarity. Husserl will continue to denounce Heidegger in the margins of *Being and Time* as "unclear."

For the present I would not dispute Granel's assessment that Heidegger's treatment of his relation to Husserl is "out of focus," or Souche-Dagues's assessment that Husserl's treatment of Heidegger is a "crude misinterpretation," or even insulting. Indeed, at one juncture she even considers "the misunderstanding . . . so dense that one would abandon to futility [*inanité*] the dialogue between the two thinkers."[27]

Nonetheless I shall try to reinstate a dialogue of sorts by seeking out junctures at which they can be said to find themselves, not futilely but significantly, at cross-purposes. Philosophers sometimes are. When John Searle, for instance, reports, "Derrida has a distressing penchant for saying things that are obviously false,"[28] the insulting imputation of perversity can be taken as evidence that the distressed reporter is likely to be a philosopher, affronted by another philosopher. But the relation between Heidegger and Husserl is a much more striking case of cross-purposes, since they were (as I pointed out earlier) former collaborators and promoters of the same brand of philosophy—phenomenology.

SIX

The Shift in Method

There is . . . a great difference between . . . pure
dedication to the requirements of the subject and
being clear in reflection about . . . the authentic
meaning of the method employed.—Husserl

The Priority of Method

In dealing with the relation between Heidegger and Husserl, previous expositors (Granel,
for example) have been primarily concerned
with the shift in *subject* to the question of
"the meaning of being" from the analysis of
"meanings." I shall try rather to bring Heidegger's relation to Husserl into focus as a
shift in *method*. So drastic a shift in *subject* as
that I have just traced could not have been
carried out without a concomitant shift in
method.

I begin with an adjustment in the relation
between subject and method, for it involves a
complication which demonstrates how much
the two philosophers are at cross-purposes—
so much so that we must recognize what is at
issue is the very character of philosophy itself
as an undertaking. The complication can be
compared with the complication we encountered with Husserl's expectation that Heidegger could be recruited as a follower. This
expectation could be said to have been frus-
trated not simply by Heidegger's refusal as a
matter of fact to become a follower of Husserl's; "following" itself was a role Heidegger
denied could be played in philosophy. Somewhat similarly, the differences in method between them can hardly be assessed without
anticipating that later in his career Heidegger
explicitly denies "the priority" (*Vorrang*) that
Husserl accorded to method. This denial is
associated with a certain indifference on Hei-

degger's part to differences in method. Thus, having admitted that Hegel's and Husserl's methods are as "different as they could be," he asserts, "But the subject" for both of them "is the same."[1] That is Heidegger's sole concern, as we shall eventually see. Hence he does not bother to specify what the differences in method are. Specific differences between Heidegger's and Husserl's methods will nevertheless remain my concern throughout my exposition.

All that concerns me at present is to anticipate how much at cross-purposes Heidegger and Husserl turn out to be with respect to the adjustment of the distinction between method and subject. In *Ideas I* Husserl avows, as "the principle of all principles," his commitment to the "things" (*Sachen*) which are immediately (intuitively) given as essential to consciousness—that is, to its intentional structure as "consciousness of something." This principle, Heidegger concludes, accords a "priority" to method (which he will not concede) because it "determines which subject [*Sache*] can satisfy [the requirements of] method," and thereby entails the abandonment of Husserl's other principle of proceeding directly "to the subject [*Sache*] itself." (That this "subject" of Husserl's is, according to Heidegger, "the subjectivity of consciousness" is not my present concern.) Thus Heidegger eventually discards Husserl's "principle of all principles" as inconsistent with Husserl's other principle, which Heidegger would retain as conferring priority instead on "the subject itself."[2] But for Husserl the two principles in effect coalesce: to proceed "to the things [*Sachen*] themselves" is to apply "the principle of all principles" and arrive at essences which will be immediately given.

To the reader who is alarmed by the sweep of Heidegger's argument, I repeat that my concern will remain with specific differences between his method in *Being and Time* and Husserl's method. I am not trying to ascertain the precise relevance of this later argument to Heidegger in the twenties, but I suspect that its very sweep betrays how completely Husserl loses the earlier relevance that he enjoyed for Heidegger.

Another reason for my anticipation is that an adjustment in the relation between method and subject also occurs in the course of Husserl's career. The later Heidegger's explicit denial of "the priority of method" permits an initial broad contrast with Husserl, who became in *Ideas I* what he had not been in the *Logical Investigations*—a proponent (in Heidegger's terms) of "the priority of method." (Recall Heidegger's endorsement of the *Investigations* at the expense of *Ideas I*.) Now I am emphasizing that Husserl's later misgivings regarding the *Investigations* were predominantly methodological. He felt he had failed there to recognize fully the importance of "the eidetic reduction" (terminology itself which he had not yet arrived at) as a procedure for carrying out the shift in level to essences, and he had not yet even discovered there the phenomenological reduction with which the shift to a transcendental level is to be carried out.

In the unpublished introduction (1913) to the second edition of the *Logical Investigations*, Husserl explains why these methodological considerations did not emerge more definitely:

> There is, after all, a great difference between making novel theoretical discoveries . . . in pure dedication to the requirements of the subject and being clear in reflection about . . . the authentic meaning [*eigentümlich Sinn*] of the method employed.[3]

Husserl could think of himself as having made "novel theoretical discoveries" in the *Logical Investigations*. But what only becomes "clear in reflection" (an obvious instance is *Ideas I*) is "the authentic meaning of the method employed." Indeed, in *Ideas I* method can be said to acquire a priority it did not have in the *Logical Investigations*. The first part of *Ideas I* is largely taken up with the eidetic reduction, and the second part is taken up with the phenomenological reduction. Thus the priority that method acquires in *Ideas I* is illustrated by his devoting the first two parts (119 pages) to method. We can even add the third part (145 pages more), since it is entitled "To the Procedures [*Methode*] and Problematic of Pure Phenomenology."

Husserl was well aware of his increasing preoccupation with method. He ruefully would tell the story of how as a child he had been given a pocketknife. Instead of using it, he kept sharpening the blade, not noticing that it was becoming ever smaller, until it vanished.[4]

The Components

Heidegger must have been prepared, when *Being and Time* was published in April 1927, for readers to expect some reference to Husserl's famous reductions in a section entitled "The Phenomenological Method of Investigation." The absence of any reference must have seemed a puzzling oversight. Even students who had deserted Husserl in Freiburg for Heidegger in Marburg would have wondered what had happened to the reductions. Whether or not they actually confronted Heidegger with questions, he seems to be making up for the omission when, in his 1927 summer course, published as *The Basic Problems of Phenomenology*, he discusses the "three basic components" of phenomenology as a method. He offers an explicit comparison with Husserl only with respect to the first component, the phenomenological reduction, and with the warning that though he is "adopting a crucial term of Husserl's phenomenology," it is "only verbally, and not with regard to the subject [*wortlaut, nicht aber der Sache*]."[5] Thus the comparison he makes would hardly survive the application of the principle of proceeding directly "to the subject itself," and may help explain why he had not felt it necessary to make the comparison in his section on phenomenological method in the introduction to *Being and Time.*

This is how Heidegger presents the second component:

Being [*Sein*] does not become accessible as a being [*seiende*] does. We do not just find it in front of us. . . . It is always to be brought into view in a free project [*Entwurf*]. This project . . . we designate phenomenological *construction.*[6]

In the case of this second component, Heidegger does not offer a comparison with Husserl, as he did with the first. Indeed, there is no similarity—not even "verbally"—that Heidegger could have relied on. The very idiom of "construction" (used by neo-Kantians before Heidegger came on the scene) was repugnant to Husserl, with his commitment to knowledge as immediately given.

Heidegger's presentation of method in the introduction to the *Basic Problems* ends with the anticipation that we shall be "led back" in the final part of the lectures to the "starting point." We are also promised, in his initial outline of the course, a final discussion of the same "three basic components." Thus, before we consider any of them, let us patiently wait —as students then would have—for the end of the course. In the intervening lectures he neither comments on his method nor mentions any of these components. What he does treat in his last lecture is "the phenomenological method of ontology," but we are not "led back" there to his "starting point." Having repeated his commitment to what "the things themselves require," he begs off: "We cannot now go any further into the essential basic components of this method."[7] Does the "now" suggest merely that he is running out of time at the end of the semester? This rather frequently happened to Heidegger in his courses. Still we cannot put the entire emphasis on the "now," for he never found time in his later courses to go any further into the three components. Method would seem to be already losing for him the priority it had acquired for Husserl.

Having begged off with his "now," Heidegger comments, "As a matter of fact we have applied this method continually. What we would have to do would be merely to go over the way already pursued, but now with explicit reflection [*Besinnung*] on it."[8] Husserl, we have seen, is committed to explicit reflection on his method. If Heidegger is not, it is because of the different interpretation he puts on the principle he inherited from Husserl of going directly "to the things themselves." Heidegger's different interpretation involves a different adjustment in the relation between subject and method. He explains that "in the essence of all genuine method, as a way toward the disclosure of objects, is its always directing itself toward what through it is to be disclosed."

Way

What I have just shown is that by the end of the *Basic Problems* method no longer seems to enjoy the priority it did at the beginning of this course. Did it enjoy priority there only because Heidegger undertook a comparison with Husserl? I raise this question because it may seem that I too am assigning priority to method in Heidegger for the purpose of undertaking the comparison with Husserl.

The question as to Heidegger's method I shall settle by spreading out the specific evidence in my ensuing exposition. Since this will entail "grubby work," I would anticipate now the scope of the issues associated with method's losing later in Heidegger the priority it has in Husserl. What happens most obviously is that references to "method" are superseded by references to the "way" that Heidegger thinks of himself as following. The idiom of "way" does not become prominent in *Being and Time* until the end of the portion published. But in the only preface he added later (the preface to the seventh edition of *Being and Time* in 1953), he claims that "its way still remains necessary today." Heidegger flourishes this idiom in his later titles: *Holzwege, Feldweg, Wegmärken, Unterwegs zur Sprache*. Indeed, when he finally offers an appraisal of his relation to Husserl, he does not refer to phenomenology as the "method" it was in *Being and Time*, and his essay is entitled, "My Way to Phenomenology." He insists, "We must learn to distinguish between way and method. In philosophy there are only ways; in contrast, in the sciences there are only methods—that is, procedures."[9] Thus one large-scale issue here between Heidegger and Husserl is Husserl's programmatic commitment to "philosophy as rigorous science."

Sequence

My eventual concern is to salvage the significance of method in what might be called (if a label is needed) the procedural sense, and to do so by bringing out in my exposition of *Being and Time* the differences between Heidegger's method and Husserl's that Heidegger himself does not explicitly acknowledge. To begin, I would single out a difference that has a direct bearing on my own procedure. At the outset of Heidegger's final discussion in *The Basic Problems*, he states, "The method of ontology is nothing but the sequence of steps [*Schrittfolge*] in gaining access to being as such and the working out [*Ausarbeitung*] of its structures."[10] This generalization may seem unpromising. What philosopher does not have a method in the broad sense that he takes a sequence of steps in working out his philosophy? But a sequence can have a stronger sense which is not philosophically neutral. There are different kinds of sequences. I cite the obvious examples. When Descartes commits himself in his *Discourse on Method* to "following a sequence [*ordre*] in my thinking, starting out with the simplest object and easiest to know, in order to arrive little by little as by steps [*par degré*] at the knowledge of the most composed, and assuming sequence even between those matters which do not proceed naturally one from the other,"[11] we recognize that he is following the sequence which since Aristotle has been distinguished as the epistemological order of knowing rather than the ontological order of nature. But he is not following that sequence as Aristotle envisaged it, since Descartes found his inspiration in an affiliate: "Those long chains of reason, altogether simple and easy, which the geometricians are wont to employ in order to arrive at their most difficult demonstrations, had been the occasion for my imagining that all things which could come within the scope of human knowledge follow each other in the same fashion." But this is not the sequence which Spinoza follows when he employs his own geometrical method. Although Husserl (as we have seen) took geometry as an affiliate which encouraged his adoption of an eidetic method, he does not thereby proceed in either Spinoza's or Descartes's fashion.

Although my examples illustrate that philosophers may follow different sequences, the significant methodological difference which I would now recognize between Heidegger and Husserl is that Husserl does not follow a "sequence of steps" in Heidegger's sense. Husserl "proceeds in a zigzag." As he himself explains, "One starts out, goes a certain distance, then goes back to the beginning, and what one has learned one applies to the beginning."[12] Husserl concedes that any "discipline would seem to require following out the order of things [*Sachen*] step by step," but then adds that "the security of our investigation requires breaking repeatedly with systematic sequence."

One justification Husserl gives for these interruptions is a "difficulty" which he explains is encountered "in all disciplines which are reflexively related to themselves." An example of such "reflexive relatedness" (*Rückbezogenheit*) is "the thinking of the psychologist," which "is itself something psychological"; another example (Husserl's own case) is "the thinking of the logician," which is itself logical. Because of this difficulty, "the first investigative entry into these disciplines must operate with methodological resources which can only subsequently be given a scientifically definite form."[13] This is a recurrent juncture at which Husserl is committed, as I indicated in my introduction, to *Umarbeitung*—to "working over again" what he had undertaken earlier; only at this juncture what he is "working over again" are specifically his "methodological resources," intentional analysis and the reductions. With the interruptions of his treatment of substantive problems, and his "working over again" of his "methodological resources," method obtains in Husserl the "priority" to which Heidegger takes exception.

As an illustration of Husserl's commitment to subsequent reflection on what he had already worked over, I take intentionality. It is, he stresses, "completely indispensable at the start of phenomenology,"[14] because it is not just a substantive problem but determines the character of his method as intentional analysis. Thus he formulates the concept of intentionality in the first of his *Logical Investigations,* but he is led back to it in the fifth, and again later in *Ideas I,* where some of the difficulties in formulating it he deals with by carrying out his two reductions.

The difference between Husserl's zigzagging and Heidegger's commitment to "a sequence of steps" is associated with two differences between them we have already observed. First of all, it is associated with Husserl's according a certain priority to method and thus to its explicit formulation and subsequent reformulation, whereas Heidegger leaves his method largely implicit in its application. The increasing explicitness that method gains from Husserl's reflecting on it in turn helps explain a second difference between him and Heidegger. If Husserl sought a "following," if he could expect to train his students to become a "team," it was (I have already suggested) because his method could be explicitly set forth.

The sequential character of Heidegger's method in *Being and Time* is evident in how frequently he indicates the step at which he is in the sequence he is following. Thus he announces at the beginning his "provisional aim" in this work. We have also seen that in the section entitled "The Phenomenological Method of Investigation" he settles down to formulating "The Preliminary Concept of Phenomenology." Division 1, which follows the introduction, is entitled "Preparatory Fundamental Analysis of Dasein."[15]

What holds for this long-run sequence holds also for the short run. We shall often find Heidegger drawing attention to the step he is at in the sequence of his analysis. Indeed, when *Being and Time* was published, Oskar Becker (a student of Husserl's who often attended Heidegger's lectures) "was irritated by the pedantic scholasticism of the reiterated outlines and advance announcements of paragraph divisions replete in *Being and Time.*"[16] Becker is overlooking how intrinsic to Heidegger's method is following a sequence of steps. Hence Heidegger's indicating to the reader the step he is at (in relation to a previous step or a subsequent step) is a prominent feature of his reiterated outlines and advance announcements.

I have not yet gotten very far in my contrast with Husserl's method, since I have been delayed by having to explain why Heidegger's method is less readily discerned. Thus I would recall the recommendation in my introduction regarding the pace at which it is appropriate to proceed in an exposition of Heidegger. Here the most obvious contrast is with Sartre. In *Method and Imagination* (Volume 2 of this work) I had to cope with what Simone de Beauvoir describes as "the extreme rapidity" with which Sartre wrote—"breathless from following with his pen the movement of his thought."[17] Sartre was in such a hurry that he did not usually take time out, as Heidegger does, for "outlines and advance announcements." In my exposition of Sartre I was more patient than he was.

Heidegger, in contrast, is an unusually slow thinker, and he seems to have been sensitive to Sartre's rapidity. It may be no accident that the final sentence in Heidegger's "Letter on Humanism," which can be regarded as a criticism of Sartre (if Heidegger's works lent themselves to so easy an allocation) compares the "furrows" left by "thinking" to the "furrows the peasant, *slow of step*, draws through the field" (my italics).[18] It is true that I am quoting the later Heidegger, who even rebukes the earlier Heidegger for having gone "too far too fast" in *Being and Time*."[19] But his rebuke might also be taken as cautioning the expositor not to go too far too fast in his exposition.

We also have an additional argument, besides that I adduced earlier, for staying as closely as we can with *Being and Time:* the sequence of steps there would not be respected if we attempted to conflate its statements with similar statements in other writings. An indiscriminate conflation is a temptation, with the spate of lecture courses recently published, but references to other writings, helpful as they sometimes can be, should be kept subordinate to recognizing the sequence of steps in *Being and Time*.

This is not to claim that the sequence there is sacrosanct. When, at the end of *Being and Time*, Heidegger plays up the idiom of "way," it is with the comment, "Whether this [the way he has been following as "a *way*" of illuminating the fundamental question of ontology] is the *only* way, or even the right way at all, can be decided only *after one has gone along it*." As a matter of fact, he had followed other ways in his earlier writings. (The sequence in his *Introduction to Phenomenological Research* [1923–24] is radically different.) He himself later admits that there were "many places where he was halted, took detours, and wrong ways [*viele Aufenthalte, Umwege und Abwege*]."[20] But such an admission itself is still a measuring up to the criterion of sequence.

Exposition

Heidegger does not identify such "places" specifically, but there can be little doubt that he would discount as *Umwege* und *Abwege* my expository departures from the sequence he himself follows. Indeed, they have already illustrated some of the hazards of dealing with the relation between two philosophers, as compared with the exposition of a single philosophy.

These hazards are so considerable that I find myself condemned to an *apologia pro via sua*. A philosophy is never elaborated parallel to another philosophy. Crossing from one to the other is never as straightforward as crossing from a sidewalk on one side of the street to the sidewalk on the other. Instead we confront cross-purposes separating the two philosophies. (Some of these I have already pointed out.) In comparing philosophies, one is usually consigned to *Abwege*. I offer one example from my present exposition. In my introduction I observed how, for Husserl and Heidegger alike, phenomenology was "difficult work." But this comparison was complicated by their different conceptions of a "difficulty," which were implicit in their different conceptions of the "work" that was necessary to cope with a "difficulty." I did attempt a broad contrast between their different conceptions of "work," but more specific differences in their conceptions of a "difficulty" I had to postpone. I have just alluded to *Rückbezogenheit* as a specific "difficulty" Husserl encountered, which precluded his proceeding in sequence as Heidegger does. But only in the next chapter shall I finally be able to deal with Heidegger's conception of a "difficulty." I shall not be able to reach Husserl's conception again until Chapter 11.

The expositor who criss-crosses between philosophers in this fashion is not zigzagging back and forth as Husserl does, for Husserl remains committed, even when he zigzags, to the principle of proceeding "to the things themselves," whereas I have been prompted, by the breakdown in communication between him and Heidegger, to get at the issues separating them—including the different fashion in which each proceeds in accordance with the principle "to the things themselves." But then I have to grant that neither Heidegger (despite the "gross errors" which he detected as having "cropped up" with respect to "the relation of my thought" to Husserl's) nor Husserl (despite his hope that some student might build a "bridge" between him and Heidegger) would show much sympathy with my detouring from this principle.

When some contrast of mine seems feasible at some juncture, there is still a risk, on the one hand, that my exposition may seem to have faltered, that I should have gone on with the exposition in order to clarify that philosophy more fully. On the other hand, when I do arrive at the other philosophy, I may seem to have been too involved with the first philosophy and to be undertaking an exposition of the other which is cluttered by pieces of my exposition of the first philosophy that are still clinging. In order to rectify my exposition, I must be even more irritatingly pedantic (as my present apologia illustrates) than Becker complained Heidegger was. I must keep acknowledging my own detours from Heidegger's sequence in order to focus on his relation to Husserl, and then I must indicate how I would reinstate Heidegger's sequence.

In short the relation between their two philosophies cannot be explained in a fashion that would fit it smoothly to both philosophies. If that could be done, it would leave unexplained how the breakdown of communication occurred between them.

SEVEN

: *The Retrieval*

*Ancient ontology . . . represents the first necessary
step that any philosophy as such must always
retrieve.—Heidegger.*

The First Step

In view of the hazards of exposition I have
been acknowledging, the safest expedient for
getting at Heidegger's method, as "nothing
but the sequence of steps" he takes, is to begin
with Heidegger's first step in *Being and Time.*

But what is his first step?

As late as page 52 of *Being and Time,*
Heidegger himself admits "the difficulties in
carrying out an existential analytic of the
Dasein—above all with respect to the start
[*Ansatz*]." (This "existential analytic" is his
initial undertaking in his treatment of "the
question of being.") I am, of course, citing his
own admission to extenuate how long it has
taken me to jockey for a starting position vis-
à-vis him and Husserl. But the admission is
also a reminder of how Heidegger, like Husserl, is beset with "difficulties."

Heidegger's most obvious first step is
the first section, "The Necessity for an Explicit Retrieval [*Wiederholung*] of the Question of Being." Granel may speak of the
"brusqueness" (albeit "suppressed") of the
"assertive moments" when Heidegger alludes
to Husserl. But brusqueness and assertiveness
are characteristic not of these moments alone.
This title of the first section of *Being and
Time* confronts us brusquely with an asserted
"necessity," and that is followed up in the
first sentence with an assertive announcement: "The aforesaid question is today forgotten, though in our time it is accounted

progress to endorse 'metaphysics' again." The qualification is not a concession that weakens the opposition. Rather it reinforces the starkness of the opposition with an ironic shrug, indicated by his use of quotation marks.

Heidegger's brusque assertiveness is not merely a matter of his personal temperament—something which would have to be explained psychologically. It is associated with "oppositional logic" (as Derrida would call it), although that takes (like the logic of sequence) such varied guises that I see little value in lumping them together. Here the opposition is between the "retrieval," as the procedure Heidegger would undertake, and the forgetfulness against which it is to be pitted. To bring out its methodological force, I have already borrowed an idiom from a contemporary review of *Being and Time:* what transpires here, with respect to the phenomenological movement, is a "lurch in a new direction" (*Ruck in eine neue Richtung*).

This idiom, in effect, is elaborated later by Heidegger himself:

> To the sciences there is always an immediate transition and access, starting from everyday representation. If one takes everyday representation as the measuring stick of all things, then philosophy is always something out of whack [*Verrücktes*]. The shifting [*Verrückung* of the attitude of thought can be carried out only with a lurch [*Ruck*].[1]

Perhaps we can more readily appreciate the methodological force of this "lurch" if I employ a comparison. I have already argued that a trait of a philosophy will sometimes emerge more distinctively when that philosophy is compared with another of demonstrable relevance. In Sartre's introduction to *Being and Nothingness* (whose very title betrays his emulation of *Being and Time*), there is no "lurch." Consider Sartre's initial sentences: "Modern thought has achieved considerable progress in reducing the existent to the series of the appearances which manifest it. Its aim was to eliminate a certain number of dualisms which were embarrassing philosophy." Instead of being initially brusque and oppositional, Sartre's first step is a standard, conciliatory academic procedure of falling into line with the "progress" which has already been made by his predecessors, whose contributions to eliminating dualisms he is ready to recognize before he himself takes any initiative.

The Step Backward

When Heidegger qualifies his initial assertion with "though in our time it is accounted progress [*Fortschritt*] to endorse 'metaphysics' again," he is not offering a genuine qualification, for he discounts "progress" by opposing to it, as a "step forward," the "step backward" (a *Schritt zurück,* as he will later term the retrieval) which he takes (in the next sentence) to the "battle of the giants over being" in Plato's *Sophist.* The initial "lurch [*Ruck*] in a new direction" thus becomes a *Rückgang* (going back).

The necessity of making the first step a "step backward" is explicitly proclaimed in the first chapter of the lecture course that Heidegger gave in the summer of 1928: "Ancient ontology . . . represents the first necessary step that any philosophy as such must always retrieve."[2] He had endorsed such a retrieval as early as his *Introduction to Phenomenological Research* (1923–24), whose first chapter is entitled "Clarification of the Expression 'Phenomenology' by Going Back [*im Rückgang*] to Aristotle."

That Husserl found such a *Rückgang* arbitrary is evident from his protest that Heidegger took some "question which first arose in Husserl's philosophy" and then read "it back into Aristotle."[3] To Husserl, a *Rückgang* was too incomprehensible to be a procedure, because his own procedure was to arrive at knowledge which is immediately given to consciousness.

Before we can get any further with this contrast with Husserl, we have to determine how Heidegger takes his "step backward"—conducts his retrieval—for it is not listed or discussed as one of the three components of phenomenological method in *The Basic Problems of Phenomenology.* We shall eventually find out why.

To begin by ascertaining certain traits of a retrieval, we do not have far to go. In fact we have already gone too far too fast. Even before the brusque announcement of the first section ("The Necessity for an Explicit Retrieval of the Question of Being") and the brusque assertion (the question "is forgotten") are followed up by the reference to the "battle of the giants" in Plato's *Sophist,* the retrieval is underway. Two paragraphs precede the first section, and the first sentence is a citation from Plato's *Sophist:* "For it is obvious that you have known this all along (what you would indicate when you say 'being'), but we who used to think we did, now we have gotten into difficulty." The two paragraphs do not compose a designated section of *Being and Time* proper, but as a matter of convenience I shall refer to them as a "preamble."

The Citation

If the citation from Plato were elevated over the start of the text (in the fashion my present volume amply exhibits), it could be regarded as a conventional epigraph. Since it is not (and since Heidegger elsewhere denies that it is "decoration"),[4] there is justification for John Sallis's concluding, in his essay "Where Does *Being and Time* Begin?" that it begins "in the middle of a Platonic dialogue."[5] I am not treating this conclusion as a quip. In the concluding chapter of my next volume, I shall still be asking how feasible is the comparison, which Heidegger may seem to invite, of his undertaking with a Platonic dialogue.

As further evidence for regarding *Being and Time* as beginning "in the middle of a Platonic dialogue," I would myself observe that the first German word in *Being and Time, Denn,* is a translation of the Greek conjunction *gar* (for). The survival of this conjunction has no grammatical justification in its new context. Its survival as a dangling remnant of the Greek sentence translated suggests that this citation is not cleanly cut out from its original context in the *Sophist.* The possibility that Heidegger is beginning in the middle of a Platonic dialogue is overlooked by his English translators, Macquarrie and Robinson, when they enable Heidegger to speak for himself by indenting a new paragraph after the citation and its translation. (The indentation survives in the Stambaugh translation, which is identical, except that the entire preamble is downgraded into smaller type than the rest of *Being and Time.*) Not only is there no indentation in the German edition, but there are also no breaks. In the same line as the Greek citation ends, the German translation continues, and in the same line as the German translation ends, Heidegger goes on to his own questions about the question in the *Sophist:* "Have we today an answer to the question as to what we authentically mean by the word 'being'? In no way. Are we then today even in difficulty over our not understanding the expression 'being'? In no way."

When these questions are assigned to a new paragraph, not only is it less evident that Heidegger is beginning in the middle of a Platonic dialogue, but the opposition also becomes less blunt between the Greek "we" in the final clause of the citation and its German translation ("now we have gotten into difficulty") and the "we today" who are not "even in difficulty." This is the opposition that is to be picked up in the first section with the demand for a retrieval to overcome our forgetfulness.

This matter of format seems trivial until we recognize that there are also problems with the citation and its German translation. The citation itself is not exactly a citation; Heidegger rearranges the original Greek. As for the translation, let me intervene and attempt to translate what Plato had actually said: "Then since we have gotten into difficulty, do you explain to us what you would signify when you say 'being.' For it is clear you have known this all along, whereas we who used to think we did, now have gotten into difficulty."

The Addressee

Although in Heidegger's rearrangement the citation and translation end with the "we" clause of the Platonic text unaltered, a phrase from the preceding "we" sentence in the Platonic text is interpolated parenthetically in the "you" sentence. Is Heidegger's rearrangement simply a matter of economy? Is he only shuffling together in one sentence two sentences in an effort to achieve the impact of the compact? There is something more to the impact, for one result of the rearrangement is that the final emphasis is on "we have gotten into difficulty," so that we get the blunt opposition between the "we" who are "in difficulty" in the citation and the "we today" —who are not "in difficulty."

Another result is to displace the initial "we" in Plato, so that the "you" is addressed at the start of the citation. Recognizing that the "we" turns up again as contemporary philosophers in the two questions after the translation, we might ask what happens "today" to the "you"? It may also acquire contemporary reference—perhaps to the philosopher to whom Heidegger has just addressed the dedication—"To Edmund Husserl in grateful admiration and friendship." Thus I would infer that a relation to Husserl may emerge with Heidegger's rearrangement of the citation. This inference is encouraged by a page, handwritten by Heidegger, which Husserl pasted on the verso of the flyleaf when he received a presentation copy of *Being and Time* from Heidegger. On this page Heidegger offered the quotation from the *Sophist* and a less inaccurate translation, which is followed by a dedication to Husserl, instead of being preceded by it, as in *Being and Time*.[6]

Of possible pertinence as well is that two years after the publication of *Being and Time,* Heidegger presented Husserl with a *Festschrift,* which Heidegger himself had edited. He had selected as its epigraph another citation from the *Sophist* in which the Stranger offers a description of "the philosopher" (that is, Husserl for the purpose of the *Festschrift*). If Heidegger adopts the Stranger on this occasion as his spokesman, could he not already have done so at the start of *Being and Time?* If the "we" in Heidegger's questions comes to refer to a different "we" today, is it not possible that the "you" may come to refer to a different "you"—the philosopher to whom *Being and Time* is dedicated? If two years later Heidegger attaches to Husserl a description of "the philosopher" from the *Sophist,* could he not be commenting with his citation from the *Sophist* on what is at issue in the relation between them as philosophers—the question of being?

I have already mentioned a comment of Heidegger's on his relation with Husserl during the period he was working on *Being and Time,* but it is worth quoting now in full. It is from the *Prolegomena,* the lecture course which he had given two years before the publication of *Being and Time,* and which he used as a draft when writing *Being and Time:*

> It is characteristic of Husserl that his questioning is fully in flux so that we must in the final analysis always remain cautious in our critique. I should mention that Husserl is aware of my objections from my lecture courses . . . and from conversations and is essentially taking them into account. Thus my critique today no longer applies in its full trenchancy. . . . It almost goes without saying that even today I still regard myself as a disciple in relation to Husserl.[7]

Given that the conversations with Husserl were still going on while Heidegger was writing *Being and Time,* may not the ostensible citation from a Platonic dialogue be an invitation to continue their dialogue? But even if the "you" in the citation and translation is obliquely a reference to Husserl, it is still not easy to decide whether this is to be taken as merely a personal nod toward Husserl or the philosophical invitation to dialogue that it was in Plato. If Heidegger is indeed issuing an invitation, he did not have to wait long for an answer of sorts. I mentioned earlier that while Heidegger was working on *Being and Time,* Husserl had invited him to collaborate on the article "Phenomenology" for the *Encyclopaedia Britannica.* Heidegger accepted Husserl's invitation as "an opportunity to characterize the fundamental tendency of *Being and Time* within the transcendental problematic."[8] But, as I also mentioned, Husserl found it impossible to use any of Heidegger's contributions. Husserl was on his way to the conclusion he would reach when retirement accorded him the leisure to read *Being and Time* more carefully than he had before: "I cannot include [*einorden*] the work within the framework of my phenomenology. . . . I also must reject entirely its method, and in its essentials its content [*sachlich*]."[9] What I shall continue to focus on are the differences in method which prompted Husserl's rejection.

EIGHT

· *The Translation*

> *Who better than Heidegger has taught us to think about what is involved in this problem of translation?—Derrida*

Eidos

Before I return to the citation and deal with the problem of Heidegger's German translation of the Greek, I would recognize another complication with respect to Heidegger's relation to Husserl. I have already indicated that Husserl found Heidegger's retrieval incomprehensible. Now I would add that Husserl does not encounter any problems of translation which can be dignified as philosophical, as are those Heidegger encounters when he carries out the retrieval. The knowledge that is to be attained as immediately given in Husserl is eidetic, and with regard to it we reach the same conclusion as holds with respect to its affiliate, the eidetic science of geometry. In that instance we have heard his claim:

> The Pythagorean theorem, geometry as a whole, exist only once, however often and even in whatever language they can be expressed. Geometry is identically the same in the "original language" of Euclid and in all its "translations."[1]

Husserl accordingly regards translation as in effect merely a kind of *Ausarbeitung* similar to that performed by his assistants when they transcribed his not easily decipherable shorthand into publishable German. Such *Ausarbeitung,* we have seen, is different in kind from the conceptual "work" required for phenomenology in the first place.

Nevertheless, a Greek term, *eidos*, does seem to be retrieved and enjoy prominence in *Ideas I*, where it is imported in Husserl's preface. It is worth considering his explanation. He imports *eidos* in order to translate the German term *Wesen* (essence), and he explains that *Wesen*, during the history of its philosophical use in German, has become "infected with ambiguities which are sometimes vexatious." As "an alien word," *eidos* has the advantage that it is "terminologically unspoiled."[2] In effect, it is not a translation, for its having been used in Greek philosophy can be dismissed as having nothing to do with modern philosophy. Greek is a dead language. Accordingly Husserl can assign the meaning which he finds philosophically appropriate—the unambiguous, essential, identical meaning which is indispensable to any term in his philosophy, particularly in the instance of *essence*, since the essential is what is identical. If Husserl resorts to *eidos* as early in *Ideas I* as the preface, it is because he envisages as his first undertaking in *Ideas I* the design of the procedure with which he will eliminate vexatious ambiguities generally: the reduction of any meaning he will entertain in his philosophy to its *eidos*—including the meaning of *essence* itself. This procedure he characterizes as the "eidetic" reduction, as we are already well aware.

Latin Translation

Although the problem of translation has come to the fore in *Being and Time* with how Heidegger translates a Greek citation, it is only the later Heidegger who deals explicitly with this problem. When he does so, there can be no overlooking the importance of the problem to him. Despite his effort to disassociate himself from the existentialist implications which were read into *Being and Time*, he himself made a statement with a rather existentialist ring: "Tell me what your attitude is toward translation, and I will tell you who you are."[3] It almost sounds as if one's authenticity were at stake. We might prefer to have had him say, "Tell me what your attitude is toward Nazism," and if he had told us, we would have thought we knew better who he was. I am not now trying to insert a political point; I am only playing up, as he himself does, how important translation is to him.

I begin with his later general statement of the problem of translation:

> The translation of Greek words into Latin is in no way the inconsequential process it is still held to be to this day. Beneath the seemingly literal [*wörtlich*] and thus trustworthy translation [*bewährenden Übersetzung; bewährenden* conveys the implication that the translation is "trustworthy" because it has been "put to the test" and can be accepted as "truthful"], there is concealed rather a trans-lation of

Greek experience into a different way of thinking. Roman thought takes over [*übernimmt*] the Greek words without a corresponding, equally original experience of what they say. . . . The groundlessness of Western thought begins with this translation.[4]

Heidegger would regard Husserl's "literal" translation of *Wesen* (which Husserl does not bother to notice derives from the Latin *essentia*) back into *eidos* as Husserl's having taken over a Greek word without taking into account the original experience of what the word says.

"Who better than Heidegger has taught us to think about what is involved in this problem of translation?" asks Derrida, when he himself would offer "a timid prolegomena" to this problem.[5] One should never overestimate Derrida's timidity, or underestimate, even when he is ostensibly proceeding in Heidegger's wake, the differences between them. Derrida's own commitment is to "*plus d'une langue,*"[6] but Heidegger, in making his translations of Greek into German, assumes that, along with Greek, German is, "with regard to the possibilities of thought, the most forceful and most spiritual of languages."[7]

We are now prepared to deal with Heidegger's German translation at the start of *Being and Time*.

Ambiguities

Just as Heidegger's citation is not exactly a citation in the usual sense, so his translation is not exactly a translation in the usual sense—not even of his own rearranged Greek. His procedure itself is ambiguous. We have seen that, on the one hand, his not omitting the "for" in his translation suggests that he intends to link his retrieval into the Platonic dialogue. On the other hand, not only does he omit other words in the Greek he cites, but there are also discrepancies between the Greek he cites and his German translation.

Macquarrie and Robinson do not seem to have been disturbed by these discrepancies. Indeed they dodge them by negotiating a sort of compromise in their English between translating the Greek and translating Heidegger's German: "For manifestly you have long been aware of what you mean when you use the expression 'being.' We, however, who used to think we understood it, have now become perplexed."[8] Perhaps they are assuming that the German translation is undertaken simply for the benefit of the illiterate.

A more accurate English translation of Heidegger's German translation would be, "For obviously you have been confident as to what you authentically [*eigentlich*] mean when you utter the expression 'being,' but we who believed we understood it, now have gotten into difficulty."

I begin with *eigentlich,* since there is no precedent for it in the Greek. We may be suspicious because *Eigentlichkeit* becomes a prominent concept later in *Being and Time,* so *eigentlich* here seems a very Heideggerian intrusion. Macquarrie and Robinson succumb to the temptation to correct Heidegger's German translation by not translating his *eigentlich* into their English, though they do translate it in the question Heidegger asks next—presumably because they would concede that "today" Heidegger can be allowed to say what he should not be allowed to get away with in translating Plato. Their not translating the first *eigentlich* (like the indentation with which they separate Heidegger's questions from his preceding translation) interrupts the argumentative continuity that Heidegger intends to achieve between the Platonic dialogue and what is to be undertaken "today."

Their translation of the second *eigentlich* is an innocuous "really." We do not discover why they adopt this translation until they later supply a note in which they are commenting on Heidegger's employment of *eigentlich* in section 2:

> The adverb *eigentlich* occurs very often in this work. It may be used informally where one might write "really" or "on its part," or in a much stronger sense, where something like "genuinely" or "authentically" would be more appropriate. It is not always possible to tell which meaning Heidegger has in mind.[9]

We are not now concerned with section 2, but this comment by Macquarrie and Robinson points up a recurrent problem in translating Heidegger himself. It is often not possible to tell which meaning—the informal, colloquial meaning or the stronger, conceptual meaning he is on the way to— is appropriate because (I shall argue) Heidegger would not dissociate them but would allow the meaning to stretch ambiguously from the colloquial to the conceptual.

Often he starts out, as he does here, with the colloquial meaning, and only further along his way does he arrive at the conceptual meaning. "Authentically" is an example, but unfortunately I shall not get so far in *Being and Time* as the corresponding concept itself. Another example of a colloquial term becoming a concept is *Umgang* (dealings). I shall come to it in Chapter 17, and I postpone until then this particular kind of stretch in meanings that appeals to Heidegger.

I am not about to violate Heidegger's sequence of steps by skipping from his first step to his later concept of "authenticity." But I can observe another kind of stretch which takes place at this first step itself by comparing how he proceeds at the start of *Being and Time* with how he proceeds at a comparable step in his summer-semester lecture course in 1928.

The comparison suggests that his retrieval is not a simple *Wiederholung,* a "fetching back" of some "Greek experience" from the past intact—just as it then was. His behest for a "retrieval" in this lecture course is, "Philosophy can be recognized only from and in historical recollection [*Erinnerung*], but this recollection is only what it is, is only living, in the present moment of self-understanding—that is, with one's own [*eigen*] free, productive grasp of the task philosophy harbors in itself."[10] (My comparison is justified, since *eigen,* if still colloquial, may carry the implication that the requisite "self-understanding" is an application of the eventual criterion of "*Eigentlichkeit.*") Thus Heidegger presumably uses the term *Erinnerung* here, rather than "retrieval," because he wants to bring out the reflexive "internalizing" required if the retrieval is also to be the "free, productive grasp" of "self-understanding," given that what is to be grasped is not anything distinctively personal but the task that philosophy "harbors in itself."

In the next sentence of the 1928 lectures, the inseparability of the recollection from the free, productive grasp is emphasized: they are not "two ways, but are both essential parts of the way" on which Heidegger would proceed. This emphasis helps us appreciate the continuity displayed by the transition in *Being and Time* from the question raised by the "we" in the *Sophist* to the questions of "we today" to which Heidegger would proceed.

The Way

In the lecture course we have another instance of a stretch of meaning between the Greek "we" and "we today" whereby the two procedures, which one would assume to be opposed—"historical recollection" and "self-understanding" sought at "the present moment"—are presented as inseparable. In this instance the question of sequence itself is encountered as embodied in the idiom of "proceeding along a way." This idiom, whatever other associations it may have, Heidegger obtains by a retrieval: he is translating the Greek *met-hodos* as "going along a way after."[11] The pertinence of this idiom may not be so immediately apparent at the start of *Being and Time,* but it comes abruptly to the fore (as I earlier indicated) at the end of *Being and Time:*

> One must seek a way of illuminating the fundamental question of ontology, and this is the way one must go. Whether this is the only way or even the right way at all, can be decided only *after one has gone along it.*[12]

The passage at the end of *Being and Time* continues, "The conflict over the interpretation of being cannot be allayed, because it has not yet been ignited." Heidegger is bringing to an end here a work he has been unable to finish, and he is doing so by returning to his starting point, where he commented on our assumption today that "we have been exempted from the struggles of igniting anew 'the battle of the giants over being.'" But he is returning to this starting point, with "explicit reflection" on the way he has been following, in the fashion he commends at the end of *The Basic Problems.*

The prospect of such reflection is suggested by his picking up the idiom of "way" again in an "Preliminary Remark," which he slips in at the beginning in the seventh edition of *Being and Time,* when he explains the new edition: "The way taken there still remains necessary today, if our Dasein is to be moved on its way after [*bewegt . . . nach*] the question of being." The "after" [*nach*] would seem to echo his retrieval of the idiom of "way" from the Greek *met-hodos.*

With this exegesis I am drawing attention to the ambiguous stretch of meaning that afflicts Heidegger's proceeding along a way. Too often it is supposed that Heidegger's adoption of this idiom is a refusal to employ a philosophical "method," which would involve a pretension, such as Husserl's, of being "scientific." Heidegger prefers to be humble and homespun, especially when his way later becomes a *Feldweg* (a path through the field). But a "way" in the usual colloquial sense is a single way, and cannot become "two ways," as it does in the lectures. "Way" can become so in Heidegger because it becomes as much a philosophical concept as does the similarly humble *Umgang,* which likewise embodies the idiom of "going," as I shall later emphasize.

Aporia

My present concern, however, is with another complication regarding Heidegger's idiom of "proceeding" (or "going"). In my introduction I pointed out that phenomenology was "difficult work" for Husserl and Heidegger alike, but that they have different conceptions of a "difficulty." These differences I have been preparing to examine. What so far has been recognized is merely that Heidegger's proceeding along a way (and being unable to decide if it is the right way until after having gone along it) is a very different procedure from Husserl's proceeding toward an experience which will be immediately given.

With my translation of the last, climactic term in the Greek citation, *ēporēkamen*—"we . . . now have gotten into difficulty"—I would seem to have accepted what amounts to a translation as well of Heidegger's "*sind wir in Verlegenheit gekommen.*" But there is an ambiguous stretch of meaning between the Greek and the German, and the implications of each have to be examined.

I restrict my attention initially to the Greek. The Greek noun corresponding to the verb in the citation is *aporia,* which did come to mean "difficulty" or "question" in Greek philosophy. But with the Greek, Heidegger is in effect commenting on the meaning which "question" has when it is "the question of the meaning of being." It becomes "that toward which [philosophy] is proceeding on its way and to which it never finds access [with *den Zugang nicht findet,* he is translating *ēporēkamen*]."[13]

But I cannot, to be consistent with my own interpretation of Heidegger's usage, skip over a range of prephilosophical, colloquial implications which Heidegger deploys for *aporia* in his 1935 summer lectures. There he comments on what he identifies as "essential words" in a chorus of Sophocles, *pantoporos aporos.* The *a* of *poros* is privative. *Poros* itself originally referred to a "ford" or "ferry" across a river. It acquired the extended meaning of "passage way," and thus the noun *aporia* came to imply an "impasse." Heidegger himself translates *poros* as "passage way through [*Durchgang durch*]."[14]

He similarly comments in his 1925 lectures on the *Sophist:*

> *aporein: Aporos* is what is without *Durchgang,* where one does not come through. *Poros* means originally the passage way through [*Durchgang durch*] a stream at a shallow place. *Aporia* means the investigation . . . does not come through, finds no way out. . . . No *Ausgang* is found.[15]

The "met-hodological" implications (I adopt this coinage temporarily by way of acknowledging Heidegger's etymological effort to retrieve the "Greek experience" of "method" as a proceeding along a "way") of Heidegger's double stress on *Durch* are not Greek and are further brought out by a definition: "*dialegesthai* [to engage in dialogue, 'talk with,' 'argue with,' or 'discuss a question with'] is to *diaporeuesthai dia ton logon*—'to proceed through' [*durchlaufen*] what is said."[16] My present interest in this definition is that the prefix *dia* is combined with the root *ēporēkamen,* which we have encountered in the citation at the start of *Being and Time,* so that the emphasis on the *Durchgang durch* which Heidegger reads into *poros* ("passage way through" or "proceeding through") is a specification with respect to the idiom of "way."

In my next chapter, when I turn to the German translation of *ēporēkamen,* I shall reconsider Heidegger's specific emphasis, when he wields the prefix *durch,* on the direction (*Durchgang durch*) in which he would proceed. For the present I would only recognize that the translation "we . . . now have gotten into difficulty" is insufficient as a rendering of what Heidegger finds implicit elsewhere in the Greek *aporia;* an alternative translation is needed. We can hardly retain the term *aporia*, since the trouble with this "ancient Greek term," as Derrida points out when he adopts this term for his own purposes, is that it has been "worn threadbare." Yet he admits it has "imposed itself on me for many years."[17] It thereby acquired new life as a technical term widely used by deconstructionsts. Thus it has become threadbare again. Since I would also avoid possible confusion between deconstructionist procedure and Heidegger's, I must look for another term.

Let me concede the larger problem. In order to appreciate Heidegger's German translation from the Greek, his convictions should be taken into account that there is an "inner relationship of the German language with the Greek language" and that, along with Greek, German is "the most forceful and most spiritual of languages." His comment on the "inner relationship" was prompted by how the French "when they begin to think, speak German, for they are sure that they cannot get through [*kamen nicht durch*] with their own language."[18] Those who speak English (I suspect he assumes) are little better off.

Accordingly I must draw attention to the "question of the 'question'"—in a different sense from that in which Derrida has posed it.[19] I have been relying on the translation "question," when I refer to "the question of being" as an *aporia*, but *quaestio* was already threadbare in medieval scholastic usage. Its survival (along with so many other Latinisms) in English, as in French, may cripple us philosophically if we take seriously Heidegger's warning that in a Latin translation "is concealed rather a *trans-lation* of Greek experience" with which "the groundlessness of Western thought begins."

Indeed if Heidegger had been up against the English (or French) term *question*, as the Latin translation for *aporia* which had been "transmitted" by the "tradition," he would have lamented this translation when he undertook to retrieve the original "Greek experience" of the *aporia* which is the question of being.

The Impasse

As for an English translation of *aporia*, I would take care of some of the implications of Heidegger's elucidation by settling for "impasse." Thus I translate the Greek phrase at the start of *Being and Time* as "we have come into an *impasse*."

Before I proceed, I should pause to admit the reorientation I am imposing on Heidegger. He is concerned to retrieve with his citation from the *Sophist* "the question of being" as an *aporia*. But I am reconnoitering a different impasse: there is "no passage way through" to Heidegger's philosophy, which he is starting to work out in *Being and Time* with this citation, from Husserl's philosophy. With respect to their relation, I began by embroidering on Granel and Souche-Dagues, but there are many steps to come, and I shall not complete my argument until the end of Volume 4.

So far the most obvious evidence of the impasse has been Heidegger's depriving us in *Being and Time* of the evidence as to their relation which he provided in the *Prolegomena*. Indeed Heidegger's not citing passages from Husserl in *Being and Time* will become, in retrospect, not only a matter of Heidegger's personal caution, but also of his recognizing that there is no "passage way through" from Husserl's philosophy to his. This was a "difficulty" he did not fully recognize in the *Prolegomena*.

My comments now are not conclusions, but have to do only with the availability of evidence. Here let me amplify the comparison with Sartre I offered before. When Sartre, like Heidegger, acknowledges his debt to Husserl, he does so by translating from Husserl numerous passages, which he incorporates in his own phenomenology. These passages enabled me to find a "passage way through" from Husserl to Sartre, and back again, for it was easy to demonstrate that Husserl would have had a misgiving regarding Sartre, which would have been pretty much the same as his misgiving regarding *Being and Time*.[20] Husserl would have envisaged Sartre's phenomenology too as a "trans-lation" in which his phenomenology was no longer an eidetic and transcendental science, since Sartre "transposes or transfers" phenomenology into the empirical science of psychology.

My own point is still that my exposition of the relation between Sartre and Husserl was facilitated by Sartre's actually having translated into French several passages of Husserl's German. The implications they acquire in Sartre's own phenomenology could be determined. Sartre's French translations of passages from Husserl were occasionally mistranslations in the "literal" sense; they were more often mistrans-lations in that the passages are arbitrarily selected, recklessly truncated, and wrenched away from the implications they had in their original context.[21] By reinstating this original context, I was able to get at specific methodological differences by showing how Sartre employs intentional analysis and the eidetic and phenomenological reductions, but not in Husserl's fashion.

I intend to show that specific methodological differences are also at issue in Heidegger's trans-lation of Husserl. My first strenuous effort will be a comparison of the analysis of signs in *Being and Time* with Husserl's analysis. I anticipate this attempt now, because it illustrates the limitations of relying on the *Prolegomena*: the analysis of signs there does not yield clues to the differences at issue between Heidegger and Husserl, as does the analysis of signs in *Being and Time*.

Verlegenheit

I resume my exegesis of the citation. There is still the problem to be faced of Heidegger's German translation of *ēporēkamen*: *"sind wir in Verlegenheit gekommen."* The Macquarrie and Robinson translation of the Greek and the German ("we . . . have now become perplexed") is a sloppy compromise between the Greek and the German. It does justice neither to the distinctive implications Heidegger finds in the Greek, nor to the German *"sind wir in Verlegenheit gekommen,"* especially if we taken into account the distinctive implications that *Verlegenheit* soon acquires in *Being and Time.* Although I have used "difficulty" to translate *Verlegenheit,* this is a different term from Husserl's *Schwierigkeit.* Like *aporia, Verlegenheit* can broadly mean a "difficulty." But it is not for Heidegger a "difficulty" in the sense that a *Schwierigkeit* is a "difficulty" for Husserl.

The reader may remember the piety with which I introduced Husserl in my introduction: "Any philosophy worth understanding is difficult to understand, and to understand it is to understand why it has to be difficult." But when Heidegger's philosophy is brought into the picture, and the expositor attempts to understand the relation between their philosophies, he must recognize that in Heidegger's philosophy we encounter difficulties which are themselves differently conceived from those in Husserl's philosophy.

My argument with respect to Heidegger's conception of a "difficulty" in the citation is that a stretch of meaning between the Greek and the German is to be accommodated. The two are to be taken together, inasmuch as the Germanm *Verlegenheit* helps explain the Greek *ēporēkamen*—why "we are unable to find a passage way through."[22] The "way" is obstructed" (*verlegt*). This is one reason it is misleading for the Stambaugh English translation of *Being and Time* to separate the citation by a blank space and a curlicue from its translation. Not only is the citation thereby transformed into an epigraph, so that Heidegger is no longer beginning in the middle of a Platonic dialogue, but any prospect of interplay between the different implications (Greek and German) of "difficulty" is removed.

But I too have done something I should not have: I have skipped over the very first word of Heidegger's Greek citation, and the second word is his translation, *offenbar* (openly, obviously). It is opposed in retrospect to the implication of "obstruction" in the phrase *"sind wir in Verlegenheit gekommen,"* as the final and climactic phrase of Heidegger's translation. Another reason I should not have skipped over *offenbar* is that it is far from inevitable as a translation of the Greek *dēlon,* which is usually translated *"klar"* (clear). Heidegger may well be avoiding this translation because *"klar"* seems too definitely associated with the criterion implemented by Husserl's phenomenological method as a "Method of *Klärung* [clarification]" in the title of section 67 of *Ideas I*. It is also presented as "The Method of the Perfectly Clear Grasping of Essences" (the title of section 68) and as "The Method of Eidetic Clarification" (the title of section 70). In short, the criterion is not "clarity" in some vague, colloquial sense; it is a clarity achieved by a "clarification" which is "eidetic," that is, the grasping of an essential meaning as identical in all its instances.

One reason for indulging in speculation regarding *offenbar* is that Heidegger, at the middle of the first inside page of his presentation copy to Husserl, entered in handwriting a citation from Lessing: "The greatest clarity has always been for me the greatest beauty." Here I suspect he is catering to Husserl, for the citation does not express a sentiment we would ordinarily associate with Heidegger himself, and he did not brandish it on any other occasion. Indeed "beauty" is hardly a criterion in *Being and Time,* and only if we credit Heidegger with more sense of humor than I think he has could we explain why he would have begun so obscure a work by brandishing in the face of the addressee the Lessing citation. Its entry in Husserl's copy suggests Heidegger was well aware that "clarity" was Husserl's criterion and was trying to head off the prospect that Husserl would often render the verdict "(*unklar*)" in the margins of his copy—as he in fact so often does.

Indeed, we have encountered this verdict in the two appraisals I cited earlier. In the first, Husserl's reaction to *Being and Time* was, "That would be a reproduction of my own theory, if 'clarified' meant clarified in . . . phenomenological fashion"—that is, I would interpolate, by "the method of clarification" which entails carrying out the intentional analysis that becomes feasible when the eidetic and phenomenological reductions are employed.

In Husserl's second appraisal, the outcome of the "trans-lation" by which Heidegger reverts from the eidetic and transcendental levels, which Husserl had reached with the reductions, is that "the whole [of phenomenology] becomes profoundly unclear and loses its value as a philosophy."

Opening Up

Husserl's appraisals betray the impasse between them. If "clarity" is Husserl's criterion for a philosophy to be a philosophy, Heidegger is opposing to it variations on the idiom of "opening up" an "obstruction." This opposition will become thematic for Heidegger's undertaking in *Being and Time*. The colloquial *offenbar* prepares for a concatenation of concepts. I cannot anticipate all of them now. I have already cited section 7, "The Phenomenological Method of Investigation," since it culminates with his acknowledgment of his debt to Husserl. I have also already suggested that, in view of the "priority" Husserl confers on method, Heidegger's mention of him in this section is hardly surprising. But one term which Husserl did not employ in presenting his phenomenological method, and which Heidegger introduces in presenting his in section 7, is "disclosure" (*Erschlossenheit*). "Phenomenological truth" he equates with the "disclosure of being." He later defines "to disclose" as meaning "to lay open" (*aufschliessen*).[23]

How philosophically preoccupied Heidegger is with the idiom of "opening up" (and some of the variations on the idiom "obstruction," to which it is opposed) can be demonstrated by sampling section 7. Having initially defined a "phenomenon" (the subject of phenomenology) as "what shows itself, the open [*das Offenbare*]," Heidegger later draws a distinction:

> What is it that must be called a "phenomenon" in a distinctive sense? . . . Openly [*offenbar*—Heidegger would seem to be playing up his own idiom] it is such that at the outset and for the most part it does *not* show itself; [it] is *concealed*.[24]

The emphatic "not" marks a lurch—a shift in method by which he proceeds to a phenomenological method governed by a criterion opposed to Husserl's "method of clarification," which is pitted against not what "is concealed" but what is confused. One example we shall encounter later is Husserl's clarification of the meaning of the term *object*. He speaks of the "clarification" which is necessary if the terms *object* and *object region* are not to remain in a state of confusion. He speaks of "confusing unclarities."[25]

Heidegger distinguishes different kinds of concealment which are obstructions, including "what relapses and gets covered up again," and "what shows itself only 'distorted.'" His explanation brings this to bear on his own investigation, as he had set it forth at the very start of *Being and Time*: "The being of beings . . . can be covered up to such an extent that it becomes forgotten and no question remains as to its meaning [*Sinn*]."[26]

One outcome of this analysis in section 7 is an implicit criticism of Husserl's methodological reliance on intuition as access to an immediately given experience: "Because the phenomena are at the outset and for the most part *not* given, phenomenology is needed. Covered-up-ness is the counter-concept to 'phenomenon.'"[27] Again the emphatic "*not*" marks the lurch—the shift in method. Again Heidegger is conceiving his phenomenological method in terms of its implicit opposition to Husserl's phenomenological method.

Auslegung

Eventually in section 7 Heidegger introduces a term which he regards as crucial: "The methodological meaning [*Sinn*] of phenomenological description is *Auslegung*."[28] The force of the prefix *aus*- is to provide some indication as to how we are to cope with the "difficulty" we have gotten into, the impasse of *aporos*—of what is "without *Durchgang*." The etymological connection with *Verlegenheit* can be brought out by recognizing that *Auslegung* is an "interpretation" which is a "laying out." One fashion in which Heidegger's "interpretation" is a "laying out" is the "laying out" of the etymological connections which we are observing.

But what I would emphasize now is how the specific connection between *Verlegenheit* and *Auslegung* illustrates Heidegger's implicit opposition to Husserl's method. The comparison seems solicited by the fact that Heidegger is about to reach his endorsement of Husserl for having made *Being and Time* "possible" by having "laid [*gelegt*] the foundation."[29] That Heidegger is proceeding differently can be taken as implicit in his employing the idiom of "laying" here without benefit of the prefix *aus*-, which has much the same force as in Heidegger's conception of *Ausarbeitung*.

We have already seen Heidegger attach methodological significance to *durch,* and we shall later probe the significance of other prefixes. My present point is only that when knowledge is immediately given, as it is for Husserl, there is no need to specify with a prefix the direction in which you are proceeding.

My proposal that Heidegger is introducing his method as *Auslegung* in criticism of Husserl's intuitive method is encouraged by Heidegger's brusque reference at this juncture to "phenomenological description." Heidegger was well aware of how promptly Husserl had rebuked himself, after the publication of the *Logical Investigations,* for having casually referred to his method as "descriptive" in the introduction to the second volume. The most penitent moment in Husserl's revised introduction in the second edition was his confession that the original "wavering Introduction" was "so little true to the essential meaning [*Sinn*] and method" of the ensuing investigations that it had to be radically "worked over [*umgearbeitet*]." With respect to his method, he had failed in particular to distinguish it from introspective description, which was all that an immediately given experience might seem ordinarily to require. But such description only yields what we have seen Husserl came to disdain as "picture-book phenomenology." Required instead was a shift in level to reach what would be immediately given as essential for the experience to be what it is (intentional, for instance).

Insofar as Heidegger's adoption of the term *Auslegung* can be considered in terms of his relation to Husserl, Heidegger has a different misgiving from Husserl's with respect to a method which is merely descriptive of immediately given experiences. His undertaking is conveyed by the prefix *aus-* in *Auslegung*, as in the case of *Ausarbeitung*. The term *Ausarbeitung* is first encountered in the preamble itself: "The concrete working out [*Ausarbeitung*] of the question about [*nach*] the meaning [*Sinn*] of 'being' is the aim of the following treatise." I have already sought the contrast with Husserl, who characterizes as *Ausarbeitung* the merely editorial "working out" for publication that an assistant was to perform after Husserl himself had already done "the difficult work"; *Ausarbeitung* in Heidegger characterizes instead the "working out" that he himself is undertaking.

Consider that the title of the second chapter of Heidegger's introduction is "The Double Task [*Aufgabe*] of the Working Out [*Ausarbeitung*] of the Question of Being." One aspect of this "given task" is (according to the title of the first section of this chapter, section 5) "The Ontological Analysis of Dasein as the Laying Open [*Freilegung*] of the Horizon for an Interpretation of the Meaning of Being as Such." In the second paragraph of this section, *Freilegung* is "envisaged" as a matter of "Dasein becoming accessible"—in an "*Auslegung*." In the second section the other aspect of the "double task that is given" is "The Task of a Destruction of the History of Ontology." I am suggesting that the character of Heidegger's undertaking as an *Aufgabe* is a recognition that access to phenomena is obstructed; hence, he refuses to rely with Husserl on what is "given" immediately.

This recognition of an *Aufgabe* is achieved only in *Being and Time*. A curious feature of Heidegger's exposition of Husserl in the *Prolegomena* is that his own emphasis on the procedure of "opening up" is credited to Husserl. Heidegger finds there a "double requirement [*Förderung*]" implicit in the principle of proceeding "to the things themselves." The first requirement is illustrated by "how Husserl understood his philosophizing (the requirement of laying open the foundation [*Freilegung des Bodens*])" and "the second is the requirement to lay the foundation and includes [*mitliegt*] the first."[30] In *Being and Time* Heidegger does credit Husserl with having "laid the foundation," and his formulation of a "double task [*Aufgabe*]" is also anticipated by the "double requirement" in the *Prolegomena*, but in *Being and Time* the *Aufgabe* of *Freilegung* is reserved for his own "Ontological Analytic of the Dasein." In other words, in the *Prolegomena* Heidegger's own undertaking is still blurred with Husserl's—if I may thus extend the idiom with which Granel appraises Heidegger's interpretation in *Being and Time* of the relation between them. This blur is a succinct illustration of how much more sharply Heidegger effects his break with Husserl in *Being and Time* and accordingly discards there, as a preliminary to his own undertaking, the exposition of Husserl which had been in the *Prolegomena,* the "Preparatory Part." Later we shall see other evidence that Heidegger has not yet in the *Prolegomena* disassociated his undertaking from Husserl's, so that there is a certain justification for my beginning my comparison with *Being and Time,* where the issues are sharper.

TWO · DECONSTRUCTION

NINE

· *Destruktion*

· *There necessarily belongs together with the*
· *conceptual interpretation of being and its*
· *structures . . . a* Destruktion.—Heidegger

Starting Over Again

In section 6 of *Being and Time* Heidegger
confronts not the accessibility of Husserl's
immediately given but the philosophical tradition, which

> renders what it "transmits" ["*übergibt*"]
> so little accessible [*zugänglich*] that at
> the outset and for the most part it covers
> it over instead. It . . . obstructs [*verlegt*]
> our access [*Zugang*] to those original
> sources from which the categories and
> concepts handed down to us have been
> in part quite genuinely derived."[1]

The *Destruktion* is a procedure for dealing
with this obstruction.

We should also take into account his presentation of the *Destruktion* in *The Basic
Problems of Phenomenology:*

> The store of basic philosophical con-
> cepts derived from the philosophical
> tradition is still so influential today that
> this effect of the tradition can hardly be
> overestimated. It is for this reason that
> all philosophical discussion, even the
> most radical attempt to start over
> again, is pervaded by traditional con-
> cepts and thus by traditional horizons
> and points of view, which we cannot as-
> sume with unquestionable certainty to
> have arisen originally and genuinely
> from the domain of being and the con-

titution of being they claim to comprehend. It is for this reason that there necessarily belongs together with the conceptual interpretation of being and its structures . . . a *Destruktion*—a critical procedure in which the traditional concepts that must at first necessarily be employed are to undergo deconstruction [*Abbau*] back to the sources from which they were derived.[2]

Some terminological comment is needed here.

Heidegger later warns that the *Destruktion* is not a *Zerstörung*, which is a "destruction" in the negative English sense of that word.[3] I am now respecting his warning by retaining the German term *Destruktion*. But since Heidegger characterizes the *Destruktion* as an *Abbau*, I shall regard the term *deconstruction* as a synonym, and sometimes employ the adjective *deconstructive*.

Earlier we were puzzled that the procedure presented at the start of *Being and Time* as a "retrieval," which is illustrated there by his retrieving the question of being with a citation from the *Sophist*, is not explicitly listed as one of the three components of method in *The Basic Problems*. But the presentation I have just cited includes an implicit reference to the retrieval when Heidegger refers to the "deconstruction" as proceeding "back to the sources." Thus Heidegger goes on to explain that the *Destruktion* "is not a negation of the tradition . . . but the reverse—even a positive appropriation [*Aneignung*] of the tradition." We recognize that this making of the tradition "one's own" is the retrieval as it is described in the 1928 lectures, where we saw that "historical recollection . . . is only what it is . . . in the present moment of self-understanding." It is "one's own [*eigen*] . . . grasp of the task philosophy harbors in itself."

It is evident too from the presentation in *The Basic Problems* that the *Destruktion* is not only a "critical procedure," but that it is also a procedure that Heidegger adopts in criticism of the feasibility of the procedure of "the most radical attempt to start over again." The allusion to Descartes is obvious, but there is no reference to Descartes's universal doubt. Thus the allusion to Husserl is at least as obvious, since he had endorsed the Cartesian precedent without endorsing Descartes's universal doubt. Indeed Heidegger may be alluding in the passage I have cited to Husserl's claim that he was himself adopting a procedure for starting over again which was more "radical" than Descartes's.[4]

Previously I only cited part of Husserl's explanation of how he started out in *Ideas I*, which is,

> In our fundamental findings we have presupposed nothing, not even the concept of philosophy, and thus we shall also proceed in the future. Formulated explicitly, the philosophical *epochē*, which our

undertaking involves, entails our completely abstaining from any judgment regarding the *doctrinal content of any previous philosophy*.[5]

This philosophical *epochē*, I have already pointed out, is implicit in Husserl's commitment to proceed directly "to the things themselves."

Matters are more complicated with Heidegger. In order to reconsider their relation at this juncture, I would briefly pick up on how Heidegger in his acknowledgment of his debt to Husserl took over Husserl's own designation of the *Logical Investigations* as a "breakthrough" (*Durchbruch*). The implication of "breakthrough" that Husserl himself brought out was that the *Investigations* were "not an end but a start"; they were "a start" which has been followed up and superseded by *Ideas I*. But the idiom of "breakthrough" itself becomes problematic in *Being and Time*. In the *Prolegomena*, what Heidegger is undertaking is still introduced by his interpretation of Husserl's undertaking. But in *Being and Time* Heidegger is no longer the "disciple" of Husserl's that he still was in the *Prolegomena*, where he keeps referring to the "breakthrough" that took place with Husserl. In *Being and Time* he is more circumspect in his use of the idiom. Moreover, when he says in his acknowledgment that Husserl in the *Investigations* "*zum Durchbruch kam*," he may not be saying that Husserl broke through, but rather that he came up to this juncture.

Indeed if tradition "obstructs our access," if "the most radical attempt to start over again is pervaded [*durchsetzt*] by traditional concepts," there is, strictly speaking, no prospect of a breakthrough in the sense that there is in Husserl with the attainment of immediate knowledge.

Application

Before we can go further in the exposition of the *Destruktion*, we need to take into account that it is carried out in conjunction with another procedure. Recall that the *Destruktion* is introduced in *The Basic Problems* with the claim that it "necessarily belongs together with" the "construction."

I expand on my earlier comment on the difference in method here between Heidegger and Husserl. That Heidegger adopts the idiom "construction" is itself a repudiation of Husserl's repudiation of this (neo-Kantian) idiom, which Husserl finds incompatible with his "principle of all principles"—the principle which takes precedence over all other principles—inasmuch as what is given to intuition is ultimately the "source validating knowledge [that is, knowledge of essences]." Given intuitively with any act of consciousness (for example, perceptual consciousness of this chair here) is the knowledge (as I have explained before) that the structure of this consciousness is intentional—consciousness of something. It is the immediate accessibility of such intuitive knowledge which assures the feasibility of Husserl's attempt to start over again by enforcing the philosophical *epochē* and proceeding directly "to the things themselves."

Implicit in Heidegger's undertaking a "construction" (as in his undertaking a *Destruktion* in lieu of the philosophical *epochē*) is a denial of Husserl's assumption that knowledge is accessible to intuition. As Heidegger puts it in explaining "construction" as a procedure, "Being does not become accessible like a being [e.g., Husserl's "something"]. We do not find it in front of us." Thus "conceptual interpretation" has to intervene, and the concepts employed in this interpretation have to be constructed.

An initial problem of interpretation which we run into in *Being and Time* is that Heidegger does not claim at any step there that he is actually carrying out the *Destruktion*. In an "Outline" (section 8, at the end of the "Introduction") Heidegger anticipates how the *Destruktion* is to be carried out in Part 2 of *Being and Time*. But this part was never published and perhaps was never finished. On the basis of this anticipatory "Outline," von Hermann is convinced that the application of the *Destruktion* is entirely postponed, though he identifies it as undertaken in portions of other works of Heidegger's—notably in *The Basic Problems of Phenomenology*. In contrast, Thomas Buchheim asserts, "Heidegger has applied the *Destruktion* throughout his thinking in all its guises."[6]

Neither of these extreme interpretations seems tenable. Buchheim's "in all its guises" does not allow sufficient room for the other components of Heidegger's method besides the *Destruktion*. Von Hermann's interpretation requires more attention. After the "Outline" Heidegger only refers to the *Destruktion* twice in *Being and Time*, and both references are anticipatory. He interrupts his own analysis in Chapter 3 in order to undertake a contrast between this analysis and "Descartes's interpretation of the world." He cautions that his interpretation of Descartes's interpretation will be "fully grounded only when he carries out the phenomenological *Destruktion* of the '*cogito sum*'" in Part 2. The other anticipatory reference comes near the end of *Being and Time*, when Heidegger is formulating the concept of "historicity," which, he explains, "serves as preparation for the . . . complete elucidation of the task of a historical *Destruktion* of the history of philosophy."[7] He refers us in a footnote to the earlier "Outline" in which he anticipates the later unpublished part.

When Heidegger includes a presentation of his *Destruktion* ("The *Destruktion* of the History of Ontology") in his "Introduction" to *Being and Time,* is he only taking a deep breath, which he is holding until he reaches the never-to-be-reached Part 2? That seems somewhat implausible. Reconsider his first anticipatory reference, which is to the eventual *Destruktion* of Descartes. His cautionary "fully [*ausführlich*] grounded" does not exclude the possibility that his handling of Descartes in *Being and Time* may be to some extent a *Destruktion,* and scholars have often interpreted it as a *Destruktion.* At any rate, I shall demonstrate that Heidegger's construction of certain concepts in *Being and Time* itself can be interpreted as the deconstruction of concepts of Husserl's.

The Concept

The demonstration cannot be offered yet. I earlier cited Heidegger's cautioning in *The Basic Problems* that the procedures composing his method can only be discerned in their application. We cannot be misled by the "priority" Husserl accords to method and thus to its explicit statement. Heidegger, consistent with the problem of access (as it emerges from his denial that knowledge is immediately accessible) has to proceed, in applying his method, in a "sequence of steps." What I thus have to locate for the purpose of my demonstration is a specific step at which his construction of a concept involves "the critical deconstruction" of a concept of Husserl's. Heidegger's commitment to a method which is "a sequence of steps" has induced us to begin with the first step he took at the start of *Being and Time.* The safest comparison may then be with the first step Husserl takes at the start of the first of the *Logical Investigations,* as the work in which, Heidegger has told us, "the foundation" was "laid" for *Being and Time.* What Husserl deals with in its first section is indicated in its title: "An Ambiguity in the Term 'Sign.'"

There is a further justification for proposing this comparison. The first reference to Husserl (after the general acknowledgment in the introduction of debt for the "foundation") is in a footnote to section 10. The issue at this juncture is the analysis of a "person," but any attention Heidegger might have paid to Husserl is quickly diverted. He links Husserl with Scheler, whom he actually discusses, because Scheler is "in print" and "emphasizes what Husserl [only] suggests." Thus any confrontation with Husserl here is skirted.[8]

The next occasion on which Heidegger refers to Husserl is in section 17. To a paragraph in which Heidegger is beginning to construct his concept of "sign," he attaches a footnote in which he cites specific analyses of Husserl's and in particular "the analysis of signs and meaning" in the first of the *Logical Investigations.*

Even if we rely on this footnote, there is a qualification to be acknowledged. Is not the *Destruktion* of "traditional concepts" (as it is presented in *The Basic Problems*) undertaken in order to arrive at "the [Greek] sources from which they were derived?" Is the application of this procedure then not short-circuited when we are taken no further back than Husserl's use of a concept? But I can appeal to Heidegger's own procedure in *Being and Time*. Admittedly the *Destruktion* is not "fully grounded" until it is carried back to these sources, but it can still be applied, short of reaching this outcome, as it is in the instance of Descartes. Thus I shall argue that Heidegger does in fact carry out quite specifically in *Being and Time* the *Destruktion* of Husserl's concept of the "sign," even though it is not until a later work, *On the Way to Language,* that he carries the *Destruktion* of this concept back to Greek sources.[9]

TEN

The Edge

Every time we go over the edge of the text of the
first of the Logical Investigations, *it is to indicate*
the principle of a general interpretation.
—Derrida

Kinks

Now that I am poised to examine Husserl's
analysis of the sign, as preparation for examining Heidegger's *Destruktion* of this analysis, I run into one of those kinks in the history
of philosophy which can get in the way of any
well-intentioned pressing ahead, but which
cannot be circumvented entirely. Recognize
where we are. I have explained that I was focusing on the relation between Heidegger and
Husserl as deserving attention because of the
breakdown in communication between them.
I have explained too why I would bring to the
fore how differences in method contributed
to this breakdown. Because method for Heidegger imposed a "sequence of steps," I have
respected sequence by beginning with the
procedure with which he starts in *Being and
Time,* the retrieval, but then I discovered the
"difficulty" in carrying out this procedure
was that "access" is "obstructed." I was anticipating that the construction of concepts
would involve the *Destruktion* of traditional
concepts. As an example I have justified taking the sign, since I proposed to argue that in
constructing this concept Heidegger would
be undertaking specifically the *Destruktion*
of Husserl's concept, as "pervaded by [to impose the phrasing with which Heidegger describes the necessity of his *Destruktion*] . . .
traditional horizons and points of view."

Man proposes but history disposes. The
history of philosophy cannot be pulled out

straight any more than history can in other guises. The particular kink I now encounter is of a different kind from the one to which I accommodated my interpretation when I recognized that the foundational works of phenomenology—Husserl's *Logical Investigations* and Heidegger's *Being and Time*—had to wait to be translated until after the major works of their disciples, Sartre and Merleau-Ponty. That kink I took as chronological evidence indicating an access route which had been followed in the understanding of phenomenology.

The different kind of kink I am up against now is that Derrida has undertaken in *Speech and Phenomena* a deconstruction of Husserl's treatment of the sign, and this deconstruction has become far more influential than Husserl's original treatment. Bluntly put, since Derrida's *Speech and Phenomena* was published, many more have read it than have read Husserl's *Logical Investigations,* and most readers who have read them recently have been much more interested in Derrida's deconstruction than in phenomenology—that is, in *Speech and Phenomena* as a founding work of deconstruction as a movement rather than in the *Logical Investigations* as the founding work of the phenomenological movement.

What is particularly disconcerting is that it never seems to have crossed Derrida's mind that Heidegger (as I claim) had undertaken the deconstruction of Husserl's "analysis of signs and meaning." Yet Derrida is usually more than generous in acknowledging his debts to him.

I know how distracting Derrida can be, but my problem is not just to keep him at bay while I undertake an exposition of Husserl's analysis. Derrida is so much in the way that I must also bring out the differences between Derrida's deconstruction and my own procedure as an expositor who is committed to deconstruction in the broad and loose, but not flagrantly subversive, sense of exposing the structure of a philosophy.

The most obvious difference is that my procedure involves me in comparing Heidegger and Husserl, whereas Derrida tends to treat them separately, as I indicated in my introduction. He launched his career with interpretations of Husserl in 1962 and 1967, in which references to Heidegger were minimal, and undertook in 1968 an interpretation of Heidegger in which there were no references to Husserl. So obvious a difference between us may seem not worth making any philosophical fuss about. After all, I anticipated in my introduction that this separation of Heidegger from Husserl took place at a time when the influence of Sartre and Merleau-Ponty, and thus of their reconciliations of Husserl and Heidegger, was waning.

The General Interpretation

Nevertheless, more than vagaries of scholarly fashion is involved in Derrida's case. He explicitly justifies his treating Husserl separately in *Speech and Phenomena*:

> The present essay analyzes the doctrine of meaning as it is constituted, starting with the first of the *Logical Investigations*. In order to better follow the difficult and tortuous itinerary, I have generally abstained from comparisons, rapprochements, and oppositions which seem here or there to impose themselves between Husserl's phenomenology and other theories of meaning, ancient or modern.[1]

This is presumably why Derrida conducts his interpretation of Husserl's analysis of signs without alluding to Heidegger's analysis.

It is difficult to believe that so astute a scholar as Derrida, and one so committed to deconstruction, would not have noticed that Heidegger in effect deconstructs Husserl's concept of the sign. Whether Derrida noticed or not, comparisons, rapprochements, and oppositions are intrinsic to my procedure, for my claim is that with them we can obtain, by virtue of the priority that method enjoys in Husserl—and the explicit attention he pays to it—a more adequate understanding of the method which in Heidegger remains largely implicit in his actual application of it. Indeed what has already emerged as obvious is that Heidegger's *Destruktion,* presented as a "deconstruction" in *The Basic Problems of Phenomenology,* is to be recognized as undertaken in criticism of Husserl's philosophical epochē.

Before I go on with further "comparisons" (and so forth), from which some understanding will emerge of other procedures of Heidegger's, I return to the ostensible justification for Derrida's abstention from them. It is that Husserl's itinerary is "difficult and tortuous," and he would follow it closely, unimpeded by other philosophers. This conventional academic justification may seem irrefutable, but it may not fully explain Derrida's procedure, for he completes his argument for refusing to go outside of Husserl by anticipating a further objective to be attained by going outside: "Every time we go over the edge [or boundary: *débordons*] of the text of the first of the *Logical Investigations,* it is to indicate the principle of a general interpretation of Husserl's thought and to sketch out that systematic reading of it we hope to undertake some day."[2] What strikes us here is first that Derrida has never quite carried out this undertaking, although he has published prolifically since *Speech and Phenomena*. The publications do include an early version of what might have been this undertaking, but he has disowned it.

"Some day" often does not come. But perhaps I might speculate as to why it has never come in this instance. The "principle" which it is Derrida's "purpose" to indicate is a commitment on Husserl's part to what Derrida identifies as "the metaphysics of presence," which he finds implicit in Husserl's "principle of all principles"—whereby "things" are immediately present to consciousness as what we are intentionally conscious of.[3] My speculation is that this commitment has never become the principle of the general, systematic interpretation of Husserl's thought which Derrida initially hoped to undertake, because it has become the principle in terms of which Derrida has instead gone on to undertake a general interpretation of the philosophical tradition at large.

Presence

In *Speech and Phenomena* Derrida is proceeding toward this interpretation at the point where he does mention Heidegger and acknowledge a certain debt to him for his conception of metaphysics as traditionally committed to the doctrine of presence. Derrida adds that he would ask "above all else, whether Heidegger's thought is not liable to the same questions as the metaphysics of presence."[4] The "metaphysics of presence" is not itself my concern, since the elucidation of what is at issue would involve in Heidegger's case his attempt to bring the problem of being within the horizon of time, and this attempt (as I earlier explained) would take me on to later steps in the sequence of *Being and Time* than I shall reach.

Nevertheless, it has long since been evident that I am not concerned with "questions" which are "the same" for Heidegger and Husserl. When I go over the edge of Heidegger's philosophy, it is only far enough to reach Husserl's philosophy, so as to bring out by my comparison the specific differences between them in a way that allows the edge of each philosophy to retain its sharpness as a delimitation, so that I can explain how communication breaks down between them. These specific, limiting differences even include how a "question" itself is conceived as a "difficulty." But when Derrida generally abstains from such comparisons, it is not simply to concentrate on Husserl's own thought. As is indicated by the reference to Heidegger I have quoted, Derrida would eventually go over the edge of Husserl's philosophy in a fashion which Rudolph Bernet has described in his appraisal of *Speech and Phenomena* as "the first step of a thought [Derrida's] which would make use of Husserl's philosophy for the purpose of taking aim on the metaphysical tradition as a whole, guilty of the same commitment to the metaphysics of presence."[5]

Where Derrida is particularly relevant to my exposition is in the broad similarity between his interpreting a text of Husserl's as a first step toward a sweeping interpretation of "the metaphysical tradition as a whole" and Heidegger's procedure, which is also sweeping. Since I have not gotten very far yet in my exposition of Heidegger, I offer a swift assessment of his procedure by Walter Biemel, whereby Heidegger interprets a text "so to speak from within," while "rendering present to it the *entire tradition* in which the text is located" (my italics).[6]

This doctrine of presence (as I would invidiously characterize it) is of course not the doctrine of presence that Derrida attributes to Husserl and Heidegger alike, but it is the doctrine which I would, as it were, deconstruct, for I doubt that the tradition is significantly present in the same fashion in two philosophies as different in their methods (I am arguing) as Heidegger's and Husserl's. I shall eventually (in Chapter 20) be able to bring out the methodological differences between what I shall acknowledge as the doctrine of "presence" in Husserl and the doctrine of "proximity" in Heidegger. Derrida seems to me to blur the two together.

"Significantly" is question-begging. What I take to be methodologically significant in the relations between philosophers are the specific differences in subject, method, level, and affiliation which I have sought out in the preceding volumes and am again concerned with in this volume. (I lump these specific differences together as "methodological" in a broad sense.) These differences are junctures at which one philosopher, inside his own philosophy, goes "over the edge" (*bord*) of another philosophy and in effect deprives it of its specific structure. I am pursuing an argument on behalf of specificity of interpretation as compared with the pursuit of "a general interpretation."

With respect to the broad similarity between Derrida's and Heidegger's resort to tradition (a similarity that itself would justify bringing in Derrida at this juncture), I cite Derrida's own comment at the start of *Of Grammatology:* "The history of metaphysics, despite all the differences, not only from Plato to Hegel, but also outside its apparent limits, from the Presocratics to Heidegger, has always assigned to the logos the origin of truth in general."[7] The logocentrism at issue here is closely associated with the metaphysics of presence, and it too is not directly my concern. The "not only" clause covers the scope of the metaphysical tradition as envisaged by Heidegger; the "but also" clause extends this scope (in criticism of the "limits" accepted by Heidegger) so as to include Heidegger himself as well as the pre-Socratics whom Heidegger had exempted.

Umarbeitung

What I would bring out by comparing Derrida's deconstruction and my own procedure is how he can often become largely indifferent, when he can get over the edge of a philosophy, to the differences between its proce-

dure and those of other philosophies. His procedure also leaves him relatively indifferent, as a matter of history, to the methodological differences
between the successive works of one philosopher. Consider Derrida's first
step at the start of *Speech and Phenomena:*

> The *Logical Investigations* (1900–1901) have opened a way
> [*chemin*] in which, we know, *all* of phenomenology has followed.
> . . . In *Crisis* [Husserl's last work] . . . the conceptual premises of the
> *Investigations* are still at work, notably when they concern *all* the
> problems of meaning and language in general. In this area more than
> elsewhere, a patient reading would bring out in the *Investigations*
> the seminal structure of *all* of Husserl's thought. *On each page* can
> be read the necessity—or the implicit operation [*pratique*]—of the
> eidetic and phenomenological reductions, the discernible presence
> of *everything* to which they will give access. (My italics)[8]

One trouble with this appraisal (for my purposes as a historian concerned
with methodological differences) is that it disavows, without explanation,
those appraisals of Husserl himself in which he betrays his own sensitivity
to the differences between his successive works.

I have already admitted that Husserl is often forgetful of his earlier
works. But a second edition of the *Logical Investigations* compelled him
to pay attention. Recall his misgiving in the introduction to this second
edition: "Anyone who knows the old work" will see that it was impossible
to "lift it entirely to the level of the *Ideas.*"[9] When Husserl refers to the
"hesitant and timid" author of the old work, he is thinking primarily (as I
have already pointed out) of his characterization of his method there as
"descriptive" and thus of his failure to achieve an adequate formulation of
the eidetic reduction (which Derrida finds implicit in the old work) as a
procedure for carrying out the shift in level from empirical facts to
essences as boldly as he should have done, and would do in *Ideas I.* Furthermore, Husserl does not think of himself as even having conceived, until several years after the *Logical Investigations,* the phenomenological
reduction (which Derrida finds implicit in the old work) as a procedure for
carrying out the shift in level to the transcendental.

In dealing with any philosopher, I am reluctant to suppose he is entirely wrong about the character of his philosophy. I prefer to allow the
philosopher himself to be his own spokesman as long as I can. This response I would maintain as to another individual—to his own "otherness"—to which Derrida can be responsive, as I noted in my introduction.

I cannot go into more detail as to crucial respects in which Derrida
downplays how *Ideas I* differs from the *Logical Investigations.* I have already admitted that I often overlook differences between successive works

by a philosopher when they would demand single-minded attention to that philosopher himself and their elucidation is not advanced by comparison with another philosopher. If I shall eventually be concerned, unlike Derrida, with the differences between the *Logical Investigations* and *Ideas I*, it is not just out of courtesy to Husserl but because Heidegger (as we shall see) emphasizes these differences even more strenuously than Husserl himself does.

For the moment, however, I restrict myself to Derrida's indifference to these differences. He is disregarding not only evidence they would yield as to how Husserl's "itinerary" became "difficult and tortuous," but also Husserl's distinctive conception of a "difficulty" and his characteristic procedure, which I would allege helps to explain his tortuousness as *Umarbeitung* (the "working over again" of what he has done before)— and often his "starting over again," and even his discounting of an earlier work, as he discounts the *Logical Investigations* in his introduction to the second edition.

The Boundary

*Starting out from what question are we to . . .
read this distinction when so much seems at
issue?—Derrida*

The First Step

My interest in Derrida's interpretation of
what Heidegger identifies as Husserl's "analysis of signs and meaning" is not to assess
Derrida's accuracy as an interpreter, but to
help me present my own procedure of deconstruction. I am accordingly fitting my interpretation onto Derrida's interpretation of
Husserl's first step, which Husserl takes in the
first of the *Logical Investigations*. There
Husserl draws a distinction between two
kinds of sign.

This distinction Derrida goes behind by
raising the following question: "Starting out
from what question [*Depuis quelle question*]
are we to take over and read this distinction
when so much seems at issue?"—that is (Derrida has just finished arguing), virtually all of
Husserl's phenomenology.[1]

I have already raised "the question of the
question" itself by recognizing that a relevant
sense of "question" for Husserl and Heidegger alike is a "difficulty." I have claimed that
if we further recognize how different are their
conceptions of a "difficulty," we will be better able to discern the differences in the procedures each adopts to cope with difficulties.

Prompted by Derrida, however, I would
first sift out a cluster of issues which can sur-
round the question with which a philosopher
begins. I have already demonstrated my ad-
herence to the principle in my exposition of
Heidegger, "*C'est le premier pas qui coûte.*" I

am now extending this principle to Husserl. Since this question of a starting point is the first question Derrida himself raises in *Speech and Phenomena,* it can be regarded as also his starting point.

What Derrida asserts (as he himself puts it) is the "lack [on Husserl's
part] of a question on the starting point." Derrida is able to justify his going behind Husserl's ostensible starting point—the distinction between
two kinds of sign—to a question that "Husserl seems to repress, with dogmatic haste." This is the question as to what the sign is "in general"—the
question which Husserl's distinction presupposes, according to Derrida.[2]

I am trying to go behind Derrida's own starting point by suggesting
that he has betrayed as an interpreter a certain dogmatic haste. At least
there would seem to be a more obvious way of determining what is at issue for Husserl himself when he starts out. The interpreter can go behind
the first of the *Logical Investigations* to the explanatory introduction
which preceeds it. He might even go behind this introduction, which is to
the second volume of the *Logical Investigations,* and take the first volume
into account. After all, the first phrase in *Speech and Phenomena* is "The
Logical Investigations (1900–1901)," so that, although Derrida concen-
trates on the first of the six investigations which were published in the second volume in 1901, the first volume (1900) would seem to be included in
the work he is interpreting.

The first volume, *Prolegomena to Pure Logic,* like the second, is provided with its own introduction. I shall refer for convenience to the two introductions as his "first" and "second." With Husserl, one respect in
which the *Umarbeitungen* pile up is in a multipication of introductions,
which I disc ıssed in my own introduction, and this second introduction is
not to be confused with the unpublished introduction (1913) that I cited
earlier.

In a sense that I would consider defensible, Husserl's starting point is
the first section of the first introduction, and this section is entitled "The
Controversy Regarding the Definition of Logic and the Essential Content
of Its Doctrines." In this section Husserl starts out with a citation from
John Stuart Mill's *Logic:* "There is . . . as much difference of opinion in
regard to the definition of logic as there is in the treatment of the subject."[3] This question of the definition of logic thus becomes Husserl's
starting point. He assumes, like Mill, that the question of the definition of
his subject has to be resolved before the logician can settle down to the actual treatment of this subject.

This question of definition Derrida seems to be overlooking deliberately when he asks, *"Depuis quelle question?"* He also overlooks the "difference of opinion in regard to the definition of logic," because any
difference here makes no difference to him. He can spare himself compar-

isons—for example, Husserl's comparison between himself and Mill—since any definition of logic would presumably illustrate to Derrida the "logocentric" character of the entire philosophical tradition. Hence Derrida would go behind Husserl's starting point in order to "go over the edge" of his logic and reach the tradition. For this purpose, he presumably could also have used Mill's logic. Derrida chooses Husserl's not only because of the vogue Husserl was enjoying as Derrida was launching his career, but also because it will enable him to reach more promptly his own starting point—as we shall later see.

Psychology

To Husserl himself, what lies behind and renders relevant his distinction between two kinds of sign (the "indicative sign" and the "expressive sign," which he will abbreviate to the "expression") is that the definition of logic is still at issue. Husserl cites Mill's definition: "Logic is not a science separate from and coordinate with psychology. To the extent that it is a science at all, it is a part or branch of psychology. . . . It owes all its theoretical foundations to psychology." This definition Husserl opposes because he would distinguish logic from psychology. According to Husserl, Mill's definition confuses logic as an eidetic science with psychology as an empirical science. (The distinction is slippery because Husserl, on the one hand, finds Heidegger guilty of a similar confusion of phenomenology with an empirical science, whereas Heidegger, on the other hand, regards Husserl as having failed to distinguish logic from psychology—as we shall see in Part 5.) This is the confusion which is still the issue when Husserl complains later in the first investigation that Mill "confuses distinctions which should in principle be separated. Above all he confuses the distinction between the indicative sign and the expression."[4]

To characterize in my own terms the issue of "principle" here, Husserl is carrying out a shift in *subject*: logic is no longer for him, as it is for Mill, "a part or branch of psychology"; it is not what Husserl himself calls a "psychological logic" or a "psychologistic logic" but a subject to be kept separate from psychology.

Of course the issue between Husserl and Mill as to the relation between logic and psychology is, in the fashion in which they state it, nowadays so *démodé* for American logicians as to be almost incomprehensible. But my concern here is with Husserl (and later with Heidegger's relation to him), and the issue is pivotal to Husserl, since logic, as he conceives it, like psychology, deals with consciousness. Husserl's first volume is entitled, *Prolegomena to Pure Logic* because the logic he is proposing is to be purified of psychologism (the confusion of logic with psychology). This purification he will eventually achieve, this confusion he will eventually eliminate, by the shift in *level*, which is more fully clarified in *Ideas I* as a shift to the transcendental level as well as to the eidetic.

Derrida is of course entirely aware of Husserl's opposition to psychologism. If it does not come to the fore in his interpretation, it is because Derrida (insofar as he can be considered still a philosopher) is preoccupied with carrying out a different shift in *subject*. Derrida quotes from the concluding paragraph of the second introduction, in which Husserl carries out (what he will call in *Ideas I*) the philosophical *epoché* that is indispensable to his starting an investigation. Derrida's quotation here is selective. On the one hand, he does not cite Husserl's specification that "no metaphysical or physical assertions or specifically psychological assertions are to be allowed to function as premises"—a specification that carries over from the first volume Husserl's opposition to psychologism.

On the other hand, what Derrida does quote is the further specification, "The meaning [*Sinn*] and worth of the ensuing analyses are independent of there really being languages which are used by men in their dealings with each other."[5] Thus, as we have already seen, there can be for Husserl no philosophical problems with respect to translation from one language to another, as there are for Derrida and Heidegger.

Boundary Disputes

What is at issue in this citation for Derrida himself emerges with his challenge that "Husserl has had to postpone, from one end to the other of his itinerary, any explicit meditation on the essence of language in general." It is mainly to dramatize the scope of this postponement that Derrida has emphasized at the beginning of *Speech and Phenomena* that "the conceptual premises of the *Investigations* are still at work [in his writings throughout his career], notably when they concern all the problems of meaning and language in general." Husserl's postponing the problems of language is not arbitrary, and this is implicit in his assertion: "The meaning and worth of the ensuing analyses are independent of there really being languages." The analysis of language and its use in men's dealings can be left in Husserl to psychology. Thus to include analysis of language in logic is ultimately to lapse into psychologism.

The issue here for Derrida, however, is different. When he refers to "problems of meaning and language in general," he is showing his own hand. Husserl is treating as his subject problems of meaning as separable from problems of language. If Derrida criticizes Husserl for postponing "problems of meaning and language in general," it is because Derrida himself finds problems of meaning inseparable from problems of language.

Derrida may seem to be suggesting that Husserl should have considered, as an alternative to *Logical Investigations,* linguistic investigations —a philosophy of language instead of a philosophy of logic. But such designations are doubtless a more forceful delineation of the shift in *subject* than can be attributed to Derrida. I am not going so far as to claim that my own expository procedure in terms of shifts is directly applicable not just to Husserl but also to Derrida's interpretation of Husserl, for my focus is not on Derrida. I am only claiming that if Derrida is to go over the boundary of Husserl's *Logical Investigations* to where the imputation can be escaped of being a philosopher, his deconstruction has to be distinguished from the boundary disputes—and the attendant reconstructions (such as Mill's or Husserl's reconstruction of logic)—which have recurrently taken place during the history of philosophy.

The risk of Derrida's deconstruction being contaminated by its being confused with traditional reconstructions may not be entirely avoidable. But one way in which the risk might be minimized is by explicit comparison with the traditional reconstructions in which philosophers have been engaged, for these regularly involve the deconstruction (in some sense) of predecessors and, on occasion, ostensibly of the entire philosophical tradition.

A difference that can be observed without more ado is that Derrida's deconstruction is to a considerable extent the deconstruction generally of boundaries *(bords)* as such. I am restricting myself to Husserl's controversy with Mill, but it illustrates how philosophy has been taken up with boundary disputes in which boundaries are not only moved around, but also are still assumed to be necessary. The issue in this controversy for Husserl illustrates his preoccupation with ambiguities and attendant confusions, which promotes his employment of a method that is a "method of clarification." Husserl specifically defends boundaries in general by explaining in his first introduction that "a dangerous fault" in "the delimitation of domains" is "the confusion of domains, the mixture of the heterogeneous in a domain which is supposed a unity." Husserl cites Kant: "We . . . subvert the sciences, if we allow their boundaries to run together."[6]

That Derrida's own commitment is to the subversion of boundaries suggests that he does not himself have a definable subject to which he is shifting. Certainly Derrida does not have a subject that can be defined as "pure," as is Husserl's "logic." In fact Derrida endorses "contamination," not out of *nostalgie de la boue* but (I would suspect) inspired by Husserl's commitment to the purity that he would obtain for logic by his reductions, although Derrida does not just have Husserl in view, for he would find the entire philosophical tradition puritanical—tainted by the tantalization of purity.

One reason Derrida bypasses Husserl's first volume is in order to avoid not simply Husserl's answer to the question, "What is the subject of logic? but the question of subject itself. It is a question which Derrida has never attempted to answer. Derrida's concern, as I have already conceded, is not with logic (and thus not with a "difference in opinion" as to its subject), but with the logocentrism of the tradition at large, and one guise taken by this logocentrism is the delimiting of the boundaries of a subject.

Although Derrida's break with tradition may not be a commitment to a subject—linguistic analysis, or whatever—yet it is still feasible to locate how he conceives his break with tradition: "In general," he asserts, "although . . . the philosopher may appeal amply to experience, whether he consults experience or finds the concept of experience a problem, traditionally he does not make explicit the experience of language."[7]

The Threshold

For the purpose of recognizing the oppositional structure which may be implicit in Derrida's performance, I have been stressing how language in Husserl is irrelevant to logic, and how problems of meaning are separable from problems of language. But in a certain respect language does have a particular relevance for Husserl. In my concern with Husserl's starting point, I have already quoted from the first section of his introduction to the first volume—the section entitled "The Controversy Regarding the Definition of Logic." Husserl cites Mill's definition at the beginning of this section. We have seen that in this first volume the separation of logic is sought, as opposed to Mill's verdict that logic "is a part or branch of psychology." Its separation is further sought in the introduction to the second volume. Again in the first paragraph of his second introduction, as in the first paragraph of the first introduction, Husserl cites Mill.

I would infer that Husserl cannot define the subject he is investigating except in terms of his opposition to Mill. Thus Derrida's rebuke of "postponement" would seem to gain additional force if it were recognized that the chapter of Mill's *Logic* from which Husserl now quotes is entitled "Of the Necessity of Commencing with an Analysis of Language."[8] This is Husserl's quotation from the first paragraph of the second introduction: "Language . . . is evidently one of the principal instruments or helps of thought, and any imperfection in the instrument, or in the mode of employing it, is confessedly liable . . . to confuse and impede the process." Thus Mill emphasizes, as Husserl himself puts it, "the necessity of starting out logic with linguistic analysis." As in his first volume, Husserl cites Mill in order to deal again with the problem of "subject-delimitation," or (as I would put it) with the problem of carrying out a shift in *subject* from the subject of logic as delimited by Mill.

Logic does not become linguistic analysis in Mill. His instrumentalist conception of language enables him to distinguish linguistic analysis from logical analysis. But he still envisages problems of linguistic analysis as encountered when we reach what he calls the "threshold" of logical analysis. What we must take into account, if we would deal with a philosophy not just as traditional but as an individual philosophy, is that there are different kinds of boundaries. A "threshold" is not just a rendering of the claim that it is necessary to start out logic with an analysis of language; it also implies a different kind of boundary from the sharply defined boundary Husserl is concerned to achieve in delimiting a "logic" which is "pure" and does not depend on the fact of "there really being languages." A "threshold" would compromise the opposition he maintains between logic and psychology.

THREE · THE SIGN

TWELVE

The Ambiguity

Meaning in communicative speech is always entangled with an indicative relation.—Husserl

The Difficulty

Now that I am ready at last to deal with where Husserl starts out, I would do so in a fashion that will enable me to pursue in my next chapter the comparison I long since proposed with Heidegger. If a "difficulty" comes up where Heidegger starts out in *Being and Time*, "in the middle of a Platonic dialogue," a "difficulty" also comes up in the first section of the first of Husserl's specific *Logical Investigations*. I have already mentioned this section, which is entitled, "An Ambiguity in the Term 'Sign.'" The kind of difficulty Husserl finds himself up against at the start is an "ambiguity."

In my introduction I recognized that, for Husserl, phenomenology is "difficult work," but then I became preoccupied with Heidegger's conception of a "difficulty." Husserl's different conception of a "difficulty" is worth probing for the same reason that it was worth probing Heidegger's conception: the method a philosopher adopts is usually shaped to a considerable extent by how the philosopher conceives the difficulties that are to be resolved by it.

I have already anticipated how Husserl would eliminate ambiguities: the outcome of his varying examples with an eidetic reduction is that intuitive insight into an identical structure (such as intentionality) emerges as essential to what the examples are examples of. In the first of the *Investigations* we shall be watching Husserl employ this procedure in dealing with examples of the sign.

A contrast with Heidegger's procedure also becomes evident. We watched Heidegger, with his translation of *ēporēkamen* by *sind wir in Verlegenheit gekommen,* seeking interplay within a range of ambiguities. Even when Heidegger uses the same word for "difficult" as Husserl, *schwierig,* Heidegger plays up an ambiguity. Thus he explains elsewhere that "it is in the essence of philosophy never to make things *leichter* [easier/lighter], but only to make them *schwerer* [more difficult/heavier]," for its "function" is to "give beings back their *Gewicht* ["importance"/ "weight"] (being)."[1]

Ambiguities are, of course, all around us, but we usually do not have to recognize them as such. The ambiguity in the use of "the term 'sign'" which Husserl is concerned to recognize at the start of the first of the *Logical Investigations* is an "ambiguity" which is "dangerous." The danger is a "confusion" that would infect the subject of logic.

The Shift in Subject

Husserl would eliminate the ambiguity in the use of the term *sign* by drawing with an eidetic reduction a distinction between two kinds of sign—the distinction in which we have seen Derrida finds "so much at issue." The distinction is the implementation of the distinction required for the shift to the subject which logic is to become.

I earlier began examining the shift in *subject* that takes place at the start of *Being and Time* as over against Husserl. It was broadly a shift from an analysis of "meanings" to the question of "the meaning of being." A comparison of Heidegger's analysis of signs as over against Husserl's will enable me to be more specific about this shift.

My interest may be in the shift that takes place in Heidegger as over against Husserl, but to take Husserl himself into account is to recognize that he was involved in a shift in *subject,* which he carried out in some measure in relation to Mill. Because there is little interest nowadays in Mill as a logician, I have supplemented my illustration of the shift in *subject* which Husserl undertakes vis-à-vis Mill with the shift which Derrida undertakes vis-à-vis Husserl. Aside from illustrating some of the procedural problems to be encountered with a shift in *subject,* the comparison with Derrida has the additional advantage that he deals explicitly with Husserl's analysis of signs. Heidegger does not. My argument will be that his own analysis of signs is implicitly a deconstruction of Husserl's analysis.

Before I can pursue this argument, I must further explore Husserl's analysis. The two kinds of sign (*Zeichen*) he distinguishes are the "indicative sign" and the "expressive sign," or the "expression." He draws the distinction with the claim that an "indicative sign" (*Anzeichen*) "indicates" something but does not express a "meaning" (*Bedeutung*). This claim is puzzling to us, since we are accustomed to say, for example, "Smoke means fire." Husserl would correct our ordinary usage and have us say, "Smoke indicates fire."

Indication

Here we have an illustration of how, no matter how anxious we may be to disregard what the progress of history has left behind, facing it may sometimes be worthwhile. Husserl's claim is made with a succinctness that can perhaps be explained partly by his assumption that the claim is hardly controversial and that the reader is already familiar with it as a claim advanced by Mill, although Husserl does not cite him by name. He assumes his audience would know.

Husserl's argument is that it is "only in the case of those indicative signs which are deliberately and artificially brought about, that one speaks of *designation* [*Bezeichnen*] . . . both with regard to the action which produces the marking (the branding, or chalking, and so forth) and in the sense of indication [*Anzeigen*] itself."[2] Here the reader is expected to catch the allusion to marking and chalking not because he has read the *Arabian Nights* but because he has read Mill.

Mill details the claim in a more leisurely fashion. I have already given Husserl's quotation from the first chapter of Mill's *Logic*, "Of the Necessity of Commencing with an Analysis of Language." Having accepted this analysis as a "threshold," Mill singles out in his second chapter "the name." He takes over Hobbes's definition: "A name is a word taken at pleasure to serve for a mark which may cause in our mind a thought like to some thought we had before, and which being pronounced to others, may be to them a sign of what thought the speaker had before in his mind." The argument that this "sign" is meaningless, and the example of "the robber's chalk mark," come in the paragraph that precedes another paragraph which Husserl cites later. This is Mill's argument:

If, like the robber in the *Arabian Nights*, we make a mark with chalk on a house to enable us to know it again, the mark has a purpose, but it does not properly have any meaning. The chalk does not declare anything about the house; it does not mean, "This is such a person's house," or "This is a house which contains booty." The object of marking the mark is merely distinction. I say to myself, "All these houses are so nearly alike that if I lose sight of them I shall not again be able to distinguish that which I am now looking at from any of the others.[3]

I will not continue with Mill's analysis, for he is concerned with propositional meaning, and Husserl is not. That difference may explain why Husserl does not actually quote Mill here.

Having taken over Mill's conclusion that the sign does not "have any meaning," Husserl will go on with his own analysis, in which an "indicative sign" is a sign whereby "certain objects or states of affairs of whose existence someone has actual knowledge indicate to him the existence of certain other objects or states of affairs, in the sense that his belief in the being of the one is experienced [erlebt] as a motive . . . for the belief in, or presuming, the existence of the other."[4] Thus smoke is a sign which indicates fire.

We now see why Husserl, in carrying out the shift to the subject of logic, puts the indicative sign aside. What an indicative sign indicates cannot be immediately given as a meaning. Thus he speaks of "the indicative relation." The relation in which an indicative sign is caught up belongs to an empirical science—for example, the proposition, "The canals on Mars are signs of the existence of intelligent beings on Mars." More important to Husserl, the belief in this proposition belongs to empirical psychology: "The mental facts in which the concept of the indicative sign has its 'origin,' in which it can be grasped by abstraction, belong to the wider group of facts which fall under the rubric of the 'association of ideas.'"[5] We have learned to associate smoke with fire, and canals with intelligent beings. Husserl's interest in the association of ideas is not a matter of its plausibility or implausibility as a psychological analysis but of the threat that psychologism—as the encroachment of a psychological analysis—poses to the separation of logic as a subject.

Objective Meaning-Content

Securing this separation involves not only the shift in *subject* which I have been describing, but also a shift in *level,* which is completed when Husserl's attack on psychologism in the *Prolegomena* reaches a certain climax in the second of the *Logical Investigations*. There he is no longer at the level of such particular facts as fire, smoke, and canals, but reaches the eidetic level. To illustrate this climax, I single out his criticism of Mill's nominalistic analysis of abstraction. Husserl upholds the generality of general names (or universals) "in the full, genuine sense . . . that is shown to be evident by an analysis of the objective meaning-content of thought." The danger he fears is lapsing from this insight through a "misunderstood psychological analysis."[6] The nominalistic analysis of abstraction may be plausible as a psychological analysis, but it is "a misunderstood psychological analysis when it is understood as a logical analysis."

In other words, however convincing the psychological analysis may be as an explanation of how subjectively we arrive at a general concept, the danger is in allowing it to explain away the generality of the concept—its "objective meaning-content," which we experience immediately. Thus the psychological explanation has nothing at all to do with phenomenological facts:

> Here and now, at the moment when we meaningfully utter a general name, we mean [*meinen*] what is general, and this meaning is different from what we mean when we mean what is individual. This difference must be shown in *the descriptive content of the isolated experience,* in the individual, actual carrying out of the general assertion. What is causally connected with such an experience, what psychological consequence may follow from it, all this does not here concern us. It concerns the psychology of abstraction, not its phenomenology. The essence of nominalism . . . resides in the fact that its attempted clarifications overlook the proper character of consciousness [*das eigentumliche Bewusstsein*], which yields us the authentic [*eigentlich*] presentation of the general—in other words of the ideation with its insight in which the general "itself" is given to us.[7]

"Ideation" is the procedure Husserl will later relabel "the eidetic reduction," as I noted in my introduction.

I have regularly cited intentionality as the crucial illustration of the insight to be obtained by an eidetic reduction: "In perception, something is perceived; in imagination, something imagined; . . . in desire, desired; and so on."[8] As the examples are freely varied, I become conscious of what remains invariant, identical—that my consciousness in each case is consciousness *of* something. This is the "experience" which the eidetic reduction has "isolated" as logical—as the experience of an essential structure, an "objective meaning-content."

The Shift in Method

I have anticipated Husserl's argument in the second investigation not only as an argument on behalf of the shift in *subject,* whereby logic is to gain independence from psychology that it does not enjoy in Mill, but also as an argument which illustrates the concomitant shift in *method* to the eidetic reduction from the procedure of empirical generalization. This shift involves the shift in *level* which renders Husserl's logic an eidetic science as opposed to an empirical science.

With an empirical generalization, concepts are reached by abstracting from particular cases, so that the "general concepts make it possible for us to treat things in bundles, as it were."[9] But a general concept, conceived as the outcome of a process of generalization, is not "isolated" as an "experience" and thus has no status that is independent of the particular cases that have been bundled together during the process. Husserl is opposing to this notion a general concept that is an essence, an *eidos,* which is "isolated" as an experience that is immediately grasped at the outome of an eidetic reduction which leaves the particular cases behind. Husserl has already employed the eidetic reduction in the first investigation, but it is more readily understood when the process of generalization to which it is opposed is considered as relegated to empirical psychology. Thus the first investigation has to be followed up by the second investigation.

Now we can go back to the opposition in the first investigation between the logical expression and the indicative sign. Looking at the introduction to the *Prolegomena* in the first volume of the *Logical Investigations* and glancing on to the second investigation in the second volume have helped bring out a certain continuity (which will be interrupted at the beginning of the third investigation). At stake throughout is the unity of the subject of logic—what Husserl refers to in the introduction to the second investigation as "the very essence of logic," which is itself the outcome of an eidetic reduction by which it is recognized that "meanings as such . . . constitute the domain of pure logic." Recall that the full title of the first section of the introduction to the *Prolegomena* is "The Controversy Regarding the Definition of Logic and the Essential Content of Its Doctrines." Husserl can define logic because it has an essential content of its own, and the essentiality of this content is to be assured by drawing what the title of the first chapter of the first investigation refers to as "essential distinctions"—eidetic distinctions which are essential to the delimitation of logic as a subject. The first of these is the distinction between the expression and the indicative sign.

We saw in the last chapter that Husserl does not start out, strictly speaking, with a distinction (as Derrida regards him as doing) in the first section of the first investigation, but with an "ambiguity" which is "dangerous" because it encourages the confusion of logic with psychology. Thus he does not begin his first volume with a definition of logic in terms of its subject, its essential content; instead Husserl reaches its subject by a shift in *subject* from the confused subject of a "psychologistic logic." Indeed this confusion is so dangerous that, before undertaking the first investigation, he has devoted an entire volume to refuting this "psychologistic logic."

We also saw that this shift is designed to ensure that his logic, as an analysis of meanings, is independent of the empirical fact that "there really are languages which are really used by men in their dealings with each other." In the first section of the first investigation, these dealings involve more specifically communication, and Husserl explains how the confusion between the expression and the indicative sign occurs: "Meaning in communicative speech [*mitteilender Rede*] is always entangled [*verflochten*] with an indicative relation."[10]

The difficulty encountered in my last chapter—the difficulty of "subject-delimitation," of separating logic from psychology—thus becomes the difficulty of disentangling meanings from the process of communicating them. Here we see again how Husserl's method is what he calls a "method of clarification." Husserl's methodological commitment to eliminating ambiguities is a commitment to clarifying what is confused by disentangling what is entangled. Here he would disentangle the "expression," as the sign which expresses a meaning, from its usual entanglement with the "indicative sign."

Husserl's interest is not in indicative signs themselves or in the part they play in communication, but in arriving at "the logical distinctions which are essential to expressions," that is, essential to their expressing meanings. What is essential becomes more evident in the section with the double title, "Expressions as Meaningful Signs: The Setting Aside [*Absonderung*] of a Sense of Expression as not Relevant Here." Here he sets aside "facial expressions and the various gestures that involuntarily accompany speech without communicative intent [*Absicht*]," and which are "not expressions in the sense in which spoken expressions [*Rede*] are." I considered the exclusion of facial expression from Husserl's definition of "expression" in Volume 2, in order to bring out a shift in *subject* that takes place in Sartre's phenomenology, in which faces and their expressions enjoy crucial significance.[11] This shift in *subject* in Sartre is not arbitrary. When in Volume 4 I pick up Sartre again, we shall see that he is committed to the relevance of communication, which Husserl would exclude as a matter irrelevant to logic.

Interruptive Transformation

Let me again bring Derrida in to provide illustrations of some of the procedural problems encountered in dealing with the relations between philosophers. We can see more definitely what is at stake in Husserl's disentanglement of "expressions as meaningful signs" from the "communicative function" of language if we compare Derrida's effort to regain the "experience of language" by undercutting Husserl's distinction between logical and linguistic meanings. Derrida cites *Ideas I* at a point where

Husserl refers to the *Logical Investigations* and recalls the title of the first investigation by arguing that "the problems of expression and meaning come first for philosophers" who are "guided by general logical interests." At this juncture Husserl arrives at the problems of distinguishing logical expressions by emphasizing, "All the acts [of meaning] considered up until now are interwoven with [*verweben sich/s'entrelacent*] the levels of acts of expression."[12]

Husserl then acknowledges that "the general and unavoidable ambiguity of the terminology" which he is employing is "apparent wherever the relations are expressed in language," and hence "is naturally also found in the terms 'expression' and 'meaning.'" This ambiguity and attendant confusion he would eliminate by distinguishing the deeper level of logical expression as prelinguistic.

When Derrida reaches the phrase "expressed in language," he interrupts his citation, for he would arrive at his own conception of a "text":

> The interlacing [*Verwebung*] of language, of that which is purely language, with other threads of experience, constitutes a fabric. . . .
> *Fabric* [*tissu*] means *text*. *Verweben* means *texere*.[13]

My excisions may gut Derrida's argument, but my only point is that an entanglement, which is to be disentangled in Husserl as a confusion to be clarified, is in contrast accepted by Derrida as an "interlacing" or "weaving" which becomes the "text"—the "experience of language."

I am not merely concerned to illustrate the shift in *subject* that Derrida could be said to carry out (if he were a philosopher) when he restores the fabric that was cut up by the distinctions with which Husserl delimited his subject. I also find relevant to my own purposes certain traits of the procedure Derrida employs. He concedes that deconstruction entails an interruptive transformation, as illustrated in the passage I have just quoted from him. There he is interrupting Husserl, who is arriving at a distinction between logical and linguistic expression, and the interruption becomes transformative in that Derrida would regain "the experience of language." This interruption involves the long-run interruption of Husserl's analysis at a juncture as late in the *Logical Investigations* as the second volume.

Such interrupting is a *forçage* (forcing) which is hardly unique to deconstruction, though it is not often so frankly conceded.[14] In one respect such a procedure is entirely traditional in philosophy. Almost any philosopher's interpretation of another philosophy is deconstructive in the loose sense that he damages the structure of that philosophy by interrupting its construction, because he is undertaking to construct his own philosophy.

I have adopted the idiom "interruptive transformation" partly because it is one way in which communication can break down. We are well aware that the other party's interrupting a conversation we are having with her involves her transforming the implications of what we have just said and that this can lead to a breakdown in communication.

I began the present chapter with a minor illustration of an interruptive transformation: in the *Arabian Nights* example Husserl takes over a conclusion reached by Mill but in an analysis in which he is departing from Mill. Husserl does not explicitly cite Mill, and of course the demonstration of *forçage* is easier when the predecessor is cited. Thus I was able to show in Volume 2 how Sartre (whom Derrida would regard as a thoroughly, even tiresomely, traditional philosopher), in elaborating his philosophy of the imagination, interrupts Husserl's *Ideas I* at a very late juncture and transforms the implications of the passage he cites from Husserl.[15]

Another illustration of an interruptive transformation is, of course, my bringing to the fore in the present volume the problem of communication by focusing on the breakdown in communication between Heidegger and Husserl. The impasse which I recognize each reached in relation to the other is not the kind of "difficulty" which Heidegger acknowledged when he translated the *aporia* encountered in the *Sophist* by *Verlegenheit,* any more than it was the kind of "difficulty" that we are about to watch Husserl disentangle as a "dangerous confusion."

Disorganization

In my last chapter I showed how Derrida with his "Starting out from what question . . ." belatedly interrupted the analysis Husserl had been conducting in the *Logical Investigations.* That the transformation he would promote is to regain "the experience of language" is evident when he cites the actual examples Husserl provides of indicative signs and claims that "Husserl should have cited writing in general, which would be for him, beyond any doubt, *indicative* at its own level." He explains that Husserl's "silence" is "prudent," for if language "is indicative in the sense that Husserl gives to this term, it has a strange privilege which would risk disorganizing all his essential distinctions."[16] Husserl would have inflicted deconstruction on himself *avant la lettre.*

I shall not try to follow this argument of Derrida's. It is relegated to a footnote, with the qualification, "We do not insist here on this problem; it belongs to the ultimate horizon of this essay,"[17] where I have already suggested that Derrida's concern soon became less with Husserl himself as an individual philosopher than with general characteristics of the tradition which Derrida finds illustrated by Husserl.

Suffice it to say, for my own purposes, that what transpires when essential distinctions (distinctions which are essential to one philosophy) are at risk of being disorganized by the intervention of another philosopher is what I have identified in Heidegger's case as a "lurch." It may also be identified with what Derrida characterizes as Husserl's "prudent silence," which could also be characterized with the term *Versäumnis* (negligent omission), which Heidegger uses in the first section of *Being and Time* with reference to how "the question of being" has been forgotten by philosophers.

The "danger" that Husserl envisages in the first section in the first of his *Logical Investigations* ("An Ambiguity in the Term 'Sign'") he had already envisaged more generally in his second introduction (preceding this first section) as due to the ambiguity of words, which will impede his formulation of concepts: "At the start what is logical [for example, the concept of "sign"] is given in imperfect shape" as "a more or less wavering meaning." Then "unnoticed ambiguities may allow other concepts to slip subsequently underneath [*nachträglich . . . unterschieben*] our words."[18] This kind of slippage of course becomes endemic when Derrida undercuts Husserl's "essential distinctions" in order to regain "the experience of language."

The general threat of slippage is further examined in a section of *Ideas I,* "Faithful Expression of Clear Data. Unambiguous Terms." There Husserl explains, "Words [especially if "they derive from the common language"] may be ambiguous, and their changing meanings [*Sinne*] may be vague."[19] Thus it is necessary for him to capture conceptual meanings with an unambiguous terminology of his own—a univocal terminology in which what is essential is conveyed, for example, by the concept of "sign" in the first of the *Logical Investigations.*

Communication

The requirements of scientific communication are laid down by Husserl: "Science is possible only where the results of thinking can be stored up in the form of knowledge and used for later thinking in the form of a system of statements." For this purpose meanings which have been first fixed "*conceptually*" by a pure phenomenological analysis must then be adhered to "terminologically."

The "clear data" in question are meanings; the conceptual procedure by which they have been clarified is primarily the eidetic reduction, but even when this result has been supplied with a terminological expression, "there is a continuing need for caution and for reexamination to see that what was fixed [conceptually] in the earlier context is actually employed with the same meaning [*Sinn*] in the new context."[20] (Once again *Umarbeitung* will be necessary.) Husserl's insistence on univocal meanings, as opposed to ambiguous meanings, is insistence on keeping meanings fixedly identical, as opposed to those which are changing, wavering.

In his next sentence Husserl postpones further discussion: "But this is not the place for going more precisely into . . . rules—including those, for example, relating to science as a product of intersubjective collaboration."[21] Communication of insights is not a scientific procedure in the same sense that the phenomenological analysis is by which they were first obtained. This conclusion of Husserl's I shall explain in detail in Chapter 24.

· *The Indicative Sign*

· *What is a sign in general?—Derrida*

· *Examples*

· Encouraged by Heidegger's footnote refer-
· ence in section 17 of *Being and Time* to Hus-
· serl's "analysis of signs," I anticipated that
· examining Heidegger's own analysis would
· enable me to begin determining Heidegger's
· relation to Husserl, and specifically the sense
· in which Heidegger's "construction" of his
· own concept of the sign could be taken as
· entailing a "deconstruction" of Husserl's
· analysis.
·   If scholars have not been more tempted
· in this way by section 17, it may be because
· the later Heidegger, in the Zähringen seminar,
· emphasizes his relation to Husserl with re-
· spect to the analysis of categorial intuition in
· the sixth and last of the *Logical Investiga-
· tions*. Heidegger finds there (as I have already
· mentioned) that Husserl "grazes slightly the
· question of being."[1] But the sixth investiga-
· tion is too late to work out a comparison that
· can be kept under control; too much has tran-
· spired in the previous investigations. It is
· safer to begin where Husserl himself starts
· out in the first—and Heidegger accords a
· footnote reference.
·   That Heidegger's footnote offers some-
· thing in the way of an invitation is suggested
· by the contrast with the *Prolegomena,* where
· Heidegger makes only a noncommittal refer-
· ence to Husserl's analysis: "Some things are
· done by Husserl in . . . the *Logical Investiga-
· *tions,* where the first investigation deals with

signs in connection with the delimitation of the phenomenon of linguistic meaning as opposed to the general phenomena (as he says) of signs."[2] Here Heidegger picks no quarrel; there is no demonstration of what opposes his analysis to Husserl's.

Section 17 even betrays an interest in what Husserl "says" that is not evident in the *Prolegomena*, despite the fact that Heidegger generally in the *Prolegomena* seems so much more explicitly interested in Husserl than in *Being and Time*. But a close and patient textual exegesis is necessary to support the claim, which I anticipated making in my introduction (borrowing from Sartre's appraisal of the relation between him and Merleau-Ponty), that Heidegger's analysis is deliberately at this juncture "a startling deviation" from Husserl's.

The first indication that Heidegger has in mind here in *Being and Time* what Husserl "says" is a certain awkwardness in how Heidegger gets his analysis of signs underway. He supplies two separate lists of examples of signs. After defining signs [*Zeichen*] as "prima facie [*zunächst*] [pieces of] equipment whose specific character is *Zeigen* [to "indicate," or to "show"]," he supplies his first list—"such signs as signposts [*Wegmarken*], boundary stones, the ball for the sailor's storm-warning, signals, flags, symbols of mourning, and so forth."

Two paragraphs later he supplies a second list of examples:

Among signs [*Zeichen*] are indicative signs [*Anzeichen*], warning signs and signs indicating what has happened in the past [*Vor- und Rückzeichen*], signs which are marks, signs by which things are recognized. Each of these has a different way of indicating, regardless of what is used as a sign. Among these "signs" are to be distinguished trace, remains, commemorative monument, document, testimony, symbol, expression, appearances, meaning.[3]

Why two separate lists of examples?

With the two lists Heidegger is making two different points. He follows up the first with a definition: "*Zeigen* can be defined as a 'kind' of referring." This definition ties the analysis of signs in with his preceeding analysis of "reference" (*Verweisung*). The sequence is brought out by the title of section 17, "Reference and Signs," and since I have argued that sequence is a crucial issue in *Being and Time*, I shall consider in Chapter 14 how the analysis of signs fits into the sequence Heidegger is following. I again stress that I am now beginning with "signs" (and for the present am skipping "reference") because Husserl started out with "signs" in the first of his *Logical Investigations*, and I wanted to pursue the comparison I had initiated by first examining how Heidegger had started out in *Being and Time*.

With the second list, Heidegger conveys a point by the sentence with which he introduces the list: "We cannot adequately investigate the multiplicity of signs." But having made this point, Heidegger makes no further explicit use of any of the examples on either list. I would intervene with my suggestion that we may interpret the compilation of examples more as a criticism of Husserl's analysis of signs than an advance in Heidegger's own analysis. Even the number of examples is anomalous in *Being and Time,* which includes no other compilation of such length.

Is Heidegger emulating Husserl's eidetic reduction as a procedure which relies on examples? Husserl did in fact compile a list of indicative signs at the beginning of his analysis of signs: "A brand is the sign of a slave, a flag is the sign of a nation. . . . Here all marks belong as characteristic qualities suited to help us in recognizing the objects to which they attach." Later he adds "signs to aid memory, . . . memorials, etc."[4]

Even if Heidegger's list is a demonstration of the "multiplicity" which Husserl has not succeeded in subduing, it is not just a miscellany. Indeed his admission that his list is not exhaustive suggests that he is being selective. In beginning with "indicative signs," he is beginning where Husserl began. But Husserl did not bother to mention the next two kinds listed by Heidegger, because to him they would simply be examples of the indicative sign. Heidegger, however, is bringing signs, like other phenomena in *Being and Time,* within the "horizon" of time.[5] Thus Heidegger is introducing *Vorzeichen* as conveying a reference to the future, and *Rückzeichen* as conveying a reference to the past.

After *Rückzeichen* Heidegger introduces "signs which are marks" (*Merkzeichen*) and "signs by which things are recognized" (*Kennzeichen*). Here his terminology is so specific that it can easily be accounted for only as alluding to Husserl's subsuming under "indicative signs" what he described as "all marks as characteristic qualities suited to help us in recognizing [*Kennzeichen zumachen*] the objects to which they attach." There may also be an allusion to Husserl's list in Heidegger's including "expression," which comes to the fore in Husserl (the title of his first investigation is "Expression and Meaning"); however, "expression" is relegated to nearly the end of Heidegger's list and receives no attention in section 17. Later we shall see that its fate is not finally determined until section 34 of *Being and Time.*

The issue, however, is not whether we may detect echoes of Husserl's examples in Heidegger. The issue Heidegger raises at the end of his second list of examples is that "each of these [signs] has a different way of indicating." The implication is that the problem with signs is not just that their "multiplicity" itself eludes adequate investigation, but that the differences in their ways of indicating cannot be corralled in an eidetic reduction. In the long run it is the fate of that procedure in Heidegger's analysis that concerns me.

Let us accordingly glance back at how Husserl carries out the reduction with which he defines the way an indicative sign indicates. The title of the subsection in which he compiles his list of indicative signs is "The Essence of Indication." Thus it is clear that his compilation is not just a compilation but an eidetic reduction of the multiplicity. The outcome is the italicized conclusion: "Certain objects . . . of *whose existence [Bestand] someone has actual knowledge* indicate to him *the existence of certain other objects* in the sense that *his belief in the existence of the one is experienced* (though not with insight [available only when a meaning is immediately given]) *as motivating a belief . . . in the existence of the other.*"[6]

The Shift in Method

The deconstruction that Heidegger undertakes in section 17 of Husserl's definition of the indicative sign is a deconstruction of the distinction which is essential to Husserl's logic—the distinction by which he opposes the (logical) "expression," with which a "meaning" is immediately "given," to the "indicative relation," which is instituted by an "indicative sign." One respect in which this distinction is "essential" in Husserl is that when it is reached, the temporal distinctions do not have the relevance they will enjoy when Heidegger distinguishes from "indicative signs" *Vorzeichen* and *Rückzeichen.*

The methodological commitment implicit in Husserl's distinguishing two kinds of sign is something he himself draws attention to with the title of the first chapter of his first investigation: "Essential Distinctions." But what I would make explicit is the kind of analysis with which he arrives at these distinctions—beginning with his distinction of the (logical) expression of a meaning from the indicative sign.

Here more methodological background is needed to appreciate what is at issue. We have already seen that Husserl draws distinctions in order to eliminate ambiguities when the attendant confusions are "dangerous." I would emphasize now that his "essential distinctions" are characteristically one-sided: he draws them in order to treat in his analysis what falls on one sided of the distinction as opposed to the other side. Thus, for example, he eliminates in this first section "an ambiguity [*Doppelsinn*] in the term 'sign,'" by drawing a distinction which cuts one way, in order to exclude as irrelevant to logic one sense of this term (the indicative sign) and with it those considerations which he regards as merely linguistic and psychological. Thus he does not find it incumbent on him to answer Derrida's question, "What is a sign in general?" He would not be disturbed by what Derrida characterizes as "this absence of a question about the starting point."[7]

All Husserl's "essential distinctions," we have learned, are essential in that they are arrived at by an "eidetic" reduction, in which particular matters of fact can finally be left out of account; the outcome is the grasping of an "essence." These essential distinctions are essential to logic, which is essentially an analysis of meanings in which empirical sciences can be left aside as generalizations from particular matters of fact.

I think we are better prepared to deal with the shifts in *subject* and in *method* that Heidegger would carry out if we bring Derrida back in, even though he does not himself compare Husserl's analysis of signs with Heidegger's. The juncture I have just reached is one at which Derrida challenges Husserl's undertaking: "How in the first place justify the *decision* to submit reflection on the sign to a logic? . . . What gives authority to a logic or a theory of knowledge to determine the essence of language?"[8] We recognize that Husserl's justification would be that only one kind of sign is to be reflected on in logic; the other kind can be left to the empirical sciences of linguistics and psychology, which, as generalizations from particular matters of fact, lack the authority of an eidetic science. If language itself does have a certain initial relevance for Husserl, it is (we have seen) because it afflicts us with the ambiguities which must be eliminated from logic.

In the last chapter we heard Derrida refuse to accept Husserl's distinction, which "disentangles" expressions from indicative signs. But then Derrida goes on to privilege the indicative sign where Husserl had privileged the (logical) expression. We heard Derrida argue that "if we suppose that writing is indicative in the sense Husserl gives this word, it has a strange privilege which risks disorganizing all his essential distinctions." At that point he accuses Husserl of a "prudent silence"[9] in thus neglecting the other side of his distinction. According writing its privilege involves the shift in *subject* which Derrida would carry out if he were a philosopher and responsive, as Husserl is, to Kant's behest: "We subvert the sciences, if we allow their boundaries to run together."[10]

I am not pausing to determine if "writing" (in Derrida's sense) is "indicative in the sense Husserl gives this word." Derrida is rightly tentative about this supposition, which he may toss off lest we think of him as simply moving to the other side of Husserl's own distinction. My general conviction is that it would be unusual for a successor to move in this fashion to the other side of a predecessor's distinction and leave intact the distinction itself or even how it was drawn.

Interplay

My present concern is that the distinctions drawn with Husserl's eidetic reduction are essential in that they are one-sided oppositions. This characterization deserves further probing. Derrida lumps together significantly different kinds of structure as "oppositional structure" or "oppositional logic." Let me propose here first a contrast between Husserl and his "disciple" Sartre, because this contrast is easier to get at. In Volume 2 Sartre was seen to elaborate what I would call two-sided distinctions. Thus Sartre found that "intrinsic" to an act of imagining is our consciousness of what we were imagining as "not being there"—as it would be if we were conscious of perceiving it. Given this duplicity of consciousness, Sartre's subject is not simply the imagination. He is dealing with what is imagined as being inseparable in our consciousness of it from what it is opposed to—what is perceived. Thus he is able, as I pointed out earlier, to annex his treatment of the imagination to Husserl's treatment of perception.

The shift in *subject* with which Sartre secures this annexation involves as well a shift in *method*. Sartre's analysis is not conducted in the fashion which Husserl regards as phenomenological, but in a fashion which amounts (as I argued in Volume 2) to a rudimentary dialectic: he gets his analysis underway by ticking off the traits of *l'imaginaire* in terms of the *interplay* which takes place between a physical image that we perceive (a work of art, a photo, a caricature, an impersonation, and so forth) and what can then be imagined in conjunction with perceiving it. The *interplay* depends on the other side of the opposition remaining relevant, so that the analysis can profit from the ambiguity (the *Doppelsinn*, to use Husserl's term) whereby an image can be a physical image or a mental image. Thus Sartre's pivotal example is the impersonation, inasmuch as it is the juncture at which *interplay* is so pronounced as to become an unstable opposition between the traits of the impersonator we perceive (a small, plump, dark-haired female) and the impersonated to be imagined (a tall, thin, blond male—Maurice Chevalier). It is the unstable ambiguity of this *interplay* which preoccupies Sartre, not simply because, as he explains, it "is obviously what is most entertaining for a spectator in an impersonation," but (more important, I would add) because he is on his way at this juncture to a further shift in *subject* whereby role-playing (or play-acting) becomes prominent in his later works. This subject in turn exhibits unstable ambiguity: when I play a role (as when I impersonate someone else), I am what I am not, and I am not what I am. The *interplay* thus exhibits Sartre's dialectic of being and nothingness.[11]

My reviewing Sartre's analysis is designed only to bring out with a contrast the different character of Husserl's analysis. Husserl's methodological commitment to the elimination of ambiguities, in order to identify univocally what he is treating and to keep its meaning fixed throughout his analysis, is a commitment to a "setting aside" with a one-sided distinction, as is illustrated by his section title, "The Setting Aside [*Absonderung*] of a Sense of Expression as not Relevant Here." He is proposing "to employ the term 'expression' restrictively"—that is, to restrict it to a sense which is distinctively relevant to logic. Accordingly he would "exclude much that ordinary speech would designate an 'expression.'" Then he makes the methodological claim with which we are already acquainted: "One must often do violence in this way to language in order to obtain terminologically fixed concepts, where only ambiguous terms are available."[12] When Husserl therefore in his analysis of expressions specifically "excludes facial expression," what he is excluding will come to the fore in Sartre's analysis as expressive of what he terms "affective meaning."

The violence of Husserl's exclusion of what "ordinary speech [and Sartre] would designate an 'expression'" helps explain how difficult it is for us to grasp what Husserl means by a (distinctively logical) expression, and it lends a justification to my pursuing first Sartre's more accessible procedure.

There is a shift in the *subject* in Sartre (even though he is not cognizant of it) with regard not only to "expression" but also to "meaning." Sartre undertakes his analysis in *L'imaginaire* by looking at a caricature of a friend as opposed to a photo. The example is designed to demonstrate that an affective reaction is necessary to trigger the act of imagination. When I respond affectively to a caricature which has "caught" the friend's expression as the photo fails to do, I recognize in the caricature what the friend "means" to me. Similarly I respond to the impersonation—"That really is him"—when "the affective meaning on the face of Chevalier" emerges on the face of the impersonator. Again the shift in *subject* involves a shift in *method*. "Meaning" itself thus becomes two-sidedly dialectical: it is still cognitive, in that perceptual ingredients still yield necessary information (the impersonator is wearing a tilted straw hat and thrusting out her chin), so that I know she intends to impersonate Chevalier, but the impersonation succeeds—the mental image of Chevalier emerges—only when triggered by the affective meaning with which I would react to Chevalier himself.[13]

Recalling Husserl's relation to Sartre has suggested that there is one danger Husserl did not envisage, when he found an ambiguity "dangerous" because it could promote a confusion, and proceeded to avoid that danger by drawing a one-sided distinction. Another philosopher can come along, as Sartre does, and induce the distinction to become two-sided, thus opening up the prospect of ambiguous *interplay* between the two sides. Husserl's one-sided distinction is endangered in a different way by

Heidegger, but I have recalled the danger in Sartre's case because there it is more readily discernible.

My further point is that there may be no general philosophical answer to a question of the order, What is the "sign" in general? or What is "expression" in general? or What is "meaning" in general? and so forth. Different philosophies yield different answers to such questions. With further illustrations, I shall eventually conclude that the different answers cannot be corralled in an overall philosophical tradition.

Oppositional Logic

Just as significant as the shifts in *subject* that punctuate the philosophical tradition are the shifts in *method*. One of the general traits which we have seen Derrida considers to pervade the tradition is reliance on "oppositional logic" or "oppositional structure." The structure of Husserl's logic is oppositional: his starting point in the first of the investigations is structured by the opposition indicative sign/expression; the eidetic reduction is geared to the opposition fact/essence; the phenomenological reduction to the opposition worldly/transcendental.

Nevertheless, "oppositional structure" or "oppositional logic" are too vague as verdicts. The differences between individual philosophers as to how each of them handles oppositions is sufficient to suggest that, when they are lumped together as "logocentric," the lump is too lumpy to be of much philosophical interest until we recognize that different "logics" are at stake, as I have already shown in the cases of Husserl and Mill.

A decisive characteristic of the oppositions which are essential in Husserl is that they are one-sided: one member of the opposition is to be excluded from the analysis insofar as it threatens the autonomy and authority of his logic. The structure of Sartre's phenomenology is also oppositional, but the oppositions are two-sided, so that the analysis can focus on *interplay* between the two sides—for example, between perception and imagination, being and nothingness. The excluded side of Husserl's one-sided distinction of expression from facial expression is rehabilitated by Sartre so that his analysis can latch onto the *interplay* between the two sides. Derrida too rehabilitates the other side of Husserl's distinction, but in a different fashion and for different purposes. It is risky to generalize about someone so flexible in his performance as Derrida, but he is not my concern here. Yet I would point out (as Derrida does not) that Heidegger (like Derrida) rehabilitates the indicative sign, which Husserl excludes from his analysis as having no meaning once he has opposed to it the expressive sign as the logical expression of a meaning. I shall also argue that Heidegger handles oppositions in a significantly different fashion from Husserl—and from Sartre for that matter.

The Indicator

Dasein is always somehow directed and on its way.—Heidegger

Examples

Since Heidegger makes no further use of his second list of examples of a sign, I have sought to interpret it largely as an implicit criticism of Husserl rather than as a step toward his own analysis. In the paragraph after the second list Heidegger does launch his own analysis by concentrating on a single example of a "sign." His preceding emphasis on the "multiplicity of possible signs" thus has the effect of playing up the extent to which he relies on this single example, for he does not even bother to subsume his example under any of the kinds of sign he has listed.

This is the example: "Automobiles are sometimes fitted up with an adjustable red arrow whose position shows the way the vehicle will take at a cross-road."[1] There is no generally accepted technical term for this "arrow in English. But its function can be brought out by referring to it as a "directional signal" or as an "indicator." (In French it would be an *indicateur*.) In Husserl's analysis the indicator would be an example of an indicative sign. Thus the prominence Heidegger confers on this example is an implicit criticism of Husserl's setting the indicative sign aside. In Heidegger's own list the example would be more specifically a *Vorzeichen* (a "warning signal") and thus is evidence of the shift in *subject* taking place in *Being and Time*, for when Heidegger brings phenomena within the "horizon" of time, the dimension of time which will acquire priority is the future. But if Heidegger does not identify his example as a warning signal or even as an indicative sign, it seems to be because he does not want the implications of his analysis of the indicator confined to any single kind of sign on his list.

Otto Pöggeler, a diligent expositor of Heidegger, acknowledges in "Heidegger Heute" the remarkable particularity of this example, by explaining Heidegger's selection of it as due to his "obvious astonishment at a new gadget."[2] But although Heidegger commends "astonishment" when it is identified in Greek with the origin of philosophy, his own philosophy does not give him much encouragement to be astonished by new gadgets. He does pay considerable attention in *Being and Time* to the *Zeug* ("the piece of equipment"). But the most prominent example of a piece of equipment in *Being and Time*, previous to the indicator, is the common and unastonishing example of a hammer. In fact, in dealing with the indicator Heidegger recalls this example, and I shall take it into account later.

Of course philosophers, at least since Socrates, have relied on examples. But the comparison in Volume 2 of Husserl with Sartre has alerted us to methodologically significant differences in how different phenomenologists employ examples. In the case of Husserl's eidetic reduction, the essence that the examples all exemplify emerges with the elimination, through a free variation of the examples, of any particularities which attach to them as matters of fact. Particular facts, we have already seen, are excludable as irrelevant by his one-sided distinction between essence and fact. Since the particularities are to suffer elimination, Husserl keeps his examples simple. Consider again the examples he ticks off in arriving at the essence of intentionality as consciousness of something: "In perception, something is perceived; in imagination, something imagined; in affirmation, something is affirmed; in love, something is loved."

In Husserl examples should be "arbitrary" (*beliebig*) so that the essence emerging will not be contaminated by their contingent characteristics but grasped as necessary.[3] In contrast, the particularities of Sartre's crucial examples are not entirely deprived of their significance. Husserl's one-sided distinction is weakened with which eidetic reduction opposes essences to particular facts. Thus in Volume 2, *Method and Imagination,* we saw Sartre rely on the particular traits which differentiate a succeeding example from a preceding example in order to advance his analysis.[4]

The Exemplar

Heidegger's example of the indicator advances his own analysis in a fashion which we can also contrast with Husserl's procedure. The example is not "arbitrary," but deliberately chosen: "As an example [*Exemplar*] of a sign, we have chosen one which will function as exemplary [*exemplarisch*] in a later analysis." Heidegger's "example" is not Husserl's rather humdrum *Beispiel*, but the more portentous *Exemplar*, as is emphasized by *exemplarisch*. Heidegger does use the term *Beispiel* later, when he mentions a particular occasion of the indicator's employment "at a cross-roads, for example."[5] He is thus acknowledging that it could be employed by the driver for a different purpose on other particular occasions—to indicate he is pulling off the road to park, for example.

What is of explicit concern to Heidegger are the implications of his *Exemplar* itself. When he identifies the indicator as "a piece of equipment for indicating" [*Zeig-Zeug*], he explains that it "gets used in a *very special* [*Vorzüglich*] fashion." Thus "the ground and the sense of its privileged status [*Vorzug*] must be explained."

Before going on to Heidegger's explanation of this status, I would observe that Husserl does not enter a marginal comment on the present passage, no doubt because he has already commented on the methodological issue in the one previous passage in which Heidegger had insisted on the exemplary and privileged character of an example. This is the crucial passage in which Heidegger raises the questions which he will answer by committing himself to an existential analytic of the Dasein:

> From which being is the disclosure of the meaning of being to start out? Is the starting point arbitrary, or does some particular being [*bestimmtes Seindes*] have priority [*Vorrang*]? Which being shall we take as exemplary, and in what sense does it have priority?[6]

Heidegger's choice of the Dasein as this exemplary being has preoccupied Derrida and other interpreters of Heidegger. But it earlier caught Husserl's attention.

What Husserl may already have suspected is illustrated by his later marginal comment (page 13), which I quoted in Chapter 8. We saw there that he regards Heidegger as perversely lapsing from the eidetic and transcendental levels to the empirical level of anthropology. Indeed by page 11 he had concluded that Heidegger's Dasein is to be equated with man. Husserl's comment on Heidegger's choice of the Dasein, which I have cited from page 7, explicitly accuses him of failing to respect the exigencies of an eidetic reduction. This is Husserl's first fairly direct methodological protest against Heidegger's procedure. Quite possibly Husserl was struck by "arbitrary," since in his eidetic reduction the arbitrariness of an example is a criterion for recognizing the limitation of any example, as opposed to the "necessity" of the essential structure which the example exemplifies, which cannot be eliminated by the variation. His entry opposite Heidegger's two sentences reads, "In a general question bearing on essence, can the priority of an example be given? Is it not rather excluded?" No example can in Husserl triumph over its arbitrariness and gain priority; the generality of the essence it exemplifies would then be contaminated by the particularity of the example.

Heidegger's second exemplary example enables us to recognize further respects in which his method differs from Husserl's. Again it is the Dasein which is in question as Heidegger explains the privileged status of the indicator as an example of the sign:

> The conduct (being) which corresponds to the sign that is encountered is either for the vehicle to "give way" or to "stay where it is" as over against the vehicle ahead with the arrow. Giving way as taking a direction belongs essentially to the being-in-the-world of the Dasein. The Dasein is always in some fashion or other directed and on its way: staying where it is, is only a limiting case of this directional "on its way."[7]

The parenthetical "(being)" draws our attention to the ontological character of Heidegger's analysis of this mode of "conduct." Our attention is further drawn by the "essentially" to how this mode of "conduct" is the "taking [of] a direction" and even to how "staying where it is" is "only a limiting case of this directional 'on its way.'"

Sequence

To appreciate how direction is so privileged in Heidegger's analysis, his conduct of this analysis should itself be taken into account. Reconsider Becker's irritation at "the pedantic scholasticism of the reiterated outlines and advance announcements of paragraph divisions replete in *Being and Time.*" Heidegger's indicating where he is on his "way" and the "direction" he is taking cannot be blamed on scholasticism. Nor is it just a quirk of his. It betrays a commitment, if not to the Dasein as man and to anthropology (as Husserl supposed), then to the Dasein as "always directed and on its way." But direction is not just an essential characteristic of the subject Heidegger is treating; it is also a met-hodological problem for him. Thus, having raised the question of being in the first section of *Being and Time,* Heidegger recognizes that "the question itself is obscure and without direction [*richtunglos*]." If the question were merely "obscure," method could be "clarification" (*Klärung*), as it is for Husserl.

The contrast with Husserl can be taken further if we observe, as we did when we were first exposed to Becker's irritation, that the direction in which Heidegger proceeds on his way involves following a sequence. Here what I have so far neglected is that Husserl's analysis of signs came at the start of his first investigation, whereas Heidegger arrives at his analysis only in section 17. Earlier I did emphasize (as a difficulty with their comparison) that different philosophers are not likely to start from the same point in their respective philosophies or to proceed from this point in the same direction. We then saw that the "first step" Heidegger takes is a retrieval. Let us reconsider what he retrieves with the citation from Plato: "For it is obvious that you have known this all along (what you would indicate [*sēmainein*] when you say 'being') . . ."

There is a term here which I did not scrutinize when I first considered the citation, since Heidegger himself did not exploit its possible pertinence. The term *sēmainein* means "to give a signal or sign [*sēma*]," as well as more broadly "to signify," "show," or "indicate." The indicator, as the example of a sign which we have watched Heidegger deploy in section 17, is a signal. But Heidegger did not deal at the start with the question of indication, as Husserl did at the start of the *Logical Investigations*. Instead Heidegger avoided having the term *sēmainein* take on specific significance when he translated it with the vague term *meinen*, which means "to mean" in the loose sense which might be rendered in English by "to have in mind." So vague a translation contrasts with the weighty significance *ēporēkamen* acquired from his translation, *sind wir in Verlegenheit gekommen.*

My speculation is that if Heidegger did not bother initially to make anything of *sēmainein*, if he is not undertaking an analysis of signs until section 17, if he is not facing up to the question, "What is a sign in general?" to which Derrida would award priority, it is because Heidegger is committed to a specific "sequence of steps."

Let me offer a further clue to his sequence. When in the introductory section, "The Phenomenological Method of Investigation," he constructs his "preliminary concept of phenomenology," it is with another retrieval: "The Greek expression *phainomenon*, to which the term 'phenomenon' goes back [*zurückgeht*], is derived from the verb *phainesthai*, which means 'to show itself' [*sich zeigen*]. Thus *phainomenon* means that which shows itself, the self-showing."[8]

The delay until section 17 of Heidegger's arrival at the sign is itself, broadly speaking, an implicit dislocation of Husserl's analysis of signs. As such it contributes to the "critical" procedure which Heidegger identifies as a "deconstruction." Heidegger is in effect cutting back behind Husserl's phenomenological starting point by finding ontologically prior to it the phenomenon which "shows itself" as over against the later phenomenon he takes up in section 17, with the definition (in the paragraph to which the footnote referring to Husserl is attached), "The intrinsic character of *Zeichen* ["signs"] . . . is *Zeigen* ["showing" or "indicating"].[9] Indeed, after placing his emphasis on "what shows itself from itself," Heidegger asserts the principle in terms of which his sequence is an outmaneuvering of Husserl. It is the principle he takes over from Husserl of proceeding directly "to the things themselves."

We must acknowledge here another contrast with respect to how Husserl applies this principle. I have already explained how Husserl's method does not follow a "sequence of steps" in Heidegger's fashion. What still needs to be explained is why Husserl does not even encounter in the conduct of his analysis the difficulty of determining its direction in the sense that Heidegger encounters it. If we can regard Heidegger's earlier admission that "the question [of being] itself is obscure and without direction" as a criticism of Husserl's phenomenology, we should also recognize that direction is not the difficulty for Husserl that it is for Heidegger because he can count on arriving, in accordance with his application of the principle of proceeding directly "to the things themselves," at something immediately given to consciousness. At the moment of arrival, direction itself is "immediately given: consciousness as 'in-tentional' is 'direction toward an object' [*Richtung auf ein Objekt*]."[10] The problem for Husserl is not the direction itself but determining the status conferred by it on an "object"—as we shall see in the next chapter.

FOUR · RELATIONAL ANALYSIS

The Context

What makes science science . . . is certainly not . . . any real context to which acts of thought are ordered, but a certain . . . ideal context.—Husserl

An Object

Heidegger's allusion in a footnote to Husserl's "analysis of signs" has solicited a comparison with Heidegger's second list of signs in the third paragraph of his section, "Reference and Signs," and with his handling of the indicator in the fifth and later paragraphs. But we must pay some attention to the second paragraph, to which the footnote is actually attached. From that paragraph I did cite Heidegger's first list of signs [*Zeichen*] as leading up to the definition, "*Zeigen* can be defined as a kind of referring," and I suggested that with this definition Heidegger is fitting his analysis of signs to a sequence in which this analysis follows his previous analysis of reference. But after this definition, he takes a further step:

> To refer, taken in an extremely formal sense, is to *relate*. . . . A relation [*Beziehung*] is a formal determination which may be read off directly by way of "formalization" from any kind of context, whatever its subject-matter or its mode of being.[1]

"Formalization," as a concept "which plays such a large role in, for example, mathematical analysis," Husserl defines in section 13 of *Ideas I,* along with "deformalization," which is "'filling out' an empty logico-mathematical form."

Heidegger could be said to be engaged

in a "deformalization" as opposed to "formalization" when he goes on with the example of the indicator, except that he is not dealing at any step with a "logico-mathematic form." He is not concerned with any "relation" as a merely "formal determination."

The differences here between Heidegger and Husserl become more apparent if we follow out the two other allusions to Husserl which are found in the same footnote: "Cf. E. Husserl, *Ideas I*, section 10 ff., as well as his *Logical Investigations*, vol. 1, chapter 11." We are fobbed off with this "cf." without any explicit explanation as to what is specifically pertinent. Our only guidance is that the two allusions precede the allusion in the footnote to "the analysis of signs and meaning" in the first of the *Investigations*. Let me hazard an interpretation as to the broader issues they bring to bear on the relation between Heidegger's and Husserl's analyses of signs.

In sections 10 ff. Husserl is elaborating his "formal ontology." In section 10 itself the concept of "an object" acquires unlimited scope:

> "Object" is a rubric for many formulations which yet belong together—for example, "thing," "property," "relation," "substantive content. . . . Obviously they are not on a par with each other but rather in every case refer back to a kind of objectivity that has priority as the *primal objectivity (Urgegenständlichkeit)* so to speak. . . . Naturally the thing itself has the priority as over against the property, the relation, and so forth.

"Priority" in a philosophy is never natural, and Husserl's "naturally" betrays an assumption which is implemented by his ontology.

Husserl's general claim is that "anything and everything is an object in the sense proper to formal ontology," which is "the eidetic science of any object whatever." With this claim, Husserl upholds the priority of the concept of an "object" over such a competing concept as a "relation," which he deals with as subordinate to an "object."

Before I consider Heidegger's different account, I would follow out his second reference to Husserl. In Chapter 11, "The Idea of Pure Logic," in the *Prolegomena* to the *Logical Investigations*, Husserl seeks purity with a reductive discrimination of the essence of science. Here again Husserl is denying the relevance of the empirical sciences, specifically of the empirical science that threatens the autonomy of logic. He is not interested in "what in particular makes a science psychological," but in "what makes science science, which is certainly not its psychology, nor any real context to which acts of thought are ordered, but a certain . . . ideal context."[2]

Intentionality

Heidegger's analysis of the example of the indicator is an analysis of a "real context" as opposed to Husserl's "ideal context." This shift in *subject* is at the same time a shift in *method* which undermines Husserl's analysis as an intentional analysis with which "an object" gains priority. Consider that the indicator is in German an "arrow." In choosing this example, Heidegger may have been alert to the metaphor with which Husserl elucidates his concept of intentionality and which he could have justified by appealing to one of the meanings of the Latin *in-tendere,* "to aim at."[3] Thus the in-tentional act, as "consciousness of something," as "direction to an object," singles out this object as its "target." Given this metaphor of Husserl's, it is worth observing that Heidegger treats the "arrow" simply as a sign in general (*Zeichen*), not as the "indicative sign" (*Anzeichen*) it would be for Husserl. Heidegger's deconstructive motive may not just be to undercut Husserl's distinction, whereby an "indicative sign" is only one kind of sign, and indeed the kind Husserl excludes from his analysis as irrelevant to logic. Heidegger may also want to avoid the specific implication, which could be associated with the prefix *an-* of *Anzeichen,* that to "indicate" is to single out, so that what are "indicated" are (as Heidegger protests with respect to Husserl's analysis of intentionality) "isolated, pointlike objects."[4]

If the driver of the following vehicle which is being signaled by the indicator were to become "conscious of something" (as required by the intentional character of Husserl's analysis) by following out the direction indicated by the indicator, it would be some object in the field beside the road. Instead of singling out an object as its target, the indicator, in Heidegger's analysis of its functioning, indicates by articulating certain relevant relations which compose a portion of its real context, which he had earlier identified as our *Umwelt* ("the world about us," "our surroundings," "our environment"). I cite from Heidegger's own analysis of the example of the indicator:

> Even if we look in the direction [here "direction" could be construed in Husserl's sense of "direction toward an object] indicated by the arrow and look at something . . . in the region indicated, then the sign is not authentically encountered. . . . The looking about [*Umsicht*] which goes along with it, following its pointing out [*Weisung*] brings into an explicit "survey" [*Übersicht*] whatever roundaboutness the world about us may then have.[5]

In this *Umwelt* of Heidegger's, *Umsicht* and *Übersicht* supersede Husserl's *Einsicht* (in-tuitive "in-sight").

To do justice to this shift from Husserl's intentional analysis, in which objects are "targeted," to Heidegger's *Umwelt,* my terminology requires adjustment. It would be misleading to speak of a shift in *subject,* comparable to the shift from psychology to logic, which Husserl seeks at the start of the first of his investigations by eliminating "an ambiguity in the term 'sign.'" Heidegger's shift should rather be characterized as a shift in context from an "ideal context" to a "real context," which is a context in the strong sense of a relational context.[6]

In Husserl's analysis, in-tuitive "in-sight" into immediately given meanings (such as the intentionality of consciousness) is feasible. The characteristic of an indicative sign, in contrast, which merits its exclusion from his logic, is its "lack of insight" [*Uneinsichtigkeit*],[7] since it is indicative of something else. (The existence of one object, a canal on Mars, "indicates" the existence of other objects, the existence of intelligent beings on Mars.) But an "indicative relation" of this sort finds its place in Heidegger's relational analysis, where *Einsichtigkeit* is no longer a relevant criterion but is displaced by *Umsicht* and the *Übersicht* which survey relations.

My earlier terminology survives inasmuch as the shift in context involves a shift in *method,* as I have already mentioned. When Heidegger constructs the concepts with which he secures an analysis that is relational, he is also deconstructing, not just concepts of Husserl's (such as the concept of "sign") but at the same time Husserl's procedure of intentional analysis. This is a further illustration of how together with the construction there necessarily belongs a *Destruktion.*

This application of Heidegger's procedure of *Destruktion,* not only to concepts that have been constructed, but also to the procedure for constructing them, seems not to have been observed by previous expositors. Certainly Heidegger's *Destruktion* of Husserl's intentional analysis is not explicit. I cite another instance in which Heidegger would deconstruct a procedure: he alludes to "dialectic" as having been "a genuine philosophical obstruction."[8] Since he is alluding to Plato, it is striking that this is Heidegger's first use of *Verlegenheit,* after he employed the term in translating Plato's "*ēporēkamen*" by "*sind wir in Verlegenheit gekommen.*" I postpone until Volume 4 interpreting this *Destruktion,* since my present concern is only with the deconstruction of Husserl's procedure of intentional analysis as implicit in Heidegger's relational analysis.

The rest of Heidegger's analysis, as to how the indicator indicates, is a further laying out of the relations composing a sector of the *Umwelt.* Like what the indicator indicates, the vehicle itself is not an isolated, pointlike object, but composes, along with other vehicles, "traffic" (*Verkehr*), which has its rules of met-hodos (for proceeding along a way)—traffic regulations (*Verkehrsordnungen*), which determine where and when vehicles are able to "turn" (*kehren*), "at a cross-roads, for example."

In assigning to the philosopher his eidetically distinctive task in Chapter 11, Husserl explains, "The philosopher is not content with the fact that we find our way about in the world, . . . he would clarify the essence of a thing, an event, a cause, an effect, of space, of time, and so forth." But we shall see in the next chapter that it is by an analysis of how we find our way about in the world that Heidegger achieves, even before reaching section 17, an analysis of the world as a real context.

Husserl was in effect turning his back on this real context with his eidetic reduction when he claimed on behalf of his *Logical Investigations,* "It can be easily seen that the sense and epistemological worth of the following analyses does not depend on the fact that there really are languages, and that men really make use of them in their dealings with each other [*Wechselverkehr*]."⁹ Such "trafficking" and its languages are relegated by him to the empirical sciences.

Restriction

The difference I am bringing out is between Husserl's intentional analysis, in which intentional "direction toward an object" is immediately given, and Heidegger's relational analysis, in which direction is not immediately given, and Heidegger therefore faces a problem of the direction in which he is to proceed along his way. This is more specifically a problem of what relations he is to "lay out" at any particular step of his analysis.¹⁰ Consider as an example how he reaches his analysis of signs. This step becomes feasible only as the result of a "restriction" (*Beschränkung*) with which Heidegger begins the fifth paragraph (the paragraph in which he starts this analysis with a list of signs) of section 17: "If the analysis which lies before us is to be restricted to the interpretation of the sign . . ."

What matters here for my purposes is that without this "restriction," it would not have been feasible for me to undertake the comparison with Husserl to which we have been led by Heidegger's footnote. Without this "restriction" in the broader scope of his analysis, he would not have provided me with a starting point for my comparison with the starting point of Husserl's analysis in the first of the *Logical Investigations.* Heidegger could have proceeded directly from his earlier analysis of reference in sections 15 and 16 to its continuation in section 18, where he does reinstate that earlier analysis. The deconstruction of Husserl in section 17 is to this extent an interlude which could be compared with the deconstruction of Descartes that is undertaken after section 18.

More generally speaking, in a relational analysis a philosopher can follow out only certain relations at the temporary expense of others; thus "restriction" pro tem is a necessary trait of his method. When Heidegger in the sixth paragraph takes the indicator as an example, he is accepting

a further restriction of his analysis to a limited sector of the *Umwelt*—
"traffic."

What are the relevant broader relations which Heidegger temporarily
excludes from his analysis in order to consider signs? The most relevant is
singled out in the title of section 17, "Reference and Signs." The restriction which temporarily excludes reference is arrived at with a transition
from the last sentence of the fourth paragraph to the first sentence of the
fifth:

> Eventually we shall have to show that "relations" themselves . . .
> have their ontological origin [*Ursprung*] in a reference [*Verweisung*].
>
>   If the analysis that lies ahead of us is to be restricted to the inter-
> pretation of the sign, separated from (*im Unterschied vom*) the phe-
> nomenon of reference . . ."[11]

This separation, which is accepted temporarily, is removed in section 18,
when the phenomenon of reference is reinstated, as I have indicated and as
Heidegger's "eventually" anticipates. Any philosopher of course often has
to accept certain restrictions on the broader scope of his analysis in order
to get on with the analysis. But we must still recognize a distinction in
terms of the comparison with Husserl: when Husserl, for instance, undertakes "to employ the term 'expression' restrictively" and to "exclude much
that ordinary speech would designate 'expression,'" what is at stake is one
of his "essential distinctions," which must be permanently fixed in order
to delimit one-sidedly the subject of logic. This restriction is not a temporary separation that is to be overcome "eventually," as is Heidegger's
"restriction."

The phenomenon of reference, which Heidegger reintroduces in section 18, he first treated in section 15, as he recalls at the beginning of section 17, before he undertakes the restriction of his analysis to signs: "In
our interpretation of that structure of being which is the ready-to-hand
(equipment), the phenomenon of reference became visible, but we merely
indicated it, and in outline."

Heidegger's recalling what he had previously "indicated," but merely
"in outline," and his later anticipation of what will take place "eventually" are rather mild instances of the procedure which Becker took exception to as obsessive when he was (in Kisiel's paraphrase) "irritated by the
pedantic scholasticism of the reiterated outlines and advance announcements." I repeat Kisiel's defense of Heidegger:

> Heidegger, sensitive to years of critique of the incomprehensible
> opaqueness of his style, wanted to make himself clearly understood.
> He wanted to communicate, and the obsessive architectonic of the
> book was one way of subverting the anticipated misunderstanding

of his intentions. Besides, the hurried deadline under which *Being and Time* was drafted and printed dictated the stability of a fixed advance outline.[12]

Heidegger did, of course, want to communicate. Philosophers usually do, or the breakdowns in communication between them would hold no interest. But I have already offered a supplementary explanation of his obsession—his methodological commitment to a sequential analysis.

Sequence

Although my own attentiveness to sequence is even more explicit than Heidegger's, and may seem even more like pedantic scholasticism, I would note some specific traits of the sequence in section 17. The sequence he is following is not linear, but can entail, since his analysis is relational, a circling back on an earlier step. For example, in the first sentence of section 17 Heidegger speaks of himself as having earlier merely "indicated" the phenomenon of reference; now "indication" will itself be the topic of his analysis with the example of the indicator. Thus he is circling back on his own analysis. At the beginning of the next (the second) paragraph in section 17, he offers an explicit motive for his circling back: "We shall again [as in section 15] take as our starting point [*Ausgang*] the being of the ready-to-hand, but this time with the purpose of grasping the phenomenon of *reference* itself more precisely [*scharfer*]." Any philosopher can move from an outline to an analysis which is more precise, but in a sequential analysis in which the philosopher circles back, an outline has the more specific justification that a certain array of relations must first be circumscribed to do justice to their scope, but precision can only be achieved when, within this scope, a certain "restriction" is accepted—in the present instance, a restriction to the analysis of signs.

Another illustration of the relational and sequential character of Heidegger's analysis is provided by his more deliberate introduction of the indicator as an example of the sign. He emphasizes, "As an example [*Exemplar*] of a sign, we have chosen one which will function as exemplary in a later analysis, though from another point of view."[13] When Husserl introduces an example, it is not with the prospect, which lends additional significance to an example in Heidegger, that he will later reemploy it "from another point of view [*Hinsicht*]." What matters in the conduct of his analysis is the moment of immediate insight [*Einsicht*], gained with an eidetic reduction, into an essential structure—such as intentionality. The structure which is then grasped is to remain "fixed" conceptually, as he goes on to allow other essences to become "fixed" conceptually by utilizing other examples.

Moreover, the character of the example Heidegger has chosen is not extraneous to the conduct of his analysis, in which we can look forward to the later reemployment of this example "from another point of view." This adjustablility of the example to a later step in his analysis, at which other relations will emerge, may well be a higher-level consideration that influenced his choice of the "arrow" as an example, which by virtue of its own adjustability can perform its function as a "directional signal."

Reference

Before moving on to section 18, where the "restriction" is removed and the phenomenon of reference resumes its place in Heidegger's analysis, I would make a further attempt to bring out Heidegger's procedure by drawing another contrast with Husserl's procedure. In his analysis of the indicative sign, Husserl distinguishes the kind of indicative relation it entails and employs for this relation the term "reference" (*Hinweis*). The force the prefix has in Husserl's analysis might be rendered by translating his *Hinweis,* not by the loose terms "reference" or "indication," but by "pointing at." At any rate, only the root, not the prefix, survives in Heidegger's analysis of the indicator, when he describes how the driver of the vehicle behind, in "looking about," is "following" the "pointing out [*Weisung*]" of the indicator. I cannot press this contrast, since indicative reference remains outside the scope of Husserl's analysis, except to the extent that it needs to be considered briefly while he is securing its exclusion. Yet it is evident that Heidegger conceives "reference" differently, as shown by the relational context indicated by the indicator.

The comparison between them is also rendered more complicated by Heidegger's providing his own term for "reference," *Verweisung,* which is not used by Husserl. I have still to take into account the implications that *Verweisung* acquires earlier and later in Heidegger's analysis, but I would speculate that Heidegger deliberately avoids *Hinweis* in order to maintain his shift in *subject.* He might well not want his analysis to incur the implications acquired by *Hinweis* in Husserl from its having a psychological "origin" in "the association of ideas."[14] This psychological origin betrays the irrelevance of the indicative sign in Husserl's analysis of "expression and meaning"—in short, to logic as he conceives the subject. Thus Heidegger's adoption of the term *Verweisung* to convey his own concept of reference may imply a criticism of Husserl for finding a psychological origin for reference, whereas Heidegger would find for relations (and for signs as relational phenomena) "an ontological origin in reference." (I shall consider in Chapters 21 and 22 how Heidegger would, with his resort to an "ontological origin," go behind Husserl's distinction between the logical and the psychological.) If Heidegger had retained here Husserl's term, *Hinweis,* there would have been some risk that pieces of Husserl's well-known analysis might stick to it and clutter up Heidegger's own analysis. Here we have an illustration of a difficulty which the expositor of what is at issue between philosophers may encounter: the successor may dodge a predecessor's term.

Expression and Meaning

Another term which Heidegger is more obviously dodging has to do, not with what Husserl would exclude as psychological from logic, but with what he would include in logic. I have emphasized in my comparison so far that the "essential distinctions," which are played up by the title of the first chapter of the first of Husserl's *Logical Investigations* are an objective for Heidegger's *Destruktion.* Prominent among these is Husserl's distinction of the logical sense of "expression," for the title of the first investigation itself is "Expression and Meaning." Yet "expression" is omitted when Heidegger alludes in his footnote to this first investigation as "an analysis of signs and meaning." (I have so far abbreviated the allusion to Husserl's "analysis of signs" because signs are Heidegger's actual concern in section 17.)

The prominence of "expression" in Husserl's title—and in his first chapter itself—was reinforced in *Ideas I* by Husserl's retrospect which justified the first investigation's having come first: "Problems of expression and meaning" are "the most immediate for philosophers guided by universal logical interests," so that "they are . . . the first to require phenomenological investigation." When Heidegger alludes to Husserl's "analysis of signs and meaning," he may be not just dodging the term "expression"; he may also be clinging to the sequential character of his own analysis, in which only at a much later step (section 34) can he replace Husserl's term "expression" with a term of his own. I consider this replacement in Chapter 23.

At least we can anticipate now what will happen in Heidegger to Husserl's term "meaning," which Husserl pairs in his title with "expression." If section 17 is a deconstructive analysis of Husserl's concept of "signs," section 18 is a deconstructive analysis of Husserl's concept of "meaning." Thus the two concepts are dealt with which Heidegger brings together when he characterizes Husserl's first investigation as an "analysis of signs and meaning." Moreover, the pairing in the title of section 18, "Involvement [*Bewandtnis*] and Meaning," can be elucidated by a comparison with the pairing in the title of section 17, "Reference and Signs." I have anticipated that in section 18 the "restriction" is removed which enabled Heidegger to concentrate on signs, and the concept of "reference" is reintroduced. Without going into the details of section 18, we can also anticipate that Heidegger's construction of the concept of "involvement" (the first concept in the title of section 18) is a further exploration of the relational context he previously explored by constructing the concept of "reference" (the first concept in the title of section 17).

This is how the concept of reference is reintroduced and the concept of involvement is introduced in conjunction with it:

> What then does reference [*Verweisung*] purport? . . . . A being . . . is discovered when it has been referred to something. . . . *With* any such being there is an involvement which it has *in* something. . . . The relation of the "with . . . in" shall be indicated by the term reference.[15]

In this relational context, "meaning" is introduced as a concept with which relations are grasped: "The relational character of these relations of referring, we conceive as *mean-ing* [*be-deuten*]." The intrusion of the hyphen is deconstructive of Husserl's concept of "meaning"; it indicates that Heidegger would disrupt the immediacy with which meaning is given in Husserl's intentional analysis and would suggest that meaning itself is a relational phenomenon, whereas for Husserl the eidetic reduction eliminates relational phenomena insofar as they are mere variations.

That I cannot proceed further than this scattering of definitions becomes clear from the summation in the next two sentences:

> In its familiarity with these relations [in particular those indicated by the term *reference*], Dasein 'means to itself.' . . . These relations are . . . what they are as this mean-ing in which Dasein gives itself beforehand its being-in-the-world as to be understood. The relational totality of this meaning we call *meaningfulness*.[16]

Against Husserl's logic, as an intentional analysis of meaning, Heidegger would array his conception of the *logos* as that which "becomes visible in its relation to something else in its 'relatedness,'" so that "*logos* acquires the meaning of *relation* and *relationship*."[17]

Before we can examine this conclusion, a problem to be faced is "familiarity." It may seem itself merely a familiar, colloquial term. But we saw earlier that Heidegger often preempts familiar, colloquial terms and stretches their meaning with his construction of a concept. "Familiarity" was introduced as a concept back in section 12. That it is a concept of some consequence for the purpose of my contrast with Husserl might be surmised, inasmuch as "familiarity with . . . relations" acquires its relevance in Heidegger because he cannot count on, as Husserl does, the immediate givenness of an in-tentional object.

"Familiarity" will have to wait until Chapter 19. I was encouraged to skip to sections 17 and 18 by the specificity of Heidegger's allusion to Husserl's "analysis of signs and meaning." I seized on this allusion, since it referred to the starting point of Husserl's analysis, and I had already considered how Heidegger himself started out. But if the sequential character of Heidegger's method is to be respected, sections 17 and 18 must be related to the preceding steps in the sequence of Heidegger's analysis.

Der Weg der Abhebung

*Being-in-the-world . . . is not pieced together;
rather, it is originally and constantly a whole.*
—Heidegger

Being-in-the-World

In the sequence of steps Heidegger is following, section 18 is a climax and conclusion, as
indicated by its subtitle—"Involvement and
Meaning: The Worldliness of the World."
This subtitle reproduces the title of Chapter 3
as a whole, "The Worldliness of the World."
This is the only two-tiered title in *Being and
Time*. There are eighty-three section titles,
and the colon here, separating the general title from the two specific concepts constructed
in the section, is the only colon employed in a
title.

When in sections 19–21 Heidegger interrupts his construction of his own concepts in
order to take on Descartes, these sections are
separated from the preceding sections and
given the overall title, "The Bringing into
Relief [*Abhebung*] of the Analysis of Worldliness [which he has just completed] by Opposing It to Descartes's Interpretation of the
World."

Heidegger first employed the term *Abhebung* in *Being and Time* at the start of
"Division One"—"Preparatory Fundamental Analysis of Dasein." This division begins
with a "preamble." I resort to this designation because there is no direct transition here
to the ensuing analysis, any more than there
was in the paragraphs which I designated a
"preamble" at the start of *Being and Time*.

In this second preamble Heidegger explains that "being-in-the-world" is a "funda-

mental structure of Dasein" and that "this structure . . . affords us different ways of looking at the moments which are constitutive for it"; thus "if
the whole of this structure is kept constantly in view, . . . it will be feasible
to bring into relief [*abzuheben*] these moments as phenomena."[1] Heidegger's terminology deserves further examination, for there are certain debts
here to Husserl that initially warrant interpreting Heidegger's procedure,
in the steps he takes from here through sections 17 and 18, by reference to
his relation to Husserl. These debts are to terminology Husserl employed
in the third of the *Logical Investigations,* "On the Theory of Wholes and
Parts."

In Husserl's intentional analysis, having accorded priority to objects,
he has to deal with their relations—as he admits at the beginning of the
third investigation: "Objects can be related to one another as wholes to
parts; they can also be related to one another as coordinated parts of a
whole." But before dealing with these relations, he insists (as he insists
again in *Ideas I*) on the priority of the object, "These kinds of relations
have an *a priori* foundation in the idea of an object."[2]

We are prepared to recognize the particular relevance that this third
investigation will have for Heidegger, given the relational character of his
own analysis. But there is another crucial methodological difference I have
emphasized between the two phenomenologists: Heidegger follows a "sequence of steps," whereas Husserl departs from sequence and zigzags.
Husserl admits in his second introduction that "systematic clarification
. . . would seem to require a following out step-by-step of the ordering of
things [*Sachen*] . . . to be clarified." But he then explains that "our investigation can only proceed securely if it repeatedly breaks with systematic sequence" and proceeds "in a zigzag fashion."[3]

Wholes and Parts

It is no accident that Husserl repeats this explanation in his introduction
to the third investigation, in which he proposes to deal with "wholes and
parts." There he disavows the prospect of subordinating "parts" to
"wholes" by recognizing a difficulty which requires him to accord priority
to method:

> Our analytic investigation cannot be allowed to wait upon the sys-
> tematic treatment of things [*die Systematik der Sachen*]. . . . Diffi-
> cult concepts, which we employ in research that would clarify
> knowledge and be made to work rather in the manner of a lever, can-
> not be left unexamined until they emerge themselves in the system-
> atic context of the realm of logic. For we are not here engaged in a

systematic exposition of logic, but in an epistemological clarification, as well as preparation for any future exposition of logic.[4]

This explanation of Husserl's is also pertinent to his later depressed appraisals of himself as "a miserable beginner." We have seen that even his
supportive former assistant, Edith Stein, doubted his ability to bring together "in a grand unity, all [his] isolated investigations."

The idiom of "leverage" is not an idiom Heidegger would adopt, since
it implies a degree of separation of method from subject that he could not
tolerate.[5] The difference between them at this juncture is not merely temperamental. When Heidegger begins his "Division One," he too, in effect,
"guides the look of the phenomenologist starting out," as Husserl explains he does in the first investigation. But instead of according priority to
the object, as Husserl does, and postponing what Husserl calls "the systematic context," Heidegger accords priority to the context. I now fill in
the details of the second preamble from which I previously quoted selec-
tively:

> A fundamental structure of Dasein is [to be] laid open—being-in-
> the-world. This structure is a priori. It is not pieced together [*zusam-
> mengestükte*]; rather, it is originally and constantly [*ständig*] a whole
> [*ganze*]. But it affords us different ways of looking at [*Hinblicke*] the
> moments which are constitutive for it. If the whole of this structure
> is kept constantly in view [*Im-Blick-behalten*] as prior [*vorgängig*],
> it will be feasible to bring into relief [*abzuheben*] these moments as
> phenomena. And thus objects for analysis emerge: the world in its
> worldliness (Chapter 3), being-in-the-world . . .[6]

Heidegger is proceeding in roughly the opposite direction to Husserl. Having proposed to start out with the "whole" as "a priori," Heidegger then
faces the methodological problem of singling out within this whole "objects for analysis"—a problem Husserl does not face, since intentional
consciousness *of* something is given from the start of his analysis as the
singling out of objects.

The comparison between Heidegger and Husserl can be pulled together because the details of this passage from the second preamble betray
unmistakable terminological debts to Husserl's analysis of "wholes" and
"parts." But let me note first some terms that Heidegger discards. In dealing with "parts," Husserl distinguishes between an "independent part" or
"piece" (for example, the leg of a table) and a "part" which is "a non-independent part" or "moment" (for example, the color of the table, which
I cannot be conscious of apart from the surface of the table). A synonym
which he introduces for a "non-independent part" is its being in "need of
supplementation by a whole" (*Ergänzbedürftigkeit*).[7] In the last chapter I

anticipated Heidegger's discarding Husserl's term "expression." Now Heidegger drops other terms of Husserl's. Since Heidegger accords priority to the structure as a whole, he does not encounter any "need of supplementation," and he does not retain Husserl's concept of *Ergänzbedürftigkeit*. Since the whole itself as "a priori" can no longer be conceived as "stuck together out of pieces" (*zusammengestükte*), there is also no application to be found for Husserl's concept "piece" (*Stück*)—that is, "part" (*Teil*) in the sense of "independent part."

There would be no point to my comparison if there were not two concepts from the third investigation which Heidegger does retain. One is *Momente*, which comes to apply in Heidegger to the relations within the whole. Thus, though Heidegger speaks of "the objects" which emerge "for analysis," these are not "objects" in Husserl's sense; rather (as illustrated by the first one that Heidegger lists, "the world in its worldliness"), they are nexuses of relations. (Thus *Momente* cannot be translated as "items" [Macquarrie and Robinson]; "dimensions" would be more suitable, but I retain the cognate.) The second concept Heidegger retains also betrays his holism, but it is more distinctively procedural. In Husserl's third investigation, since he allows for "parts" which are not separable and independent, "to bring into relief" has a special application to such "parts." But in Heidegger's relational analysis, "bringing into relief" becomes a general procedure which can be characterized (in a passage I shall examine later) as *der Weg der Abhebung*.

Abhebung does not qualify in Husserl as a "way" to be followed generally. Yet we shall see that Heidegger derives the general methodological character of his analysis from the specific character of an analysis in Husserl for which Husserl does not claim any general methodological character. In Heidegger *Abhebung* is a "way" which has to be followed generally because "separable" and "independent" parts are not encountered, as they are in Husserl's analysis; instead relations are encountered in Heidegger as "constitutive moments." Moreover, given this relational character of Heidegger's analysis, the *Hebung* of each of these "moments" (or "dimensions") encountered, is ultimately a *Mithebung;* it "brings into relief along with it" other moments, unless some "restriction" is imposed, as happens in section 17. Here we might note that what Heidegger could not obtain from Husserl—what is an innovation of his own—is the employment of hyphens to render this *mit*—as in the instance of his fundamental concept, "being-in-the-world."

Relations

As I have long since acknowledged, the problem for the expositor who would ascertain Heidegger's method is that he usually refuses to present it separately from its application "to the subject itself." I would therefore not go so far as to endorse the Macquarrie and Robinson translation of *der Weg* in *der Weg der Abhebung* by "method." I would rather draw attention to the two occasions in *Being and Time* when the term *Abhebung* is elevated into prominence in a section title. After Heidegger has brought his analysis of "worldliness" to a climax in section 18, he pauses in the sequence of his analysis in order to provide what is indicated in the overall title for the next three sections: "The Bringing into Relief of the Analysis of Worldliness by Opposing It to Descartes's Interpretation of the World" (*"Die Abhebung der Analyse der Weltlichkeit gegen die Interpretation der Welt bei Descartes"*).

The other occasion is the penultimate section of *Being and Time,* which is entitled, "The Bringing into Relief of the Existential-Ontological Interrelation [*Zusammenhang*] between Temporality, Dasein, and World-Time, by Opposing It to Hegel's Conception of the Relation between Time and Spirit."[8] Heidegger's relations to Descartes and Hegel are not my present concern. But what interests me is that at steps in his analysis when he is dealing with the relation between it and the analysis of another philosopher, his following *der Weg der Abhebung* becomes more prominent, for he does not proceed directly "to the subject itself," but instead takes into account the treatment of the subject by another philosopher. At these junctures his method becomes more separable from its application, since he is dealing with a relation which can be brought into sharper relief (in terms of the opposition between his philosophy and the other philosophy) than can the relations that in his own philosophy are discerned as composing being-in-the-world.

It has become evident that in order to interpret Heidegger's relation to Husserl, I am by and large grafting my own procedure onto Heidegger's procedure for following out relations—*der Weg der Abhebung*. At this juncture I might well interrupt this interpretation in order to consider alternatively how Husserl interprets his relation to Heidegger by grafting in effect his interpretation on his *Methode der Klärung*. Recall Souche-Dagues's verdict on Husserl: "A crude misinterpretation, lacking in any generosity . . . dominates [his] entire reading of *Being and Time*." However, what is dominating here, I would suggest, is not simply some kind of personal arrogance on Husserl's part. It is his *Methode der Klärung,* which we have seen is a commitment to "essential distinctions" (to recall the title of the first chapter of the first of the *Logical Investigations*) which are reached by eliminating dangerous ambiguities and grasping essential meanings as identical. Here I would also recall Granel's appraisal: "*Being and Time* . . . is swamped in a kind of *flou* with respect to what has to do with its relation to Husserl's phenomenology." In translating this appraisal, I have come to prefer "out of focus" to the metaphor of "blur," for "blur" suggests that clarification is in order. If this were construed as any kind of approximation to Husserl's *Methode der Klärung,* we would have to recognize that an eidetic analysis is essential to it. I cite from the section *"Der Methode der Klärung"* in *Ideas I:*

> Where ... the *graspings of the essence* ... have a low degree of clarity ... correlatively what is *grasped* is, with respect to its sense, "unclear"; it has its hazinesses [*Verschwommenheiten*], its ... separations which are not decisive [*Ungeschiedenheiten*]. ... One cannot ascertain what [its] components "really are," which are perhaps already shown by vague contrast [*Abhebung*] or are suggested in a wavering fashion.
>
> What floats before us in fluid unclarity ... must be *made perfectly clear* before it can be employed for a correspondingly valuable eidetic intuition.[9]

It is hardly necessary to explain what happens when a "vague contrast" is discredited and this procedure of clarification is in effect applied by Husserl to interpret his relation to Heidegger.

In other words, Husserl's "lack of generosity" betrays his commitment to an eidetic procedure for grasping an essence, which yields only the options illustrated by the marginal comments we examined earlier—of interpreting Heidegger's philosophy as, on the one hand, essentially identical with his own or, on the other hand, as a perversely ambiguous distortion of his own, whereby Heidegger "transposes or transfers the clarification which is ... phenomenology," so that it lapses to the level of an empirical science.

In the present chapter I have lingered with Heidegger's assertion that being-in-the-world is a relational structure, and with *der Weg der Abhebung* as his procedure for dealing with relations. What we have not yet examined is his assertion, "This structure is a priori." Since it is not empirical, the comparison between Heidegger's and Husserl's procedure cannot be pursued further without taking into account differences in how each maintains a distinction of level.

SEVENTEEN

Umgang

*Beings are in every case the preliminary and
accompanying theme.*—Heidegger

The Shift in Level

In *Ideas I* the first shift in *level* is carried out
by the eidetic reduction. It is a shift from the
empirical level to the level of essences. The
distinction itself between the two levels is indicated in the title of the first chapter in *Ideas
I*: "Fact and Essence." We have already seen
that this distinction of level, like Husserl's
other "essential distinctions," is a sharply one-
sided distinction: the eidetic reduction is the
elimination of the contingent particularities
of examples at the factual level, so that the
essence will emerge at the ideal level. To illustrate this one-sidedness, I quote Husserl's italicized claim from the first chapter: "*Essences
imply not the slightest positing of any individual factual existence.*"[1]

Heidegger's concern to dispose of this
claim seems evident from a footnote in section 15. The footnote may appear innocuous.
Being and Time includes about three hundred
footnotes, but this is the only one which is
self-referential: "The author may remark that
this analysis of the *Umwelt* and in general the
'hermeneutic of facticity' of Dasein have been
presented repeatedly in lectures since the win-
ter semester of 1919–1920." Why this footnote? Is he soliciting a certain confidence in
his analysis of the *Umwelt* on the ground that
he has worked on it so long? But why does he
still flaunt "hermeneutic of facticity" when
he no longer employs this terminology in the
text itself of *Being and Time?*

A possible explanation is that the terminology is suited to conveying his commitment to cutting across and dismantling Husserl's one-sided separation of essence from fact. The terminology implies that the factual is itself essentially charged with meanings requiring interpretation. If the footnote thus conveys a sense of what is at issue here between Heidegger and Husserl, it may be more than a coincidence that it comes just before the footnote to section 17 in which he refers to Husserl's "analysis of signs and meaning."

In any case the footnote to section 15 suggests the appropriateness of a brief backward glance at his 1919–20 lectures. There Heidegger had explicitly objected to the one-sidedness of Husserl's eidetic analysis: "The distinctive character of phenomenological knowledge is demarcated in phenomenology up until now as 'essence-knowledge' or 'eidetic knowledge.' But the meaning [*Sinn*] of eidetic is *too sharply separated*" (my italics).[2] In the *Prolegomena* (1925) Heidegger is still criticizing the eidetic reduction in that "the *what-content* [the essence exemplified by the examples] is brought out in relief [*herausgehoben*] without any questioning with respect to the being of the acts [the intentional "acts" of consciousness in Husserl] in the sense of existence."[3]

The shift in *level* with which essence is to be separated from fact (existence) in Husserl by an eidetic reduction is a "free variation." Here a comparison can be made with how "the geometer operates in relation to figures and models."[4] The phenomenologist operates in a similar fashion:

I can in imagination imagine the brown bench as painted green; there it remains an individual existent in this lecture hall, only imagined as changed. But I can as it were transform each and every fact into a fiction in free arbitrariness. I can imagine as a pure fiction a bench with a mermaid sitting on it, *in no place and no time, free from all weight of actuality,* free from any restriction to the factual world.[5]

Achieved here is the separation of essence from fact which Heidegger would undercut with his "hermeneutic of facticity."

Observe too the implication for my original theme of the difference between Heidegger's and Husserl's conception of a "difficulty." I pointed out that when Heidegger uses the same word as Husserl for a "difficulty," *Schwierigkeit,* he plays up the ambiguity whereby "it is in the essence of philosophy never to make things *leichter* [easier/lighter], only to make them *schwerer* [more difficult/heavier]," for the "function" of philosophy is to "give beings back their *Gewicht* [importance, weight] (being)."[6] Heidegger's "making things heavier," his "giving beings back their weight," is not mere byplay (as it may have seemed in Chapter 12) with an ambiguity.

Heidegger's weightiness remains prominent later when he is apparently giving Husserl no further thought and is pitting "the heaviest burden" (*Schwergewicht*) in his exposition of Nietzsche against "the experience that all things have lost their weight":

> Nietzsche's "thought of thoughts" is at the same time "the most burdensome thought" . . . in several respects. It is most burdensome, for instance, with respect to that which is to be thought in it, that is, being as a whole. . . . That has the heaviest weight and so is the most burdensome in the sense of the weightiest. Thus it is the most difficult.[7]

Examples

I return to Heidegger and Husserl by reconsidering the status of examples in each analysis. I have already emphasized that in arriving at concepts, Heidegger and Husserl alike rely on examples, and I shall continue to try to determine more definitely the differences   between Heidegger's construction and Husserl's eidetic reduction by considering differences in the examples each relies on. The directional signal in section 17 has illustrated how the particularities of examples matter in Heidegger. To this extent I am proceeding as I did in Volume 2. There I compared Sartre's examples and Husserl's, and found that in Sartre, too, the particularities of an example retain a relevance which examples in Husserl are supposed to lose when the level of essence is reached.

My argument for the attention I have paid to an example such as the directional signal can be put to the test again in section 15, since more examples are analyzed in detail there than in any other section of *Being and Time*. I shall examine those examples in section 15 with which Heidegger constructs the three concepts he needs to recall in the first sentence of section 17: "With our interpretation of being which is the *ready-to-hand* (*equipment*), the phenomenon of *reference* became visible" (my italics). In this examination I am trying to bring out the methodological character of his analysis as a sequence by filling in steps which I previously skipped in order to begin with what seemed the most obvious comparison between Heidegger and Husserl—a comparison of section 17 and the analysis of signs with which Husserl began.

The analysis of the *Umwelt* in section 15 is perhaps the most frequently expounded stretch of *Being and Time*—at least in pragmatic America. I am not threatening just another exposition, for I am trying to expose methodological implications which do not usually receive much attention and which have a bearing on what is at issue in Heidegger's relation to Husserl. The one work I am aware of which is dedicated entirely to the exposition of this stretch does not even mention Husserl,[8] so that this stretch seems an appropriate occasion for gauging my general proposal that we can gain a more definite understanding of the distinctive character of Heidegger's analysis when differences between Heidegger and Husserl are taken into account.

The broadest issue between Heidegger and Husserl that is pertinent to section 15 I have already anticipated. It was raised by Husserl's claim, "What makes science science . . . is certainly not . . . any real context to which acts of thought are ordered, but a certain . . . ideal context." I have also pointed out that when Heidegger undertakes to analyze the *Umwelt*, he is dealing with a real context in which real actions (such as driving, in section 17) are performed.

Ambiguity

These real actions are subsumed by Heidegger under the concept of *Umgang*. There is no comparable concept in Husserl. One difference between them that this concept illustrates, I have already recognized, is how Heidegger deploys an ambiguous range of meanings with his concepts.

Ambiguity often demands attention when we face the problem of translating Heidegger. Macquarrie and Robinson translate *Umgang* as "dealings" and mention as an alternative translation "trafficking," which might have the advantage of suggesting the relation between this earlier step in the analysis and the step taken in section 17, in which the context is "traffic" (*Umkehr*). But "trafficking" would not allow for the differences between the context of the analysis in section 15 and the more restricted context sought in section 17. Rorty volunteers "coping"; "intercourse" tempts Kisiel.[9] I shall respect ambiguity by usually settling for the more colloquial and etymological "going about."

A range of ambiguity in Heidegger of considerable philosophical significance is the close affinity, which is associated with the inseparability of his method from the subject to which it applies. The affinity might even be characterized as a certain kind of overlap. Thus, when Heidegger analyzes the directional signal as an example, he observes with respect to his subject (the Dasein as being-in-the-world) that "taking a direction belongs essentially" to it, but it was also to be observed that with respect to Heidegger's conduct of his analysis, he too, like the driver conducting a vehicle, is "going along a way" and faces a problem of the direction to take.

This affinity or overlap is implicit in Heidegger's own initial appraisal of the analysis of *Umgang* he is about to undertake in section 15: he extends the idiom of "going" to his own proceeding: "Our investigation will take its course [*Gang*] . . . toward the idea of worldliness in general. We shall seek the worldliness (*Umweltlichkeit*) of the *Umwelt* in going through [*Durchgang*] an ontological interpretation of those beings within the *Umwelt* that we encounter as nearest to us."[10] It is not, then, just to bring out Heidegger's manipulation of prefixes and prepositions (as themselves indicating direction) that I favor for *Umgang* the translation "going about." Retaining the root brings out the overlap between method and the subject to which it is applied—or rather from which it cannot be separated.

We have just been confronted with a criterion for how Heidegger "goes about" his analysis. Proximity ("nearest") is a criterion which I shall have to compare more carefully later with Husserl's criterion of "immediate givenness." But it is already evident, not only that proximity is a criterion for determining the direction in which Heidegger is to proceed, but also that he is respecting in some sense this criterion when he constructs a concept of *Umgang*. The word itself is used colloquially, and it is also used in the compound *Umgangs-sprache* (colloquial usage). A difference between Husserl and Heidegger is that the ambiguities Husserl would eliminate often arise, as he himself admits, in familiar colloquial usage. Again I cite the instances when Husserl eliminates facial and linguistic expressions in arriving at the concept of "expression."

Consider too Heidegger's most famous example in section 15: "The mode of being of [the hammer as] equipment . . . we call readiness-to-hand [*Zuhandenheit*]"[11] (one of the three concepts he carries over in section 17). Rather than a sharp distinction, as in Husserl, there is a certain affinity between the example of the hammer and the concept to be exemplified. The hammer's *Handlichkeit* (manipulability) is retained not only in constructing the concept "readiness-to-hand," but also in reinvigorating the abstract concept of "concept" (*Begriff*) itself: "The more we take hold of [*je zugreifender*] the hammer, the more primordial our relation to it becomes."[12]

This affinity between the example and the concept exemplified is also found in the case of the directional signal, whose mode of being is also "readiness-to-hand." The directional signal is itself manipulable. Indeed, in the *Prolegomena*, Heidegger points out that the directional signal takes the place of the hand, which used to be "stretched . . . out of the vehicle to point in one direction or another."[13]

Granted the colloquial ambiguities of *Umgang*, the term brings with it what might almost be characterized as a philosophical commitment. It is only used in the singular and thus, when taken over for philosophical purposes, can encourage the expectation that our miscellaneous array of "dealings," as we "go about" ("trafficking," "coping," and engaging in "intercourse"), can be embraced in the conceptual unity of a mode of being.

Moreover, the distinction in *level*, even if it is no longer so sharply delineated as in Husserl, does itself survive in Heidegger. Husserl had initiated his eidetic reduction with an example of what Heidegger would refer to ontologically as some being. However, "in the disclosure and explication of being" in Heidegger, "beings are in every case the preliminary *and the accompanying theme* [*das Vor- und Mitthematische*]" (my italics).[14] The examples Husserl begins with are merely preliminary, but one characteristic—"manipulability"—of the two examples I have just cited, the directional signal and the hammer, is a theme which accompanies the construction of the concept *Zuhandenheit*.

Equipment

The hammer is not Heidegger's first example in section 15. "Equipment" (the second of the three concepts he will carry over in his analysis of signs in section 17) is the first concept he constructs:

> We shall call those beings which we encounter in concern *equipment*. In our *Umgang* we come across equipment for writing, for sewing, working, transportation, measurement.[15]

These examples are not "arbitrary" (*beliebig*) as examples are required to be in Husserl. The first example ("equipment for writing") I postpone, since it turns up again in the next list of examples, which Heidegger adduces to construct the concept of "reference." The second example, "sewing," obtains a certain relevance as *Handwerk,* as will emerge after he has constructed the concept of "reference" and offers as an example "the reference to whomever is to wear and use" the clothing, when it is made to measure. "Transportation" prepares us for the example of the directional signal. With the final example, "measurement" (*Messzeug*), we may have a further instance of affinity between subject and method, for he is looking for the "fitting [*angemessenen*] structural concepts." A clock will turn up later as an "instrument for measuring time" (*Zeitmessung*)—an instrument which will be of some interest in an analysis whose "horizon" is time.[16]

I return from these examples of "equipment" to the concept. Heidegger claims, "Strictly speaking, there 'is' not *an* equipment. To the being of any equipment, there always belongs a totality of equipment in which it can be this equipment that it is."[17] This holistic qualification I am trying to render in English with the circumlocution "(piece of) equipment."

With his list Heidegger has deployed totalities of equipment. "Equipment for transportation" in that list is a totality which will be seen in section 17 to include vehicles, roads, and traffic regulations. The relations composing this totality are then brought into relief as implicated in his example of the directional signal as a (piece of) equipment.

In dealing with the relational character of any of these totalities, Heidegger makes a transition: "Equipment is essentially 'something in-order-to' [etwas-um-zu] in which it can be this equipment that it is.[18] Other relations can now be brought into relief. The zu probably should remind us that the principle of proceeding directly "to the things themselves," inherited from Husserl, still presides over the Gang of Heidegger's analysis—over the direction in which he is "going" and over his effort to obtain access [Zugang]. But the zu can now be hitched to the prefix um. We are well acquainted with um, since the entire analysis is of Umgang in the Umwelt. But the um of Umwelt has seemed so far to merely characterize what is topologically "round about" one; um-zu now characterizes what one is "about" in the practical sense of what one is "up to" as one "goes about."

Reference

Once the teleological character of this relational structure has been recognized, Heidegger can construct the concept of "reference": "In the structure 'in-order-to' [um-zu] there lies a reference [Verweisung] of something to something."[19]

"Reference" is the third concept which is carried over at the start of the analysis of signs in section 17. Its construction is indispensable to the articulation of the relational context, which he has been committed to analyzing ever since he introduced the fundamental concept of "being-in-the-world" in his methodological preamble.

This is the list of examples with which Heidegger reaches his concept of "reference":

> Provisionally it is sufficient to take a look phenomenally at a multiplicity of references. A (piece of) equipment in its equipmentality is always in terms of [aus] its belonging together with other (pieces of) equipment: equipment for writing, pen, ink, paper, blotting pad, table, lamp, furniture, windows, doors, room.[20]

Heidegger's procedure here is similar to his procedure in constructing the concept of "sign" in section 17. At both steps he offers a list of examples which is longer than the lists Husserl provides at comparable junctures. We have already seen that the "multiplicity" in the case of the list of signs can be taken as implying that Husserl is oversimplifying when he is satisfied with distinguishing only two kinds of sign. The criticism of Husserl that is implicit in the present list will emerge after I have compared this list, with which Heidegger constructs his concept of "reference," with the first list, with which he constructed the concept of "equipment."

The present list is linked to his first list by his taking over from it the first example—"equipment for writing." The first example in the first list now becomes itself a totality of (pieces of) equipment. The distinctive implication that is sought with the second list is the "belonging to [*Zugehörigkeit*]" of any (piece of) equipment with other (pieces of) equipment, by virtue of the referential relations composing the totality.

Schreibzeug is ambiguous. I have translated it "equipment for writing," since it needs this breadth of meaning to convey its character as a "totality," but when it is taken over as the first example in the second list, it does not just provide a link with the first list. *Schreibzeug* also shrinks in the scope of its meaning to "inkstand" (the Macquarrie and Robinson translation) so that it becomes as specific as the succeeding "pieces" on the list, "pen, ink, paper, blotting pad," which are all "equipment for writing" in the broad sense *Schreibzeug* had in the first list.

Intentionality

Is this second list just a contribution to the construction of the concept of "reference"? In answering this question I argue that we should not forget another instance where the criterion of *Zugehörigkeit* emerges from Heidegger's relational analysis. His procedure of construction is related to another procedure: "There necessarily belongs together with" the construction "a *Destruktion*."[21] So far I have found the justification for Heidegger's selection of examples in terms of his own analysis; now I shall find its justification at the same time in the deconstruction of Husserl's analysis as conveyed by his examples.

The first example in Heidegger's list of (pieces of) equipment can be compared with the example Husserl starts out with in arriving at his concept of intentionality in *Ideas I*—the example of perceiving a sheet of paper. Since Sartre too starts out in *L'imagination* with almost the same example as Husserl, I have commented on it in Volume 2. This is how it is presented by Husserl: "Let us start with examples. Before me [*Vor mir*] in the semidarkness there is this sheet of paper. I am seeing it . . ."[22] Of course no example is perhaps more natural for someone writing to offer. But there was another reason why Sartre would start with this example: he was promoting an intentional analysis, and was very much aware of Husserl's having started with this example in his intentional analysis. It is equally clear why Heidegger, who is promoting a relational analysis, would disregard this first example of Husserl's, for the piece of paper is singled out in Husserl's analysis as an object—that is, as something "before me." This mode of being Heidegger defines in section 16 as *Vorhandenheit*. With his selection of this example, Husserl is committing himself to what Heidegger regards as the traditional conception of a "thing" as an ob-ject *vor mir.*

If I consider it permissible to speak of Heidegger's disregarding Husserl's first example, it is because he in effect refurbishes Husserl's second example, though without mentioning Husserl. This is Husserl's example: "Round about [*Rings um*] the sheet of paper lie books, pencils, an inkstand [*tintenfas*], and so forth, also 'perceived' in a certain fashion." But "while I was turned toward the paper [in his first example] . . . they were not . . . grasped singly [*herausgegriffen*], not posited for themselves." It is the paper which is singled out; they remain in the "experiential background."[23] The second example could attract Heidegger because it begins, not with the "*vor mir*" of Husserl's first example, but with "*rings um,*" so that it could be adapted to Heidegger's analysis of the *Umwelt.* Husserl almost approaches a relational analysis, insofar as the items envisaged, he explains, are "not grasped singly, not posited for themselves" as objects. But he pulls back from a relational analysis by treating them as merely "experiential background" against which the paper is singled out.

Heidegger does alter in both his lists Husserl's *tintenfas* to *Schreibzeug,* presumably so that his own list can begin with something which colloquial usage (*Umgangs-Sprache*) explicitly designates as "equipment" and which could be expanded in the first list to include (consistently with the other totalities listed there) more than an "inkstand" and then in the second list contracted to an "inkstand" as a single piece of equipment.

Direction

That Heidegger is undertaking the *Destruktion* of Husserl's in-tentional, object-targeting analysis is confirmed by his following up the second list with the claim that it does not "add up to a sum" of *realia* (real "things"— Heidegger has already in section 15 alluded to the Latin *res*) which "fill up a room." The most obvious difference with respect to this second list is that the example of the "room" completes it. A "room" is round about us in a different fashion from that in which Husserl observes that "round about the sheet of paper lie books, pencils, an inkstand, and so forth." The "room" in Heidegger is not only a relational totality; it is also described as not "'between four walls' in the sense of geometrical space." It is instead "living quarters" (*Wohnzeug*—literally "equipment for dwelling"), which exhibits its relational character as a "totality of equipment" (*Zeugganzheit*) by its "arrangement" (*Einrichtung*).

In Heidegger's second list of examples, *Einrichtung* would be "furniture" (*Mobel*), which can be itemized and listed, but in the "arrangement" of the furnishings, any single item finds its place as "(a piece of) equipment for dwelling." Now that *Einrichtung* has emerged in this analysis, we can anticipate the concept of "directionality" (*Ausrichtung*), which emerges later in his *Destruktion* of the Cartesian concept of geometrical space.[24] Heidegger is already on his way toward this *Destruktion* when he denies that the "room" we occupy as "living quarters" is "'between four walls' in the sense of geometrical space."

I have anticipated his later concept because I would bring out the general "direction" in which Heidegger is himself going in *Being and Time*. We have seen that *Richtung* ("direction") is itself a met-hodological criterion that Heidegger raised in the first section of *Being and Time* ("the question of being is . . . without direction"). But "direction" is not just a met-hodological criterion. We have learned from the example of the indicator that "taking a direction" is a trait of the subject to which method is being applied, and from which method cannot be separated—the Dasein which is "going about" (*Umgang*) the world round about it (*Umwelt*).

EIGHTEEN

Ausgang

*The starting point for the analysis has to be
secured by the proper method.—Heidegger*

Direction

I have already noted that the incommensura-
bility of Heidegger's and Husserl's philosophies is shown in Husserl's general complaint
that Heidegger "has not understood . . . [the]
direction" in which I "had proceeded." Instead he has "interpreted my phenomenology
backward from the level which it was its entire meaning to overcome."[1] The "direction"
which Husserl has in mind here is not the "direction to an object," with which I have been
preoccupied, but the direction in which he
proceeds by carrying out his phenomenological reduction.

Before turning to consider this reduction,
I must explain that I have emphasized the
problem of direction ever since I dealt with
the example of the directional signal not just
because of the prominence of this problem in
Heidegger; it is a problem that any expositor
is likely to encounter whenever he compares
philosophies. I put the problem earlier in a
homely fashion: if a philosophy is interesting,
the philosopher has not elaborated it parallel
to the other philosophy, so that to cross from
one to the other is never as straightforward as
crossing from a sidewalk on one side of the
street to the sidewalk on the other. I have
meantime improved on mere homeliness by
bringing out the respects in which Heidegger
and Husserl are at cross-purposes, in that
they proceed in different directions in their
philosophies.

Our attention is drawn to these differences in direction by Heidegger's criticism in the *Prolegomena* of "the starting position [*der Ausgangsstellung*] of the reductions."[2] Here as often elsewhere Heidegger is not respecting what an expositor should respect: the separation in Husserl of the two reductions and thus the difference between the two directions in which Husserl himself proceeds—from "fact" to "essence" (guided by the eidetic reduction) and from the level of the natural attitude to the transcendental level (guided by the phenomenological reduction).

In Chapter 17 I considered what happens to the distinction between fact and essence (in Chapter 1 of Part 1 of *Ideas I*) to which Husserl's eidetic reduction is geared. I would now reconsider the factual level as the natural attitude from which Husserl again starts in Part 2. Heidegger's actual references to this "starting position" in *Ideas I* are to Part 2, where Husserl elaborates his phenomenological reduction. But Part 2 does not follow Part 1 sequentially; instead Husserl zigzags back in Part 2 to what had been his starting point in Part 1.

Heidegger was well aware of how sensitive Husserl was on the issue of the phenomenological reduction. (So many of his presumed followers had disavowed this reduction that Husserl had himself, we recall, disavowed "the phenomenological movement.")[3] Perhaps for this reason Heidegger's criticism of this reduction is not explicit in *Being and Time,* and I shall sometimes have to turn to the *Prolegomena.* Even there Heidegger does not bother with most of the details of Husserl's account. I shall fill in some of them in before I turn to Heidegger's criticism.

Section 1 of Part 2 of *Ideas I* is entitled, "The World of the Natural Attitude: I and My *Umwelt,*" and he proceeds as follows:

> We begin our considerations as human beings living naturally, who are representing [*vorstellend*], judging, feeling, willing *"in the natural attitude."* What that means we shall make clear in simple meditations. . . .
>
> By my seeing, touching, hearing, and so forth, in the different modes of sensory perception, physical things [*Dinge*] are . . . *simply there for me,* . . . "on hand" [*"vorhanden"*].

Sequence

Heidegger does not acknowledge the simplicity of these "meditations." They constitute in his own terms an answer to his question of the meaning of being, and he regards what Husserl takes as "simply there" as in the mode of being *Vorhandenheit.* Having started out with human beings who are *vorstellend,* and with things which are *vorhanden,* Husserl only reaches at the end of his inventory "things" which "are there as objects of use." Although Husserl acknowledges their "value-characteristics and practical characteristics," he still identifies them as "objects '*vorhanden*.'"

Husserl may have thought of himself as offering no more than an inventory, but out of his own commitment to sequence, Heidegger would detect a covert sequence in the priority Husserl accords the *vorhanden*. If human beings are first of all *vorstellend*, it is because Husserl supposes (and now I quote the *Logical Investigations*) that "every intentional experience" is "an objectivating act," or "is founded upon such an act," which has "the unique function of providing other acts with the *represented object* [my italics], to which other acts may then refer in their new ways"— for example, by judging it, having an affective reaction to it, and so forth.[4]

This sequence Heidegger cannot accept. Thus he asks in section 15, "Suppose one characterizes these 'things' as invested with value? . . . Aside from the obscurity of this structure of investiture with value, have we thereby come upon that phenomenal characteristic which we encounter in our concerned going about [*Umgang*]?"[5] To appreciate that Heidegger regards as belated Husserl's arrival in his inventory at "objects of use," we have to recognize that Heidegger himself starts out instead with an analysis of *Umgang*. His claim in the section, "The Phenomenological Method of Investigation" is that "the *starting point* [*Ausgang*] for the analysis has to be secured by the proper method, just as should the *access* [*Zugang*] to the phenomena and *passage* [*Durchgang*] through what is prevalently covering them up."[6]

So far we have been preoccupied with the problems of *Zugang* and of *Durchgang*, as problems to be dealt with by the *Destruktion*. But implicit in Heidegger's appraisal of Husserl's *Ausgangsstellung* is Heidegger's own commitment to an analysis of *Umgang* as his *Ausgang* in the sequence he follows. Heidegger finds Husserl's belated arrival at "objects of use" a *Verlegung*—a "misplacing of the prior understanding of being to being as *Vorhandenheit*." This *Verlegung* is an obstruction which Heidegger would deconstruct by following in his own *Auslegung* the sequence in which the *zuhanden* is encountered first. The sequential character of this *Verlegung* is bluntly described in Heidegger's *Prolegomena* as a matter of how, "with the perverted direction of interpretation [*der verkerten Interpretationrichtung*], we explain our encounter with the world . . . from our apprehension of it," instead of "the latter as founded on the former."[7] The latter sequence Heidegger's *Auslegung* respects by rectifying this "perverted direction of interpretation" in Husserl.

Handlichkeit

Having recognized the respect in which Heidegger's *Ausgang* is an analysis of *Umgang*, we can resume our interpretation of this analysis as a *Destruktion* with which Heidegger gains "*Zugang* to the phenomena" by a "*Durchgang* through what is prevalently covering them up." We should now be able to discern how he would rectify the sequence he ascribes to Husserl.

The rectification is prepared for by Heidegger's analysis in section 15 of the example of the hammer as a (piece of) equipment. We saw that the *Handlichkeit* of the hammer remained an "accompanying theme" for the construction of the concept of *Zuhandenheit,* but we could not follow out all of the implications, since the concept of *Vorhandenheit* is not deconstructed until section 16. Glance back at the example in section 15:

> The hammering . . . has appropriated this [piece of] equipment in a fashion which could not be more fitting [*angemessener*]. . . . The less we just stare at the hammer-thing, and the more we take hold of the hammer, the more primordial our relation to it becomes and the more unveiledly is it encountered as what it is—[a piece of] equipment. The hammering itself discovers the specific manipulability [*Handlichkeit*] of the hammer.[8]

Heidegger is poking fun at the visual idiom of staring, not only for its ineffectuality, but also for its isolating the hammer as if it were an object *vorhanden* to be contemplated in detachment from its relation to its user and from its relation to what it is being used for: "Where something is being put to use, our concern takes a subordinate place [*unterstellt*] in relation to the 'in-order-to' [*um-zu*]"—that is, in a referential context.

The forcefulness that the root *hand* acquires from the *Handlichkeit* of the hammer contributes some of the strenuousness needed to rectify Husserl's "perverse direction," so that *Zuhandenheit* regains its priority by displacing the concept *Vorhandenheit,* in which the root has gone slack because the experience of what is "before" us as "on hand" is construed by Husserl as typically visual, as shown in his example of the "sheet of paper"—*vor mir.*

We can discern the slackness if I restore a qualifying clause I previously excised from Husserl's descriptive inventory of the natural attitude: "By my seeing, touching, hearing, and so forth, in the different modes of sensory perception, physical things are . . . *simply there for me* [in a literal or metaphorical (*bildlich*) sense]—'*vorhanden.*'" Husserl is allowing for an ambiguity: a thing may be "on hand" literally or "on hand" in the broader, metaphorical sense that it "exists." (*Vorhandenheit* had become in philosophy a traditional translation of *existentia*.) Husserl does not regard it as a "dangerous" ambiguity, because in either case the thing is to enter his analysis only as an intentional object. Heidegger, in contrast, is taking advantage of this ambiguity. With his example of the hammer he revives the "literal" tactile force of the root of *Zuhandenheit* in order to display how dead this metaphor has become in *Vorhandenheit*. Heidegger even pits the phrase "the more the hammer is taken hold of [*Zugreifender*] in being used" against the weak metaphorical "grasp" of a merely theoretical conception of a concept (*Begriff*).

Heidegger also has the eventual aim of prying *existentia* (in philosophical Latin) away from the traditional translation, *Vorhandenheit,* so that he will be able to reserve *Existenz* for the Dasein, and to revive the force of its root in turn by a retrieval of the Greek *ekstasis.*[9] But at the present step in his analysis, all that interests me is that the *Destruktion* Heidegger is undertaking in *Being and Time* is of the traditional concept *Vorhandenheit* and of the priority it had traditionally acquired. Here I am pushing my own cumulative argument that Heidegger's *Destruktion* gains its purchase only if we recognize that Heidegger is not simply up against the tradition at large, although this is how he presents his analysis. Too many traits of it can only be accounted for by recognizing that he is more specifically taking on Husserl.[10]

The maneuver we watched earlier in the example of the indicator in section 17 is similarly deconstructive: "The sign is *not* [the "not" is italicized, I would suggest, to emphasize that a *Destruktion* is taking place] authentically 'grasped' [the quotation marks remind us that the con-cept of the "sign" is at issue] if the driver of the vehicle behind just stares at it and identifies it as something which is *vorhanden."* It became evident too that what the indicator indicates is also not authentically "grasped" if the driver simply follows out with his look the direction in which it points— toward something *vorhanden* in the field beside the road. His conduct must instead respond to the referential relations indicated by the specific adjustment of the indicator. With this example too, as an example of a (piece of) equipment which is "ready-to-hand," Heidegger can give the root its literal force by reminding us in the *Prolegomena* (as I noted earlier) that before the indicator was invented, "the hand had the same function, whenever the driver stretched it out of the vehicle to point in one direction or another."

I am not suggesting that the force of Heidegger's *Destruktion* is only a matter of his reinvigorating the root *hand.* Heidegger is at the same time pitting the prefix *zu* (already introduced in terms of the relation *um-zu* in constructing his concept of "reference") against the prefix *vor.* Here too we can detect the play of affinities between levels which, as we saw in the

last chapter, becomes feasible in Heidegger. The prefixes are (as I mentioned) directional signals, as it were, and I have taken them as indicating
the difference in direction in which his analysis is proceeding, as compared
with Husserl's. But Heidegger's employment of prefixes also exhibits (as I
also mentioned) the flexibility of his analysis—a flexibility which can be
contrasted with the fixity Husserl would secure for his concepts with his
analysis. Thus having constructed the concept of *Zuhandenheit* in section
15 and obtained for it the priority which would discredit in advance the
concept of *Vorhandenheit*, Heidegger takes a further step in section 16
which permits him to adjust his direction and accommodate the concept
of *Vorhandenheit*. In section 16 he provides examples of how "ready-to-
hand equipment" can exhibit "in a certain fashion unready-to-handed-
ness." When it is unutilizable it becomes "conspicuous." It is singled out
as *vorhanden:* "being only an object before us, it comes to the fore [*das
Nur-vorhandensein zum Vorschein kommt*]." At this step Heidegger completes his outmaneuvering of Husserl's analysis. He is pulling off the coup
a successor often does with a predecessor, whose analysis is allowed to enjoy limited relevance from being relocated within the more comprehensive
scope of the successor's philosophy.

This allowance I am sure Heidegger did not regard as reconciling his
analysis with Husserl's. Heidegger is still opposing "the perverted direction of interpretation" in which Husserl had proceeded.

Hands

In my exposition of Heidegger I have followed *der Weg der Abhebung* by
bringing recurrently into relief his opposition to Husserl, in somewhat the
same fashion as Heidegger himself brings "into relief" his analysis of "the
worldliness of the world" (the analysis we have been sampling) in terms of
his "opposition" to Descartes. But I would pause now in order to present
a further misgiving of mine with regard to Heidegger's conceiving his *Destruktion* as a procedure for dealing with the tradition at large. So conceived, it does not do justice to the different ways in which the relations
between philosophers are structured. These relations take many different
guises besides the relation of opposition, which emerges as Heidegger's relation to Husserl.

The guise which can most pertinently be illustrated here is an overcoming with an *Aufhebung* an apparent opposition. A notoriously facile
combination of Heidegger and Husserl (which I anticipated earlier when I
sketched out the history of the relation between them in later philosophy)
is Sartre's overcoming of their opposition in a dialectical "synthesis" in
Being and Nothingness.[11] That combination is indeed not only facile, but

also impossible, as my present exposition has demonstrated. Yet we should not overlook the work Sartre has put into a literary "synthesis." For my purposes here I can be brief. I cite first an example in which Sartre is elaborating on Heidegger before I go on to a second example of how he blends Heidegger with Husserl.

Sartre's protagonist in *Nausea* reflects,

> In my hands, for example, there is something new, a certain way of taking hold of my pipe or my fork. Or rather it is the fork which has, now, a certain way of making itself be taken.[12]

I suspect that the novelty felt here is not just a matter of the pathology of the character portrayed—that it is due in some measure to the conceptual novelty Sartre felt when he encountered Heidegger's concept of *Zuhandenheit*. With the correction "or rather," the initiative passes (in a fashion which Heidegger inspired) to a (piece of) equipment as imposing its own requirements on anyone who handles it.

Another example of Sartre's is likely to have been modeled on an example which Heidegger employs in section 15, but which I have not yet considered. I quote Heidegger: "When I open the door, for example, I make use of the knob." Sartre's example incorporates Heidegger's emphasis on *Handlichkeit:*

> Just now I was about to enter my room. I was halted suddenly, because I felt in my hand a cold object which held my attention by a sort of personality. I opened my hand, I looked: I was merely holding onto the doorknob.[13]

We have seen how in Heidegger a (piece of) equipment *zuhanden* can become an object *vorhanden*—something which is initially given, as in Husserl's analysis. Something can become "conspicuous" in Heidegger's analysis because it is unutilizable and holds my attention. Sartre undertakes a reversal: his protagonist did not utilize the (piece of) equipment in order to open the door, because the piece itself held his attention.

This reversal Sartre carries out with some assistance from Husserl. But first of all there is Sartre's own literalizing of the idiom of *Handlichkeit:* the object is "felt in my hand," and I then "opened my hand"—not the door. What Husserl assists Sartre with is the explanation that "the object held my attention by a sort of personality." An object which is given to perceptual consciousness in Husserl, is "given in person [*in eigener Person* or *Liebhaftig*]." "*En personne*" is Sartre's translation elsewhere.[14] The "metaphorical" extension which Husserl's terminology involves may help explain the hesitancy of Sartre's "a sort of."

I am pressing the philosophical implications of a novel (more specifically of what Sartre would characterize as the *travail du style*) in order to push an analogy between the work that is implicit in a philosophical method and this *travail*.[15] This analogy has encouraged me to examine more carefully more of the details of a philosophical method than is customary. I have presented the analogy in preceding volumes, and I reintroduce it in the next chapter as pertinent to the interpretation of Heidegger.

FIVE · BEING-IN

NINETEEN

Concept Construction

> *Where the region of being to be disclosed is*
> *ontologically far more difficult, . . . so will the*
> *complexity of the concept construction be*
> *aggravated.—Heidegger*

Direction

Before I reintroduce my analogy between
method and style as applicable to Heidegger's procedure of concept construction, I
should reemphasize one trait of his procedure—its holistic scope. I did cite earlier Heidegger's methodological behest, "If the whole
of this structure [being-in-the-world] is kept
constantly in view," the "moments which are
constitutive for it . . . can be brought into relief." But I have not been able to keep the
whole constantly in view, because my focus is
on Heidegger's relation to Husserl, and in
Husserl's analysis "objects" are singled out by
the in-tentional acts of consciousness. Thus
in maintaining my focus I had to compromise
and give a certain preference to examples (the
indicator, a hammer, a furnished room, opening a door) which may have seemed to limit
the scope of the implications of the concepts
Heidegger used these examples to construct.

In order to do more justice to Heidegger's
holism, I would now consider the perspective
put forth in the title of his Chapter 2, "Being-
in-the-World in General as the Fundamental
Constitution of Dasein," and by the title of
its first section, "A Preliminary Sketch of
Being-in-the-World, in Terms of [*aus*] an Orientation toward Being-In as Such." This orientation leads to the analysis of *Umgang*
which I have already sampled. But it also supplies direction to Heidegger's analysis for a

longer stretch in the sequence he is following than I am able to survey: while this first section of Chapter 2 offers "a preliminary sketch," Chapter 5 is entitled, "Being-In as Such."

It is evident that "in" qualifies as one of the "elemental words," which Heidegger claims it is "the ultimate business of philosophy to preserve in their truth [bewahren]."[1] The "in" is in fact preserved even when it involves Heidegger in misreading Husserl. The first section of Part 2 of *Ideas I* (the section we were examining in the last chapter) has the title "The World of the Natural Attitude: I and My *Umwelt*." But when Heidegger refers to this section in his *Introduction to Phenomenological Research* (1923–24), he intrudes his own elemental word: "Husserl . . . starts out from 'I in My *Umwelt*.'"[2] In this misreading is implicit Heidegger's different orientation, which involves him in a *Destruktion* of Husserl's analysis of "I and My Umwelt." The "and" itself is too weak to qualify as a relation for Heidegger. But the weaker "and" is appropriate for Husserl, inasmuch as his undertaking in Part 2 is to carry out the phenomenological reduction, with which the "I" along with its realm of intentional meanings can be "disconnected" in order to receive eventual recognition as a transcendental ego.

Since Heidegger goes so far as to substitute his own "in" for Husserl's "and," the comparison with Husserl cannot be renewed until we have taken into account the concepts Heidegger constructs which orient his analysis toward being-in:

> *"In"* is derived from *"innan"*—"to dwell," *"habitare,"* "to stay." *An* means [*bedeutet*] "I am accustomed to," "I am familiar with," "I look after something"; it has the meaning [*Bedeutung*] of *colo* in the sense [*Sinn*] of *habito* and *diligo*. The expression *"bin"* is connected with *"bei"* ["by"], and so *"ich bin"* ["I am"] signifies in turn "I dwell," "I stay by [*halt mich auf bei*]" the world as that which is familiar to me in such and such a way. "Being" [*Sein*], as the infinitive of *"ich bin,"* . . . means "to dwell by, . . ." "to be familiar with." . . . Thus *"Inbeing"* is accordingly the formal existential expression for the being of [Dasein], which has as its essential structure being-in-the-world.[3]

The importance of this step in Heidegger's analysis is evident in that the conclusion he has reached here is his first extended resort to italics in sixty-three (German) pages of *Being and Time,* since the passage concerning *"a system of categories"* which is *"blind and perverted."*[4]

I am recalling that passage because, as we shall see in the paragraph after the present passage, Heidegger is again criticizing what he calls "traditional ontological categories." To take their place, he constructs in the present passage existential categories which in the next paragraph he will commend as "fitting [*angemessen*] structural concepts."

Acrobatics

The passage I have quoted is the one in which Heidegger's construction of concepts is most enmeshed in what Souche-Dagues designates, on Husserl's behalf, as "philological acrobatics."[5] If Husserl makes no comment on this passage, I would guess he may have felt (as most commentators apparently have who neglect it) that its philology is not Heidegger's own but is lifted from Jacob Grimm. Yet we should not forget that Heidegger himself not only does the lifting but also redeploys the philology acrobatically.

I cannot renew more specific comparisons between Heidegger's concepts and Husserl's until I have resolved the problem the passage poses as an extreme example of what I shall label Heidegger's "style." Probably I should not have earlier so blithely brushed aside Kisiel's comment regarding *Being and Time*: "Heidegger, sensitive to years of critique of the incomprehensible opaqueness of his style, wanted to make himself clearly understood. He wanted to communicate."[6] Given my own interest in the problem of communication, little may have been more surprising in my exposition of Heidegger than my having proceeded as far as I have without facing up to this problem of incomprehensible opaqueness. But the present passage seems to have been worth waiting for as a particularly impressive illustration.

Before I get down to this question of Heidegger's style, I admit that my own attention to style in conjunction with method has been partly a protest against the preposterous conception that there is a single philosophical method, whether it is conceived to be identical with scientific method or distinguishable from it. The conception is clearly preposterous once we take into account the actual, empirical evidence of the differences in method between philosophies.

When I insisted on differences in method, even though the philosophies I was dealing with were ostensibly employing the same "phenomenological method,"[7] I sought an analogy between a philosophical method and a style. There is, I proposed, no more a single philosophical method than there is a single literary or artistic style. The analogy gained further relevance in dealing with philosophies whose affiliations are not with science but with literature (as is Sartre's) or with painting (as is Merleau-Ponty's).

Ausarbeitung

A comparison of Heidegger's "style" with Husserl's may seem unpromising. Husserl does not seem to have a style in the obtrusive sense that Heidegger does. Husserl writes in a fashion which sometimes has been found innocuous, even by some fairly austere analytic philosophers. In contrast, when Sartre explains how he was converted first not to Heidegger but to

Husserl, he mentions how he was put off by Heidegger's "barbaric" phi-losophy.[8] (He never comments, when he later succumbs to Heidegger, that his own style also became barbaric.) If the problem of style is inescapable in dealing with Heidegger—at least in *Being and Time*—it was so little a problem for Husserl that he was willing to delegate to his assistants the *Ausarbeitung* (the "working up") of his manuscripts into the "literary" form (as he calls it) which would make them ready for publication. This division of labor, as I have explained, was not accidental. Its philosophical justification was Husserl's conviction that pure phenomenological investigation could be carried on as a conceptual analysis independently of its receiving linguistic expression—indeed of "there really being languages." Husserl could delegate the *Ausarbeitung* to his assistants because he drew a one-sided, sharp distinction between problems of the (logical) "expression" of meanings, which are proper to phenomenology, and problems of linguistic expression.

What we must take into account, however, are differences not just in the styles of different phenomenologists but in their conceptions of "style." I am not presenting "style" as a court of last resort in which to render philosophical judgments, for it is itself a conception which, like the conception of method, is subject to vagaries as we move from one philosophy to another. One consequence of Husserl's philosophical indifference to "style" in the "literary" sense is that he can preempt the concept of "style" in a different sense for a philosophical purpose of his own. Given the resistance to be encountered in overcoming the natural attitude, when Husserl undertakes the "shift" [*Umstellung*] to a transcendental attitude, he would confer on "attitude" [*Einstellung*] itself a philosophical significance that the colloquial term does not convey. Accordingly Husserl resorts to the term *style:* "Attitude in general means a habitually fixed style of willing life, comprising directions of the will or interests that are prescribed by this style, comprising the ultimate ends, the cultural accomplishments whose total style is thereby determined."[9] "Style" thus acquires for Husserl a broad, quasi-methodological implication which can be associated with his effort with the eidetic reduction to keep the meanings of concepts "fixed" throughout the course of his investigation. Husserl's conception of "style" as "a habitually fixed style of willing life" enables us to appreciate the disdain Souche-Dagues attributes to Husserl with respect to the agility of Heidegger's "philological acrobatics."[10]

The Step

Heidegger was himself well aware of the misgivings regarding what he refers to in the *Prolegomena* as his "style in the use of language."[11] Before I consider the implications of his defense of his style, I would determine the step in the sequence of his analysis where he finds this defense appropriate. He has completed his exposition of Husserl in the "Preparatory Part," has begun his own phenomenology in the "Main Part," and makes his defense at the start of the chapter "Dasein as Being-in-the-World," in which he constructs the concepts of "being-in," "dwelling," "familiarity," and so forth—the concepts which appear again in the parallel passage I have already quoted from *Being and Time*. It seems plausible to suppose that he may have found the defense appropriate at the moment he left Husserl behind. With this transition, Husserl's use of language (or even Heidegger's own use in his previous exposition of Husserl) is likely to be compared favorably to Heidegger's use of language in elaborating in the "Main Part" his own phenomenology—particularly in elaborating the concepts which he is about to derive from Grimm—on the next page.

In *Being and Time* the "Preparatory Part" is dropped, and Heidegger relocates the defense to the final paragraph of the introductory section, "The Phenomenological Method of Investigation." The defense thus comes when Heidegger is dealing with method and just after the paragraph in which he acknowledges his debt to Husserl. Again, its location at this step may not be accidental.

One revision in *Being and Time* of the defense in the *Prolegomena* is that the explicit reference to "style" is dropped, so that the issue becomes simply Heidegger's "use of language." I would guess he discards "style" not because the reference is out of keeping with the earnestness of his undertaking but precisely because in this paragraph he finds (as we shall soon see) comparison with a literary narrative irrelevant—as well as any literary criteria.[12] I shall nonetheless take advantage of the reference in the *Prolegomena* and label (for convenience alone) the paragraph in *Being and Time* "the paragraph on style." The conclusion Heidegger reaches there is that

> if a reference is permissible to earlier researches in the analysis of being which are incomparable at their level, then the ontological sections in Plato's *Parmenides* or the fourth chapter of the seventh book of Aristotle's *Metaphysics* may be compared with a narrative section from Thucydides, and then it is seen how unprecedented those formulations were. . . . Where our strengths [*Kräfte*] are essentially less [than those of the Greeks] and where the region of being [*Gebiet*] to be disclosed is ontologically far more difficult [*schwieriger*] than that the Greeks were given, so will the *Umständlichkeit* ["complexity"] of the concept construction be aggravated and the *Härte* ["hardness" or "harshness"] of expression."[13]

This conclusion I can hardly overlook, given my stress on the difficulty of Heidegger.

More than the issue of style itself may be discernible here. There is a famous accusation against Heidegger that he was philosophically "predisposed" to join the Nazi Party in 1933 by his "yearning for the difficult and the hard."[14] In making this accusation, Winfried Franzen finds the most pertinent philosophical evidence in a 1929–1930 lecture course of Heidegger's. Whether or not the passage I have just cited is earlier evidence of a philosophical predisposition to Nazism, I do not pretend to decide. But it may be evidence worth recognizing of a predisposition to stylistic violence. The function of this violence I have not brought out, since it is adduced only at a late step in *Being and Time:*

> The *mode of being* of the Dasein *demands* that any ontological interpretation . . . should *conquer [erobert] the being of this being in opposition to its own tendency to cover itself up.* The existential analytic therefore has constantly the character of *exercising violence* [*Gewaltsamkeit;* Vézin, in *Être et Temps,* translates as "*coup de force*"] against the pretensions of the everyday interpretation, its complacency, and its tranquilized commitment to what goes without saying [its *Selbstverständlichkeit*]."[15]

This opposition to complacency and tranquillity may help explain some of the force of the *Aus* in *Ausarbeitung* and in particular Heidegger's adopting the idiom of *Destruktion.*

Umständlichkeit

Less evident is what *Umständlichkeit* itself entails. *Umständlich* Heidegger had already employed in the first sentence of the paragraph on style in the *Prolegomena,* where he admits, "We shall come upon a series of formulations" which are "perhaps characterizable as being complicated." In *Being and Time* the "perhaps" is omitted, and the admission is unqualified. As a matter of fact, the concepts in *Being and Time* are generally more "complicated."

I have been responsive to the Vézin translation of *Umständlichkeit* as *complexité.* Kisiel's translation of *Umständlich* as "involved" is preferable, but I have already reserved "involvement" for *Bewandtnis,* which is particularly difficult to translate. The two kinds of "involvement" are themselves not unrelated, but I want a translation that does not further complicate the complications.

Umständlich implies that the "complexity" is "elaborate," even "labored," and thus is a trait that can be associated with Heidegger's *Ausarbeitung.* The *Umständlichkeit* can extend to "details" and imply "intricacy." Macquarrie and Robinson translate *Umständlichkeit* as "minuteness of detail." Albert Hofstadter adds the implication of "fussy."[16]

I need not plead my finding in this ambiguous range of implications a certain vindication for my unremitting scrutiny of certain detailed intricacies in Heidegger's text, as well for whatever impression of fussiness on my own part this may have given. But I would press the point that Heidegger's commitment to *Umständlichkeit* suggests that any exposition of *Being and Time* that was a bald summary and did not attend to the "work" he has expended on details in constructing his concepts he would himself regard as a misleading oversimplifying of their complexity.

Of course I would not maintain that my own *Umständlichkeit* is simply a matter of respecting Heidegger's. But my *Umständlichkeit* (like my more general consideration of style itself) takes on different implications from my dealing with different philosophers. No one ever bothered to sift as minutely as I did in Volume 2, *Method and Imagination,* the details of Sartre's analysis in *L'imaginaire* in order to get at the relation between him and Husserl. Presumably most previous interpreters either felt that Sartre merited consideration simply in his own terms or felt that he was a sloppy writer who merited only sloppy generalizations. My fussiness was feasible, not by virtue of any *Umständlichkeit* attributable to Sartre himself, but rather by virtue of a certain "bookishness" on his part to which he almost confessed with his pronouncement, "I began my life, as I shall doubtless finish it—in the midst of books."[17] This "bookishness" was betrayed by his often seeming to take over from predecessors more terminology than was needed to convey his own less complicated philosophy. One result of my respecting his "bookishness" was that I was able to dispose of the oversimplifying presumption that to qualify as "existential" it is necessary to have pristine experiences as evidence that they are authentically one's own.

I am recalling my previous diligence, not to congratulate myself on what I accomplished, but because one of my claims in the present volume is that Heidegger is more attentive to some of the details of Husserl's phrasing than has previously been supposed, and that he is not simply dealing in *Being and Time,* as he pretends, with "traditional ontological categories," but with Husserl.

Still I would not have my *Umständlichkeit* in the present volume too closely identified with my previous diligence when I was trying to deal with the clutter of Sartre's "bookishness." Heidegger exhibits much more conceptual integrity than Sartre in the working out of his own philosophy. But this does not preclude ascertaining debts to Husserl which Heidegger does not himself acknowledge.

Joints

First I must take into account the explanation Heidegger offers of the *Umständlichkeit* of his concepts:

> With regard to the awkwardness [*Ungefüge*] and "inelegance" [*Unschöne*] of expression in the analyses to follow, the comment can be adjoined [*angefügt*] that it is one thing to report in narrative fashion about beings, but another to grasp beings in their *being*. For the . . . task [of grasping beings in their being] we lack not only mostly the words, but above all the 'grammar.'"[18]

The "awkwardness" is due in part to Heidegger's undertaking the shift from the "ontic" level, where a Thucydides can "report in narrative fashion about beings [*Seiende*]," to the "ontological" level, where Heidegger would "grasp [conceptually these] beings in their being [*Sein*]." Our attention is drawn to the root of *Ungefüge* by the verb *angefügt*, especially since it seems itself awkwardly "adjoined." One might be tempted, with some help from Shakespeare and Derrida (commenting on the later Heidegger's use of the word *Fug*), to translate *Ungefüge* as "out of jointness."[19] But Heidegger's later usage is too intricately complicated for that word to be anticipated now, though it justifies noticing the idiom on this rare occasion of its use in *Being and Time*.

The difficulty in carrying out this shift in *level* is also emphasized in the *Prolegomena:*

> Our language . . . in following its natural traction [*Zug*] . . . is at the outset oriented in its meaning [*Sinn*] toward beings. But even when we attempt to explicate the being of the being . . . the world as it is there for us, even here there are enough difficulties in finding a fitting [*angemessen*] formulation for the structures of being in the being.[20]

Here we have a specific illustration of what I had in mind when I warned in my introduction that to understand a difficult philosophy is to understand why it has to be difficult.

The most obtrusive fashion in which Heidegger would make up for the deficiencies of grammar is his resort to hyphens, which I have so far interpreted as merely enjoining a relational analysis, to be contrasted with Husserl's intentional analysis in which objects are targeted. By inserting hyphens, Heidegger would also compose a context in which he joins up what is disjoined by the orientation of Husserl's analysis of intentionality toward beings. The hyphens indicate joints, which seem "awkward," "out of joint," because they defy "the natural traction" of language. This defiant use of hyphens can be a deconstructive as well as a constructive procedure. One example we have already encountered is Heidegger's resort to hyphenation of *be-deuten* to dislocate Husserl's conception of *Bedeutung* ("meaning") as immediately given.

In order to bring out the complication Heidegger encounters with his shift in *level*, I earlier undertook a comparison with Husserl, who would enforce one-sided distinctions in level with his eidetic and phenomenological reductions. Examples of his one-sided distinctions were the meanings he secured for "expression" and "meaning" in the first of the *Logical Investigations*. Heidegger, however, in order to "grasp beings in their being," would not leave the ontic level behind when he reaches the ontological level, although the ontic orientation toward beings has to be overcome— and may even require the exercise of violence in the use of language. This complication was illustrated by two of Heidegger's examples. In the case of the hammer, Heidegger was formulating the concept, *Zuhandenheit*, both to make up for the lack of a word and to secure priority for this concept as over against the concept of *Vorhandenheit*. We also saw that the example remained an "accompanying theme"; it enabled him to allow the theme of the *Handlichkeit* of the hammer to accompany him to the higher level, where it reinvigorated the dead metaphor in the traditional conception of a "con-cept." In the case of the indicator, "the conduct (being)" of the driver remained pertinent when Heidegger reached the ontological conclusion that "taking a direction belongs essentially to the Dasein's being-in-the-world."

Modes of Conduct

Now that the "difficulties" have been summarized that Heidegger encounters in constructing concepts, we are better able to resume consideration of the particular concepts which turn up in that singularly complicated and awkward passage I have quoted from his analysis of being-in. We can see that he is "bringing into relief," with the concepts constructed in this passage, different relations that being-in entails. It is in the next paragraph that he mentions *der Weg der Abhebung,* and he may well do so, lest it seem random that he has deployed in such rapid succession relations so multifarious.

What he is grasping as relational are modes of conduct. In the first clause of the passage they are *wohnen* (to dwell [in]), *habitare* (to inhabit), and *sich aufhalten* (to stay by). The examples in the second clause—"*an*" means *ich bin gewohnt* (I am accustomed to), *vertraut mit* (I am familiar with), and *ich pflege etwas* (I look after something)—are reached reflexively, as is emphasized by the relation between his initial examples in the two listings: *wohnen* in the first clause and *ich bin gewohnt* in the second clause. The reflexive character of this move from one formulation to the other is brought out in the third sentence: "The being [the Dasein] to which being-in with this meaning belongs is the being which has been characterized as the being which in each case I am [*ich bin*]." I comment in the next chapter on this reflexivity.

First, however, there is a concept here which demands special attention if we would determine what is afoot with Heidegger, for he does not take it over from Grimm, as he does all the other concepts, and he employs it frequently later. It is "familiarity" (*Vertrautheit*). (We have already encountered it in section 16.) It is introduced with *vertraut mit* in the first sentence I have quoted, but it attains prominence in the third sentence, when Heidegger reaches the conclusion with respect to his crucial concept in *Being and Time*: "The expression '*bin*' is connected with '*bei*' ["by"], and so '*ich bin*' ["I am"] signifies in turn 'I dwell,' 'I stay by [*halt mich auf bei*]' the world as that which is familiar to me in such and such a way." It retains this prominence in the fourth sentence: The expression "'*ich bin*,' . . . means 'to dwell by, . . .' 'to be familiar with.'" Why does Heidegger in this sentence drop the expression *sich aufhalten* (which is the most likely candidate for the expression that he replaces with dots), while he retains *vertraut mit*? His preference seems the more surprising inasmuch as he is able to use *aufhalten*, as he does *wohnen*, with both the prepositions *in* (which he is analyzing and had already begun analyzing in the preceeding paragraph) and *bei* (which he will make more of two paragraphs later), and he cannot use *vertraut* with either preposition. In fact the two prepositions had supplied Grimm with a title for his article, "'*In*' und '*Bei*,'" whereas there was no reference in his article to being "familiar with."

Before explaining why Heidegger would construct this concept, I would compile more evidence regarding how he employs it. In the parallel passage of the *Prolegomena*, its general significance is evident:

> The expression *bin* is connected with *bei*. Being as being-in and "I am" thus amounts to "I dwell," "I stay by the world as with something familiar. . . ." "In" primarily does not mean anything spatial but signifies primarily "*being familiar with*."[21]

A possible explanation for the prominence of *vertraut sein mit* (and for the italics it is awarded) is that there is more risk of taking "I dwell" or "I stay by" in a merely spatial sense. (I return later to Heidegger's concern to avoid this risk.) There is also a certain suppleness about the term—the ambiguous range of senses it supports. In colloquial German *vertrauen* means "place one's confidence in," "rely on," "put one's trust in." Some of the broader implications of *vertrauen* are suggested by the English cognates of its root: "trust," "troth" ("truth"). These different senses can be corralled very roughly: one puts one's "confidence" in something with which one is "familiar" and has come to "trust" as "true."

Primary Familiarity

The status of *Vertrautheit* is further illustrated by the adjectives at times attached in order to distinguish the specific senses Heidegger would have it convey from more trivial senses. Thus he specifies in *Being and Time* that it is a matter of what Dasein is "primordially [*ursprünglich*] familiar with." In *The Basic Problems of Phenomenology* (in a passage in which Heidegger provides us with a summary version of the analysis of the *Umwelt* in *Being and Time*), he alludes to what can "only be grasped in terms of [*aus*]" the "structure of primary familiarity [*Struktur der primären Vertrautheit*]," and he goes on to claim that "primordial familiarity with beings lies in going about them fittingly [*in dem ihm angemessen*]"—that is, in a fashion which is commensurate with their requirements as (pieces of) equipment in the mode of *Zuhandenheit*.[22] This claim is offered in protest against "the usual approach in the theory of knowledge," which "does not do justice to the primary facts." We recall the analysis of the *Umwelt* which Heidegger carried out on behalf of what he takes as prior in his own approach: "We shall seek the worldliness of the *Umwelt* in going through an ontological interpretation of those beings [the *zuhanden*] within the *Umwelt* that we encounter as nearest to us." This analysis, we have seen, is a deconstructive analysis in which he deprives the object *vorhanden* of the priority it enjoys in Husserl.

We have already seen other relevant evidence of the priority which Heidegger would accord *Vertrautheit*. His German translation of the citation at the start of *Being and Time* I rendered, "For obviously you have been confident as to [*vertraut mit*] what you authentically mean when you say 'being,' but we who believed we understood it, now have gotten into difficulty." Instead of translating Heidegger's German translation, as I have tried to do, Macquarrie and Robinson (and Stambaugh) alike translate *seid . . . vertraut mit* as "been aware of." Perhaps the translators are uneasy over how blatant a mistranslation of the Greek Heidegger's German is, and so dilute the German. But they dilute the Greek as well. The use here of the reduplicative past tense of *gignōskō* is not a matter of mere awareness; rather, it implies, "you know."

My particular concern, however, is that "you have . . . been aware" does an injustice to Heidegger's German translation—if his later use of *Vertrautheit* in *Being and Time* is taken into account. The relevance of this later use is a possibility these translators do not entertain, since they assume that all Heidegger is up to here is translating the Greek.

In contrast, the Vézin translation, *tout à fait familiarisés,* entirely disregards Plato's Greek in favor of Heidegger's German. When, in Chapter 8, I considered Heidegger's mistranslations, I suggested he did not necessarily intend to obliterate the original Greek. After all, Heidegger quotes the original Greek. I propose that he may want us to surmount an incongruity. Let me put it in crude English: your "confidence" (in German) that "you know" (in Greek) becomes merely a matter of what you are "familiar with" (in German). The playing up of an incongruity of this sort might plausibly be regarded as a procedure of the Platonic Socrates.

A methodological specification is also involved. The answer to the question raised by Sallis, "Where does Heidegger begin?" is perhaps not just "in the middle of a Platonic dialogue." The primordiality he later accords *Vertrautheit* suggests that Heidegger is beginning where he must begin as a philosopher if this primordiality of *Vertrautheit* is to be respected, as it is in the *Basic Problems.* If so, he may be protesting implicitly against what he characterizes as "the usual approach in the theory of knowledge." I defer that protest until Chapter 22. But I can anticipate now that what is at issue is the *ordo cognoscendi*—the "sequence" in which knowledge is obtained. A methodological conception of how it is obtained sequentially often emerges at the first step. In his 1923 summer course he italicizes *unabgehobenen,* when he speaks of "the *unabgehobenen Selbstverständlichkeit der Vertrautheit.*"[23] *Der Weg der Abhebung*—his "method of bringing into relief"—is thereby pitted against what has "not [yet] been brought into relief," because it seems so "obvious" as to "go without saying." But its seeming "obvious" is merely a matter of its "familiarity."

A Difficulty

At this juncture I would resume my initial argument that Heidegger's break with Husserl is not simply reducible to the shift in *subject* with which he poses the question of being, which (according to Granel) "is not and cannot be a question for Husserl."[24]

Concomitantly involved as well is a shift in *method,* inasmuch as the question of being is for Heidegger a "question" which is *mehrdeutig* (involving a "multiplicity of meanings"). In treating this question, Heidegger accordingly cannot commit himself methodologically, as Husserl does, to eliminating ambiguities and formulating concepts with univocal meanings. If this is the case with "the meaning of being," it is more specifically the case with the meaning of "being-in," and the complications of the passage we are considering are an attempt to do justice to the multiplicity of the different relations that need to be brought successively into relief as "moments" in the structure of being-in, toward which his analysis is now "oriented." Once again we see how following *der Weg der Abhebung* entails recognizing *Mithebung*.

A further step in this comparison must now take into account a distinction Husserl would draw. When I was, in my introduction, concerned to bring out their respective conceptions of a "difficulty," I consulted Husserl's introductory section, "The Difficulties of Pure Phenomenological Analysis." Since I have been dealing more recently with the "difficulties" Heidegger encounters in the use of language, I single out now Husserl's acknowledgment in this section of "the difficulty in the *statement* [*Darstellung*] of . . . results." This difficulty is that "the essential content [of a concept which has been] established by the most adequate analysis . . . has to be stated in [linguistic] expressions which are wide-ranging in their differentiation [*weitreichender Differenzierung*]."[25]

We have seen how the meaning of a concept (such concepts as "intentionality," "perception") is originally established by an eidetic reduction, which eliminates variations in meaning in favor of what is identical and thus can be taken as essential. This eidetic reduction is carried out prelinguistically—that is, conceptually and independently of "there really being languages."

The danger of ambiguities, of variation in meanings, recurs when the meanings that have once been established by the reduction are provided with linguistic expressions—"wide-ranging in their differentiation." An illustration we have had is Husserl's beginning the first of his *Logical Investigations* with a section entitled, "An Ambiguity in the Term 'Sign.'" We watched him overcome this ambiguity by an eidetic reduction in which he disentangles a univocal concept which defines a "sign" in the sense that is relevant in logic—as immediately expressing a meaning.

Here a comparison I offered earlier can be renewed. Heidegger does not appreciate Husserl's difficulty with "expressions which are wide-ranging in their differentiation." Indeed, he deploys such expressions in the complicated passage in which he is formulating what he describes in the next paragraph as "fitting [*angemessenen*] structural concepts." They would not fit, be commensurate with, the structure of "being-in" if they did not exhibit this structure by bringing into relief varied relations.

After having eliminated variation in meaning by an eidetic reduction and obtained a concept with a fixed univocal meaning, "there is," Husserl warns, "a continuing need for caution and for frequent reexamination to see whether what was fixed [the meaning assigned a concept by an eidetic reduction and carried over in the linguistic expression] in the earlier context is actually employed in the same sense in the new context." The danger is (as I observed earlier) that "unnoticed ambiguities may allow other

concepts to slip subsequently beneath and be substituted for our words,"
so we are no longer employing these words with the identical meaning.
But this is no longer a danger that is to be avoided in Heidegger. Thus he
employs the concept "being-in" with the different meanings which it acquires in different contexts: for instance, when he finds *in* related to *an* and
expounds *an* as having "the meaning of *colo* in the sense of *habito* and
diligo." Here Heidegger is not attempting to keep the meaning of *in* fixed.
Since *Abhebung* becomes the recognition of *Mithebung,* he is "bringing
into relief" an overlap in meaning between *in* and *an,* and overlaps between *colo, habito,* and *diligo.* With *colo* itself Heidegger could have moved
from the agri-cultural context, which originally gave the term much of its
meaning, into other contexts where the "cultivation" which takes place is
more "cultured." We thus see how the methodological criterion of fittingness (or "commensurability") is conceived by Heidegger when he seeks
"fitting structural concepts" and keeps adjusting their application to successively different structures of "being-in."

The difficulty Husserl finds with respect to the philosophical use of
language is not just that the expressions of ordinary language are "wide-
ranging in their differentiation," but that they also "only fit familiar
[*vertrauten*] natural objects." When he speaks of "familiar natural objects,"
he is speaking rather casually and colloquially, as befits these objects,
which belong to the realm of what he characterizes later in *Ideas I* as
"the natural attitude." These objects are not the aim of his analysis; ideal
objects, "essences," are, and "familiarity" never could become for him a
philosophical concept.

The case, however, for Heidegger's having derived his concept from
Husserl's use of "familiar" is somewhat strengthened by evidence that
Heidegger may have been responsive to another expression of Husserl's in
this section, "The Difficulties of Pure Phenomenological Analysis." I shall
examine this evidence before I continue with Heidegger's concept of "familiarity" and consider how his following *der Weg der Abhebung* becomes the expansion in successive contexts of the implications of this
concept in a fashion which illustrates what Husserl would stigmatize as
deploying meanings which are "wide-ranging in their differentiation."

TWENTY

Aufgehen In

In these analyses the *seeing* of a primary structure
of Dasein's being is at issue.—Heidegger

The Ambulatory Idiom

In Husserl's introductory section, "The Difficulties of Pure Phenomenological Analysis,"
the "origin of them all" is located in

> the counter-natural direction of intuition
> and thought which phenomenological
> analysis requires. Instead of becoming
> absorbed in the *carrying out to comple-
> tion* [*im Vollzuge . . . aufzugehen*] . . . of
> acts [of consciousness] and thus naively
> positing the existence of the objects re-
> ferred to [*gemeinten*], . . . we must rather
> "reflect"—that is, make these acts them-
> selves and their immanent meaning
> content [*Sinnesgehalt*] into objects.[1]

So comprehensive an explanation requires
considerable comment.

But first I would point out that Heidegger
is likely to have derived from it another concept. In the next sentence after the complicated passage regarding *in* and *bei,* in which
Heidegger adds "familiarity" to the concepts
he derived from Grimm, he introduces the following: "'Being by' ['*Sein bei*'] the world, in
the sense of being absorbed in the world
[*Aufgehens in der Welt*]—a sense still to be
laid out more closely—is an *existential* cate-
gory [that is, a concept needed for the analysis of the Dasein] founded upon being-in."[2]
"Absorption" is the other concept, besides
"familiarity," which Heidegger did not find in
Grimm. "Absorption" is no more a concept

in Husserl than is "familiarity," and he is not concerned to specify its sense "more closely," as Heidegger is. In this instance, too, Husserl is satisfied with the colloquial expression, for he is not interested in "natural objects" but ideal objects—essences. He is interested in the natural direction of consciousness (in what he will call in *Ideas I*, the "natural attitude") only to the extent that the "direction . . . which phenomenological analysis requires," is "counter-natural."

Going About

When Heidegger considers his own analysis (in the sentence after the sentence in which he first introduces the terminology *aufgehen in*) we are in effect reminded of its root: "In these analyses [of 'being-in' and of 'being-by'] the *seeing* of a primary structure of Dasein's being is at issue [*es geht um*]." The force of the root of *aufgehen in* is lost with Macquarrie and Robinson's translation "absorbed in," just as the root meaning of *es geht um* is almost lost with their translation of *es geht . . . um* as referring to what is "at issue," though they have in mind that *issus* is a past participle of *ire* ("to go").[3] On first translating this terminology, Macquarrie and Robinson do observe that "expressions of the form '*es geht . . . um*' appear very often in this work," but they do not explain what is "at issue" in these expressions themselves. Kisiel does explain, with a triple translation of Heidegger's characterization of the *Dasein* as "ein Seiendes, dem es in seinem Sein *um* dieses Sein selbst geht": "a being which *in* its being goes *about* this being, is concerned *about* this being, *has* this being as an issue."[4]

If this relational nexus is implicit in the ambiguities of *es geht . . . um*, the fact that such "expressions" do "appear very often" is to be explained by the reflexive character of Heidegger's analysis in *Being and Time*. I emphasize this now, not just because of the reflexive move we observed in the complicated passage in the last chapter, but also because the *reflexivity* of Heidegger's analysis is to be distinguished from the *reflective* character Husserl asserts of his analysis, when he demands, "instead of becoming absorbed in the carrying out . . . of acts [of consciousness]," we must "reflect."

We have already watched the ambulatory idiom, which emerges in *es geht . . . um*, undergo a different elaboration in section 15. There Heidegger's analysis becomes an analysis of "going about" (*Umgang*) the *Umwelt*. There, as I have already noted, the Macquarrie and Robinson translation of *Umgang* by "dealings" unfortunately eliminates the force of the root—as indeed do most translations.

This ambulatory idiom is also employed in *Being and Time* to characterize the procedure Heidegger follows in treating the subject "going about," but with considerable specification as to how he goes about "going about." The methodological requirement which is satisfied by his treatment of *Umgang* is to reach the right "starting point [*Ausgang*] for access [*Zugang*] to the phenomenon of worldliness." The treatment itself, we recall, takes "its course [*Gang*] . . . toward the idea of worldliness in general . . . in going through [*im Durchgang*] an ontological interpretation of . . . beings within-the-*Umwelt.*"

The "way" or "ways" Heidegger follows are heralded in such later titles as *Unterwegs zur Sprache, Wegmarken, Holzwege, Feldweg, Mein Weg in die Phänomenologie.* What I am bringing out is how he is "on the way" toward this later usage when he deploys the ambulatory idiom in *Being and Time,* where it involves the *Destruktion* of Husserl's analysis. As I have often urged, the comparison with Husserl cannot be restricted to the shift in *subject* which takes place when Husserl's acts of consciousness, as a subject for phenomenology, are displaced in *Being and Time* by how the Dasein "goes about" the world. The comparison has to be extended to the differences between Husserl's and Heidegger's methods. Here I single out the specific trait of Heidegger's deployment of the ambulatory idiom. When Heidegger, in explicating "being-by," introduces *Aufgehen in,* it elicits from him the parenthetical comment that he is using it in "a sense still to be laid out more closely [*noch näher*]." He then looks forward to the destructive implications of this closer analysis with a generalization: "[The] structure of Dasein's being is in principle one which cannot be grasped by the traditional ontological categories; this 'being-by' must be examined still more closely [*noch näher*]." This criterion of "proximity" of course also applies to the shift in *subject* (or rather context) which I have already dealt with as taking place when the subject becomes what is nearest [*nächst*]—the *Umwelt*—and when Heidegger goes "through an ontological interpretation of those beings within-the-*Umwelt* that we encounter as nearest"—that is, (pieces of) equipment.

Criteria

The vigor of the criterion of "proximity" (*noch näher*), which is repeated here in two successive sentences, can only be appreciated when the force it acquires *im Durchgang* is recognized as its displacing of the methodological criterion of "immediate givenness," which presides over Husserl's analysis, as his "*principle of all principles,*" whereby "*every intuition* [of a meaning] *that is immediately given is a legitimating origin* [*Rechtsquelle*] of knowledge."[5] This "legitimating origin" is to be implemented in overcoming "the difficulties [of pure phenomenological analysis]" whose "origin [*Quelle*]" is our being "absorbed in the carrying out . . . of acts [of consciousness] and thus naively positing the existence of the objects referred to." This opposition of knowledge, as immediately given, to our having becoming "absorbed," is undercut by Heidegger.

One claim I keep making on behalf of my focus on Heidegger's relation to Husserl is that it may help bring out what is distinctive in Heidegger. Thus it is worth pausing here to remark on Derrida's elision of Heidegger's criterion of "proximity" together with the criterion of "presence" enforced by Husserl's appeal to immediate givenness—inasmuch as both alike betray nostalgia for origins. I cite again Derrida's asking in his deconstruction of Husserl's analysis of the sign: "Does Heidegger's thought not often raise the *same* questions [my italics] as the metaphysics of presence [as illustrated by Husserl]?" I add this time Derrida's commentary on the "starting point" in *Being and Time* of Heidegger's existential analytic, where his commitment to an existential analytic is itself legitimated:

> The originary, the authentic, is determined as the *propre* (*eigentlich*), that is the *proche* (*propre, proprius*) the *présent dans la proximité de la présence à soi*. It could be demonstrated how this criterion [*valeur*] of proximity and of presence to oneself intervenes at the start of *Being and Time*. . . . The weight of metaphysics in such a decision could be demonstrated.[6]

This elision of the two criteria apparently adds to the weight of Derrida's own effort to see established an overall metaphysical tradition as meriting deconstruction. But he does not allow for the decisive implications of the differences between the criterion of "proximity" (or "nearness"—to avoid the Latinism) in Heidegger and the criterion of "presence" (immediate givenness) in Husserl. The methodological implications reach into every corner of their respective philosophies. To deprive Heidegger's criterion of "proximity" of its decisiveness is to deprive him of the prospect to which he most earnestly clings in his thinking, of going "along a way" (*der Weg der Abhebung* or any other "way"). How decisive this criterion is to him can hardly be appreciated until we see how it is pitted against Husserl's criterion of immediate givenness, which ensures the legitimacy of his eidetic reduction.

The different implications here, I have suggested, receive another illustration when Heidegger brings out the ambulatory idiom implicit in the terminology *Aufgehen in* in the sentence after the one in which the concept of *Aufgehen in* is first introduced. I cite this next sentence: "In these analyses the *seeing* of a primary structure of Dasein's being is at issue ["gone about"/*es geht . . . um*]." Heidegger's italics draw our attention to the visual idiom. Heidegger's explicit *Destruktion* of the visual idiom will only be undertaken in section 36, where he gets back to the origin of the philosophical tradition as a cognitive tradition. He then cites Aristotle as he starts out with the proposition, "All men desire by nature to know [*eidenai*]." I have supplied the traditional translation of *eidenai*, but Heidegger himself would also translate its root-meaning, "All men desire to see." To this traditional assimilation of "knowing" to "seeing," Heidegger opposes his *Destruktion* as requiring a *Durchgang* with which he in effect opposes the criterion of *Durchsichtigkeit* to Husserl's *Einsichtigkeit*.[7]

This is one of the junctures at which the specific relevance of Husserl to Heidegger's analysis should be taken into account, even though Heidegger himself is undertaking a *Destruktion* of the tradition at large and is quoting Greek. The examples Husserl prefers to analyze at the "natural" level are taken from the visual perception of objects, and when in this analysis he reaches the level at which he distinguishes the "eidetic," he is deliberately borrowing the Greek term *eidos* for "essence," and coining the term "eidetic" for the procedure with which he reaches this level.

Heidegger has quoted Aristotle in Greek. I am not claiming that Husserl rather than Aristotle is his antagonist, only that Husserl is his "nearer" antagonist (to apply Heidegger's own criterion) and that Husserl had asserted the visual idiom more vividly than perhaps any predecessor:

> *Immediate "seeing . . . ,"* not the mere sensory experience of seeing, but *seeing überhaupt as originary given consciousness* . . . is the ultimate justification of all rational assertion. . . . To assign no validity to "I see it," as an answer to the question, "Why?" is nonsensical [*Widersinn*].[8]

Such confidence in the visual idiom betrays almost unprecedented confidence in the immediacy with which essential meanings can be intuited and seen to be eidetic knowledge.

Double Meaning

I return to the ambulatory idiom displayed by Heidegger's going along *der Weg der Abhebung* and reinforced by his also taking over the terminology *Aufgehen in*.

When I characterize Heidegger as employing *Aufgehen in* with a "double meaning" (much as he does in translating the Greek *eidenai*), the nomenclature I am adopting, *Dopplesinn*, is Husserl's. I have pointed out that it enjoys the considerable prominence of appearing in the title of the first section of the first chapter of the first of his *Logical Investigations*—

"A Double Meaning of the Term 'Sign.'" *Dopplesinn* in Husserl has the pejorative sense of "ambiguity" (Findlay's translation), and as such it is to be eliminated. His methodological objection to ambiguities is discussed in Chapter 5 in terms of his commitment to keeping "our meanings unshakably identical." The danger he is warning against is allowing "meanings" to "pass over and flow into each other." This characterization of an ambiguity (although elaborated in the *Logical Investigations*, long before *Being and Time* was written) would describe how Husserl would react to Heidegger's employment of *Aufgehen in* as a concept. According to Husserl, such "wavering blurs boundaries."[9]

To apply Husserl's use of the terminology "double meaning" to Heidegger is misleading if it is taken as implying that Heidegger fails to distinguish what Husserl would distinguish. Rather, Heidegger is cutting back behind Husserl's distinction between the conceptual analysis of "meanings" and physical "signs" (such as the spoken or written word, or the brand of the slave, canals on Mars, fossils) and arriving at the concept *Aufgehen in*, which could never become a concept in Husserl, who uses it with reference to the natural attitude in the merely metaphorical, psychological sense of becoming "absorbed."

Heidegger cuts back behind in his analysis of "being-in," even before he resorts to the ambulatory idiom. One example that Heidegger uses is a garment.[10] When we refer to it as "'in' the closet," an external relation is conveyed between two physical objects which are both *vorhanden*. The garment can be separated from its relation to the closet and remain what it is as an object. The Dasein, however, cannot be separated even analytically from its "being-in-the-world" as its mode of being. Thus (if I may embroider on Heidegger's example), when we recognize that Heidegger follows "a way" (for instance, "in phenomenology"—later I'll adjust this translation of the *in* in Heidegger's title "Mein Weg in die Phänomenologie" [My way to phenomenology]) or that "Jack is in trouble," or that "Jill is in love again," we are not envisaging them as being distinct and separable from what he or she is "in" in the sense that the garment is separable from the closet it is "in," and can be taken "out" and remain the same object. Matters become more complicated when the garment is left "in" the closet because it is no longer "in" fashion. Then the Dasein's being-in-the-world is implicated. This difference in Heidegger's and Husserl's use of language is not philosophically arbitrary. When Husserl distinguishes the conceptual meaning from its physical expression, he is delimiting the subject of phenomenology; when Heidegger cuts back behind this distinction, as a distinction of the psychological from the physical, a shift in the *subject* (or rather context) of phenomenology is taking place.

Consider as a consequence of this shift in *subject* Heidegger's use of the seemingly innocuous methodological criterion "more closely" [*noch näher*] when he justifies the further analysis of "*Aufgehen in.*" Closeness here is not measurable by a physical distance (say, by the number of pages devoted to the analysis) any more than it is when we say Jill feels "close" to Jack, now that she is "in" love with him and he is "in" trouble.

Psychologism

The whole of this is too psychological; make more discernible . . . inbeing and the presiding ontology.—Heidegger

Psychological Conduct

In my introduction I indicated that I could not do justice in this volume to the internal development of Heidegger's philosophy, for my undertaking was to bring into focus the relation between Heidegger's philosophy, as presented in *Being and Time,* and Husserl's philosophy. Yet since I hope to explain the breakdown in communication between Heidegger and Husserl, I conceded I could not entirely overlook the change which took place in this relation between the *Prolegomena* and *Being and Time:* in the *Prolegomena* Heidegger is still an avowed "disciple in relation to Husserl,"[1] and he devotes a "Preparatory Part" to a critical exposition of Husserl before he undertakes in the "Main Part" an exposition of his own philosophy, whereas in *Being and Time* there is no exposition of Husserl—not even a single-sentence quotation. I have acknowledged that this change may involve prudence or cunning on Heidegger's part. But one matter which is philosophically at issue is a shift in *subject,* whereby he "depsychologizes" phenomenology. This characterization is clumsy, but it has the advantage of suggesting that Heidegger continues Husserl's critique of "psychologism," but in a more strenuous fashion. I would cite as a justification for my characterization a marginal behest which Heidegger entered in the manuscript of a 1923 course: "The whole of this is too psychological; make more discernible . . . inbeing [*sic*] and the presiding ontology."[2] The behest has a certain pertinence to *Being and Time* since it was in this course that Heidegger first constructed the concept "being-in." The emphasis on "whole" is evidence of the holistic breadth of the shift. To get under this breadth, I would concentrate first on a very specific illustration of the shift. It is provided by Heidegger's somewhat different use in the *Prolegomena* of the terminology *Aufgehen in*, which we have been examining in *Being and Time*. Citing the marginal comment in the 1923 lectures is an admission on my part that depsychologization is a development that antedates the *Prolegomena*, but I can compare the *Prolegomena* and *Being and Time* with more confidence, inasmuch as Heidegger employed it as a "draft" for writing *Being and Time*.

Here I would take into account the subject Heidegger initially proposes to analyze in the *Prolegomena*: "Let us present an exemplary and easily accessible case of 'psychological conduct' ['*seelischen Verhaltung*']: a concrete and natural perception, the perception of a chair which I find on entering a room."[3] I grant that the quotation marks may be a warning that depsychologization is under way. But in *Being and Time* this sort of warning is no longer necessary, because Heidegger is no longer analyzing "psychological conduct" but "conduct" ontologically. Thus the ontological character of his analysis is indicated by his parentheses after "conduct" in the example of the driver: "The conduct (being) which corresponds to the sign that is encountered, is . . . to 'give way.'"[4] His entire analysis of "going about" (*Umgang*) is an undercutting of any psychological characterization of his subject, such as still survives to some extent in the *Prolegomena*, as we shall see.

We have already seen that this undercutting is undertaken in *Being and Time* with an analysis of being-in and with the concepts he constructs in that analysis—including *Aufgehen in*. This is why I would next compare his use of this terminology from the *Prolegomena* in *Being and Time*. When Heidegger presents in the *Prolegomena* his initial example of "psychological conduct," he does emphasize that I am "absorbed in a concrete practical dealing [*Umgehen*] with things [*Sachen*]." But there is no explicit emphasis on the root of either *geht auf* or of *Umgehen*. *Aufgehen in* itself is not a concept which he constructs when he borrows from Grimm's philology in the *Prolegomena* (section 19), as it is in the parallel section in *Being and Time*.

Nevertheless the *Prolegomena* yields more definite evidence than *Being and Time* that Heidegger derived the terminology *Aufgehen in* from Husserl. Consider his exposition of how the reduction intervenes in Husserl:

> When I reduce the concrete experiential context [*Erlebniszusammenhang*] of my life . . . after the reduction I still have the same concrete experiential context. . . . But now I do not have it in such a

fashion that I am absorbed in the world, following the natural direction of the acts [of consciousness] themselves.[5]

Holism

In order to be more specific, I single out in the last sentence what seems certainly an echo of Husserl's use of terminology with respect to the natural direction of our acts of consciousness. The difference between Heidegger's usage and Husserl's is that (as in *Being and Time*) I am, according to Heidegger, "absorbed in the world" instead of in acts of consciousness. With "in the world," as well as with *Erlebniszusammenhang*, we recognize how Heidegger is blending his own holism into what is ostensibly just an exposition of Husserl.

Although we are "absorbed in the world" already in the *Prolegomena, Aufgehen in* does not yet have in the *Prolegomena* the "double meaning" (as I have called it for the purpose of pursuing my comparison with Husserl) that it will acquire in *Being and Time*. The ambulatory meaning of the root is not yet brought into play in the *Prolegomena*.

Let me press this point. The first instance in which *Aufgehen in* is employed in the "Main Part" of the *Prolegomena* is in section 22, "How the Tradition Bypassed the Question of the Worldliness of the World." What is striking is that when Heidegger employs in this "Main Part" the terminology *Aufgehen in*, the debt to Husserl, which was so apparent in the "Preparatory Part," is no longer apparent, for his undertaking is to deal instead with the tradition at large. At this juncture I would renew the argument, which I have offered with respect to *Being and Time*, that how Heidegger deals with the tradition at large cannot be accounted for unless we sometimes recognize that he is not dealing with the tradition at large but specifically with Husserl's individual philosophy.

This is not just a scholarly quibble. It is Heidegger's holistic ambition to deal with the tradition as if it were a homogeneous whole. I am protesting that the history of philosophy is no longer the history of philosophy if we do not acknowledge the differences between individual philosophies, as I would, for instance, acknowledge the differences between Heidegger and Husserl.

The Visual Idiom

In the "Main Part" of the *Prolegomena, Aufgehen in* assumes a certain prominence. Indeed it is awarded italics in the course of his explanation that in the tradition,

> the original way of encountering the *Umwelt* evidently cannot be directly grasped; . . . this phenomenon is instead bypassed in a char-

acteristic fashion. This is no accident, inasmuch as Dasein as being-in-the-world is *absorbed* in the world in which it is concerned, is so to speak exhausted [*mitgenommen*] by that world, so that . . . the world in its worldliness is not experienced thematically at all.[6]

Thus "the world in its worldliness" is "bypassed" and is denied the holistic priority which we have already seen it receives in the sequence of steps followed in *Being and Time*.

There is, however, at this juncture a difference between the *Prolegomena* and *Being and Time*. In the *Prolegomena* Kisiel appropriately translates *aufgeht in* in the passage I have quoted by "absorbed," since there is no attempt by Heidegger to bring out the force of its root. In fact Heidegger's applying "so to speak" to the accompanying concept, *mitgenommen*, implies that it too should be construed in a psychological sense and not in any merely physical sense.

The next time the term "absorbed" is employed in the *Prolegomena* is in subsection 23a:

> The genuine relation to the (piece of) of equipment is to be occupied in using it [*der gebrauchende Umgang*]; it is absorbed in [*geht in . . . auf*] the reference. Here is something essential: The concern looks away [*sieht auf*] in a certain sense from the tool as thing.[7]

I have retained Kisiel's translations "occupied" and "absorbed." Just as my "literal" translation, "going about," which brings out the force of the root of *Umgang* in *Being and Time*, would seem inappropriately stilted here, so also would the translation, "the (piece of) equipment goes out into the reference."

Furthermore, when Heidegger then states "something essential" about "the concern," "*sieht auf*" prevails as an idiom over "*geht . . . auf.*" To this extent, the predominant idiom is still visual, as in Husserl, granted that it is no longer a matter of visual consciousness as a singling out of something it is consciousness *of,* as in Husserl's intentional analysis. Heidegger's analysis instead becomes relational as soon as "concern looks away . . . from the tool as thing."

In section 23a the things themselves qualify as ambulatory:

> Things step back [*treten zurück*] constantly into the referential totality, or, more properly stated, in the closeness of everyday *Umgang*, they never even initially step out of the referential totality, which itself is primarily encountered in the form of familiarity. . . . Things step back into relations.[8]

This passage is embarrassing, with things stepping back into the referential totality when they never step out of it. Things stepping back, or not stepping out, are apparently dynamic variations on the standard idiom (also found in section 23a), whereby things "stand out" in a visual field or do not "stand out." Heidegger is apparently attempting to render an experience of the visual field in which the initiative is transferred to things themselves and away from our consciousness of them, on which Husserl relies. In *Being and Time*, however, the significant use of the ambulatory idiom is reserved for the Dasein (or some surrogate), which becomes the grammatical subject of whatever form of *aufgehen* is employed, so that it can display its "double meaning."[9]

If the ambulatory idiom thus tends to displace in *Being and Time* the visual idiom, which Husserl found appropriate to analyzing acts of consciousness, it is not just that "going about" displaces acts of consciousness as the subject for phenomenological analysis in *Being and Time;* the ambulatory idiom (as we saw in Chapter 16) also comes to apply to the conduct of the analysis itself in *Being and Time*.

Relational Analysis

In section 23a of the *Prolegomena*, Heidegger lists the "phenomena of encounter" to be analyzed: *"reference, referential totality, the closed character of the referential context, familiarity of the referential whole, things not stepping out of referential relations . . ."*[10] The roughly corresponding stretch of the analysis in *Being and Time* is section 15, "The Being of the Beings Encountered in the *Umwelt*." There too Heidegger analyzes "reference" and "referential totality."

However, revisions of the "draft" should be noticed. Certain "phenomena of encounter" are no longer encountered in *Being and Time*. I have already mentioned "things not stepping out." There is also "the closed character of the referential context" and its "familiarity." Heidegger's example of this "referential totality" is a room in the *Prolegomena*, as it is also in *Being and Time*. Its "closed character" is a conclusion which Heidegger obtains in the *Prolegomena* as follows:

> The multiplicity of things encountered here is not an arbitrary multiplicity of incidental things; it is at the outset only present in a definite context of references. This referential context is itself a *closed whole*. It is out of this whole that the individual piece of furniture shows itself [*sich zeigt*]. . . . Primarily I see a referential totality as closed, from which the individual piece of furniture stands out. Such an *Umwelt* with its character of a closed referential totality is at the same time distinguished by a specific *familiarity*.[11]

Moving on from this "draft" to the roughly corresponding analysis in *Being and Time*,

What we encounter as nearest to us . . . is the room; and we encounter it, not as "between four walls" in a geometrical sense but as equipment for dwelling [*Wohnzeug*]. Out of this the "arrangement" emerges, and it is in this fashion that any "individual" piece of equipment shows itself.[12]

The room acquires its "closed" character in the *Prolegomena* because Heidegger is still analyzing what is familiar in visual experience; it is a room which I am looking around, and to which my looking around is confined. But the room loses its closed character as a familiar referential totality in *Being and Time*, because it is identified as a *Wohnzeug*, and thus becomes another (piece of) equipment. Thus the analysis becomes entirely an analysis of the mode of being of (pieces of) equipment.

At the same time, what is undergoing analysis in section 15 of *Being and Time* is no longer a matter of looking around a room, as in the *Prolegomena*; it is a matter instead of the spatial "arrangement" (*Einrichtung*) in which the furniture (also *Einrichtung*—perhaps another instance of "double meaning") is implicated as (pieces of) equipment which are used "in-order-to." There is no play in the *Prolegomena* with the word *Einrichtung*, such as we found in section 15 (a piece of furniture remains in the example of the room in section 23a of the *Prolegomena* simply a *Möbelstück*), so that we are not tempted to find in the analysis of this example (as we are tempted in *Being and Time*) an anticipation of the later analysis in both works of "the spatiality of being-in-the-world" in terms of *Ausrichtung* ("directionality"). As compared with the *Prolegomena*, the analysis in *Being and Time* is depsychologized so that ontology will preside.

Weglos

Having suggested that Heidegger would have found the *Prolegomena* still "too psychological" when he employed it as a "draft" for *Being and Time*, I would associate this criticism with Heidegger's own later criticism of Husserl. Here I would anticipate the retrospect the later Heidegger provides in "My Way to Phenomenology" (1963). There he reports how he had responded as a student to Husserl's *Logical Investigations*. He acknowledges that Husserl had, in the first volume of the *Logical Investigations*, "refuted psychologism in logic by demonstrating that the theory . . . of knowledge could not be based on psychology." (A phase of this refutation, the attack on John Stewart Mill's nominalism, I dealt with in Chapter 10.) But Husserl had then faltered, according to Heidegger:

The second volume . . . comprises the description of the acts of consciousness as essential to the structure [*Aufbau*] of knowledge. So psychology after all. . . . Accordingly, Husserl falls back [*fällt* . . . *zurück*] with his phenomenological description of the phenomena of consciousness into the position of psychologism which he has previously refuted. But if so crude a confusion cannot be attributed to Husserl's work, then what is the phenomenological description of the acts of consciousness?[13]

That Husserl's description of acts of consciousness (in the six investigations in the second volume) was inconsistent with his attack in the first volume on psychologism—this was a standard accusation against Husserl, before Heidegger ever appeared on the scene as a philosopher. In the *Prolegomena* Heidegger reports the accusation as made by the neo-Kantian Marburg school. He mentions the review of the *Logical Investigations* by a leader of that school, Paul Natorp, who "praised only the first volume." The second volume, Heidegger continues, Natorp "left unexamined" except "for the claim that it was a falling back [*Rückfall*] . . . into psychology, whose translation [*Übertragung*] into philosophy had been explicitly rejected by Husserl in the first volume."[14]

Natorp's accusation may have rankled in Husserl's mind, for we note how similar were his own appraisals when he dismissed in a marginal comment the phenomenology of *Being and Time* as "a translation of my own," and when in 1930 he accused Heidegger of "misunderstandings and ultimately of interpreting my phenomenology backward from the level [the empirical level] it is its entire meaning to overcome." Heidegger thereby is "falling [*Verfallen*] into . . . 'psychologism.'"[15]

Heidegger himself may have heard an echo of Natorp's criticism of Husserl when he encountered a version of Husserl's 1930 accusation in a 1931 public lecture. At any rate Heidegger alleges (in the *Der Spiegel* interview, conducted three years after "My Way") that the public lecture had led to the break in their personal relation. (I'll consider Heidegger's allegation in Chapter 25.) In any case, the accusations are not just tit-for-tat. At issue is a boundary dispute—the delimitation of philosophy as a subject.

Here, however, I come up against the fact that Heidegger does not press the accusation further in "My Way." This may not just be the reluctance he expresses to attribute "so crude a confusion to Husserl." He may also be conceding his own early confusion. In retrospect he admits, "I could hardly grasp the questions [raised by the *Logical Investigations*] with the definiteness [with which] they are now formulated." He admits he found himself "*weglos*"—not knowing how to proceed.

When Heidegger began lecturing in 1919, he began finding his way. In his first lecture course, *Zur Bestimmung der Philosophie* (1919), he began with the topic "Knowledge and Psychology" (the editor's title). Heidegger announces, "Knowing is a psychological process," but then insists, "Psychology as an empirical science is not a philosophical discipline."[16] By the time he wrote "My Way," Heidegger had become indifferent to any such simple opposition as a resolution of the boundary dispute.

Faltering, falling back into the position one has been attacking, and confusion deserve some attention as occurrences in the history of philosophy. But indifference sometimes also deserves attention, which I take as explaining why Heidegger does not report in "My Way" how his early confusion over the relation between the theory of knowledge and psychology was definitely remedied. "My Way" itself must wait for interpretation until my conclusion. What we can deal with now is the extent to which his indifference is due, not only to the repudiation ("the whole of this is too psychological"), but also to his contempt for "the theory of knowledge."

: # The Theory of Knowledge

*A fundamental phenomenological illusion . . .
consists in having its theme determined by its
mode of investigation.—Heidegger*

The Shift in Subject

Even in the *Prolegomena,* when Heidegger
has cited Natorp's criticism of the second volume of the *Logical Investigations,* it is another criticism of his own which he goes on to
make—of Husserl's "choice of the subtitle,
'Theory of Knowledge' [for the sixth of the
Logical Investigations]." He explains that it
"happened *solely* out of dependency [*ledig-
lich in Anlehnung*] on the tradition."[1] I have
introduced the italics in order to suggest that
even in the *Prolegomena,* where he is ostensibly still Husserl's "disciple," he can interpret
Husserl's conception of philosophy as the by-
product of the tradition and thus elicit my
protest that no philosophy worthy of attention should be discounted in this fashion.

Heidegger's attempt to rescue phenomenology from that dependency is consummated
in *Being and Time,* to which I turn before I resume my comparison with the *Prolegomena.*
In section 12 (the section which we have sampled because Heidegger there introduces the
concepts of "familiarity" and *Aufgehen in*)
Heidegger explains that "the phenomenon
of being-in has for the most part been represented exclusively by a single exemplar—
knowing the world." The "starting point
[*Ausgangspunkt*]" the tradition has accordingly found "for problems in the theory of
knowledge [*Erkenntnistheorie*]" is "the relation between subject and object." Heidegger asks sarcastically, "What is more obvious

[*selbstverständlich*]?"[2] I detect the implication, "What is more unphilosophical?"

The problems in the theory of knowledge (Heidegger's sarcasm continues) are then problems as to "how knowing makes its way 'out of' [*hinaus*] this inner sphere" of the subject. They are, in effect, problems in the relation between psychology (as an investigation of this inner sphere) and the object. But these are the problems to which Heidegger becomes indifferent when he finishes undercutting in his ontology the distinction between the (psychological) subject and (the physical) object, in the fashion I have already illustrated by his analysis of *in*.

Since 1927, when Heidegger vented his sarcasm, nothing has become "more obvious" than the validity of his criticism. If Heidegger's ensuing analysis in the rest of the chapter, "The Worldliness of the World," has elicited more commentary in Anglo-America than anything else in *Being and Time*, it is in some measure because this analysis has been recruited for the widespread repudiation of what I have so far characterized as "depsychologization." This term loses its appropriateness when the issues no longer derive primarily, as they do in the *Prolegomena*, from the critique of psychologism with which Husserl attempts to distinguish "logic" from "psychology." I would now recharacterize the shift in context in Heidegger as "desubjectivation" in order to do justice to the broadening of Heidegger's critique into a critique of the "subjectivism" of modern philosophy. (The term *subjectivation* has already been accommodated in French philosophy.) Heidegger's critique of subjectivism will be implemented historically when the context becomes in the later Heidegger "the history of being"—as I shall anticipate in my concluding chapter.

Once Heidegger has discredited the theory of knowledge in *Being and Time* and his own analysis has become fully ontological there, he need no longer press his criticism of his work as "too psychological." He is no longer preoccupied with the delimitation of the subject of phenomenology from psychology as he was in the *Prolegomena*. There "the question of being" was conjoined with "the question of the being of the intentional," because "Brentano recognized in intentionality the structure which constitutes the authentic nature of a psychological [*psychisch*] phenomenon." Heidegger remains preoccupied in the *Prolegomena* with how "phenomenology is demarcated from psychology [*gegen Psychologie abgrenzt*]."[3]

The shift is evident if we reconsider the example with which Heidegger constructs his concept of "reference" in *Being and Time*: "A (piece of) equipment in its equipmentality is always *in terms of* [*aus*] its belonging together with other (pieces of) equipment: equipment for writing, pen, ink, paper, blotting pad, table, lamp, furniture, windows, doors, room." I suggested that Heidegger is here refurbishing, in the context of his own relational analysis, the second example with which Husserl elaborates his concept of "intentionality": "Round about the sheet of paper lie books, pencils, an inkstand, and so forth, also 'perceived in a certain fashion.'" But "while I was turned toward the paper [in Husserl's first example] . . . they were not . . . grasped singly."[4]

This example was in Husserl an example of a "turning of the look" (*Wendung des 'Blickes'*) which he identifies as the turning "not . . . merely of the physical, but rather of the *mental look.*" In *Being and Time* this psychological "turning" is superseded when Heidegger constructs the concept of *Bewandtnis* as applicable to a "turning" in which one piece of equipment is "involved" with another piece. I suspect that he is deliberately attempting to construct a concept which has the same root as *Wendung.* If so, we have still another concept that he specifically adapted from Husserl. The adaptation suggests he was no longer *Weglos*—he had finally found a "way," an exit from an analysis that was "too psychological" to an ontological analysis.

The Mode of Investigation

In order to examine one stretch of this "way," I resume the citation, which I began in my last chapter, from the account of "reference" in the *Prolegomena:*

> These primary phenomena of encounter—reference, referential totality . . . things not stepping out of referential relations—are of course seen only if the original phenomenological direction of look [*Blickrichtung*] is taken and above all carried out—that is, letting the world be encountered in concern. This phenomenon is bypassed straightaway when the world is approached from the start as given for observation or, as it is for the most part even in the case of phenomenology, when the world is approached just as it shows itself in an isolated, so-called sense-perception of a thing, and this isolated, free-floating perception of a thing is now interrogated with respect to the specific mode of givenness of its object.[5]

Granted that Husserl's psychological idiom of *Blickrichtung* survives here, Heidegger is seeking a break with Husserl with his "that is" explanation.

The conclusion may suggest that this break is merely a shift in *method* that is concomitant with the shift in *subject*—to a relational analysis in which a perception is no longer "isolated" and "free-floating" in the fashion illustrated (we recall) by Husserl's initial example in *Ideas I* of intentional consciousness which singles out a sheet of paper.[6] But I have interrupted the citation from the *Prolegomena* too soon:

There is [in the attempt to isolate sense-perception and treat it in terms of the givenness of its object] a fundamental phenomenological illusion [*Täuschung*], which is peculiarly frequent and persistent. It consists in having its theme determined by the mode of its investigation. For inasmuch as phenomenological investigation is on its side theoretical, the investigator is thereby easily motivated to make its theme conduct toward the world which is specifically theoretical. Thus a specifically theoretical apprehension of the thing is put forward [*ansetzt*] as an exemplary mode of being-in-the-world, instead of phenomenologically putting oneself [*versetzen*] straightforwardly into the traction and accessible context of everyday preoccupation with things [*in den Zug und den Zugangszusammenhang des alltäglichen Umganges mit den Dingen*].[7]

The disparagement here of having the theme "determined by the mode of investigation" is not just a shift in *method* but a premonition of Heidegger's later denial of "the priority" which method enjoys in Husserl.

The issue for me is not whether the "mode of investigation" (or method) is prior, in the sense to which Heidegger is objecting, as determinative of the theme (or subject), or whether the theme (or subject) is prior, in the sense that it should be determinative of the "mode of investigation" (or method). My claim is only that method and subject are to be distinguished, because neither is unilaterally determinative, and that their respective functions—and thus the relation between them—can differ from one philosophy to another.

In *Being and Time* we have already discovered that it is feasible to distinguish Heidegger's method from his subject, but not to separate them, for there is an affinity between his "mode of investigation," as determining the direction in which his investigation should proceed, and the "theme," whereby being-there is "always directed and on its way."[8] This "theme" is already illustrated by the prominence of *Blickrichtung* in the *Prolegomena*.

Obstruction

The evidence in the *Prolegomena* as to the direction in which the investigation is proceeding encourages a comparison with Husserl, inasmuch as Heidegger is still committed there from the outset to an intentional analysis, even though his analysis also becomes relational.

Consider the first example Heidegger introduces in the *Prolegomena*:

Let us present an exemplary and easily accessible [*zugänglichen*] case of "psychological conduct": a concrete and natural perception, the perception of a chair which I find when entering a room in my way and push out of the way. I stress that in order to point out that we would get at the most everyday kind of perception and not perception in the accentuated [*betonten*] sense in which we observe for the sake of observing. Natural perception as I experience it in moving in my world is for the most part not an autonomous [*eigenständiges*] observation . . . of things, but rather is absorbed [*geht auf*] in a concrete practical dealing [*Umgang*] with things. . . . I do not perceive in order to perceive but in order to orient myself, to open a way [*Weg zu bahnen*] in order to do something.[9]

If this example can be commended as "easily accessible," its selection also betrays the direction in which Heidegger is proceeding—toward gaining access, and on a "way" which is obstructed and which he would open up.

In Chapter 8 I examined this procedure of Heidegger's in terms of his translation of *ēporēkamen* by *sind wir in Verlegenheit gekommen.* I had suggested then that nothing may be more intimate to a philosophy than its conception of a "difficulty." Heidegger's conception is built into the present example from the *Prolegomena,* even though the ambulatory idiom itself (in the instances of *aufgehen in* and *Umgang mit,* as I have already pointed out with respect to other passages in the *Prolegomena*) does not yet take on the more "literal" sense it gains in *Being and Time.*

That Heidegger's "mode of investigation" (in his terminology) in the *Prolegomena,* as in *Being and Time,* is a matter of gaining access is also evident in Heidegger's higher-level explanation there as to why he is bringing the problem of intentionality to the fore: "We want to treat intentionality first, precisely because contemporary philosophy . . . even now finds it a genuine obstacle [*Anstoss*], because intentionality impedes an immediate and unprejudiced reception of what phenomenology would undertake."[10] In particular he emphasizes that "for the Marburg School . . . intentionality remained the real obstacle, obstructing access to phenomenology." When Heidegger deals with this obstacle, he encounters a further obstacle in another prejudice:

It should first be noted that in this undertaking to make intentionality clear—that is, to see and to grasp what it is—we cannot hope to succeed in a single move [*Schlag*]. We must free ourselves from the prejudice that because phenomenology requires us to grasp the things themselves, these things must be grasped with a single move, without any preparation. Rather the movement forward toward the things is complicated [*Umständlich*], and before anything else has to remove the prejudices which *verbauen* things ["obstruct" our way to "things," by the "faulty construction" imposed on them].[11]

A specific obstacle that Heidegger here encounters as an obstructing prejudice is the procedure of a "single move."[12] This move is not attributable to Marburg but is the philosophical *epochē* with which Husserl seeks to free himself from prejudices in order to proceed at once "to the things themselves." The "single move" Heidegger would replace by "preparation" in the guise of a "sequence of steps." An instance of this "preparation" in the *Prolegomena* is, of course, the "Preparatory Part," and in *Being and Time* we have "Division One: Preparatory Fundamental Analysis of Dasein." In his "sequence," I focus in the "Preparatory Part" and in the "Preparatory Fundamental Analysis" on the steps which are deconstructive of Husserl.

Interpretative Tendencies

The example of the "chair" does not reappear in *Being and Time* because it is in the *Prolegomena* an example of an intentional object we are conscious of, and Heidegger's analysis in *Being and Time* is no longer an intentional analysis. Nevertheless, gaining access is still characteristic of his "mode of investigation." He only needs a different example:

> When I open the door, for example, I make use of the knob. Gaining phenomenological access to the beings . . . encountered entails much more pushing away the interpretative tendencies which keep pushing themselves upon us and running along with us, and which conceal . . . those beings themselves. . . . These clutching misconceptions become plain, if we now in our investigation ask, What beings shall become our preliminary subject [*Vorthema*]?
> One answers, things [*Dinge*].[13]

In my previous exposition of section 15 I overlooked this example of opening the door because I was comparing Husserl's eidetic reduction with Heidegger's procedure for constructing concepts, and no concept is constructed with this example, although we would have expected from the precedent of Husserl's eidetic reduction that an example would only be brought up in order to arrive at a concept.

Heidegger, however, would seem to be playing up instead the methodological problem of "gaining phenomenological access." The affinity thereby displayed between method and subject is comparable to the affinity (in contrast with the distinction of level maintained by Husserl) displayed between the met-hodological direction taken in *Being and Time* and "the taking of a direction" which "belongs essentially to the being-in-the-world of the Dasein."

With the emphasis of his "much more," Heidegger further plays up the extent to which he cannot gain access without undertaking the *Destruktion* of misconceptions. Recall that the second German word of *Being and Time, offenbar,* called attention to itself because it was not the usual translation of the Greek *dēlon.* I then supposed that Heidegger might be avoiding the usual translation "clear," since he did not want to concede that his procedure was "clarification" in the sense that Husserl's was. But "openly" could also be played off against the implication of an "obstruction," for the "difficulty" he faced was conveyed by his translation, *Verlegenheit,* as an explanation of why there was an *aporia,* an impasse; there was "no passage way through."

The *Destruktion* itself is visualized in section 15 as the "pushing away," which is incumbent on us, of "interpretative tendencies that keep pushing themselves upon us." Our hand is, as it were, not just on the knob; it is also "pushing away" these "tendencies." There are (it might almost be said) other hands on hand, for the "misconceptions" are "clutching misconceptions" (*verfänglichen Misgriffe*).[14]

At the same time, the "interpretative tendencies" are "running along side of us [*mitlaufenden*]." Their pace rather overtakes the example itself. There we were ostensibly only about to go into the room. But continue the citation: "One answers, things [*Dinge*]." When this designation is accepted for the beings that are "given as nearest" (*zunächst gegebenen*), one "goes astray ontologically." The misconception is intruded by the tradition in the guise of the Latin *res* for "things," which Heidegger goes behind to the "appropriate term" which "the Greeks had . . . for 'things': *pragmata*—that is, what one has to do with in one's concerned *Umgang* (*praxis*)."

The Latin translation *res* provides a succinct illustration of how the tradition "renders what it 'transmits' so little accessible that at the outset and for the most part it covers it over." Here we can again anticipate the later Heidegger's complaint, "The translation of Greek words into Latin is in no way the inconsequential process it is still held [to be] to this day."[15]

Straightforwardness

My interest now, however, is in Heidegger's behest in the *Prolegomena* for straightforwardness, which accompanies his warning there that the "fundamental phenomenological illusion . . . consists in having its theme determined by the mode of its investigation."[16] This warning I take not only as a premonition of Heidegger's later denial of "the priority" that method enjoys in Husserl, but also as a rebuff to my own attempt to get at the differences in their methods. I would accordingly review the implications emerging from my exposition.

My claim is that if we would appreciate the distinctive character of Heidegger's undertaking in *Being and Time,* we cannot accept its presentation as his coping with "things" (*Dinge* as bequeathed him by the Latin language and the tradition at large). Despite the fact that Heidegger never cites a sentence from Husserl in *Being and Time,* certain specific steps that Heidegger takes can only be accounted for adequately by bringing into relief his opposition to Husserl. Thus at the step Heidegger takes with the example of opening the door, I am arguing that the "interpretative tendencies" which he is "pushing away" are specifically Husserl's. That is where the *Destruktion* in section 15 is headed—toward the undercutting in section 16 of Husserl's conception of the intentional object as given *vorhanden.* This claim, which I made in Chapter 17, I am renewing in order to assess Heidegger's behest for straightforwardness.

The behest is less blunt in *Being and Time* than in the *Prolegomena,* but the passage in *Being and Time* is the only version which was available for Husserl to comment on. I cite the passage:

[This phenomenological interpretation] as an investigation of being, is the bringing out . . . explicitly . . . that understanding of being which belongs already to Dasein. . . . The beings which are phenomenologically our preliminary theme, those which are used, . . . become accessible when we put ourselves into the position of concern with them. But strictly speaking, 'putting ourselves [*Sichversetzung*] into such a position' is misleading, for the mode of being which belongs to such concerned *Umgang* is not one into which we need to put ourselves first [*erst zu versetzen*]. This is the way everyday Dasein always *is:* when I open the door, for example, I make use of the knob.[17]

Here Heidegger might well be regarded as using the *Prolegomena* as a "draft" and revising the passage on straightforwardness I cited earlier from section 23a. He is, in effect at least, correcting with his "strictly speaking" the argument there, granted that he ostensibly is correcting as "misleading" only his preceding invitation in *Being and Time* itself—"to put ourselves" into such a position. In *Being and Time* this behest becomes unnecessary, inasmuch as there the mode of being of the Dasein, as it "goes about," becomes simply determinative, as compared with what was also acknowledged in the *Prolegomena* as "the mode of investigation." All that Heidegger admits he is doing in *Being and Time* is "bringing out . . . explicitly . . . the understanding of being which belongs already to Dasein." Thus when I am using the knob to open the door to enter the room, I already understand implicitly the mode of being which is "going about." The example of opening the door in *Being and Time* obtains its cogency from the ontological emphasis of Heidegger's italicized "*is*" in the passage quoted above.

Into this comparison between the two works I would now reintroduce Husserl. When Heidegger in the *Prolegomena* drew our attention to the natural attitude as "the starting position [*Ausgangsstellung*] of the reductions," I considered the sense in which the natural attitude was for Husserl an *Ausgang*, but I overlooked the sense in which it was a "position," even though I was citing Husserl's chapter which refers in its title to "The Positing [*Thesis*] of the Natural Attitude." In contrast Heidegger's idiom of "putting oneself straightforwardly" is presented as merely colloquial straightforwardness (presuppositionless, unmethodical)—as is befitting when what is under investigation is the *Umgang* and not a philosophical "positing." But I would nonetheless interpret his "phenomenologically putting oneself straightforwardly into the traction and accessible context of everyday preoccupation" as Heidegger's positioning himself against Husserl's philosophical *Thesis*.

The "traction" in the *Prolegomena* seems designed to supersede Husserl's "positing" of a "natural attitude." Heidegger protests that the natural attitude is

> an experience which is completely *unnatural*. . . . This kind of conduct [*Haltung*] and experience [Husserl's "simple meditations" are translated into "conduct," and his usual term for "experience," *Erlebnis*, into *Erfahrung*] is rightly called an attitude [*Einstellung*]. . . . One must place oneself into [*hineinstellen*] this mode of consideration in order to be able to experience [*erfahren*] in this manner.[18]

Einstellung is Husserl's term. He is the candidate for the irony of Heidegger's "rightly called." With his translations Heidegger is thinking of himself as only yielding to the "traction."

Strictly Speaking

Although Husserl did not have the assistance of this explicit criticism of himself in the *Prolegomena*, it is evident from a marginal comment on the roughly parallel passage I have cited from *Being and Time* that he recognized the issue with respect to which Heidegger was criticizing him. Husserl underlines in the text Heidegger's phrase *in einem Sichversetzen in solches Besorgen* ("when we put ourselves into the position of concern [with things]"). In his marginal comment Husserl rejects Heidegger's "strictly speaking" and reasserts with his visual idiom the initiative the investigator cannot avoid exercising: "But of course we must represent [*vergegenwärtigen*] a concern to ourselves, or reflect on a concern which is directly taking its course [*gerade im Gange*], and indeed 'look at' it and ask about it."[19]

Husserl offers a similar marginal challenge as soon as Heidegger goes on to construct with the example of the hammer the concept of *readiness-to-hand*. Heidegger had himself commented on the example, "When we only look at things 'theoretically,' we lack understanding of readiness-to-hand." Husserl's challenge is, "But of course it is necessary to look theoretically at the (piece of) equipment in order to conceive it objectively [*gegenständlich erfassend zu haben*] as such and to explain it by describing it." Heidegger would not accept "of course it is necessary." The Dasein in its "going about" will only come to conceive the (piece of) equipment when it exhibits some un-ready-to-handness.

A general methodological issue emerges between them here, which can be formulated by turning back to Husserl's comment on the beginning of section 15, where Heidegger had stated, "The kind of *Umgang* which is nearest to us, is not mere perceptual knowledge, but rather concern which manipulates and uses things, and it has its own 'knowledge.'" Husserl asks in the margin, "Why regard this as knowledge?" What is at issue is his different conception of knowledge, as is evident from his preceding question here, "What does 'nearest' mean [*heisst*]?" This criterion is puzzling to a philosopher whose "principle of all principles" committed him to knowledge which would be immediately given.

This difference over criteria pervades their respective philosophies. I am only reviewing it now for its bearing on Heidegger's behest for straightforwardness, which he backs up with his claim that a "fundamental phenomenological illusion . . . consists in having its theme determined by the mode of its investigation." My own claim is rather that a fundamental phenomenological illusion is the presumption that straightforwardness is feasible in the undertaking of proceeding directly "to the things themselves" without making any methodological commitment. When Husserl so proceeds, he is committing himself to the prospect of their immediate givenness; when Heidegger so proceeds, he is committing himself to those things which are "nearest."

That the traditional theory of knowledge should go permanently out of business is an outcome which we have heard Heidegger encourage with his sarcasm. It is an outcome which I suspect is not very likely. But if it transpires, then we might reassign the rubric "theory of knowledge" to dealing, in the way I have illustrated in this volume, with the methodological criteria that determine what "knowledge" is—as in the question raised by Husserl's challenge to Heidegger, "Why regard this as knowledge?"

We can reach a final conclusion regarding the procedural principle of going directly "to the things [*Sachen*] themselves" only when we have taken into account the revision of this principle by the so-called "later Heidegger," so that it becomes "to the subject [*Sache*] itself." I would not, however, leave the Heidegger of *Being and Time* behind without commenting on the impasse we have reached between him and Husserl, insofar as it involves the problem of communication—the problem which I have attempted to bring to the fore.

SIX · COMMUNICATION

TWENTY-THREE

Language

> Communication is never anything like a
> transporting of experiences . . . from the inside of
> one subject into the inside of another.
> —Heidegger

The Impasse

I have focused in my exposition on the breaks
in Heidegger's relation to Husserl that are lo-
catable in Heidegger's analysis of "being-in"
and "worldliness" in *Being and Time* and at
roughly corresponding junctures in the *Prolegomena.* I have stressed the specificity of
these breaks as over against Heidegger's own
broader preoccupation with his *Destruktion*
of the tradition at large. If my exposition is to
be completed, some account is needed of what
happens to Heidegger's relation to Husserl
further on in *Being and Time,* so that it is no
longer feasible to locate breaks as specific as
those I have been eliciting.

In the sequence of steps Heidegger takes
in *Being and Time,* I have so far gone no further than the first part ("A") of the chapter,
"The Worldliness of the World." That Husserl
is then left behind, displaced by Descartes, is
indicated by the title of the second part ("B"),
"The Bringing into Relief of the Analysis of
Worldliness by Opposing It to Descartes's Interpretation of the World." When Heidegger
resumes his own analysis, Husserl is no longer
relevant as the antagonist I have argued he
implicitly was at previous steps.

Nevertheless, a later step can be singled
out as yielding evidence as to one step at
which the impasse widens between them so as
to become impassible in a new sense.

I was accepting Heidegger's own guidance in section 17 as to where Husserl was

relevant when I followed out Heidegger's footnote, which alluded to "the analysis of signs and meaning" in the first chapter of the second volume of the *Logical Investigations*. I accordingly compared with this analysis Heidegger's analysis of signs in section 17 and Heidegger's analysis of meaning in section 18. If that comparison was convincing, it now seems plausible to seek Heidegger's next footnote alluding to Husserl. We have a long wait—until section 34, "Dasein and Speech. Language." What is remarkable about this footnote, as compared with the preceding footnote, is how much less specific it is. In section 17, "Reference and Signs," the footnote specified sections of *Ideas I* as well as the first chapter in the first of the *Logical Investigations*. This next footnote alludes sweepingly to the "doctrine of meaning in the first of the *Logical Investigations* and in the fourth through the sixth."[1]

Furthermore, specific details in Heidegger's analysis of signs in section 17 underpinned the comparisons I sought with Husserl's analysis, but the sentence in section 34, to which the footnote is attached, is as sweeping as the footnote itself: "The doctrine of meaning is rooted in the ontology of Dasein. On it depends the fate [*Schicksal*] of [this doctrine] for better or worse."

If the absence of any allusions to Husserl in between these two footnotes is justification for skipping over the intervening steps in *Being and Time*, further justification can be found in Heidegger's anticipating section 34 in section 18. The sentence in section 34 to which the footnote is attached and in which Heidegger looks back over his earlier analysis, can be compared with the sentence in section 18 in which he looks forward to his later analysis:

> But in meaningfulness itself, with which Dasein is always familiar, there resides the ontological condition which makes it possible for Dasein . . . to disclose something of the sort which "meanings" are; upon these meanings, in turn, is founded the being of words and of language.[2]

When Heidegger actually reaches section 34, he draws attention with italics to "the fact that language is *now for the first time* our theme."

At this step, however, we encounter a complication of a sort I have so far dodged. In the margin next to what I have quoted from section 18 the later Heidegger entered perhaps the most explicit disavowal of any step in his analysis in *Being and Time*: "Not true. Language is not stacked up [*aufgestockt* ("added as another floor")] but is the original essence of truth as there." The issue here is sequence: "language" should not have had to wait until this section to become Heidegger's theme "for the first time." It should have been the ground floor—if he were not with his comment implicitly criticizing the idiom of "floors" itself. There are no "floors" in "the house of being"—to anticipate an idiom of the later Heidegger's.[3]

This repudiation in the margin would not concern me any more than his previous marginal comments, even though none of them was so drastic as "Not true." But here I have to acknowledge that if Heidegger had not postponed "language," as Husserl also did at the start of the first of his *Logical Investigations,* he would not have been able to accommodate the relation to Husserl which I have demonstrated held earlier in *Being and Time.* Then the comparisons I have undertaken of their respective analyses of signs and meaning would not have been feasible. Thus Heidegger's repudiation may itself help explain the remarkable fact to which I drew attention in my introduction—the disappearance for nearly thirty years of any extended treatment on Heidegger's part of his relation to Husserl.

Expression

Section 34 itself yields evidence as to how and why Husserl becomes irrelevant in *Being and Time* itself—as soon as Heidegger reaches "language." In fact the footnote to section 17 already yielded obliquely some of this evidence. The footnote referred to the first of the *Investigations* as an "analysis of signs and meaning." This reference is consistent with the sequence of topics Heidegger followed in his own analysis: "signs" in section 17 and "meaning" in section 18. But the actual title of the first of the *Investigations* is not "Signs and Meaning," but "Expression [*Ausdruck*] and Meaning." The topic "expression" is again not mentioned in the footnote attached to section 34 where Heidegger refers to Husserl's "doctrine of meaning."

"Expression" did turn up in Heidegger's long list of signs in section 17, but it was included along with eight other varieties of sign which were listed in what was hardly more than a demonstration of their miscellaneousness. "Expression" enjoyed no prominence in the list and received no further attention. I am tempted to borrow the terminology of Heidegger's footnote in which he alludes to "the fate" of "doctrine of meaning" as depending on "the ontology of Dasein." I ask, Why is it the fate of the "expression" to be discarded, once the doctrine of meaning comes to depend in Heidegger on this ontology?

The discarding was in a sense already implicit in Heidegger's treatment of what were distinguished in Husserl as "two kinds of sign": Husserl excluded as irrelevant one kind, the "indicative sign," and devoted his analysis to the other kind, the (logical) "expression." Heidegger rehabilitated the "indicative sign" in opposition to Husserl. But if Husserl excluded from his analysis the kind of sign that Heidegger included in his, the indicative sign, the exclusion from Heidegger's analysis of the "expression," which Husserl treated, has not yet been accounted for. Although Husserl made clear why he was excluding the indicative sign, Heidegger proceeded promptly to his presentation of the indicator as an exemplary example of the (indicative) sign. Thus we have to wait until section 34 in order to learn that the fate of the "expression" is its replacement by another concept, which Heidegger introduces when he explains how the two topics, which he has posted in the title of section 34 (*Da-sein und Rede. Sprache*), are related: "*Die Hinausgesprochenheit der Rede ist die Sprache* [The outspokenness of speech is language]."[4]

This sentence Macquarrie and Robinson translate, "The way in which speech gets expressed is language." (Stambaugh offers the same translation.) They defend this translation by commenting that "the verbs '*ausdrücken*' and '*aussprechen*' are roughly synonymous," so they decide "it is often sufficient to translate '*aussprechen*' as 'express.'" They do not ask why the term *Ausdruck* itself is only found in quotation marks in section 34, as if it did not belong to Heidegger's own philosophy. Regrettably, they conduct their defense by citing "connotations" they have gleaned from a dictionary as "specific" to *aussprechen*. But a dictionary is not the final adjudicator when translating a philosopher, for it is still necessary to determine what connotations are congenial to the philosophy itself. Here the differences between Heidegger's and Husserl's philosophies disturb any rough synonymy the dictionary may yield.

The problem of translation into English can hardly be separated from what I earlier dubbed the problem of philosophical "translation." Heidegger may well prefer the term *Hinausgesprochenheit* because of its root connection with *Sprache* ("language"). But I suggest he is also deliberately avoiding *Ausdruck* ("expression") because he construes it as belonging to Husserl's analysis, which he is rejecting.

To appreciate this rejection, recall how the process of communication comes up in Husserl. I grant it does not come up as such, but rather in the course of Husserl's effort to demarcate his subject. As he bluntly emphasizes in *Ideas I*, "*Logical meaning [Bedeutung] is expression*."[5] But in order to demarcate "the logical-expressive realm," he must still disentangle "meaning" from its entanglement in communicative speech with the indicative sign. In the passage of *Ideas I* in which Husserl alludes to his discussion in the *Logical Investigations,* he further elaborates the distinction between the fundamental "stratum," the logical expression of meaning, and the stratum at which meaning is expressed in language, spoken or written. With this distinction, problems of language can be postponed. When Heidegger rebukes himself in the margin for having in section 34 "stacked up" language as an "added floor," the similarity between his idiom and Husserl's suggests an implicit rejection by Heidegger of the distinction in Husserl between the stratum of logical expressions of meaning and the stratum of linguistic expression.

Transportation

In any case, Husserl's distinction cannot survive in *Being and Time*. When Heidegger in Chapter 2 originally oriented his analysis toward "being-in," it was in order to undercut ontologically the one-sided distinction in Husserl of the "inner," psychological sense of "in" from its "external," physical sense. Heidegger's primary concern, which I commented on in my last chapter, was to undercut this distinction insofar as it was involved in phenomenology having become a "theory of knowledge," in which the "being-inside of knowing" was presumed, and the question had to be asked sarcastically, "How knowing makes its way 'out of' [*hinaus*] this inner sphere."

This earlier undercutting in section 12 of Chapter 2 of the problem of the relation between "subject" and "object" prepares the way for the undercutting in section 34 of the problem of the relation between one "subject" and another "subject," posed as a problem of communication—as it is treated by Husserl in his chapter, "Expression and Meaning." Indeed, it is this earlier preparation which has enabled me to run the risk of skipping the intervening steps in *Being and Time* in order to reach this later step.

One reminder in section 34 of section 12 is that Heidegger is again sarcastic:

> Communication is never anything like a transporting of experiences, such as opinions [*Meinungen*] and wishes, from the inside of one subject into the inside of another. . . . In speech Dasein speaks itself out, not because it has at the outset been encapsulated as something "inside" over against something "outside," but because as being-in-the-world, Dasein is already "outside."[6]

A certain finality is flourished with Heidegger's "never."

Although the analysis in section 12 was ostensibly directed against the tradition, details suggested that Husserl was Heidegger's specific antagonist. Heidegger now seems to be mocking Husserl's conception of communication as presuming the distinctions between inside/outside, subject/object, subject/subject.

Heidegger's playing up the prefix *aus* of *Ausgesprochenheit* may recall how the force of this prefix was debilitated when Husserl elaborated the concept of *Ausdruck*, which Heidegger would displace. Husserl had sought a concept of the distinctively logical expression of meanings by abstracting it (with an eidetic reduction) from any "outward" reference.

What is at issue between Heidegger and Husserl at this present step deserves particular attention, inasmuch as it is a *breakdown in communication* with respect to "*communication*" itself. Indeed, Husserl is capable at this juncture of mocking Heidegger. In the 1931 lecture which Heidegger regards as an attack on him, Husserl in effect flings back the inside/outside distinction at him:

> Has this talk of "outside" and "inside," if it has any meaning [*Sinn*] at all, is it not a meaning conferred and verified by me? I should not forget that the totality of whatever I can think of as being, lies within the universal realm of my consciousness.[7]

Period

Singling out section 34 as a step in *Being and Time* is not just a matter of the problem of communication finally emerging, which I would myself bring to the fore. At this step I am halted in my exposition by a complication in Heidegger's own analysis. Of course I have already been halted by his later disavowal in the margin of section 34 of his treatment of language there. But a complication arises at this step in *Being and Time* itself, and it is betrayed by the title of section 34: "Dasein and Speech [*Rede*]. Language." There is no comparable instance in the eighty-three section titles in *Being and Time* where Heidegger resorts to a period to separate the topics he is lining up for treatment.[8]

Such a period seems anomalous, given that his analysis is relational. Heidegger often links topics with an "and"—for instance, "Reference and Signs," "Involvement and Meaning." In these two cases I have tried to bring out the relational significance of the "and" and how the "bringing into relief" (*Abhebung*) of one topic brings "with" it (*Mithebung*) the other topic. On one occasion Heidegger employs a colon, on which I commented in Chapter 16. But, I repeat, in no other comparable instance do we encounter the full stop of a period.

That this full stop is not only unprecedented but also seems grammatically unnecessary may explain why Stambaugh apparently presumes it must be a misprint and substitutes a colon. (Macquarrie and Robinson respect the period.) The full stop can be explained partly by reference to the step Heidegger will be taking next. The period is in effect an admission that he cannot proceed directly from *Rede* (the preceding topic in the title and in section 34 itself) to a treatment of *Sprache*, even though it has been defined as the "outspokenness of *Rede*." He must interrupt the sequence and take *Gerede* ("talkativeness," "loquacity") into account, which he does in section 35.

My concern is not with mere punctuation, but with the prospect of a precipice. I am alluding to Heidegger's own comparison of *Being and Time* to "climbing a mountain which has never been climbed before," for "anyone traveling that way encounters sometimes a precipice," which (Heidegger adds) "the reader may not notice," since "the page numbers continue."[9]

The break in continuity, in sequence, we are now confronting may indeed be a "precipice," since Heidegger, before going on to section 35, explicitly acknowledges the break with a commentary, introduced under the heading "B"—"The Everyday Being of the There and the Falling of the Dasein." In this commentary he concedes that "the everydayness of the Dasein has been lost sight of," and that "the analysis must regain this phenomenal horizon which was the thematic starting point." The concession can only be appreciated fully by turning back to the introduction to *Being and Time*. Heidegger had announced in the initial preamble that he was undertaking "the interpretation of time as a possible horizon for the understanding of being." In section 5 of the introduction, he characterized the "everyday" interpretation of time as "at the outset [*zunächst*] and for the most part," the temporal horizon that is "nearest" [*nächst*] to us.[10]

If Heidegger had enforced his own criterion of "proximity" from "the outset," Husserl would not have retained the relevance in chapters 2 and 3 of *Being and Time* that my exposition has demonstrated that he did. A horizon is all-embracing, and although the spatial idiom of "horizon" is itself Husserl's, there is no such temporal horizon as "everydayness" in Husserl.

I am not asserting that this postponement, any more than the postponement of "language," was necessarily intended by Heidegger to enable him to accommodate his relation to Husserl. If it were, I could more confidently pursue my original suggestion that Heidegger was attempting in *Being and Time* the dialogue that seemed proposed by the citation from the *Sophist* at the start of *Being and Time*. I do not pretend to have so conclusive an insight into Heidegger's intentions.

Once the horizon of "everydayness" is regained in "B" of chapter 5, Husserl is, as it were, over Heidegger's horizon. If this is not evident from the "everydayness" replacing the "natural attitude," which was where Husserl began, it is evident from the rest of the title of "B"—"and the Falling of the Dasein." This is the sort of thing that Husserl eventually rejects as "theological-ethical talk" in the margin of his copy of *Being and Time*.[11]

The period in the title of section 34 that has halted me does not spare me some unfinished business. Heidegger has asserted in section 34 what "communication is never anything like," and this dismissal has seemed applicable to Husserl. But what is communication "like" for Heidegger himself?

I cannot deal with this question without making an adjustment in my exposition. I can no longer continue the close comparison back and forth between them that I have previously pursued. Before I can try to deal with the problem of communication in Heidegger, I have to allow for it's being merely marginal in Husserl. Thus in the next chapter I leave Heidegger temporarily to one side and consider Husserl's treatment of the problem, and in the following chapter I go on to Heidegger's conception. It turns out to have a relevance to his relation to Husserl which could hardly have been anticipated and which I shall then take into account in Chapter 25.

TWENTY-FOUR

The Monologue

Through isolation and meditation alone does a
philosopher come into being. —Husserl

Trespassing

So far in my interpretation of Husserl I have
emphasized how he postpones the difficulties
of communicating his philosophy until the
prior "difficulties of pure phenomenological
analysis" have been overcome and essential
"insights" have been obtained which are immediately given. But a fuller account is now
needed of Husserl's conception of "communication" itself, in order to assess from his side
the impasse which we have watched open up
between him and Heidegger as a breakdown
of communication.

When Husserl's *Cartesian Meditations*
was published in French in 1931 and in German in 1950, and *Crisis* was published in
1954, there is no evidence that Heidegger read
these works with the care he had expended
earlier on the *Logical Investigations* and
Ideas I. Accordingly I make no effort to do
justice to Husserl's later works or to his
labyrinthine archives where the *Umarbeitung*
continued. I shall instead go back to the treatment of the problem of communication in the
Logical Investigations and *Ideas I.*

In his second introduction Husserl
speaks of "the persuasive communication to
others of the insights we have obtained."[1]
What I would single out here is that the communication of these insights can only be "persuasive," for the insights themselves can only
be obtained with certainty by the reader in
the same fashion in which Husserl originally

obtained them—that is, as insights into essential structures (such as intentionality) which are immediately given to the individual's own consciousness.

The distinction between pure phenomenological analysis, in the strict sense of a rigorous science, and the process of communicating its insights, which is merely "persuasive," I regard as one of the "essential distinctions" to which the title of the first chapter of the second volume of the *Logical Investigations* alludes. I have called them one-sided distinctions, since what falls on their other side is to be relegated beyond the limits of the subject of phenomenology—in particular, to the empirical science of psychology, whose encroachment on phenomenology proper we have seen Husserl attack as "psychologism."

Nevertheless, there is a qualification I have so far overlooked. Husserl admits that he has at times to "trespass beyond our prescribed limits"— those which delimit the subject of phenomenology. Thus he allows himself to "start . . . from the fact that there are languages," and does discuss "the merely communicative meaning of their many forms of expression."[2] To this purpose the analysis of indicative signs is pertinent, since they are relied on in communication, and he would distinguish from them as linguistic those logical expressions which express immediately given meanings.

Such trespassing can be tolerated: "No damage of course will be done by *gelegentliche Zwischenbemerken* [*"incidental* parenthetical (or marginal) comments"] which are *without influence* on the content and character of the analysis, nor by the many declarations [*Äusserungen*] which the author addresses to his public [*Publikum*], whose existence [like his own] is not therefore presupposed by the content of his investigations" (my italics).

It is not just Husserl's comments on the process of communication that are merely "parenthetical" or "marginal," and are to remain "without influence on the content and the character of the analysis"; the flow of any influence as such is stemmed as soon as his reader takes over, reinitiates with an *Umarbeitung* this analysis, and reaches on his own part identical, eidetic meanings which are not contaminated by the differences between the particular persons involved (the author and members of his reading public) nor by the differences between the particular languages in which the communication may be couched.

Intimation

When I began dealing in Chapter 11 with Husserl's "essential distinctions," I was concerned with their enabling him to postpone any consideration of language, for I was approaching Husserl's delimitation in terms of

Derrida's challenge that "Husserl has had to postpone, from one end to the other of his itinerary, any explicit meditation on the essence of language." Some such challenge to Husserl is almost inevitable, ever since philosophy undertook the so-called "linguistic turn."

The communicative function of linguistic expressions Husserl characterizes as the "intimating" [*kundgebende*] function. In explaining it, he is not directly interested in the function itself, but (I reemphasize) in disentangling from it the mental experiences of meanings in order to delimit the subject of logic. But in achieving this disentanglement, Husserl envisages how the intimating function is performed:

> To understand an intimation is not to have conceptual knowledge of it. . . . The hearer perceives the intimation in much the same sense in which he perceives the intimating person, even though mental phenomena which make him a person cannot, as what they are, come within the intuition of another.[3]

Whereas my perception of my own inner mental experiences is "adequate," inasmuch as it is immediately given, my perception of "an outward bodily thing" is "inadequate," for it remains subject to further confirmation or disconfirmation (as I explained in Volume 2) when we go on to perceive other "aspects" of the thing. Likewise when the hearer hears the other person speak,

> the hearer perceives the speaker as externalizing certain inner experiences, and to that extent he also perceives these experiences themselves; he does not, however, himself experience them, he has not an "inner" but an "external" perception of them. This is the huge difference between the actual grasp of what is adequate intuition and a putative grasp of the basis of intuitive though inadequate representation. In the former case we have to do with experienced being; in the latter case with presumed being, to which no truth corresponds at all.[4]

A similar analysis would hold of the reader who sees the word on the page.

In order to maintain the sharpness of his one-sided distinction between "experienced being" and merely "presumed being," as well as his disentanglement of the logical expressions of mental meanings from expressions in a particular language, Husserl has to deal with how linguistic expressions are used when one talks to oneself:

> Shall we say that even in solitary mental life, one still uses expressions to intimate something, though not to a second person? Shall we say that in soliloquy one speaks to oneself and employs words as signs—that is, as indicative signs—of one's own inner experiences?[5]

Husserl rejects such a view, which would threaten his essential distinction between (logical) expressions and indicative signs and gum up his entire analysis.

In contrast with "expressions used in communication," in the case of

> expressions used in soliloquy . . . we are content with imagined rather than actual words. In imagination the spoken or printed word floats before us, though in truth it does not exist. . . . The word's non-existence . . . has no effect on the function of the expression as an expression.

Indeed, no communication is taking place:

> In a monologue words can perform no function of indicating the existence of mental acts, since such indication would be quite pointless. For the acts in question are themselves experienced by us in the same moment.⁶

When Husserl concludes that the "word . . . does not exist," we recognize that the authority of the author of these *Logical Investigations* cannot reside in what he says there, but resides in the monologue the reader is to conduct in his own "solitary mental life." There (!) Husserl's words no longer perform the function of indicating the existence of mental acts. Thus if "the context and character" of Husserl's own analysis is to be respected, when it is communicated, it must then become for the reader the monologue it was originally for Husserl himself: the reader must disentangle the meanings mediated by the words on Husserl's page, which merely indicate what Husserl means, and these meanings must become immediately given experiences for the reader. Here Husserl's Latin tag, which I cited earlier, finds a justification: "*Tua res agitur*—"It is your own fate which is at issue."⁷

Of course, when something "intimated" is replaced by an immediately given meaning, it no longer remains just your affair. Here Husserl's phenomenology is affiliated as an eidetic science with geometry. His example, which we considered before, is the meaning of the assertion, "The three perpendiculars of a triangle intersect in a point." He explains that anyone, "asked about the meaning . . . of my assertion," will not "revert" to it as "a psychological [*psychisches*] experience" that is merely my own. "Everyone will rather reply:

> What this assertion asserts is *the same* whoever may assert it, and on whatever occasion, or in whatever circumstances he may assert it. . . . One therefore repeats what is in essence "the same" assertion,

and one repeats it because it is the one . . . way of expressing what is identical—that is, its meaning. In this identical meaning, which we are conscious of as identical whenever we repeat the statement, nothing at all about the assertion or whoever made it is to be discovered.[8]

It can be added that from this consciousness nothing at all is to be discovered about the process itself of communicating this assertion. Communication is as irrelevant to phenomenology as it is to geometry; or rather (I repeat), it is irrelevant to phenomenology except insofar as it is a process from which the phenomenologist must disentangle himself. The actual analysis of this process belongs, not to phenomenology proper, but to empirical psychology.

Solipsism

I have been quoting the first of the *Logical Investigations.* Move on to *Ideas I* and recall how there "we begin our considerations as human beings begin living naturally, . . . '*in the natural attitude.*'" What that signifies, Husserl explains, "we shall make clear in simple meditations which can best be carried out in the first person singular."[9] Like many other initial moves made by philosophers, this move may seem, in its simplicity, philosophically neutral. It was intended so by Husserl, who expected his reader would naturally go along with him.

Nevertheless, this first step betrays Husserl's longer-run commitment to meditations carried out in the first person singular. When he later adopts the title *Cartesian Meditations,* he concludes with "the Delphic motto, 'Know thyself'" and with Augustine's appeal, "'Do not wish to go outside; go back into yourself. Truth dwells in the inner man.'"[10]

This traditional twist takes on distinctive implications in Husserl. When in *Ideas I* he has carried out the phenomenological reduction in Part 2 and has applied the traditional term *cogito* to the phenomena he would analyze, he promptly turns to examples in order to carry out eidetic reductions. The first of these examples, "the sheet of paper" which is "lying in front of us," we have already considered, because Heidegger disregarded it in favor of the second.[11] Before employing this example in section 35 (or rather, I should say, in order to arrive promptly at this example), Husserl has put aside in section 34 certain problems regarding the *cogito.* In particular the "I," the ego, is "left out of consideration" in favor of the intentional direction of consciousness toward its *cogitatum* in this and other examples.

Husserl's preoccupation in *Ideas I* is to reach the eidetic and transcendental levels. He thus vindicates his announcement that phenomenology "knows nothing of [particular] persons, of my [particular] experiences or those of others, and conjectures nothing regarding them."[12] Yet phenomenology remains first personal. Husserl can even embrace the stigma "solipsism" once it becomes a rendering of the primacy of the transcendental ego. Here I would not consult further the *Cartesian Meditations,* since there is no evidence that Heidegger read with any care the French translation which came out in 1931. I would instead turn to a lecture of Husserl's in 1931, "Phenomenology and Anthropology," to which Heidegger did pay some attention (as we shall see in my next chapter) and single out one assertion:

> All modern philosophy originates in the Cartesian *Meditations.* . . . This historical proposition means that every genuine beginning of philosophy issues from meditations, from solitary self-reflection [*einsam Selbstbesinnung*]. Autonomous philosophy . . . *comes into being* in the solitary, radical taking [of] responsibility for himself on the part of the philosopher. Through isolation [*Vereinsamung*] and meditation alone does a philosopher come into being, does philosophy as necessary begin in him. (My italics)[13]

As a philosopher I can accept "only what is evident to me . . . as an autonomous ego," but with the phenomenological reduction, this "human solitude" is "transformed into something radically different: the transcendental solitude, the solitude of the [transcendental] ego."

The issue of "solitude," as it would come up for Heidegger, cannot be restricted to his relation to Husserl (as we shall see in Volume 4). It might be appropriate in Husserl's case to pursue the issue into his archives, but since Heidegger never consulted these, I am satisfied to illustrate his transcendental solitude with anecdotes, which I take as betraying not merely his personal idiosyncrasies but his philosophical commitments. Cairns tells about the relatively relaxed occasion of a Christmas party, when Husserl was asked "how he went about it to write a book." Husserl explained that "although he writes a tremendous amount, . . . the smallest part is written with any book in mind." "A tremendous amount" is "in the form of meditations, not destined for other eyes."[14] Casual as is his distinction here of writing for himself from writing for publication, the distinction yet illustrates the essentially meditative character of his philosophy. We encountered this distinction at the beginning of the present volume as a distinction between the *Umarbeitung* of "ever renewed self-reflection," which went into his "research manuscripts," and the kind of *Ausarbeitung* which could be delegated to assistants w'len they prepared manuscripts for publication.

While Husserl did not write regularly for publication, he did lecture regularly to students. Once when Husserl finished a lecture, he turned to Heidegger and said, "Today for once we had an exciting discussion." Hans-Georg Gadamer comments, "He said this after he had spoken without period or comma for the duration of the session in response to the first and only question raised." Gadamer, whose question it was, generalizes that Husserl's lectures "were monologues, but he never saw them as such."[15] This incongruity Gadamer does not bother to explain. Whatever psychological explanation might be alleged, a possible philosophical explanation is that discussion in the usual sense has no prescribed place in phenomenology. Husserl assumed that his lectures were exciting any attentive student to engage in a monologue of his own, in which he was grasping the meaning of what Husserl had said as rendering irrelevant that Husserl in particular had said it. That a particular student had raised a question was likewise irrelevant.

Heidegger told Jean Beaufret a similar anecdote. A student spent her vacation preparing a paper to be presented at a seminar, which Heidegger had organized on behalf of the students. "Husserl interrupted her and did not stop talking until the end of the semester!" Husserl commented to Heidegger, "'Never have students participated as much in the work.'" Yet "in fact they had not gotten a word in edgewise. Fundamentally Husserl was not someone who engaged in dialogue, but was a monologist without contrition."[16] The participation of his students must have been the presumed monologuing of each of them.

Collaboration

I have cited these anecdotes as background for interpreting certain instances of Husserl's inability to collaborate. The primary instance for my purposes here was the breakdown in collaboration with Heidegger over the *Encyclopaedia Britannica* article. But his seemingly successful collaboration with his assistant Eugen Fink also requires some comment, for it may shed some light in retrospect on the optimism with which Husserl initially sought Heidegger's collaboration.

Consider the extravagance of Husserl's prefatory endorsement of a lengthy exposition of his phenomenology by his assistant Eugen Fink: "It contains no sentence which I could not completely accept as my own or openly acknowledge as my own conviction."[17] What conviction of Husserl's is more remarkable than his conviction that there was "no sentence" in the exposition of his phenomenology by another philosopher which he could not completely accept as his own! Such a blanket endorsement is even more incredible than Husserl's taking over completely in response to a student's question. Such instances cannot be explained fully without bringing to bear Husserl's philosophical assumption that anyone who understood his phenomenology would arrive at conclusions which were identical with his own—just as anyone would in the instance of a geometrical proposition.

I have cited Husserl's blanket endorsement of Fink's exposition because it is collaboration of this sort that Husserl must have expected of Heidegger, whom he rebuffed when he did not obtain it for the *Britannica* article.

I have recalled this rebuff for another reason. Any expositor of a philosophy can hardly approach in good conscience the completion of his exposition without considering how his exposition would be received by the philosopher himself. There can be no doubt that Husserl, with his commitment to identity of meaning, would rebuff any exposition such as mine which accords philosophical relevance to the differences at issue between himself and another philosopher.

Husserl's blanket endorsement of Fink's exposition is also to be read in conjunction with Husserl's preceding statements in his prefatory endorsement. If his final emphasis there is on how thoroughly Fink understands his phenomenology, his preceding emphasis is on how thoroughly his critics misunderstand it: "*All* of the criticisms with which I have become acquainted miss the fundamental meaning my phenomenology to such an extent that it is *not in the least affected* by them, despite their quotation of my own words" (my italics).[18] Indeed the "words" do not count; only the meanings to be sought out behind the "words."

One more comment. If instead of answering his critics himself, Husserl has turned their "principal misunderstandings of phenomenology" over to Fink, it is, he explains, because "I regarded it as more important to deal with the demands made by problems relating to the new science."[19] Husserl is here not only proceeding directly to "the things themselves," but is also anticipating the "unassailable claim to truth" which his "work" will have when "completed."

The delegation to Fink is at the same time, like his delegation of *Ausarbeitung* generally to assistants, the relegation of the problem of communicating with others (and of dealing with their criticisms) as extraneous to phenomenology. Thus there may even be a certain impropriety in my idiom "breakdown in communication," if it is taken as implying that the process of communication is more than merely "marginal" for Husserl's philosophy.

Here, as elsewhere, my concern with the relation between Husserl and Heidegger is from Heidegger's side rather than Husserl's. Heidegger's own commitment to dialogue seems evident in his anecdote regarding Husserl's depriving his student of her right to be heard. Indeed Heidegger often stresses "dialogue," "discussion." But how committed in fact was Heidegger to dialogue? This question will continue to haunt my exposition in the rest of this volume and in the next.

TWENTY-FIVE

The Public Reckoning

What induced Husserl to set himself in opposition to my thought with such publicity, I was never able to learn.—Heidegger

The Anyone

When we reached Heidegger's treatment of the problem of communication in *Being and Time,* the mockery was evident in his pronouncement:

> Communication is never anything like a transporting [*Transport*] of experiences ... from the inside of one subject into the inside of another. ... In speech Dasein speaks itself out, not because it has at the outset been encapsulated as something "inside" over against something "outside," but because, as being-in-the-world, Dasein is already "outside."[1]

The heavy labor imputed by *Transport* suggests the impediment Heidegger finds in the inside/outside distinction.

Consistent with his having previously undercut this distinction with his analysis of being-in-the-world, Heidegger constructs in section 34 the concept of "outspokenness" to displace Husserl's concept of "expression." We also saw how Heidegger, on arriving at this step in *Being and Time,* makes so considerable a readjustment in his analysis as to amount to a break in the sequence he himself is following. With this readjustment, he seeks to regain the "horizon" of Dasein's "everydayness," which has been "lost sight of."

Heidegger fills out the analysis of *Rede* ("speech") in terms of "outspokenness" (in section 34) by undertaking (in section 35) an analysis of *Gerede* (everyday "talkativeness," "loquacity"). The addition of the prefix *ge* seems to imply a kind of collective consolidation which *Gerede* exhibits as compared with *Rede*.

My interest is in the process of communication involved in constituting *Gerede*:

> Communication is not "sharing in common" [*Mitteilung "teilt" nicht*] the primary relation of being toward the being that is talked about, but being-with each other is underway [*bewegt sich*] in talking with each other and concern with what is said in the talking. To it what matters is that the talking go on. . . . Things [*Sache*] are so because one says so.[2]

Although the process of communication remains in Husserl external to phenomenology and to its proceeding directly "to the things themselves," the process becomes crucial at this step in *Being and Time,* inasmuch as "things are so because one says so." Accordingly, the impasse between Heidegger and Husserl becomes here even more (so to speak) impassible.

The "loquacity," which thus emerges as an obstruction to applying the principle of proceeding directly "to the things themselves," is so pervasive that the idiom "obstruction" becomes insufficient to convey the difficulty, if it suggests an obstacle that might be gotten out of the way. This is not in prospect:

> From this everyday interpretedness [*Ausgelegtheit*], in which Dasein at the outset has developed, it cannot extricate itself. In it, out of it, and against it, all genuine understanding, interpreting and communication, rediscovering and appropriating anew are to be undertaken.[3]

With the "at the outset" and the "all" we recognize that there is no readily discernible justification for Heidegger's having postponed until now this climax to his analysis of "everydayness" while he brought into relief other "dimensions" of Dasein's being-in-the-world.

Whatever Heidegger intended to accomplish by the postponement, it has enabled him (as I suggested in Chapter 23) to work out his analysis of "the worldliness of the world" in opposition to features of Husserl's phenomenology. Now, however, the impasse is such that the detailed comparisons that I have undertaken at certain previous steps are no longer feasible. We arrive instead, as I pointed out before, at "talkativeness," "everydayness," and "the falling of the Dasein," and this sort of thing Husserl will eventually simply dismiss—"always theological-ethical *Rede.*"

Of course continuities still survive from Heidegger's own preceding analysis, as further "dimensions" of being-in-the-world are "brought into relief." Thus the concept *aufgehen in,* which was previously involved in his undercutting the distinction between "inside" and "outside," is reintroduced: "Dasein at the outset and for the most part goes out into and is absorbed in the anyone [*Das Man*]." Still another dimension: Dasein "goes out into and is absorbed in what has already been said," which "belongs to the mode of being of 'the anyone.'"[4]

With my translations, I have sought out "the double meaning" of *aufgehen in,* as I did when I previously dealt with Heidegger's having derived this idiom from Husserl's casual application of it to how consciousness becomes psychologically "absorbed in the carrying out of [its intentional] acts." I then recognized that Heidegger, by what Husserl would have regarded as indulgence in a "double meaning," was violating Husserl's commitment to keep "our meanings unshakeably identical," lest they "pass over and flow into each other." Husserl's misgiving, that "wavering blurs boundaries,"[5] could be brought to bear on Heidegger's use of *aufgehen in.* If Heidegger previously respected no boundary between the "within," which is what becomes available in Husserl for conceptual analysis, and the physical "without," these further "dimensions" are further violations of Husserl's commitment to keep any concept "fixed" with a single meaning.

The Lecture

We have reached a step, with the conception of communication in section 35, at which the breakdown in philosophical communication between Heidegger and Husserl might be said to be complete. But there is one matter which I may seem to have too long overlooked: When and how did the *actual* breakdown in communication occur? If so far I have restricted my exposition to the philosophical differences between them, one justification is that Heidegger himself distinguishes the philosophical from the actual breakdown. In the interview that the magazine *Der Spiegel* conducted with Heidegger, which he had withheld from publication until after his death, he puts forward this distinction. He alludes to his differences with Husserl as first "differences regarding substance [*in sachlicher Hinsicht*]." (The terminology is colloquial, but it might be taken as referring to the principle of proceeding directly "to the things themselves.") He observes that these philosophical differences had "become sharper,"[6] before he considers, quite separately, the actual personal break between them.

The distinction itself does not concern me in the present volume, since Husserl also maintains the distinction, if in a fashion quite different from Heidegger's.[7] Heidegger's explanation of the actual personal break saddles Husserl himself with entire responsibility for it:

Husserl had . . . a public reckoning with Max Scheler and me to the frankness [*Deutlichkeit*] of which nothing was lacking. . . . Husserl spoke to the students in the Berlin *Sportpalast*. Erich Mühsam reported it in one of the large Berlin newspapers.[8]

I have begun with the statements in Heidegger's explanation that are most obviously puzzling.

One puzzle is why Heidegger should single out the lecture in the Berlin *Sportpalast*. That same June, in 1931, Husserl gave the same lecture in other German cities. Moreover, Husserl did not in this lecture criticize Heidegger by name or in any manner which was particularly offensive, unless being philosophically uncompromising is offensive. What Husserl attacked explicitly was "a new kind of anthropology which is very influential at present and has even affected the so-called phenomenological movement."[9] "New kind" can be taken as an allusion to what the net result was when Heidegger had fallen back from the eidetic and transcendental levels (which Husserl is regaining in the lecture) to the level of empirical science (whether identified as anthropology or psychology). This attack is consistent with Husserl's general intolerance of "misunderstandings of phenomenology"—an intolerance that I suggest is in some measure due to his philosophical commitment to keeping meanings "unshakably identical."

Husserl's attack could not have taken Heidegger by surprise. Why did Heidegger make so much of the lecture? As a matter of fact, in a "Supplement to My Ideas" (1930), Husserl had previously undertaken what, as compared with his rather innocuous comment in the lecture, could be dubbed a franker reckoning.[10] We can hardly avoid the suspicion that one reason was that this supplement was published in a philosophical journal, and so was somehow less "public" than what was spoken in the Berlin *Sportpalast*.

If a public lecture was the occasion for their actual break, we must ask why would not Heidegger's own inaugural address two years before in the amphitheater at Freiburg qualify? Heidegger's zealous partisan, Beaufret, dates what he calls the "chill" between Husserl and Heidegger to that address, in which Heidegger uncompromisingly concluded, "Scientific rigor cannot attain the seriousness of metaphysics." Beaufret exclaims, "One can imagine how Husserl must have felt, when he heard that."[11]

It wouldn't require the intervention of a Berlin journalist to detect in the phrase "scientific rigor" a reference to Husserl's *Philosophy as Rigorous Science*. Many in Heidegger's Freiburg audience would have recognized that his address had reached its end and climax as an attack on Husserl, "to the frankness of which nothing was lacking."

One difference between the two occasions was that Husserl was seated prominently in the audience. Heidegger's frankness would have been taken in conjunction with the absence from his lecture of any reference to phenomenology or personal reference to his predecessor in the chair. Some personal reference would have been regarded as normal academic courtesy. If Heidegger had offered some variation on the "admiration and friendship" of the dedication in *Being and Time,* he would not have been interpreted as compromising himself philosophically any more than he had with that dedication.

Emendations

Before I attempt to deal with other puzzles, it is worth segregating those which are factual inaccuracies in Heidegger's report of what took place. Husserl did not deliver a lecture in the *Sportpalast.* The journalist was not Erich Mühsam, but his brother Heinrich. Erich's name may have lodged in Heidegger's memory because he died in a concentration camp, but Heidegger does not mention this, and there is no other detailed public evidence of concern for particular individuals who died there weighing heavily on his mind, as it did in the case of those who died in battle.

The factual inaccuracies in the interview were corrected when Heidegger's son published an emended version. This is the corrected Berlin passage: "In the University of Berlin Husserl spoke before 1,600 listeners. Heinrich Mühsam reported in one of the great Berlin newspapers, a "kind of *Sportpalast* atmosphere [*Stimmung*]." The emendation introduces another implausibility. As Heidegger himself knew all too well, Husserl usually read his lectures in a fashion which was at best dry and was often found boring, especially as compared to Heidegger. But anyone reading the lecture "Phenomenology and Anthropology" itself would have trouble imagining its delivery surrounded with the atmosphere of a sporting event. If there was any heightening of the atmosphere, it was more likely due to the audience being aware that they were listening to Germany's most prominent Jewish philosopher and that clouds were gathering.

Attempting to comprehend Heidegger's original version, Karl Schuhmann has supposed the appraisal may have derived from a remark of the chairman, who commented, in introducing Husserl, on the size of the crowd by making a reference to the *Sportpalast.*

Personal Conduct

Let us examine the portion of Heidegger's original report which remains intact in the son's corrected version:

Husserl had . . . a public [*öffentlich*] reckoning with Max Scheler and me, to the frankness of which nothing was lacking. What induced Husserl to set himself in opposition [*abzusetzen*] to my thought with such publicity [*Öffentlichkeit*], I was never able to learn."

One item which certainly seems specious is the final and climactic phrase, "I was never able to learn [*konnte ich nie erfahren*]." Are we supposed to visualize Heidegger diligently scurrying around what was in the thirties the very small university community of Freiburg, buttonholing colleagues and trying unsuccessfully to find out what had induced Husserl to criticize him publicly? I have never heard any evidence that Heidegger did so.

We should not, however, allow Heidegger's "I was never able to learn" to take us back to 1931. No evidence exists that Heidegger was very much concerned in the thirties with what Husserl thought about him. It was only long after Husserl's death that he became a threat to Heidegger. The "public reckoning" that Heidegger resented occurred not in 1931 but after the war. The threat was initially the confiscation of his library and then his livelihood, with the suspension of his employment as a professor as a result of denazification proceedings, in which his personal treatment of Husserl became a salient issue. This may help explain Heidegger's distorted reconstruction of the episode. Heidegger's biographer and apologist, Heinrich Petzet, recalls (with no reference to the interview in *Der Spiegel,* though he was the close friend that Heidegger singled out to be present "as a 'second'") "the bitterness that threatened to get the better of Heidegger."[12] That Heidegger should be so elaborately wrong about the occasion he alleged for his personal break with Husserl might betray bitter brooding over accusations regarding his treatment of Husserl.

One of the postwar accusations against Heidegger was his failure to visit Husserl or make any other gesture during the long period from August 1937 until April 1938 when Husserl lay sick and dying. Heidegger claimed in *Der Spiegel* to have written Husserl's widow an apology for not having attended his funeral. When he admitted on another occasion having failed to write such a letter, was it just faulty memory, or was he recognizing that it would never turn up in the files carefully kept by the widow? But so much attention to the funeral only diverts attention from its having followed the long period of sickness during which Heidegger kept his back turned on his erstwhile mentor and supporter, whom he had customarily designated his "fatherly friend."[13]

I am reluctant to bog down in an appraisal of Heidegger's personal conduct. I risk seeming to revert to narrating personal episodes, such as I canvassed in my introduction, where they seemed appropriate enough.

But now I am still concerned with the philosophical differences—*in sachlicher Hinsicht*—as I have been throughout. My present point is that even if the distinction Heidegger draws in the interview between philosophical differences and the actual break is designed to protect his philosophy from imputations derivable from his personal conduct, it does not preclude his philosophy from having influenced his personal conduct. The presumption of this influence seems to me not to have been given sufficient weight even by those appraisers of his conduct who are primarily interested in his philosophy.

I am not arguing that philosophical commitments necessarily dictate a philosopher's personal conduct nor denying that a philosopher can seek with his philosophy to extenuate his personal conduct. My argument is rather that so many incongruities (to put the matter mildly) arise in Heidegger's personal conduct and in his extenuations that it is worth clinging to what comes through it all with some philosophical coherence.

Publicity

My claim is that Heidegger's defense to *Der Spiegel* of his personal break with Husserl is not entirely ad hoc and cannot be understood fully without some reference to his philosophy. Heidegger is alleging that it was really Husserl who had broken with him. But even if that were the case, it was not so simple, as Heidegger also alleges, as Husserl's having sought "a public [*öffentlich*] reckoning," and having "set himself in opposition to my thought with such publicity [*Öffentlichkeit*]." Here a distinction must be drawn. I must reemphasize that nothing Husserl said in "opposition" to Heidegger in the lecture was outrageous or surprising. The problem for Heidegger must rather have been "such publicity." What Heidegger's allegation then brings to our attention is less what Husserl said than Heidegger's own sensitivity to *Öffentlichkeit*—as does his focusing not on anything substantive in the lecture itself, which he does not quote, but on a report of it "in one of the leading Berlin newspapers" (though again no quotation). In fact, this sensitivity may be betrayed even by Heidegger's singling out the lecture as given in Berlin, when it was also given in other less notable cities.

My immediate argument is that Heidegger's sensitivity to *Öffentlichkeit*, which seems so extravagent, so exaggerated, in his accusation against Husserl, cannot readily be accounted for without some recourse to the extent to which it involves a philosophically warranted *Stimmung* on Heidegger's part—a philosophical sensitivity. I am recognizing how crucial the concept of *Öffentlichkeit* is to Heidegger's analysis of communication, which is my own main concern in this volume. I accordingly return to the step involving "loquacity," when he regains in *Being and Time* the "horizon" of "everydayness." We saw how at this step "the Dasein is absorbed in and dominated by the anyone." Now we must add that the anyone's "distinctive mode of disclosure" is *Öffentlichkeit.* The domination by the anyone is "the domination of public [*öffentlich*] interpretedness."[14]

Macquarrie and Robinson translate *Öffentlichkeit* as "publicness," as Stambaugh also does. In the present setting I have adopted the translation "publicity," because of the reference to a newspaper report. But I have adopted it with the misgiving that this translation may conceal its status as a philosophical concept. With respect to some of Heidegger's concepts, we have already had to face up to how he stretches their meaning from the colloquial to the philosophical.

An illustration of Heidegger's distrust of "publicity" is his distrust of *Der Spiegel* itself as a popular weekly which was a vehicle of publicity—in fact more effectively so than "one of the leading Berlin newspapers." My further point is not that publicity is to be trusted, but the ambiguity in Heidegger's situation: he is accusing Husserl of having gone public over their philosophical differences by having undertaken "a public reckoning" with him, but the interview itself was Heidegger's going public by undertaking a public reckoning with his own accusers.

The conduct Heidegger usually avowed was simply to ignore publicity, as he recommended to Jean Beaufret, who had intervened on Heidegger's behalf in another weekly. Heidegger "begged him to abstain from then on from such interventions, and added that it was not only a matter of wasting his time, but he was degrading himself by replying seriously to detractors of Heidegger." On another occasion "he confided to friends not to pay any attention and to continue to work with as little publicity as possible."[15]

Heidegger's distrust of *Öffentlichkeit* was such that it ostensibly took the pressure of close friends for him to resort to *Öffentlichkeit* by exposing himself to the public in the interview in *Der Spiegel.* His son reports Heidegger's "unambiguous resistance" (*eindeutig Ablehnung*) to giving this interview. The son cites in evidence Heidegger's edict in a letter, "I will under no circumstances agree to a *Spiegel* interview that is in any way organized [*in irgendeiner Form organisiertes*]."[16] But again there is an ambiguity: when Heidegger finally did grant the interview, he insisted on having the arrangements thoroughly organized—in particular the arrangements for revision afterwards of the oral interview.

This may seem somewhat inconsistent with his "under no circumstances," just as his recommendation that publicity be ignored may seem somewhat inconsistent with is "bitter brooding" over public accusations against him.

Of course we might ask if Husserl betrays comparable philosophical sensitivity, quite aside from any personal resentment he might have felt toward Heidegger. All I would point to is how irrelevant in his philosophy the "public" was, "whose existence is not presupposed by the content of his investigations." We saw in the last chapter that it was his conviction that "every genuine beginning of philosophy issues from meditations, from solitary self-reflection." Although Husserl could be said to have been resentful—even contemptuous—of Heidegger's very public behavior when he rallied to Hitler, there is no philosophical concept Husserl brings to bear which is comparable to Heidegger's *Öffentlichkeit.*

"ISMS"

My argument regarding the extent to which Heidegger's distrust of *Öffentlichkeit* was philosophical is strengthened by the readiness with which Heidegger applied his analysis of *Öffentlichkeit* to another philosopher. Here I anticipate his first postwar publication, his "Letter on Humanism," which he wrote during the denazification proceedings against him, when he was suffering as well from most unfavorable publicity.

The "Letter" is worth taking into account if I seem to be making too much of a couple of references to "publicity" in an interview. The philosophical scope of "publicity" is more evident in the "Letter," where Heidegger recalls explicitly the passages in *Being and Time* to which I have appealed.

For the present, I cite one pertinent portion of the "Letter": "The market of public opinion [*öffentlich Meinens*] continually demands new 'isms.' One is always ready to supply the demand." In the "Letter" Heidegger later generalizes:

> One no longer thinks; one makes a business [*sich beschäftigt*] of "philosophy." In competition, such businesses publicly [*öffentlich*] offer their bids as "isms" and try to outbid each other. The domination of such terms is not accidental. It depends above all . . . upon the authentic dictatorship of publicity [*Öffentlichkeit*].[17]

The reference to "isms" is clearly to Sartre's public lecture, *Existentialism Is a Humanism,*" in which he could be taken as supplying the market demand by offering two "isms" for the price of one.

What I am drawing attention to now is not just the prominence of this charge in the "Letter," but that it is buttressed by philosophical citations. Heidegger recalls the section of *Being and Time* in which he had presented *Öffentlichkeit* as a manifestation of the "dictatorship of the anyone," although he also seeks a significant telescoping: the "authentic dictatorship" becomes in the "Letter" the dictatorship of *Öffentlichkeit* itself.[18] I do not pretend to be able to decide if this telescoping is merely postwar bitterness over the unfavorable publicity he was himself receiving.

What I can claim is that the "Letter" was Heidegger's first publication after the Second World War. Philosophers and others were impatiently expecting some account from him as to why he had supported Hitler's dictatorship; instead Heidegger is in effect reminding them that he had employed the idiom of "dictatorship" before Hitler's dictatorship. By refurbishing the idiom, and taking the title of Sartre's public lecture as an example, rather than the Nazis, Heidegger would seem to be implying a distinction, which would in effect tend to exculpate his conduct, between a mere political dictatorship and a "dictatorship" in the more fundamental guise of *Öffentlichkeit*.

Indeed, in his lengthy postwar correspondence with Jaspers regarding the period which began when he became a Nazi Party member on assuming the rectorate of the University of Freiburg in 1933, he never refers explicitly to Hitler or to dictatorship—very strange inhibitions. Moreover, to the best of my knowledge, Heidegger never permitted himself in writing, even after the war, any so superficial an illustration of the "dictatorship of *Öffentlichkeit*" as Hitler's harangues or Goebbels's manipulation of public opinion.[19] We seem to be left instead with the explicit illustrations of Sartre's public lecture as well as Husserl's going public regarding their philosophical differences. Nevertheless, when he rebukes Husserl and Sartre alike for consorting with *Öffentlichkeit*, he is demonstrating his own philosophical commitment to that concept rather than discerning anything that Husserl and Sartre might have significantly in common philosophically.

If Heidegger's explanation of the personal break with Husserl is puzzling, interpreters have also been puzzled as to why Heidegger singles out for attack a shoddy public lecture of Sartre's rather than taking on *Being and Nothingness*, which was written for fellow philosophers and would have provided, with its ample references to Heidegger, a philosophical opportunity for the discussion he had originally proposed in a cordial letter to Sartre. Heidegger's preference for the public lecture can to some extent be explained in terms of the character of the attack he wanted to launch on Sartre. At a time when Heidegger felt he was a "dead dog" in Germany[20] and was not able to publish there himself, he may have wanted to bring his concept of *Öffentlichkeit* to bear on as widely acclaimed a public figure as Sartre, especially since their philosophies were regularly linked. Beaufret was probably at the public lecture in Paris (I was) and could have told Heidegger not only about the link Sartre had made between them, but also about how the lecture room was so crowded it was difficult to breathe.

The public was there in force, and a Paris newspaper reported that three women had fainted. At least one did and had to be carried out.

Openness

I should not leave the impression that *Öffentlichkeit* is an incidental concept in *Being and Time* which I might have credited with too much scope because of my concern with the problem of communication. To appreciate the wider implications of *Öffentlichkeit*, we must recognize that, since Heidegger's analysis is relational, *Öffentlichkeit* belongs to a concatenation of concepts. I touched earlier on the second word, *offenbar*, in Heidegger's German translation of the Greek citation at the start of *Being and Time*. Heidegger, I suggested, may have been avoiding the usual translation *klar* for the Greek *dēlon* because he wanted to avoid any confusion of his procedure with Husserl's "*Methode der Klärung* ["clarification"]." What Heidegger certainly did want was to set up with his translation an initial opposition between *offenbar* at its beginning, and its last word, *Verlegenheit*, which implied that the "way" was not "open," but confronted us with an "obstruction."

This difficulty of "access," which Heidegger acknowledges at the start of *Being and Time*, becomes thematic in a fashion that warrants his adopting the *Destruktion* as a procedure. A paradox thus emerges when we recognize in section 36 that "*Öffentlichkeit* obscures [*verdunkelt*] everything and presents what is thus covered up [*verdeckt*] as known and accessible to anyone."[21] (Accordingly, in my two previous volumes, one translation I proposed for *Öffentlichkeit* was "publicly accessible.") This ostensible accessibility itself becomes the "obstruction." Thus *Öffentlichkeit* is a moment in Heidegger's explanation of how the "discovery [*Entdecken*] of the world" and the "disclosure of Dasein" are "always carried out as a removing out of the way of concealments and obscurities [*Verdeckungen und Verdunkelungen*] . . . with which the Dasein bars the way against itself."[22] As he further explains in his analysis of the "domination of public interpretedness," the "disclosure" [*Erschliessen*] of what is ostensibly "open" (or "ob-vious") "is perverted [*verkehrt*] into a closing off [*Verschliessen*]," so that the predicament is encountered which I have already cited: "From this everyday interpretedness . . . the Dasein cannot extricate itself. In it, out of it, and against it, all genuine understanding, interpreting, and communication . . . are to be undertaken."[23]

In *Being and Time* I located, as a crucial breaking off of communication with Husserl, Heidegger's mocking protest, "Communication is never anything like a transporting of experiences . . . from the inside of one subject into the inside of another." At later steps in *Being and Time* than I have been able to reach, there is an analysis of how genuine understanding and interpreting can involve extrication in a certain sense of the Dasein from "everyday interpretedness." But is there any specification at any step of what "genuine . . . communication" would be "like"?

The Other

There is a juncture in Heidegger at which genuine communication may seem in question. In his analysis of "being-with," Heidegger offers in the instance of *Fürsorge* ("care for [the other]") one extreme: "*Fürsorge* can *einspringen* [*"leap in"* or *"intervene"*] for the other" in such fashion that "the other is thrown out of his place" and "steps back in order afterward to take over what has been taken care of [on his behalf] . . . or to disburden himself of it entirely." This kind of *Fürsorge* is not genuine, since "the other becomes dependent and dominated." At the opposing extreme, *Fürsorge* "does not so much leap in for the other as *leap ahead* . . . not in order to take away his care but to give it back to him authentically as such for the first time. It aids the other to become transparent in his care and to become *free* for it."[24]

Several questions are left unsettled here. First, is the relation reciprocal and reversible, so that the other can "leap in for" or "leap ahead" in relation to me? Second, does so swift a movement as leaping even permit the emergence of a sustained relation to the other? Thirdly, can any communication be envisaged as involved—as not only imparted but also responded to?

This juncture seems rather an impasse—to adopt the idiom I have derived from Heidegger himself. Does this impasse merely betray the formalistic character of the analysis, in that it does not lend itself to any interpretation of a substantive relation between the individual and the other? The question might be justified by a comparison with the relation between the individual and the other as analyzed by Sartre and Merleau-Ponty. I smuggled their analyses into my introduction (it will now be apparent in retrospect) because there seemed to me no prospect of a comparable illustration of this relation emerging in Heidegger any more than in Husserl.

These are larger issues than that posed in *Der Spiegel*, where Heidegger set aside his "philosophical differences" with Husserl and dealt only with the issue of personal responsibility for breaking off their relation. But there is another issue here which we can illustrate by considering another episode that raises a question of Heidegger's personal responsibility. During a visit, Paul Celan supposedly challenged him regarding the Holocaust, and supposedly received no response. George Steiner resigns himself to speaking of "some kind of inhuman muteness" on Heidegger's part.[25]

Steiner's verdict of "inhuman muteness" has been challenged. What conclusion then can be reached? The evidence is apparently inconclusive. This conclusion is less easy to reach regarding Heidegger's relation to Husserl, about which the evidence seems ample. But if the judicious still prefer to treat the evidence here, too, as inconclusive, what might we then infer from this inconclusiveness? That it is itself evidence that personal relations did not have for Heidegger the philosophical relevance assigned them by such existentializing analyses as Sartre's and Merleau-Ponty's.

At any rate, the inconclusiveness is one reason why the "Heidegger controversy" continues as a controversy over his personal conduct, and I shall return to it in Volume 4.

Conclusion:
The End of Philosophy

This sort of thing is . . . wholly without relevance.—Heidegger

The Later Heidegger

A problem remains with respect to Heidegger's relation to Husserl: Heidegger's references to him disappear in the thirties for nearly thirty years, except for one statement in the "Letter on Humanism." My account of their relation from Heidegger's side would not be complete without some explanation for the disappearance.

I would take the one reference to Husserl in the "Letter on Humanism" as a large part of the philosophical explanation. Husserl, Heidegger states, failed to recognize "the essentiality of the history of being [*die Wesentlichkeit des geschichtlichen im Sein*]."[1] In order to avoid such monstrosities as "historicity in being" or "historicality in being," I shall sometimes interpolate *Geschichte* but more frequently offer in quotation marks the expression "the history of being." My quotation marks warn that the "history" which is in question is to be distinguished from "history" (*Historie*) in the ordinary sense. (I am not sure there is an ordinary sense, but Heidegger himself is indifferent to the varieties of *Historie*, which have apparently little or no bearing on "the history of being.")

The shift in context (in my terminology) from *Historie* to "the history of being" indicates a break with Husserl which is more final, more sweeping, than the breaks I located in *Being and Time*. The implications of this break are worked out in the "Letter" in terms of Heidegger's relation not to Husserl but to another philosopher, Sartre, who also is cited as failing to recognize "the essentiality of the history of being." Thus the "Letter" must be postponed until Volume 4; it does not provide a suitable occasion for rounding out the present volume to a conclusion regarding Heidegger's relation to Husserl.

Other presentations of "the history of being" in Heidegger's still later writings include references to Husserl which are not simply negative. These later references are mostly to what the relation between them was in the twenties. Some of these I have already exploited. Yet we need to reconsider them now, since the retrospect they offer is in terms of his later commitment to "the history of being." I shall not pretend that my sampling adds up to a complete account of this "history."

These references occur mostly in writings which can perhaps be segregated from Heidegger's other later writings—writings which are addressed primarily to a non-German audience. After the war Heidegger was beseiged by Frenchmen inspired in some measure by Sartre's having put Heidegger together with Husserl in his own philosophy. Thus it was the Frenchman Beaufret who asked Heidegger, "*Qui est Husserl pour vous?*"[2] Heidegger's "Letter on Humanism" was itself addressed (according to its original title) "To Jean Beaufret, Paris." "A Dialogue on Language" ostensibly took place with a Japanese visitor whose mentor had attended Husserl's as well as Heidegger's lectures in the twenties. "The End of Philosophy and the Task of Thought" was originally presented in a French translation to a UNESCO conference in Paris. The "Letter to Richardson" was written to an American Jesuit. The "Zähringen Seminar" had a francophone audience and was preserved in a French translation. I note these facts without trying to determine exactly how crucial to Heidegger, early or late, was the distinction between the Germanic and the rest of the world. What Heidegger was apparently recognizing was that Husserl was enjoying a certain vogue in France, Japan, and America.

Titles

I begin with the one occasion when Heidegger did deal with his relation to Husserl before a German audience: "My Way to Phenomenology." This very title may seem to assert its pertinence, but I believe it is too often read as if Heidegger were at last prepared, as his career neared its end, to make a proper philosophical acknowledgment of Husserl. Even though the climax of the essay is the publication of *Being and Time*, there is no mention of any of the steps there over which I lingered in arguing on behalf of the relevance of Husserl to understanding *Being and Time*. If my argument has been at all convincing, why did Heidegger himself never admit the extent to which he had tried to come to grips there with Husserl? A possible answer is that Heidegger's preference for presenting himself there as coming to grips instead with the tradition was later consolidated by the coherence the tradition acquired for him in the later context of "the history of being."

If "My Way" were a tribute to another philosopher, it would constitute a most unusual tribute, since Husserl is never cited, any more than he is in *Being and Time*. A tribute without citation is hardly a tribute. Indeed "My Way" is only obliquely a tribute to Husserl. At best the honors are to be shared with Husserl's publisher, who was also the publisher of *Being and Time*. Near the beginning of this tribute, Heidegger recalls how, on "the title page" of the *Logical Investigations,*

> I encountered the name of the publisher, Max Niemeyer. This encounter is before my eyes as vividly today as then. It was connected with that of "phenomenology," then strange to me, which appears in the subtitle of the second volume. My understanding of the title "phenomenology" was just as limited and vacillating as my knowledge in those days of the publisher Max Niemeyer and his work. Why and how both names—Niemeyer Publishing House and phenomenology—belong together would soon become clearer.[3]

Is a certain strain betrayed in this curious conjunction of the "understanding of the title "phenomenology" and "knowledge . . . of the publisher Max Niemeyer and his work"?

This brandishing of the conjunction does seem rather excessive, especially when in the last sentence of "My Way" Heidegger concludes that phenomenology "can disappear as a title in favor of the subject of thinking." But let me make a guess as to what is afoot. The publisher (Hermann Niemeyer) had previously turned up in Heidegger. "A Dialogue on Language" is ostensibly, as I have said, a dialogue with a Japanese visitor, whose mentor had been a student of Husserl's as well as of Heidegger's. His later visit to Freiburg was thus an appropriate occasion for Heidegger to deal with his own relation to his own mentor in a note he appended to the "Dialogue."

In this note Heidegger takes up what was widely viewed as his final act of disloyalty toward Husserl—after having failed to get in touch with him during his last long illness or to attend his funeral. In the note, Heidegger explains how he "agreed, on the recommendation and desire of Niemeyer, that the dedication ["To Husserl in Admiration and Friendship"] be omitted from the [1941] edition of *Being and Time*." Heidegger claims to have yielded to the publisher on the condition that the footnote be retained, which "gives the reason for the dedication." This is the footnote which was attached to the paragraph in *Being and Time* in which Heidegger acknowledged that the work "would not have been possible if the foundation had not been laid by Edmund Husserl." The footnote added,

> If the following investigation goes any steps forward in the disclosure of the things themselves, the author must first of all thank Edmund Husserl, who, by providing his own incisive personal guidance and by freely turning over his unpublished investigations, familiarized the author with the most diverse areas of phenomenological research.[4]

Since Heidegger's account of the suppression of the dedication shifts most of the responsibility onto Niemeyer, he may well have felt he should offer as compensation in "My Way to Phenomenology" a tribute in which the debt was emphasized which Husserl himself owed the publisher.

That "My Way" is to this extent a tribute to the publisher (it was privately printed for this purpose) may help explain why Heidegger could get away with dealing in so perfunctory a fashion with his own philosophical relation to Husserl. But we must still recognize that Heidegger did later include "My Way" in the last anthology of his later writings that he himself assembled. There it does seem to serve a more philosophical purpose.

Even so, an ambiguity may be detected. That the title "phenomenology" is to disappear may be cautionary regarding the title of "My Way to Phenomenology" itself. The translation of the title *Mein Weg in die Phänomenologie* is not "My Way in Phenomenology." *In* can indicate in German (as in English) the place where a movement is proceeding—when *in* is used with the dative. Evidently Heidegger would thwart this interpretation, for he is using *in* with the accusative, so that what is in question would seem to be the place he was proceeding "to" or "toward." Hence Stambaugh's translation "My Way to Phenomenology" is accurate.

Being and Time prepared us to recognize that the direction indicated by a preposition can be pivotal in Heidegger. "To" does suggest that "phenomenology" was a destination, even if it is a destination that is to disappear. Indeed, Heidegger had long since dropped the title "phenomenology" as a description of his own undertaking.

In response to Beaufret's questions about the title, Heidegger elucidated: "This title is to be understood as, 'My Way of Thinking as Putting Phenomenology to the Test' [as *l'épreuve de la phénoménologie*]' or as "How My Way Opens Up in Opening Up Phenomenology Itself."[5] Both titles would be compatible with the ambiguity, a destination which is to disappear.

Heidegger accepted the French translator's proposal, "*Mon chemin de pensée et la phénoménologie.*" But the awkwardness of the ambiguity is then discarded in favor of the laxity of the "and." With this loose juxta-position, neither *l'épreuve* is apparent, nor the double opening up.

The Shift in Context

At issue in the disappearance of the title "phenomenology" is the shift in context from *Historie* to "the history [*Geschichte*] of being." What I would bring out is what happens to *Historie* ("history" in the ordinary sense) when it is left behind with the shift to *Geschichte*.

I begin with this shift in context as it occurs in the last paragraph of the essay, providing an explanation of why the title is due to disappear:

> The epoch [*Zeit*] of phenomenological philosophy seems over. It is already considered something past, which is only taken into account historically [*historisch*] along with other movements of philosophy. Yet phenomenology is not a movement. . . . It is the possibility of thinking—at times changing and only thus remaining—the possibility of responding to the claim of thinking. If phenomenology is thus experienced and retained, it can disappear as a title in favor of the subject of thinking, whose openness [*Öffenbarkeit*] remains a mystery [*Geheimnis*].[6]

By way of briefly defending my refusal to be more precise about what happens to the relation between Heidegger and Husserl when the conclusion of this paragraph is reached, the best I can offer is to recall Husserl's unreadiness to respond to "mystery." In the early twenties Husserl had discounted an earlier Heidegger with the observation, "The war and ensuing difficulties drive men into 'mysticism.'"[7] Such "difficulties," I pointed out before, were simply not of the sort Husserl had designed phenomenology to resolve. Not even my earlier exposition of the differences between Husserl's and Heidegger's conception of "difficulty" can accommodate the difference here or measure the impasse.

At least we can see how we are led, in Heidegger's last paragraph, up to the "mystery," even if the present occasion of dealing with his relation to Husserl is not the place to succumb to the "mystery" itself. We start from *Historie,* with its recognition that "the epoch of phenomenological philosophy seems to be over," and that this philosophy is "something past, which is only taken into account historically [*historisch*]." The shift to "the history of being" is signaled by, "Yet phenomenology is not a movement."

This shift at the end of the history of phenomenology had been carried out earlier in the essay, when Heidegger was recalling the history of phenomenology as beginning with Husserl's *Logical Investigations:*

> At that time the rather obvious conclusion was often reached that with "phenomenology" a new movement had emerged in European philosophy. Who could have denied the correctness of this assertion?
>
> But such historical calculation missed what through "phenomenology" had happened.[8]

Heidegger's scorn for *Historie* is evident when its "conclusion" is brushed aside as "rather obvious." The conclusion is further disparaged by Heidegger's conceding its "correctness" as an "historical [*historisch*] calculation." This "correctness" is the Platonic and Cartesian criterion of truth to which the later Heidegger opposes his conception of *a-letheia*—of truth as the mysterious "openness" of "un-concealment."

Finally, "historical calculation missed what through 'phenomenology' had happened [*geschehen war*]." At this juncture actual history [*Historie*] is displaced, and we arrive at "the history [*Geschichte*] of being," as we will again when the essay reaches the conclusion I have already cited.

Rückblick

The disappearance in "My Way" of "phenomenology . . . as a title" is associated with the end of philosophy more generally. I accordingly seek some interpretative backup from "The End of Philosophy and the Task of Thinking," as the essay which preceded "My Way" when it was reprinted in Heidegger's last anthology. There Heidegger issues the edict, "Any attempt to obtain an insight [*Einblick*] into the task of thinking, sees itself as dependent on a looking back [*Rückblick*] over the whole of the history of philosophy." This *Rückblick* is only feasible by virtue of the place which Heidegger himself occupies at the end of this history as "the history of being." Here Heidegger deploys an ambiguity: "The old meaning of the word '*Ort*' was 'end,'" but "it has come to mean 'place.'"[9] The end of philosophy is the "place" where the "whole of philosophy is gathered together" and thus comes within Heidegger's retrospect which embraces it as a tradition.

This outcome raises an array of issues. Given the limitations of my exposition, the issue that concerns me is that this retrospect enforces Heidegger's adoption of the expository procedure characterized by Biemal as "rendering present [to a text] the entire tradition in which the text is located."

I launched my interpretation of Heidegger's relation to Husserl with Heidegger's analysis of signs in section 17 because Husserl had himself started out with an analysis of signs. If I could carry out this interpretation, it was because the entire tradition was *not* present at this step in the sense that Husserl's analysis of signs was. Matters became more complicated, however, when I went back to the earlier step in section 15, at which Heidegger began his analysis of the *Umwelt,* for at that step his analysis was a *Destruktion* of "interpretative tendencies" which he attributed to the tradition at large.[10] But I persisted in discovering that specific traits of the examples on which he relied in carrying out this *Destruktion* could not be accounted for except by reference to Husserl.

In order to remain within the confines of the present volume, I can try to suggest what has transpired by a comparison with *Being and Time:* Heidegger's resort there to tradition receives now a more comprehensive justification. To determine how the *Destruktion* has accordingly changed through the later Heidegger's having gained, at the end of philosophy, a retrospect on the tradition as a whole, we need to consider more of Heidegger's statement in the "Zähringen Seminar" regarding the *Destruktion:*

> In *Being and Time* there was already such a turning back [*Rück-kehr*], if still rather clumsy [*ungeschickt*]. In *Being and Time* the turning back is undertaken as *Destruktion*—that is, as the destructuring [*Auflösung*], as the deconstruction, of the uninterrupted succession, since the beginning [*Anfang*], of transformations to which the history [*Geschichte*] of philosophy is destined [*zuschickt*] as being. But in *Being and Time* there was no place for a genuine recognition [*Erkenntnis*] of the history [*Geschichte*] of being. Hence, the clumsiness [*Ungeschicklickeit*] and strictly speaking naïveté of the "ontological *Destruktion.*" Since then the unavoidable naïveté of the inexperienced has yielded to knowledge [*Erkenntnis*].[11]

The ambiguous wordplay indicates that the *Ungeschicklichkeit* is not any ordinary "clumsiness" or "naïveté" on the part of "the inexperienced"; it was a lack of "knowledge" of the *Geschick* ("destiny" as destination) of "the history [*Geschichte*] of being."

My concern here is not "the history of being" itself, but its implications for Heidegger's relation to Husserl. I would observe first that the directional principle Heidegger derived from Husserl in *Being and Time* is no longer "to the things [*Sachen*] themselves" (as it was in Husserl and in *Being and Time*) but is "to the subject [*Sache*] itself." (The title of Heidegger's last anthology, in which both "My Way to Phenomenology" and "The End of Philosophy" were published, is *Zur Sache des Denkens.*) When the plural is thus replaced by the singular, what is at issue becomes more definitely holistic. But the principle itself no longer derives uniquely from Husserl; Heidegger attributes it in "The End of Philosophy" to Plato (*to pragma auto*) and to Hegel, before he reaches Husserl. Indeed, he then interprets Husserl himself as not having proceeded directly "to the subject itself." Instead, he inherited the *Sache* of his philosophy from Descartes (as did Hegel and all other modern philosophers)—"the subjectivity of consciousness."[12]

Direction

I would recall now my initial emphasis on the preposition "to," in the phrase "to the things themselves," as indicating the direction in which to proceed. The issue is not just that the plural *Sachen* is replaced in the later Heidegger by the singular *Sache*, as I anticipated when I first discussed the difference between Heidegger's and Husserl's methods. Husserl's method itself finally loses its direction "to the things themselves" as soon as Heidegger undercuts Husserl's distinction between the "subject" of philosophy and the history of philosophy.

Here I would recall how Husserl conceded, when confronted with misunderstandings of the *Logical Investigations* (the misunderstandings I cited at the beginning of my present undertaking), that he should have written an introduction in which he prepared the reader *historisch und sachlich*—"historically" as well as with respect to the "subject" to be treated. The history would

> have warned the reader of all the misinterpretations which were pro-
> moted by the dominant trends of thought. In this way the under-
> standing of the uniqueness of the thoughts communicated [in the
> *Logical Investigations*] and hence of their proper effect would surely
> have been promoted.[13]

Observe the distinction Husserl maintains between such a history, de-signed to dispose of "misinterpretations" of his thinking, and his thinking itself, for the respect in which it is unique is in its dedication to the subject (the *sachlich*), which renders him indifferent toward history—except insofar as the encroachment of historical trends is likely to render his reader insensitive to the "uniqueness of the thoughts" achieved through his "dedication to the subject." But it is the distinction itself between the historical and the *sachlich* that Heidegger is undercutting when his "subject" becomes "the history of being."

To appreciate the implications of Heidegger's undercutting, we must recognize that the force of the "to" has been transformed in Heidegger's title, "To the Subject of Thinking," from the force it had, not only in Husserl's methodological principle of going directly "to the *Sachen* themselves," but even in *Being and Time*, where Heidegger took this principle over. We have seen that in Husserl the directional force of the "to" was de-

termined by the intentional character of his analysis—by the "directedness" [*Gerichtetsein auf*] of in-tentional consciousness "to" the "things"
it targets as "objects."[14] In the later Heidegger the force of the "to" in "to
the *Sache* itself" is still directional, but the direction has become the direction in which it is the "destiny" (*Geschick*) of *Geschichte* to proceed at the
end of philosophy. With this undercutting of Husserl's distinction between
the *historisch* and the *sachlich*, he finally loses the relevance for Heidegger
that I have argued he still had in *Being and Time*.

Method

My own primary concern has been with the differences between Husserl
and Heidegger with regard to method, such as the differences between
Husserl's commitment to an intentional analysis, which targets "the
things themselves" with an eidetic reduction, and Heidegger's commitment to a holistic analysis, in which different relational contexts are successively "brought into relief."

This opposition in method has been recurrent throughout the history
of philosophy—between Platonists and Aristotelians, between Spinoza
and Descartes, between Hegel and Kant. The history of philosophy is a
history in which a holistic method has been proved inadequate as regularly as it has been vindicated. But this procedural opposition cannot just
be extracted from other differences in method and simply decided by a
bold and enterprising philosopher on its own merits. Rather, each method
retains its cogency only when it is recognized to involve other differences
between philosophies, such as the differences between Husserl's commitment to "things" which can be immediately given and Heidegger's proceeding to the "things" which are "nearest." That such differences must
be tracked down in specific detail has been the warrant for the "grubby
work" of this volume.

Here I would acknowledge a more specific instance where the later
Heidegger would rebuff me. The history (*Geschichte*) on which he relies is
illustrated by his referring in "My Way to Phenomenology" only to the beginning and the end of the history of the phenomenological movement, as
if once these were clamped around the phenomenological movement,
nothing of consequence had happened [*geschenen war*] in between. I
would accordingly recall a further illustration of the point I have just
made with respect to the more general history of philosophy. The methodological opposition between a holistic relational analysis and an intentional analysis recurred during the history of phenomenology itself, and in
a version which is significantly different in its ramifications from its occurrence between Heidegger and Husserl.

Merleau-Ponty never attained the vogue of Sartre. But this is not the philosophical explanation of why Merleau-Ponty expended more effort in understanding Sartre than Sartre ever expended on him—at least until the rather special circumstance of Sartre's having to write a memorial essay on Merleau-Ponty. This effort of Merleau-Ponty's I explained in my introduction in terms of how the relation to the other takes on an intimate significance in Merleau-Ponty that it did not have for Sartre, inasmuch as the other is for Merleau-Ponty "installed athwart [à travers de] our thinking."[15]

I shall not repeat the comparison between Sartre and Merleau-Ponty from my introduction, but I would broaden it by recalling Sartre's comment that Husserl "became . . . the distance between us." By now we have perhaps sufficient understanding of Husserl to be able to measure one stretch of this distance. Sartre began his career in phenomenology with an essay he wrote in Berlin in 1933–34, "Une idée fondamentale de la philosophie de Husserl—Intentionnalité." This idea never became fundamental for Merleau-Ponty. He disparages Sartre's claim that it was "Husserl's principal discovery."[16] The concomitant conception of the intentional object Merleau-Ponty discredits with an analogy:

> To the player in action, the football field is not an "object." It is pervaded by lines of force (the yard lines, those which demarcate the "penalty areas") and articulated in sectors (for example, the "opening" between members of the other team). . . . The player becomes one with the field and feels the direction of the "goal."[17]

What Merleau-Ponty is discrediting cannot be understood fully in terms of Husserl's conception of intentionality. We must also take into account Sartre's transformation of this conception. Like Merleau-Ponty, Sartre is broadly concerned with "action," not with an "act of consciousness" in Husserl's restricted eidetic sense. This "directedness" of an in-tentional act to its object in Husserl becomes in Sartre a goal-directed action—an ad-petitio.[18] But in Merleau-Ponty, as opposed to Sartre, an intentional analysis is superseded by a holistic relational analysis. If Merleau-Ponty's "player in action" were to enter Sartre's analysis, he could not become "one with the field" in his feeling for "the direction of the goal."

The Work

I do not propose to linger over comparing Heidegger's relational analysis with Merleau-Ponty's, for Heidegger paid next to no attention to Merleau-Ponty. My present point is only that Merleau-Ponty provides a different relational analysis from the one with which we have watched Heidegger undercut Husserl by analyzing examples of actions (hammering, driving, and so forth). A climactic difference is that Merleau-Ponty repudiates analysis itself—not just Sartre's dialectical analysis but also, in effect (he is never explicit), Heidegger's sharply articulative "bringing into relief" of different relations sequentially.

Merleau-Ponty is preoccupied instead with "the wonder of interrelated experiences." His emphasis (if put in Heidegger's terms) is on the *mit* of interrelatedness, rather than on the *Hebung*—on the holding together of relations. In this respect, consider another analogy of his:

> Just as the perceived world holds together only by reflections, shadows, levels, the horizons between things, which are . . . fields of possible variation, . . . so in the same way the work and thinking of a philosopher are also made out of certain articulations between things said, . . . [which] are not objects of thinking, since, like the shadow and the reflection, one would destroy them by submitting them to . . . analysis, or to thinking that isolates.[19]

Observe how Merleau-Ponty's repudiation of analysis even extends to "the work and thinking of a philosopher," which becomes analogical rather than performed on examples, as in Husserl, Heidegger, and Sartre—albeit in a different way in each case.

Here I am renewing two arguments I have pursued in this volume. I am picking up my introductory presentation of the different conceptions of philosophy as "work" by citing the analogy Merleau-Ponty provides for "the work and thinking of a philosopher." At the same time I am bringing out how the interrelations that Merleau-Ponty endorses include the interrelations between himself and other philosophers. This is the move in the passage I have cited from "between things" to "articulations between things said," which are likewise "not objects of thinking."

In my introduction I restricted myself to the relation between Sartre and Merleau-Ponty, as differently conceived by Sartre and Merleau-Ponty. Now I would add how Merleau-Ponty is concerned not to "destroy" more generally interrelations between himself and other philosophers "by submitting them to . . . analysis, or to thinking that isolates." Thus Merleau-Ponty would not isolate his own thinking from its relations with Sartre's or Husserl's or Heidegger's. The thinking of other philosophers is "installed athwart" Merleau-Ponty's thinking—as is the other himself. It involves not just a relation but an interrelation.

Further, it is not only a matter of not isolating himself from other phenomenologists, but of not isolating phenomenology from other thinking. Thus his preface to *The Phenomenology of Perception*, although it is ostensibly a preface to phenomenology and designed to answer his initial question, "What is Phenomenology?" ends by his finding relevant Balzac,

Proust, Valéry, and Cézanne. Thus phenomenology finally "blends into [*se confond*] the effort of modern thinking."[20]

Such a state of confusion is consistent with the conciliatory tendency which Sartre characterizes as the "placid dandyism" of Merleau-Ponty's "caution," with which he "took care not to rupture anything and not let anything break loose." I have recalled this illustration of how the method a philosopher follows in his own philosophy can embrace his interpretation of the relation between his philosophy and other philosophies for the purpose of a broad contrast with the later Heidegger. His commitment "to the subject itself" shrugs off any relation to any other philosopher. It is a commitment to thinking which in effect "isolates" him. I am preparing for the next volume, in which I will spell out how this isolation is secured in the later Heidegger, so that other contemporary philosophers lose any relevance to his thinking.

When I have considered in the next and final volume what happens to the later Heidegger's relation to Jaspers and Sartre, I shall be able to recast my present conclusion as to Heidegger's indifference to differences between different philosophers' methods. This indifference is illustrated when he deals with Husserl along with Hegel in "The End of Philosophy." He admits that their "two methods are as different as possible. But the subject as such which they are to present is the same, although experienced in different ways." The qualification even leaves unsettled the question as to how these "different ways" of experiencing may be associated with the different "methods" of the preceding sentence. Heidegger himself is concerned only with the *Sache,* which is "the same" for all modern philosophy—the "subjectivity of consciousness."[21] Whatever can be associated with the "different ways" is also itself merely subjective, and is to be left behind at the end of philosophy.[22]

Heidegger would find subjectivism betrayed in my own concern with the "different ways" the *Sache* is experienced by himself and Husserl—and, I have added, by Merleau-Ponty and Sartre. By probing these differences as differences in method, I mean to renew my claim that they can no more be dismissed as merely a subjective matter than can the differences in style between individual artists. The end of philosophy has indeed been reached if such differences in method can be overridden in Heidegger's *Rückblick* over the history of philosophy.

1. The Two Traditions

1. Husserl, *An Introduction to the Logical Investigations* (1913), p. 16. I shall continue to supply this date to distinguish this unpublished introduction to the second edition of *Logical Investigations*. In addition we have his original foreword to the *Logical Investigations*, his foreword to the second edition, his introduction to Volume 1 (1900), and his introduction to Volume 2 (1901). (This introduction is considerably revised for the second edition.) Accordingly, we encounter in Husserl not only the multiplication of successive works which were introductions to phenomenology, but also more than one introduction and foreword to the *Logical Investigations* themselves.

2. Marion, *Réduction et donation*, p. 7.

3. Husserl, *Logical Investigations*, 1: 44.

4. Ibid., p. 41.

5. Ibid., pp. 254–55.

6. Heidegger, "My Way to Phenomenology," p. 74.

7. Husserl, *Introduction* (1913), p. 18.

8. Ibid.

9. This was David Hoy's oral statement at a conference in the eighties. As an illustration of how things may have changed, I cite Simon Glendinning's reference (in the preface to his *On Being with Others* [1998]) to the division between Anglo-American analytic philosophy and Continental philosophy: "I don't intend to go into why I think the division deserves ignoring. Suffice it to say that what I have found characteristic about my work is that it only gets along at all by getting along without it" (p. vii). No analytic philosopher could have contemplated getting away with such

blitheness—not so very long ago. I recall a boast by an internationally renowned "analytic philosopher" that he had never read a page of Heidegger.

10. Rorty, *Philosophy and the Mirror of Nature*, p. 8.

11. Hocking, "From the Early Days," p. 5.

12. Quoted from a letter in Richardson, *Heidegger: Through Phenomenology to Thought*, p. viii; Heidegger, *Hegel's Phenomenology of Spirit*, p. 147.

13. Heidegger and Blochmann, *Briefwechsel*, p. 120. A justification for citing Blochmann is that Heidegger seems to have treasured the relation to her, although his motives are not all that clear. He kept her letters, although his usual practice with other correspondents was to dispose of a letter as soon as he had replied to it. This information is provided in the article on their correspondence by Storck, "Martin Heidegger and Elisabeth Blochmann." Storck does not comment on the letter I have cited, but there is no previous evidence of her not having mailed a letter which she had written, and there is no precedent in the previous mailed letters for its tone.

14. Spiegelberg, *The Context of the Phenomenological Movement*, p. 107.

15. Husserl himself continued to assume that "the progress of English philosophy finds its completion in phenomenology" (Cairns, *Conversations with Husserl and Fink*, p. 104).

16. Ibid., p. 105.

17. For an account of Husserl's visit to England, see Spiegelberg, *Context*, pp. 144–61.

18. Boyce Gibson, "Freiburg Diary," p. 63–64.

19. Spiegelberg, *Context*, pp. 162–65.

20. I am citing from Spiegelberg's paraphrase, ibid., p. 190.

21. This delay is not the only time-warp which we encounter in interpreting Husserl. By the time his philosophy received enough attention in England to get the *Logical Investigations* translated in 1970, John Stuart Mill's *Logic*, which figured prominently in the *Logical Investigations* as a foil, no longer commanded much attention in England. But my Chapters 11 and 12 present evidence that it is still helpful to take Mill into account in interpreting Husserl.

2. Disciples

1. James, *The Art of Criticism*, pp. 376–77.

2. Sartre, *Situations*, 4: 192.

3. Lévinas, *The Theory of Intuition in Husserl's Phenomenology*, pp. xxxiii–xxxiv.

4. Spiegelberg, *Context*, p. 177.

5. Husserl, *Introduction* (1913), p. 17.

6. Ibid., p. 16.

7. Husserl, *Ideen 3*, p. 162.

8. Cairns, *Conversations*, p. 9. Heidegger's salutations in letters to Husserl became, "Dear fatherly friend." In his letter (October 22, 1927), accompanying his critical comments on Husserl's article "Phenomenology" for the *Encyclopaedia Britannica*, Heidegger recalled how during a holiday visit, "I truly had the feeling of being almost a son." But he then qualified, "Only in actual work [as opposed to 'mere holiday conversation'] do actual problems become clear" (quoted in Husserl, *Psychological and Transcendental Phenomenology*, p. 136). Husserl's repudiation of Heidegger's comments will be the first manifest breakdown in communication. But one of the unavowed "problems," we shall see in my next chapter, is that Husserl and Heidegger have different conceptions of the "actual work" that phenomenology is. Their earlier, almost father/son relation seems conveyed by the photograph used as a frontispiece to this volume.

9. Husserl, *Briefwechsel*, 1: 20.

10. Husserl, letter to Hugo Munsterberg, in *Husserl: Shorter Works*, p. 352.

11. Cairns, *Conversations*, p. 39.

12. Husserl, letter to Paul Natorp (1 Feb. 1922), in *Briefwechsel*, 5: 151–52.

13. Husserl, *Briefe an Ingarden*, p. 59.

14. Lévinas, "La ruine de la représentation," pp. 73–74.

15. Husserl, *Ideen 3*, pp. 161–62.

16. Husserl, *The Crisis of European Sciences and Transcendental Phenomenology*, p. 389.

17. Husserl, *Briefe an Ingarden*, p. 42.

3. Fellow Workers

1. Husserl, *Logical Investigations*, 1: 256–57.

2. Héring, "Souvenirs et réflexions," pp. 26–27.

3. Husserl, "Phenomenology and Anthropology," p. 315. I shall consider in Chapter 25 Heidegger's allegation that this lecture was an attack on him.

4. Husserl, *Logical Investigations*, 2: 554. For readily accessible illustrations of intentionality which the early Sartre provides, see Cumming, *Phenomenology and Deconstruction*, 2: 38–41; hereafter, this work is cited as *P & D*, with volume number. The epistemological objection that I may be mistaken (e.g., I thought I was seeing a mugger, but I was only imagining it—it was a hydrant) is phenomenologically irrelevant, for the original act had the structure of an act of perception.

5. Husserl, *Logical Investigations*, 1: 48. Sometimes the "phenomenological reduction" is referred to as "the transcendental reduction." I overlook certain complications in Husserl when I speak, as a matter of convenience, simply of the "phenomenological reduction."

6. The put-down *Bilderbuchphänomenologie* had become standard. It is recalled, for example, by Héring in "La phénoménologie d'Edmund Husserl il y a trente ans" (p. 370). I have argued that this would plausibly have been Husserl's

reaction to *L'imaginaire*, which Sartre wrote as Husserl's "disciple." See *P & D*, 1: 114, 144–45, 247–48.

7. Ingarden, "Edith Stein on Her Activity as an Assistant of Edmund Husserl," p. 162. This impersonal character of the phenomenological undertaking Husserl emphasized by reporting of himself that "phenomenology . . . arrived in his life as an unexpected and unsought guest" (in Schuhmann, *Husserl-Chronik*, p. 261).

8. Ingarden, "Edith Stein," p. 156. Ingarden cites Dussort's indignant discovery from the report by P. M. Schuhl in *Revue philosophique*, no. 4 (1960): 447–48.

9. Ingarden, "Edith Stein," p. 158.

10. Husserl, *Briefe an Ingarden*, p. 149.

11. Husserl, *Logical Investigations*, 1: 256.

12. Husserl, *Briefe an Ingarden*, p. 149. Although Stein's letter sounds as if it were her own spontaneous report on Husserl's situation, it may reflect Husserl's own report to her on his situation, for there are curious similarities in the phraseology he adopts in his letter to Gustav Albrecht (29 Dec. 1930) four years later: "What is tragic about the situation is that, while I have become absolutely certain, these last ten years, that I have brought my phenomenological philosophy to a . . . clarity and purity, . . . a new generation has arrived which misinterprets my published fragments and incomplete initiatives" (Husserl, *Briefwechsel*, 9: 75).

13. Ibid., p. 42.

14. Heidegger, *History of the Concept of Time: Prolegomena*, p. 121; hereafter cited as *Prolegomena*.

15. Cairns, *Conversations*, p. 16.

16. See Husserl, *Psychological and Transcendental Phenomenology and the Confrontation with Heidegger* (as Sheehan and Palmer continue the title). The breakdown illustrated here is different in character from the breakdown in communication which will concern me in *Being and Time*, for Heidegger in his comments and proposed insertions in the *Britannica* article is attempting to restate the position he took in *Being and Time* in terms more accommodating to Husserl's conception of phenomenology. I have not made use of this restatement, since Sheehan's interpretation is so thoroughly detailed that it does not lend itself to piecemeal borrowing. The successive drafts of the *Britannica* article are followed up in the *Confrontation* by the lectures Husserl delivered in Amsterdam in 1928. In these Husserl found, as Palmer points out, "a further opportunity to explain and defend his standpoint in the *Encyclopaedia Britannica* article" (p. 199).

17. Heidegger, "Phänomenologie—lebendig oder tot?" p. 47.

18. Husserl, *Briefe an Ingarden*, p. 41.

19. Cairns, *Conversations*, p. 106.

20. A detailed history of Husserl's relation to Heidegger from 1909 to 1931 is available in Sheehan's "General Introduction," to Husserl's *Psychological and Transcendental Phenomenology*, pp. 2–32.

21. Heidegger, *Introduction to Metaphysics*, p. 20. I am not pretending there is

any evidence that, when Heidegger discounted reliance on a "following" as a misunderstanding of philosophy in general, he had in mind his own refusal to be recruited by Husserl. By 1935, Heidegger had turned his back so completely on Husserl that he was no longer bothering to criticize him. But he had drawn a distinction in his 1929 *Festschrift* tribute: "The works we present you are merely a witness to the fact that we *wanted* to follow your leadership, not proof that we succeeded in becoming a following" (Husserl, *Psychological and Transcendental Phenomenology*, p. 476). One factor in Heidegger's 1935 disposal of a "following" may have been his incipient disillusionment with Nazism in 1935, so that, without being dangerously explicit about it, he may be disavowing his commitment to the *Führerprincip* in his rectoral address of 1933 and how it had become interlocked with *Gefolgschaft* in his propaganda speeches. For his Nazi commendations of a following, see, for instance, *Reden und andere Zeugnisse*, pp. 188, 204, 236, 284.

22. Husserl, *Logical Investigations*, 1: 44.

23. Heidegger, *Hegel's Phenomenology of Spirit*, p. 144.

24. Jaspers, *Philosophische Autobiographie*, p. 96.

25. Heidegger, *Pathmarks*, p. 13.

26. Arendt, *Arendt/Jaspers Correspondence*, p. 88. There is no actual reference here to Heidegger's rebuke. Jaspers is writing in 1947, when his postwar vogue is intruding distracting demands with respect to "the way I'm living now."

27. Heidegger, *Being and Time*, p. 15.

28. Cairns, *Conversations*, p. 23.

29. Husserl, *Zur phänomenologie des inneren Zeitbewusstseins*, p. 343. The labyrinth of manuscripts in Husserl's archives is evidence of his recurrent encounters with "difficulties"—of the corpses coming back to life and snickering, and of his eventual dissatisfaction even with how his previous revisions dealt with them.

4. The Work of the Other

1. As evidence I cite the cover (combining Husserl's and Heidegger's portraits) and the lead essay in the *Times Literary Supplement* for 24 June 1994. This periodical accords most of its contemporary philosophical coverage to philosophers classifiable as belonging to the "analytic" tradition, but I cannot recall any of them recently awarded a cover.

2. James, *Letters*, 4: 382–83. To my knowledge James never employs the idiom "breakdown in communication." It would be interesting to trace the process by which the idiom became established as a cliché, but that is not my present task.

3. Cairns, *Conversations*, p. 9.

4. Heidegger, *Phänomenologie des religiösen Lebens*, p. 65.

5. I rely on Kisiel's account of the *Cursus Interruptus* (*Genesis*, pp. 170–73).

6. The complainant was the *Observer*, 18 April 1948.

7. Derrida, *Limited Inc.*, p. 158.

8. Searle, "Reiterating the Differances: A Reply to Derrida," p. 198. Searle's reply begins, "It would be a mistake . . . to regard Derrida's discussion of Austin as a confrontation between two prominent philosophical traditions. This is because he . . . has misunderstood and misstated Austin's position at several crucial points, and thus the confrontation never quite takes place." I don't know what Searle would commend as a valid confrontation (unmarred by misunderstandings and misstatements) which has been achieved, by someone who is properly "Continental," with the "analytic" tradition. His assessment of Derrida in terms of the idiom also bothers me, for I am not sure that a confrontation, strictly speaking (and Searle favors strict speaking), could ever take place between Derrida and Austin or between Derrida and Searle. Derrida's procedure is a "refusal of direct confrontation, of 'frontal *contestation*,'" as Jean-François Courtine points out (quoting Gérard Granel) in *Les fins de l'homme: A partir du travail de Jaques Derrida* (p. 588). Neither of them is referring to Derrida's dealings with Austin and Searle, of which they may have been unaware at the time. I am myself referring not to Derrida's insidiousness, but to his commitment to deconstructing what he calls "oppositional logic," which is entailed by a "confrontation" strictly speaking. This strict use of "confrontation" I shall clarify with a contrast between Sartre and Merleau-Ponty, who also is not "confrontational"—I grant in a quite different fashion from that in which Derrida is not "confrontational."

9. Another confrontation in Searle's positive sense failed to take place between two "Continental" philosophers themselves—between Derrida and Hans-Georg Gadamer (the most prominent philosopher in Germany in the generation after Heidegger). A much-heralded meeting failed to yield the clashes that were expected. Such importance was attached to this failure that various interpretations of what had taken place were offered in the compilation *Dialogue and Deconstruction*, ed. Michelfelder and Palmer.

10. Boyce Gibson, "Freiburg Diary," p. 72.

11. Aristotle's original statement is, "I am reluctant to undertake an investigation [of the universal good] because the proponents of [the theory of] ideas are friends. But it would seem . . . necessary for a philosopher to sacrifice intimate relations when the truth is at stake. Both are friends to us, but the truth is to be given preference" *(Nicomachean Ethics* 2.4). I supposed the tag wielded by Husserl is Erasmus's version, but Sheehan supplies an intricate lineage (see Husserl, *Psychological and Transcendental Phenomenology*, p. 270).

12. Derrida, *Limited Inc.*, p. 157. Derrida is referring in particular to Habermas *(The Philosophical Discourse of Modernity)* as "the philosopher of consensus, of dialogue, and of discussion" who is "daring to criticize [me] without citing me or giving a reference for twenty-five pages."

13. Sartre, *Situations*, 4: 192.

14. Blanchot, *L'entretien infini*, cited by Derrida in *Adieu*, pp. 20–21.

15. Lévinas, *Totalité et infini*, p. 39. I am overlooking the distinction he draws between *l'autre* and *l'autrui*.

16. Heidegger, *What Is Philosophy?* p. 79.

17. Sartre, *Situations*, 4: 193–94.

18. In Volume 1, I offered a merely preliminary rendering of different phenomenologists' understanding of "understanding," which the phenomenological undertaking becomes in *Being and Time*.

19. Merleau-Ponty, *Signes*, p. 201; *Phenomenology of Perception*, p. 360. I have gone back to Sartre and Merleau-Ponty because each provides an explicit account of the individual's relation to the other. Lévinas is committed to the priority of "the relation to the other," and Derrida to "the irreducibility of the relation to the other" (*Points de suspension*, p. 285), but in neither case does the other as an individual enjoy the priority of irreducibility, any more than does the individual I am myself. That Heidegger also finds an analysis of the individual's relation to the other irrelevant will emerge in Chapter 25.

20. Sartre, *Situations*, 4: 189. Sartre is clearly committed to "oppositional logic," which Derrida would deconstruct, but with reference to the tradition at large. In the statement I have cited, Sartre is positioning himself antithetically to Montaigne by twisting into an antithesis his classic explanation of a friendship as solidarity—"Because it was he; because it was me" (*Essais*, 1: 197). There is a similar resort to antitheses when Sartre ticks off differences between Merleau-Ponty's life and his own: "He was a day student, I was in residence [at their *Lycée*]. . . . As for military service, I was a private, he was an officer" (*Situations*, 4: 190). I cite these antitheses as preparation for the antithetical character (according to Sartre) of the understanding "each of us" had of Husserl and thus of phenomenology.

21. Merleau-Ponty, *Signes*, p. 201.

22. Hyppolite, "Existence et dialectique dans la philosophie de Merleau-Ponty," p. 230.

23. Merleau-Ponty, *Phenomenology of Perception*, p. 354.

24. Sartre, *Situations*, 4: 258. In an earlier draft of the memorial essay (In *Revue internationale de philosophie*, pp. 152–53). Sartre sets up an antithesis between Merleau-Ponty's readiness to be conciliatory and his own readiness to be antithetical by recalling how "I used to blame him for his half-shadows, his continuities; he used to blame me for my breaks [*cassures*], my voluntarism, my brutality" (p. 16).

25. Merleau-Ponty, *Sense and Non-Sense*, p. 72.

26. Sartre, *Situations*, 4: 189.

27. Merleau-Ponty, *Phenomenology of Perception*, p. 355.

28. Ibid., p. 361.

29. The anthologies were *Durchblicke*, ed. Klostermann, and *Heidegger*, ed. Pöggeler.

30. Derrida, *La voix et le phénomène*, (translated as *Speech and Phenomena*), and "*Ousia* and *Grammē*."

31. Heidegger, *Prolegomena*, p. 121.

32. Heidegger, *Being and Time*, p. 39.

33. Bubner, *Modern German Philosophy*, p. 32.

34. Pöggeler, *Martin Heidegger's Path of Thinking*, p. 286. Heidegger's warning is directed against Gadamer's interpretation in *Truth and Method*.

35. So far in my preparatory planning I may seem to be dodging "the real issue." Heidegger's break with Husserl in the thirties, however it is to be explained, was at least solidified by Heidegger's support of Hitler. When in the interview with *Der Spiegel* the interviewers take up in succession Heidegger's break with Husserl and his break with Jaspers, who had a Jewish wife—the suspicion clearly is that anti-Semitism may have been a factor in both instances. Although my focus in the present volume is on the distinctively philosophical issues that led to the break, I shall not in Volume 4 dodge the issue of Heidegger's Nazism, once I have allowed Jaspers to challenge Heidegger's distinction between the philosophical and the personal.

5. The Shift in Subject

1. Heidegger, *Being and Time*, p. 38.

2. Husserl, *Ideas I*, sec. 18.

3. Husserl, *Logical Investigations*, 1: 43.

4. Husserl, *Ideas I*, sec. 79.

5. Ibid.

6. Heidegger, *Being and Time*, p. 27. The ambiguity of this section of *Being and Time* is recognized by von Herrmann: "the intentional *ambiguity* of certain comments, in which Heidegger speaks on the one hand in Husserl's sense and on the other hand with the same words puts himself at a critical distance from Husserl" (*Der Begriff der Phänomenologie*, p. 8). But von Herrmann does not bring out the specific ambiguities of the acknowledgment of debt to Husserl with which this section culminates. He does not deal with the issue of "the priority of method" or undertake the detailed comparisons I shall offer between the procedures composing their respective phenomenological methods.

7. Heidegger, *Being and Time*, p. 28.

8. Heidegger, "The End of Philosophy," p. 62.

9. In moving from one philosophy to another, the interpreter cannot count on any fixed adjustment in the relation between method and subject. Thus I pointed out in Volume 2 how what had been the methodological exercise of the imagination in Husserl's eidetic reduction can become substantively embodied traits of Sartre's subject, *l'imaginaire* (*P & D*, 2: 231–33). Other adjustments in the relation between method and subject I shall take up in Chapter 6 of this volume.

10. Heidegger, *Being and Time*, p. 27.

11. Cumming, *P & D*, 2: 59.

12. Sartre, "Conscience de soi," p. 76.

13. Misch, *Lebensphilosophie und Phänomenologie*, pp. 1–2. Husserl read Misch's appraisal with care, since he was becoming preoccupied, when it came out in 1928–29, with the relation between himself and Heidegger, but he did not respond to the idiom of "lurch."

14. Granel, "Remarques sur le rapport de *Sein und Zeit* et de la phénoménologie Husserlienne," p. 351.

15. Ibid., p. 350.

16. Souche-Dagues, "La lecture husserlienne de *Sein und Zeit*," p. 123.

17. Granel, "Le rapport," p. 352.

18. Heidegger, "Le séminaire de Zähringen," in "Les séminaires," pp. 460, 462. I translate from the original transcript, which was in French.

19. Rorty, "The Historiography of Philosophy," p. 52.

20. Husserl, "Randbemerkungen," p. 13. This accusation was cited in Alwin Diemer's *Edmund Husserl* (1956), and so was entirely available to Heidegger for comment, had he retained much concern with Husserl's interpretation of the relation between their philosophies. These *Randbemerkungen* have been reviewed in the original version and translated with commentary by Sheehan in Husserl, *Psychological and Transcendental Phenomenology*, pp. 254–422 (I cite the *Randbemerkungen* by reference to the pages of *Being and Time* on which they are entered; Sheehan provides the same page references).

21. Husserl, *Logical Investigations*, 1: 252; *Ideas I*, sec. 66; *Logical Investigations*, 1: 251.

22. Husserl, *Crisis*, p. 357.

23. Derrida, introduction to Husserl's *L'origine de la géométrie*, p. 61.

24. Husserl, *Nachwort* (in *Ideen 3*, p. 140).

25. Souche-Dagues, "La lecture," pp. 123, 246.

26. Heidegger, *Being and Time*, p. 11.

27. Ibid., p. 124. The juncture at which Souche-Dagues is ready to give up is when Husserl protests in the same fashion on behalf of the intentional character of his analysis, "But how can all this be clarified except through my theory of intentionality? . . . This is my own theory, only without its deeper foundation" ("Randbemerkungen," p. 62). Husserl did not know that Heidegger had attempted to give the theory of intentionality a deeper foundation in the *Prolegomena*.

28. Searle, "Reiterating the Differances," p. 203.

6. The Shift in Method

1. Heidegger, "The End of Philosophy," pp. 63–64.

2. Ibid., p. 62 (Heidegger quotes Husserl's statement of this principle from *Ideas I*, sec. 24); Heidegger, *Phänomenologie—lebendig oder tot?* p. 47. The "priority of method" was a more general issue for Heidegger than that posed by his relation to Husserl. Not only does Heidegger later pose it with reference to Hegel, too, but in the early twenties it was an issue he posed vis-à-vis Paul Natorp. See Heidegger, *Phänomenologie der Anschauung*, pp. 112–29.

3. Husserl, *Introduction* (1913), p. 16.

4. Schuhmann, *Husserl-Chronik*, p. 2.

5. Heidegger, *Basic Problems*, p. 21.

6. Ibid., pp. 21–22.

7. Ibid., p. 328.

8. Ibid. Although I have preferred to a circumlocution the considerable risk of the translation "reflection," *Besinnung* must not be confused with "reflection" in Husserl's sense. See Fell, "Seeing a Thing in a Hidden Whole: The Significance of *Besinnung*."

9. Heidegger, *Questions III et IV*, p. 487.

10. Heidegger, *Basic Problems*, p. 328.

11. Descartes, *Discourse on Method*, Part 2. There are, of course, still other kinds of sequence. In Volume 2, I introduce one kind with the example of a short-run sequence followed by Sartre (Cumming, *P & D*, 2: 128–32).

12. Husserl, *Logical Investigations*, 1: 261.

13. Husserl, *Ideas I*, sec. 65.

14. Ibid., sec. 84.

15. The problem of sequence becomes particularly acute at the step in *Being and Time* when Heidegger proposes "a renewed retrieval of the existential-temporal analytic of Dasein within the framework of a fundamental discussion of the concept of being" (p. 333). But because of my respect for the sequence Heidegger is following, I shall not be able to reach so late a step in *Being and Time*.

16. Becker's verdict is thus paraphrased by Theodore Kisiel in *Genesis*, p. 423. If Becker's implication is that Heidegger has not broken with his scholastic training, he is overlooking how much easier going were Heidegger's earlier presentations of phenomenology. Sequence in *Being and Time* accordingly deserves attention that it has not received as a commitment of Heidegger's there—a commitment reasserted in *The Basic Problems*.

17. Beauvoir, *La force de l'âge*, p. 216.

18. Heidegger, "Letter on Humanism," p. 249. In dealing with this work in Volume 4, I shall show that an allocation is not feasible that would impose on it a single interpretation.

19. Heidegger, *On the Way to Language*, p. 7.

20. Heidegger, "My Way to Phenomenology," p. 80.

7. The Retrieval

1. Heidegger, *What Is a Thing?* pp. 1–2.

2. Heidegger, *Metaphysical Foundations of Logic*, p. 10.

3. Cairns, *Conversations*, p. 5.

4. Heidegger, *Kant und das Problem der Metaphysik*, p. 163.

5. Sallis, "Où commence *Être et temps?*"

6. Sheehan (in Husserl's *Psychological and Transcendental Phenomenology*, p. 20) identifies this page that Husserl later pasted in as having been "presented to Husserl . . . on Husserl's sixty-seventh birthday, . . . April 8, 1926."

7. Heidegger, *Prolegomena*, p. 121.

8. Heidegger, quoted in Husserl's *Psychological and Transcendental Phenomenology*, p. 136.

9. Husserl, *Briefe an Ingarden*, p. 56.

8. The Translation

1. Husserl, *Crisis*, p. 357.

2. Husserl, *Ideas I*, p. xxii. Husserl's assumption that *eidos* is "unspoiled" is remarkable, considering how regularly he incurred the charge of Platonism.

3. Heidegger, *Hölderlins Hymne "Der Ister,"* p. 76. This statement about translation may not have been original with Heidegger.

4. Heidegger, "The Origin of the Work of Art," p. 23.

5. Derrida, *Margins*, p. 33.

6. Derrida, *Mémoires pour Paul de Man*, p. 38.

7. Heidegger, *Introduction to Metaphysics*, p. 57.

8. The Stambaugh translation is identical here with the Macquarrie and Robinson.

9. Macquarrie and Robinson, trans., in Heidegger's *Being and Time*, p. 5n. 3. The term *authentic*, which intrudes in Heidegger's initial translation from the *Sophist*, is not found in his translation of the same passage in his presentation page to Husserl or when he translates a portion of the same passage in the *Prolegomena* (p. 129). But Heidegger does employ it when he characterizes as *"authentic"* Plato's "central undertaking at this place [where the question is announced] and in the dialogue as a whole" in the *Sophist* lectures *(Plato: Sophistes*, pp. 446–47).

10. Heidegger, *Metaphysical Foundations of Logic*, p. 8.

11. Heidegger, *Fundamental Concepts of Metaphysics*, p. 58.

12. Heidegger, *Being and Time*, p. 437.

13. Heidegger concludes his *Kant und das Problem der Metaphysik* (p. 168) with this quotation from Aristotle's *Metaphysics* regarding the *aporia*.

14. Heidegger, *Introduction to Metaphysics*, p. 151.

15. Heidegger, *Plato: Sophistes*, pp. 126–27.

16. Ibid., pp. 195–96.

17. Derrida, *Apories, Prière d'insérer*, p. 1.

18. Heidegger, "Only a God Can Save Us," p. 113.

19. I am alluding to Derrida's famous footnote in the essay *Of Spirit* (p. 129).

20. The title of my first chapter in my introduction to *P & D*, Volume 2, "The Passage Way," referred to how these translated passages could assist us in finding a "passage way through" from Husserl to Sartre; the title of my first chapter in the work proper, "In Passing," acknowledged the room for his originality implicit in Sartre's appraisal, "Husserl treats the problem of the image only in passing." Sartre's originality even survives the later publication (1980) of Husserl's treatment of the imagination (see *Phantasie, Bildbewusstsein, Erinnerung*).

21. Of course there is nothing unusual in dealing with the relation between a

successor and a predecessor in terms of the latter's citing from the former. In "Giving Back Words: Things, Money, Persons," I latched on to Jeremy Bentham's claim, in his *Defense of Usury* against Adam Smith, that I am "giving you back your own words." (That standard procedure is not covered in John Austin's canonical *How to Do Things with Words*.) I examined the process of the restructuring of Smith that went on in Bentham's interpretation. Smith reportedly granted that Bentham had "given [him] some hard knocks," and Bentham supposed that this phrasing implied Smith's endorsement of the *Defense*. I explained, since the elderly Smith did not, why the "knocks" did not disturb his confidence in his political economy.

22. I do not pretend that the stretch in meaning which takes place here is a precedent for resolving other instances of discrepancy between Greek originals and Heidegger's translations. In particular, it does not help with the notorious discrepancy (strikingly at the end of his rectoral address, just as the present instance is at the start of *Being and Time*) between some such plausible translation of Plato's original as "All things great are liable to collapse," and Heidegger's translation, "All that is great stands in the storm." On the discrepancy here, Karl Löwith, who heard the address, is in effect commenting when he says, "At the end of the speech, one is in doubt at to whether one should start reading . . . [the] pre-Socratics, or join the Storm Troopers" (*My Life in Germany*, p. 34). Here Heidegger goes berserk (in a fashion which is not uncharacteristic of the preceding address), even though one can conjecture some such covert implication as that the alternative standing (in German), as opposed to collapsing (in Greek), depends on the decision which Heidegger is summoning the Germans to, but which they may try to evade.

23. Heidegger, *Being and Time*, p. 75.

24. Ibid., pp. 35.

25. Husserl, *Ideas I*, sec. 10, sec. 26.

26. Heidegger, *Being and Time*, p. 35.

27. Heidegger, *Being and Time*, p. 36. After the emphasis of "*not* given," Heidegger goes on to play up in quotation marks "clear" (p. 36) and "immediately" (p. 37). These criteria are not introduced in a fashion which suggests he is necessarily referring to Husserl, yet Heidegger seems to be preparing us to recognize the need for a procedure that is not Husserl's *Methode der Klärung*, which relies for clarification on bringing into focus the immediately given.

28. Ibid., p. 37.

29. Ibid., p. 38.

30. Heidegger, *Prolegomena*, p. 76.

9. Destruktion

1. Heidegger, *Being and Time*, p. 21. Heidegger would seem to be playing *übergibt* off against Husserl's conception of the immediately given.

2. Heidegger, *Basic Problems*, p. 22.

3. Heidegger, *What Is Philosophy?* pp. 70–73.

4. Husserl, *Ideas I*, sec. 31.

5. Ibid., sec. 18.

6. See von Herrmann's detailed commentary on sec. 6 in *Hermeneutische Phänomenologie des Daseins*, pp. 199–277; Buchheim, *Destruktion und Übersetzung*, p. v.

7. Heidegger, *Being and Time*, pp. 89, 392.

8. Ibid., p. 47.

9. Heidegger, *On the Way to Language*, pp. 114–16.

10. The Edge

1. Derrida, *Speech and Phenomena*, p. 3. Because Derrida abstains, in his deconstruction of Husserl's analysis of signs, from comparing it with Heidegger's analysis, I shall myself, in making this comparison, abstain from any comparison between Heidegger's procedure and Derrida's procedure (if it can be called that) of deconstruction. Any such comparison would be a complicated affair, as he and others have recognized. I have taken a stab at it in "The Odd Couple: Heidegger and Derrida."

2. Derrida, *Speech and Phenomena*, p. 4.

3. Ibid., p. 52.

4. Ibid., p. 74.

5. Rudolph Bernet, "Derrida et la voix de son maître," p. 148.

6. Walter Biemel, "Le professeur," p. 128. I am not denying grave differences between Derrida's general interpretation and Heidegger's. Perhaps the most obvious is that Heidegger's is epochal. But my present concern with differences is elsewhere. I would bring out the fate, in Derrida and Heidegger alike, of the differences in method that in my exposition separate individual philosophers.

7. Derrida, *Of Grammatology*, p. 3.

8. Derrida, *Speech and Phenomenoma*, p. 3.

9. Husserl, *Logical Investigations*, 1: 47.

11. The Boundary

1. Derrida, *Speech and Phenomena*, p. 4.

2. Ibid., p. 24.

3. Husserl, *Logical Investigations*, 1: 53.

4. Ibid., 1: 90, 296. Observe that Husserl carries out his shift in *subject* by opposing Mill's conception of the subject. His logic is structured by what Derrida characterizes as traditional—an "oppositional structure" or an "oppositional logic," which in this instance is exhibited by Husserl's opposition to another philosopher.

5. Ibid., 1: 265–66.

6. Ibid., 1: 55. See Chapter 8 above, for we are observing how the eidetic re-

duction, with which Husserl secures clarity, can be a commitment to "delimitation," as opposed to what is "dangerous"—a "confusion," a "mixture." Thus this commitment takes hold not just in Husserl's analysis of specific examples but with respect to the subject which he is delimiting as "logical."

7. Derrida, *Points de suspension*, p. 387.

8. Mill, *Logic*, Book 1, sec. 1 (cited in *Logical Investigations*, 1: 248); I have supplied the title of Mill's initial section because Husserl emulates it with the title of his initial section: "The Necessity of Phenomenological Investigations as a Preliminary to the Epistemological Criticism and Clarification of Pure Logic."

12. The Ambiguity

1. Heidegger, *Introduction to Metaphysics*, p. 11.

2. Husserl, *Logical Investigations*, 1: 270.

3. Mill, *Logic*, chap. 2, sec. 5.

4. Husserl, *Logical Investigations*, 1: 270.

5. Ibid., pp. 269, 270, 273.

6. Ibid., p. 368.

7. Ibid., p. 369.

8. Ibid., 2: 554.

9. Ibid., p. 387.

10. Ibid., p. 269.

11. Ibid., p. 275. See Cumming, *P & D*, 2: 84–87.

12. Husserl, *Ideas I*, sec. 123.

13. Derrida, *Margins*, p. 160. The idiom of *tissu* was not originally associated with a "text." It had been a regular resort of Merleau-Ponty's, who conveyed the relational character of his analysis by speaking of "phenomena" as a "fabric," of "the real as a solid fabric," of "existence" as "not a set of facts . . . but the ambiguous setting of their interrelation, the juncture at which their boundaries run into each other, or where they are woven together" (*Phenomenology of Perception*, pp. x, xii, 166). Observe how ambiguity is reinstated when phenomena, having been disentangled by Husserl, become entangled again in Merleau-Ponty, although the *tissu* of a "text" was not in question. For similar idioms in Merleau-Ponty ("net," "knot"), see my *Starting Point*, p. 227.

14. For Derrida's acknowledgment of "the necessity of *forçage*," see, for instance, *Les fins de l'homme*, p. 364.

15. Cumming, *P & D*, 2: 4–11.

16. Derrida, *Speech and Phenomena*, pp. 27–28.

17. Ibid., p. 28n.

18. Husserl, *Logical Investigations*, 1: 251.

19. Husserl, *Ideas I*, sec. 66.

20. Ibid.

21. Ibid.

13. The Indicative Sign

1. The most elaborate interpretation in English of Heidegger's treatment of the question of being is Herman Philipse, *Heidegger's Philosophy of Being*. When Philipse comments on the introductory section in *Being and Time*, "The Phenomenological Method of Investigation," he focuses on Heidegger's "dilemma with respect to philosophical method. If he [Heidegger] uses the hermeneutical technique of interpreting the way in which humans understand themselves and the world . . . his results will be limited to specific cultural epochs, and the job of the philosopher cannot be very different from that of the novelist, the historian, or the cultural anthropologist. Or, if he wants to claim that philosophical knowledge is 'fundamental and a priori,' he has to substantiate it by a convincing methodological argument, which Heidegger does not provide" (p. 337). This "dilemma" I cite for the purpose of the contrast with my own focus on the methodological argument which Heidegger does provide and which requires some attention, if one has any concern with how Heidegger himself formulates the question of being. Like many other commentators, Philipse does not respect Heidegger's method as a "sequence of steps" and instead relies initially on his concepts of "understanding" and "interpretation," although these concepts are not constructed until pp. 148–53 of *Being and Time*. A commentator who would skip in this fashion should still offer some explanation for the long delay in Heidegger. But the delay no longer matters in Philipse, since what was sequence in *Being and Time* becomes hodgepodge. Philipse does offer a section, "Ways of Interpretation," which begins, "It would be tedious to spell out all problems of interpretation concerning the question of being that are *concealed* in Heidegger's introduction to *Sein und Zeit*, let alone the problems *added* by the body of the book and by the later works" (my italics). We are spared such tedium, for it turns out "that in order to do justice to Heidegger's works, we should not apply Heidegger's own doctrine of interpretation in interpreting his thought" (p. 45).

2. Heidegger, *Prolegomena*, p. 203.

3. Heidegger, *Being and Time*, p. 77. Heidegger would associate *Zeichen* with *Zeigen*, but in English one hesitates between the translation "to indicate" or "to show." The first translation risks confusion with *anzeigen*; I shall bring out in Chapter 14 the force the prefix has for Husserl. The second translation is too vague, but would help us appreciate Heidegger's having earlier in *Being and Time* defined "phenomenon" itself as meaning "to show itself" (*sich zeigen*). Here too the implications must wait until Chapter 14.

4. Husserl, *Logical Investigations*, 1: 269–70.

5. Heidegger, *Being and Time*, p. 1.

6. Husserl, *Logical Investigations*, 1: 269.

7. Derrida, *Speech and Phenomena*, pp. 23–24.

8. Ibid., p. 7.

9. Ibid., p. 28.

10. Husserl, *Logical Investigations*, 1: 55.

11. Sartre, *Philosophy of Jean-Paul Sartre*, p. 86; Cumming, *P & D*, 2: 214–16.

12. Husserl, *Logical Investigations*, 1: 275.

13. See Cumming, *P & D*, 2: 84–85, 118, 122–125.

14. The Indicator

1. Heidegger, *Being and Time*, p. 78.

2. Pöggeler, "Heidegger Heute," p. 42.

3. Husserl, *Experience and Judgment*, p. 342.

4. See Cumming, *P & D*, 2: 131, where I summarize Sartre's argument.

5. Heidegger, *Being and Time*, pp. 78–79.

6. Ibid., p. 7.

7. Ibid., p. 79.

8. Ibid., pp. 28, 34. If I have not made more extensive use of the section entitled "The Phenomenological Method of Investigation," it is because I am singling out only the most definite references there to Husserl. I am overlooking references which I take as more particularly to Kant and neo-Kantianism—for example, when Heidegger goes on from *phainomenon* to "the kind of showing-itself" which is "what we call 'seeming' [*Scheinen*]" and to "what is called an 'appearance' [*Erscheinung*]" (p. 29). I could nonetheless have pursued even here his differences with Husserl. Most obviously, Heidegger is exploiting ambiguities, where Husserl would, for example, point out, "The term 'appearance' is, of course, burdened [*beschwert*] with ambiguities. . . . It will not be pointless . . . to line up these ambiguities explicitly" (*Logical Investigations*, 2: 860). Although I have confined my interpretation of *Being and Time* to points where his relation to Husserl is more readily exhibited, it should not be forgotten that the sequel to *Being and Time* was *Kant and the Problem of Metaphysics*, as Husserl himself recognized when he entered marginal comments on this work as well. For an incisive summary of the issues posed by these comments, see Richard E. Palmer's introduction to them in Husserl, *Psychology and Transcendental Phenomenology*, pp. 424–33.

9. Heidegger, *Being and Time*, p. 77.

10. Husserl, *Logical Investigations*, 2: 554.

15. The Context

1. Heidegger, *Being and Time*, p. 77. I am taking advantage here of Heidegger's comment on "formalization" as a reference to Husserl (see *Ideas I*, sec. 18), but at the same time I have to admit a limitation of my own exposition. Heidegger's treatment of the indicative sign could warrant examining his procedure of "formal indication" (*formale Anzeige*). This procedure is crucial in Heidegger's earlier writings, and Kisiel insists that "formal indication constitutes the very fulcrum of *Being and Time*" (*Genesis*, p. 529). Even an explanation, then, as to why it is not more explicitly presented there would have to bring in the evidence of Heidegger's earlier writings. They are, I have already explained, largely beyond my scope.

2. Husserl, *Logical Investigations,* 1: 225.

3. Ibid., 2: 563.

4. Heidegger, *Prolegomena,* p. 55.

5. Heidegger, *Being and Time,* p. 79.

6. I employed "context" in an entirely different sense in my *Human Nature and History* (1969). By that time it had become established procedure to canvass the economic and social circumstances as the "context" in the sense of the ultimate court of appeal in determining what the statements of a political theorist mean, so I tried to point out that there might intervene a "context" in the different sense of certain presuppositions and procedures which his theory involves and which also deserved explication in determining his meanings. Needless to say, my use of "context" in this sense did not take on. But I shall again be raising the issue of "circumstances" in Volume 4, where we shall see the reckless fashion in which the later Heidegger will dispose of them.

7. Husserl, *Logical Investigations,* 1: 270. To illustrate the respect in which the exclusion of relations is required for Husserl's exercise of *Einsichtigkeit,* I would cite from Chapter 11, to which Heidegger refers us: "It is a matter of *insight into the essence* of the relevant concepts with a view [*Hinsicht*] methodologically to the fixation of word meanings which are unambiguous, sharply separated" (Ibid., 1: 238).

8. Heidegger, *Being and Time,* p. 25. What I would interpret as Heidegger's deconstruction of Husserl's intentional analysis in *Being and Time* can also be considered in the light of his attempts elsewhere (most particularly in the *Prolegomena*) to reconstruct intentional analysis. See Rudolph Bernet, "Husserl and Heidegger on Intentionality and Being," and Burt Hopkins, *Intentionality in Husserl and Heidegger.* Neither scholar brings out sufficiently how drastically deconstructive of Husserl Heidegger's reconstruction is. For a succinct illustration, consider the conclusion Heidegger reaches in the *Prolegomena:* Intentionality in Husserl is "*fragmentary,* a phenomenon seen *merely from the outside.* What is referred to as intentionality—the *mere* directing itself toward, must still be laid back [*zurückverlegt*] in the *unified* fundamental structure of being-ahead-of-itself-in-already-being-by. This is above all the authentic phenomenon which corresponds to what is inauthentically and merely in an *isolated* direction referred to as intentionality" (*Prolegomena,* pp. 303–6). My italics are meant to bring out the disparagment implicit in the holistic and relational criteria which Heidegger is applying, so that Husserl's analysis is merely external to the phenomenon, its fragmentation, and its isolation from its *relata.* Heidegger's "it could be shown" is not argumentative, but a phenomenological appeal to how the phenomenon "shows itself."

9. Husserl, *Logical Investigations,* 1: 245.

10. See the section "*Auslegung*" in Chapter 8.

11. Heidegger, *Being and Time,* p. 77.

12. See the section "Sequence" in Chapter 6. The passage is from Kisiel, *Genesis,* p. 443.

13. Heidegger, *Being and Time*, p. 78. Heidegger did not arrive at this later step in *Being and Time* (as published).

14. Husserl, *Logical Investigations*, 1: 203.

15. Heidegger, *Being and Time*, pp. 83–84. Heidegger's use of italics for "*with*" betrays his commitment to a relational analysis, and in my next chapter I shall deal with *Mithebung*.

16. Ibid., p. 87.

17. Ibid., p. 34.

16. Der Weg der Abhebung

1. Heidegger, *Being and Time*, p. 40.

2. Husserl, *Logical Investigations*, 2: 436.

3. Ibid., 1: 261.

4. Ibid., 2: 435.

5. See the section "The Components" in Chapter 6.

6. Heidegger, *Being and Time*, p. 40.

7. Husserl, *Logical Investigations*, 2: 463–64.

8. Heidegger, *Being and Time*, p. 428. Heidegger could hardly have deployed a procedure which he would characterize as an "*Abhebung*" unless he had the further intention of emphasizing that he was handling relations in a fashion opposed to the dialectical fashion in which Hegel carried out the shift in *level*, for which he employed the term *Aufhebung*.

9. Husserl, *Ideas I*, sec. 67.

17. Umgang

1. Husserl, *Ideas I*, sec. 4.

2. Heidegger, *Die Grundprobleme der Phänomenologie*, p. 241. Throughout his analysis, Heidegger is dealing directly with sec. 4 of *Ideas I*.

3. Heidegger, *Prolegomena*, p. 110.

4. Husserl, *Ideas I*, sec. 70.

5. Husserl, *Phenomenological Psychology*, p. 53.

6. Heidegger, *Introduction to Metaphysics*, p. 11.

7. Heidegger, *Nietzsche*, 2: 22–25. Heidegger's own holism is a factor in this burdensomeness. He admits that "Nietzsche does not invoke 'being' as a whole." I shall return to this section in Volume 4, as a juncture at which Heidegger deals with "solitude."

8. The one work dedicated entirely to the exposition of this stretch is Prauss, *Knowing and Doing in "Being and Time."*

9. Kisiel, "The New Translation of *Sein und Zeit*," p. 245.

10. Heidegger, *Being and Time*, p. 66.

11. Ibid., p. 68.

12. Ibid., p. 69.

13. Heidegger, *Prolegomena*, p. 205.

14. Heidegger, *Being and Time*, p. 67.

15. Ibid., p. 68.

16. Ibid., pp. 70–71.

17. Ibid., p. 68.

18. Ibid.

19. Ibid.

20. Ibid.

21. Heidegger, *Basic Problems*, p. 22.

22. Husserl, *Ideas I*, sec. 35.

23. Ibid.

24. Heidegger, *Being and Time*, p. 102.

18. Ausgang

1. Husserl, *Ideen 3*, p. 140.

2. Heidegger, *Prolegomena*, p. 110.

3. See the section "The Reductions" in Chapter 3.

4. Husserl, *Logical Investigations*, 2: 468.

5. Heidegger, *Being and Time*, p. 68.

6. Ibid., p. 36.

7. Heidegger, *Prolegomena*, p. 194.

8. Heidegger, *Being and Time*, p. 69.

9. Ibid., p. 329.

10. Perhaps nowhere has Heidegger's break with the tradition in *Being and Time* been more regularly recognized than in his undercutting of the *vorhanden*. But where in the tradition is the *vorhanden* as recurrent as in Husserl's dealing with the natural attitude? See, for instance, in *Ideas I*, sec. 27: "The world is continually '*vorhanden*' for me. . . . Value-characteristics and practical characteristics belong *constitutively to the objects* '*vorhanden*' *as objects*." This is the juncture at which Heidegger would intrude his concept of *Zuhandenheit*. See also sec. 28: "The natural world remains '*vorhanden*.'" See also sec. 31, where Husserl again refers to "the characteristic 'there,' '*vorhanden*.'" The same phrasing is repeated in sec. 32.

11. Sartre, "Conscience de soi et connaissance de soi," p. 76.

12. Sartre, *Nausea*, p. 4.

13. Ibid.

14. Sartre's italicizing *en personne* even in a literary work (*Les mots*, p. 38) implies that it is a technical phrase.

15. Sartre, *Situations*, 9: 55.

19. Concept Construction

1. Heidegger, *Being and Time*, p. 220.

2. Heidegger, *Einführung*, p. 258.

3. Heidegger, *Being and Time*, p. 54.

4. Ibid., p. 11.

5. Souche-Dagues, "Lecture husserlienne," p. 132. She is interpreting Husserl's marginal reaction (two question marks and a *"gekunstelt"*), which is elicited by Heidegger's, *"hören-hörig-Hörigkeit-zugehörig-hörchen"* (p. 163).

6. Kisiel, *Genesis*, p. 423.

7. In *P & D*, Volume 1, Chapter 12, I was objecting in particular to Merleau-Ponty's preface, in which he answers the question, "What is phenomenology?" by claiming that *"phenomenology can be identified . . . as a manner or style of thinking"* and that it "is accessible only *via* a phenomenological method" (*Phenomenology of Perception*, p. viii), which he ascribes to Husserl and Heidegger alike, and to himself and Sartre as well.

8. Sartre, *Les carnets*, p. 404.

9. Husserl, *Crisis*, p. 280.

10. Souche-Dagues, "Lecture husserlienne," p. 132.

11. Heidegger, *Prolegomena*, p. 151.

12. Heidegger clearly also finds "style" of no relevance in his treatment of art. Is that remarkable temple, "standing there" in "The Origin of the Work of Art," Doric (pp. 41–43)?

13. Heidegger, *Being and Time*, p. 39.

14. Franzen, "Die Sehnsucht nach Härte und Schwere."

15. Heidegger, *Being and Time*, p. 311.

16. Heidegger, *Basic Problems*, trans. Hofstadter, p. 44.

17. Sartre, *Les mots*, p. 29. For his "bookishness," see Cumming, *P & D*, 1: 50–51.

18. Heidegger, *Being and Time*, p. 39.

19. Derrida, *Spectres de Marx*, p. 122.

20. Heidegger, *Prolegomena*, p. 187.

21. Ibid., p. 158.

22. Heidegger, *Basic Problems*, p. 304.

23. Heidegger, *Ontologie*, p. 100. The sentence I have cited in part comes at the end of a short paragraph, which illustrates how compactly Heidegger phrases what he will analyze elaborately in *Being and Time*. It also illustrates how early in Heidegger's career he found fundamental, on the one hand, "familiarity" and, on the other, an obstructed way.

24. See the section "The Blur" in Chapter 5.

25. Husserl, *Logical Investigations*, 1: 255.

20. Aufgehen In

1. Husserl, *Logical Investigations*, 1: 254–55. Husserl accords the distinction between "act" and "object" a more technical reformulation in *Ideas I* as the distinction between *noēsis* (noetic moment) and *noēma* (noematic content); see section 88. I do not deal with this reformulation, since the distinction had no implications for Heidegger.

2. Heidegger, *Being and Time*, p. 54.

3. Ibid., p. 42.

4. Kisiel, *Genesis*, p. 537.

5. Husserl, *Ideas I*, sec. 24.

6. Derrida, *Margins*, p. 64. Derrida is commenting on Heidegger's reflexive commitment in section 5 of *Being and Time*. (The question raised in this section is cited in my section "The Exemplar" in Chapter 14.) The elision is recurrent in Derrida. See also *Margins*, p. 126, where he refers to "the criterion of proximity, *that is, of presence in general*" (my italics). He similarly interprets the "concept of presence" in terms of "a being in absolute proximity to itself" (*Speech and Phenomena*, p. 58). Husserl sometimes does use the terminology "*absolute proximity* [*Nähe*]" (e.g., *Ideas I*, sec. 67). But Heidegger would never use this terminology, since "nearness" in his relational analysis is relative, as is suggested by his varied resorts to the criterion *zunächst*.

7. Heidegger, *Being and Time*, pp. 146, 170–71.

8. Husserl, *Ideas I*, sec. 19.

9. Husserl, *Logical Investigations*, 1: 307.

10. Heidegger, *Being and Time*, p. 54.

21. Psychologism

1. Heidegger, *Prolegomena*, p. 121. I have preferred the comparison of the *Prolegomena* with *Being and Time* to taking into account *The Essence of Reasons* (*Vom Wesen des Grundes*), even though the latter appeared in the *Festschrift* for Husserl (1929). Heidegger's relation to Husserl there (two years after the publication of *Being and Time*) does not differ significantly from his relation to him in *Being and Time*, whereas the differences between the *Prolegomena* and *Being and Time* (published two years after those lectures) are most significant. Indeed, it would not have been feasible for me to limit my comparison to particular passages in the *Prolegomena* and *Being and Time*, had not an array of larger problems already been dealt with by Kisiel in his article "On the Way to *Being and Time*."

2. Heidegger, *Ontologie*, p. 36.

3. Heidegger, *Prolegomena*, p. 5.

4. See the section "The Exemplar" in Chapter 14.

5. Heidegger, *Prolegomena*, p. 100.

6. Ibid., p. 185.

7. Ibid., p. 191.

8. Ibid., p. 187.

9. This depsychologization of the meaning of *Aufgehen* might be said to be carried further in the later Heidegger, when, for example, in the *Introduction to Metaphysics* (p. 14), he translates the Greek *physis* as *"Das von sich ausaufgehende"* ("that which emerges from itself"). What Heidegger would eliminate is no longer the restriction to psychology, but the "restriction of *physis* in the direction of 'physics'" (p. 16).

10. Heidegger, *Prolegomena*, p. 187.

11. Ibid., pp. 186–87.

12. Heidegger, *Being and Time*, pp. 68–69; see Chapter 17 in this volume.

13. Heidegger, "My Way to Phenomenology," p. 76.

14. Heidegger, *Prolegomena*, p. 29.

15. Husserl, *Ideen 3, Nachwort*, 140.

16. Heidegger, *Zur Bestimmung der Philosophie*, pp. 29, 38.

22. The Theory of Knowledge

1. Heidegger, *Prolegomena*, p. 25.

2. Heidegger, *Being and Time*, p. 59.

3. Heidegger, *Prolegomena*, p. 115.

4. See the sections "Reference" and "Intentionality" in Chapter 17.

5. Heidegger, *Prolegomena*, p. 187. I am overlooking how crucial the phenomenon of concern is for Heidegger. Despite his initial statement in *Being and Time* that "the modes of being-in," which he is analyzing, "have *concern* [*Besorgen*] as their kind of being," he cautions that it is "a kind of being which is not yet characterized" (p. 57). It cannot be characterized adequately until he reaches section 65, "Temporality as the Ontological Meaning of Care [*Sorge*]." "Care" is also postponed in the *Prolegomena*. When, near the end of these lectures, Heidegger has "brought the various structures of Dasein into a certain correlation with the basic phenomenon of care," he announces that "a stage has been reached which provides a place at which we could critically retrieve what we have heard about *intentionality* in the introductory treatment" (p. 303). His conclusion that this is "a place at which the way is prepared for a fundamental critique of the phenomenological problematic," does solicit an attempt to supply this critique. I have not responded, since my preoccupation is with *Being and Time*, and in the sequence followed there, the treatment of intentionality is itself deferred. Thus I have tried to explain this deferment by restricting my exposition to how Husserl's intentional analysis is in effect superseded by a relational analysis in *Being and Time*. But the publication of the *Prolegomena* has encouraged the comparison of the treatment of intentionality there with Husserl's. I have already cited in particular Rudolf Bernet's "Husserl and Heidegger on Intentionality and Being."

6. Husserl, *Ideas I*, sec. 35.

7. Heidegger, *Prolegomena*, p. 187.

8. See the section "The Exemplar" in Chapter 14.

9. Heidegger, *Prolegomena*, pp. 29–30.

10. Ibid., pp. 28–29.

11. Ibid., p. 29.

12. The phrase Heidegger uses here, "in a single move," is in fact Husserl's, though used by him with reference to the phenomenological *epochē* (see *Ideas I*, sec. 32) rather than the philosophical *epochē*. For the way Heidegger sets up the *Destruktion* in opposition to Husserl's philosophical *epochē*, see the section "Starting Over Again" in Chapter 9.

13. Heidegger, *Being and Time*, p. 67.

14. Ibid., p. 68. It is tempting to read the turmoil of the "clutching" and the "pushing away" as critical of the prompt ease with which the philosophical *epochē* is carried out in *Ideas I*.

15. See the section "Latin Translation" in Chapter 8.

16. The issue as to whether it is feasible to appeal to untainted, pretheoretical experience was extensively canvassed by neo-Kantian critics of phenomenology in the twenties. I do not examine their criticisms of phenomenology, because I am focusing on the relation between Heidegger and Husserl.

17. Heidegger, *Being and Time*, p. 67.

18. Heidegger, *Prolegomena*, p. 113.

19. It seems evident that Husserl, before making the preceding comment on *Being and Time*, p. 67, has first gone on to this passage two pages later, since he anticipates in quotation marks the verb *hinsehen* which is used there. Thus we should not infer from the impatience and brevity of many of his comments that he rushed through *Being and Time* ungenerously venting his indignation. At the same time, my exposition of *Being and Time* would vindicate (at least in the stretch I cover) Husserl's suspicion that Heidegger was quite regularly criticizing him in particular, even though I am not at all suggesting that Heidegger's preference for criticizing the tradition instead is a mere ruse. It is a commitment of his philosophy.

23. Language

1. Heidegger, *Being and Time*, p. 166n.

2. Ibid., p. 87.

3. Heidegger, "Letter on Humanism," p. 217.

4. Heidegger, *Being and Time*, p. 161.

5. Husserl, *Ideas I*, sec. 124.

6. Heidegger, *Being and Time*, p. 162.

7. Husserl, "Phenomenology and Anthropology," p. 321.

8. The only other instance in the eighty-three section titles where a period is used is in the title of section 11: "The Existential Analytic and the Interpretation of

Primitive Dasein. The Difficulties of Achieving a 'Natural Conception of the World.'" But in this instance the first half of the title designates a broad area of comparison and debate, whereas the second half refers to a single philosopher's particular formulation—as Heidegger's single quotation marks indicate.

 9. Heidegger, *Schelling's Treatise,* p. 189.

 10. Heidegger, *Being and Time,* p. 16. The "everydayness" can be said to have been "lost sight of" only after section 27, but the phrase "thematic starting point" would seem to take us back to section 5.

 11. Husserl, "Randbemerkungen," p. 307.

24. The Monologue

 1. Husserl, *Logical Investigations,* 1: 256.

 2. Ibid., pp. 265–66.

 3. Ibid., pp. 277–78.

 4. Ibid., p. 278.

 5. Ibid., p. 279.

 6. Ibid., p. 280.

 7. Husserl, *Ideen 3,* p. 162.

 8. Husserl, *Logical Investigations,* 1: 285.

 9. Husserl, *Ideas I,* sec. 27.

 10. Husserl, *Cartesian Meditations,* p. 157.

 11. See the section "Intentionality" in Chapter 17.

 12. Husserl, *Logical Investigations,* 1: 48.

 13. Husserl, "Phenomenology and Anthropology," pp. 317–18.

 14. Cairns, *Conversations,* pp. 60–61.

 15. Gadamer, *Philosophical Apprenticeships,* p. 36.

 16. Beaufret, *Entretiens,* p. 178.

 17. Fink, "Husserl's Philosophy and Contemporary Criticism," pp. 73–74.

 18. Ibid.

 19. Ibid.

25. The Public Reckoning

 1. Heidegger, *Being and Time,* p. 162.

 2. Ibid., p. 168.

 3. Ibid., p. 169.

 4. Ibid., p. 224.

 5. Husserl, *Logical Investigations,* 1: 252, 307.

 6. Heidegger, "Only a God Can Save Us," p. 98. I have checked the emended version in *Antwort* (ed. Neske and Kettering) against the original (*Der Spiegel,* May 31, 1976).

7. In Volume 4 I shall present Karl Jaspers's challenge to Heidegger's distinction.

8. Heidegger, "Only a God Can Save Us," p. 98.

9. Husserl, "Phenomenology and Anthropology," p. 315. Wilhelm Dilthey alone is mentioned by name as having influenced this anthropology. Husserl seems unaware of the public lecture in 1931 as a factor in the breaking off of the relation with Heidegger. He himself offers two dates. He writes of Heidegger's "self-initiated break in relations with me soon after his appointment [at Freiburg]." But Husserl's emphasis is on the break which took place when Heidegger entered the Nazi Party in May 1933. It hit Husserl hard. It was the "ending of the supposed bosom friendship between philosophers." He admits, "I had come to place a trust (which I can no longer understand) not just in his talent but in his character as well" (letter to Dietrick Mahnke, May 4, 1933, three days after Heidegger's entry into the National Socialist Party, *Briefwechsel*, 3: 493).

10. These criticisms Husserl published in his *Jahrbuch fur Philosophie und Phänomenologische Forschung*. They are reprinted in *Ideen 3*, p. 140.

11. Towarnicki, *À la rencontre de Heidegger*, pp. 177–78.

12. Petzet, *Encounters and Dialogues*, p. 92. I shall consider Heidegger's "bitterness" in Volume 4, Chapter 8.

13. For this and other accusations I am citing, see Karl Schuhmann's meticulous compilation of the facts in "Zu Heideggers Spiegel-Gespräch," although the interpretations here are my own.

14. Heidegger, *Being and Time*, p. 169.

15. Beaufret, *Douze questions*, pp. 37–38.

16. Neske and Kettering, eds., *Antwort*, p. 112.

17. Heidegger, "Letter on Humanism," pp. 219, 221. The application of the concept of *Öffentlichkeit* is not the only justification for the comparison with Sartre. Heidegger initiated the relation to Sartre with a cordial letter to him, October 28, 1945 (cited by Towarnicki, *À la rencontre*, pp. 83–85; I shall examine it in Volume 4). On the same day, Sartre delivered his "Existentialism Is a Humanism" lecture. The next spring Heidegger began writing the "Letter on Humanism," which is (among other things) an attack on Sartre. Is it merely a trivial coincidence that there is a certain similarity to what happened to his relation to Husserl and Jaspers—in short to all three of his relations to prominent contemporary philosophers? Each time the relation began cordially and ended with a remarkable breakdown in communication. Certainly the differences, personal and philosophical, in the three instances, are so considerable that the prospect of any comparison may seem far-fetched. But in Volume 4 I shall add the breakdowns in communication with Jaspers and Sartre to the breakdown with Husserl.

18. Heidegger, *Being and Time*, p. 126.

19. Heidegger's *Introduction to Metaphysics* ([Sommersemester 1935], p. 38) includes a reference to "when mass meetings attended by millions are looked on as a triumph," which might be taken as an allusion to Nuremberg and perhaps to Leni Riefenstahl's *Triumph of the Will*. But the allusion is in effect depoliticized by the climax: "Any incident anywhere . . . can become swiftly accessible anywhere, when the assassination of a king in France and a symphony concert in

Tokyo can be 'experienced' at the same time." These items are corralled but (since it is 1935) without benefit of any such dangerous terminology as "the dictatorship of publicity."

20. Towarnicki, À la rencontre, p. 123.

21. Heidegger, Being and Time, p. 127.

22. Ibid., 129.

23. Ibid., p. 169.

24. If a substantive illustration of this *Fürsorge* can be risked, it might be Heidegger's relation to students. Karl Löwith, the only student who did a *Habilitation* with Heidegger in the twenties, quotes Heidegger as having written him as follows: "[My concern is not] whether or not you agree with me substantively [*sachlich*] for determining acceptance or rejection, nor . . . whether or not you have understood my work. . . . In your own interest only I have made marginal comments in places where you have taken the easy way out of the critique and underestimated the difficulties of the problems and their presuppositions" (Heidegger, "Drei Briefe," p. 68). Heidegger even cautioned Löwith, "I have nothing to say to you."

Heidegger was leaping out of the way when he disavowed those students who were "Heideggereans," who "Heideggereanized." Thus Gadamer can describe Heidegger as "studentless" (van Buren, *The Young Heidegger*, p. 353). Such an accomplishment would be consistent with Heidegger's repudiation of a "following," and here I would renew my contrast with Husserl's "team."

25. Steiner, "Review," p. 137. The pertinence of this episode to the problem of communication is suggested by Steiner's assessment: "Only one thing is absolutely and despairingly clear . . . Heidegger did not answer" when Celan "came to challenge that thinker's terrible silence after 1945 (a silence far more appalling than were Heidegger's complaisant follies and self-delusions in 1933–34)." In Volume 4 I shall take up the issue of Heidegger's silence as posed by Jaspers's persistent effort to cope with Heidegger's *Unoffenheit* ("lack of openness"), which defeated communication between them and justified Jaspers's verdict that Heidegger was "*kommunicationlos.*"

Conclusion. The End of Philosophy

1. Heidegger, "Letter on Humanism," p. 243.

2. Towarnicki, À la rencontre, p. 254.

3. Heidegger, "My Way to Phenomenology," p. 75.

4. Heidegger, Being and Time, p. 38n.

5. Heidegger, "Mon chemin de pensée," in *Questions III et IV*, p. 325.

6. Heidegger, "My Way to Phenomenology," p. 82.

7. Cairn, *Conversations*, p. 9.

8. Heidegger, "My Way to Phenomenology," p. 77.

9. Heidegger, "The End of Philosophy," p. 57.

10. See the section "Interpretative Tendencies" in chapter 22.

11. Heidegger, "Les séminaires," pp. 482–83.

12. Heidegger, "The End of Philosophy," p. 62. Heidegger had cited the passage from Plato with the phrase *to pragma auto* in his tribute to Husserl on his seventieth birthday (*Reden und andere Zeugnisse,* p. 59).

13. Husserl, "Introduction" (1913), p. 16.

14. Husserl, *Ideas I,* sec. 35.

15. See the section "A Startling Deviation" in Chapter 4.

16. Merleau-Ponty, *The Phenomenology of Perception,* p. xvi. Merleau-Ponty's complaint that intentionality is "too often cited as the principal discovery of phenomenology" cannot but be taken as a criticism of Sartre's exuberant "une idée fondamentale."

17. Merleau-Ponty, *The Structure of Behavior,* p. 168.

18. Sartre, *Being and Nothingness,* p. 613.

19. Merleau-Ponty, "Le philosophe et son ombre," in *Signes,* p. 202. The philosopher is Husserl, and the interrelatedness in which Merleau-Ponty is indulging is conveyed in part by the idiom of "shadow," which derives from Husserl's phenomenology of perception in which the object is perceived in terms of its *Abschattungen*—its "adumbrations," its "aspects"—which one is successively conscious of (see Cumming, *P & D,* 2: 61). But with Merleau-Ponty's addition "and the reflection," the object itself is mirrored by its interrelations and can no longer be intentionally singled out as in Husserl. With Merleau-Ponty's move from "between things" to "articulations between things said," which are likewise "not objects of thinking," Husserl can be visualized as casting the "shadow"—the phenomenological movement—from which he can no longer be singled out in the fashion (Merleau-Ponty was then unaware) that Husserl himself insisted on. The analogy in the passage is not just to landscape, but to "landscape" as an artistic genre—notably Cézanne's. I take the opportunity to recall the issue of affiliation for philosophy, which I emphasized in dealing with the phenomenological movement in my two previous volumes. I have neglected affiliation in the present volume because it is not an issue in *Being and Time.*

20. Merleau-Ponty, *The Phenomenology of Perception,* p. xxi.

21. Heidegger, "The End of Philosophy," p. 64.

22. Heidegger's "thinking" as "subjectivity relinquishing" ("Letter on Humanism," p. 231) will be a prominent theme in Volume 4.

Arendt, Hannah, and Karl Jaspers. *Hannah Arendt/Karl Jaspers Correspondence, 1926–1969.* Edited by Lotte Kohler and Hans Saner. Translated by Robert and Rita Kimber. New York: Harcourt Brace Jovanovich, 1992.

Beaufret, Jean. *Douze questions posées à Jean Beaufret à propos de Martin Heidegger.* Edited by Dominique Le Buhan and Eryck de Rubercy. Paris: Editions Aubien Montaigne, 1983.

———. *Entretiens avec Fréderic de Towarnicki.* Paris: Presses Universitaires, 1984.

———. *Introduction aux philosophies de l'existence.* Paris: Editions Denoël, 1971.

Beauvoir, Simone de. *La force de l'âge.* Paris: Gallimard, 1960.

Bernet, Rudolph. "Derrida et la voix de son maître." *Revue philosophique* 2 (April–June 1990).

———. "Husserl and Heidegger on Intentionality and Being." *Journal of the British Society for Phenomenology* 21 (May 1990).

Biemel, Walter. "Le professeur, le penseur, l'ami." In *Martin Heidegger.* Paris: L'édition de l'Herne, 1983.

Boyce Gibson, William R. "From Husserl to Heidegger: Excerpts from a 1928 Freiburg Diary." Edited by Herbert Spiegelberg. *Journal of the British Society for Phenomenology* 2 (January 1971).

Bubner, Rüdiger. *Modern German Philosophy.* Translated by Eric Matthews. Cambridge: Cambridge University Press, 1981.

Buchheim, Thomas. *Destruktion und Übersetzung. Zu den Aufgaben von Philosophiegeschichte nach Martin Heidegger.* Weinheim: Acta Humaniora, 1989.

Cairns, Dorion. *Conversations with Husserl and Fink.* The Hague: Martinus Nijhoff, 1976.

Carr, David. *The Paradox of Subjectivity: The Self in the Transcendental Tradition.* New York: Oxford University Press, 1999.

Courtine, Jean-François, "Relève-Répétition." In *Les fins de l'homme: A partir du travail de Jacques Derrida,* edited by Philippe Lacoue-Labarthe and Jean-Luc Nancy. Paris: Galilée, 1981.

Cumming, Robert Denoon. "Giving Back Words: Things, Money, Persons." *Social Research* 48 (summer 1981).

———. *Human Nature and History: A Study of the Development of Liberal Political Thought.* 2 vols. Chicago: University of Chicago Press, 1969.

———. "The Odd Couple: Heidegger and Derrida." *Review of Metaphysics* 34 (March 1981).

———. *Phenomenology and Deconstruction.* 4 vols. Chicago: University of Chicago Press, 1991–2001.

———. *Starting Point: An Introduction to the Dialectic of Existence.* Chicago: University of Chicago Press, 1979.

Derrida, Jacques. *Adieu à Emmanuel Lévinas.* Paris: Galilée, 1997.

———. *Apories.* Paris: Galilée, 1996.

———. *Les fins de l'homme: A partir du travail de Jacques Derrida.* Edited by Philippe Lacoue-Labarthe and Jean-Luc Nancy. Paris: Galilée, 1981.

———. *Limited Inc. a b c.* Translated by Samuel Weber. Evanston, IL: Northwestern University Press, 1988.

———. *Margins of Philosophy.* Translated by Alan Bass. Chicago: University of Chicago Press, 1982.

———. *Mémoires pour Paul de Man.* Paris: Galilée, 1988.

———. *Of Grammatology.* Translated by Gayatri Chakravorty Spivak. Baltimore: Johns Hopkins University Press, 1974.

———. *Of Spirit: Heidegger and the Question.* Translated by Geoffrey Bennington and Rachel Bowlby. Chicago: University of Chicago Press, 1989.

———. "*Ousia* and *grammē.*" In *Margins of Philosophy,* translated by Alan Bass. Chicago: University of Chicago Press, 1982.

———. *Points de suspension.* Paris: Galilée, 1992.

———. *Spectres de Marx.* Paris: Galilée, 1993.

———. *Speech and Phenomena.* Translated by David B. Allison. Evanston: Northwestern University Press, 1973.

———. "The Time of a thesis: punctuations." In *Philosophy in France Today,* edited by Alan Montefiore. Cambridge: Cambridge University Press, 1983.

Diemer, Alwin. *Edmund Husserl.* Meisenheim am Glan: Anton Hain, 1956.

Fell, Joseph P. "Seeing a Thing in a Hidden Whole: The Significance of *Besinnung* in *Die Grundbegriffe der Metaphysik.*" *Heidegger Studies* 10 (1994): 91–109.

Fink, Eugen. "Husserl's Philosophy and Contemporary Criticism." In *The Phenomenology of Husserl,* edited and translated by R. O. Elveton. Chicago: Quadrangle Books, 1970; Bloomington: Indiana University Press: 1988.

Franzen, Winfried. "Die Sehnsucht nach Härte und Schwere." In *Heidegger und die praktische Philosophie,* edited by Annemarie Gethmann-Siefert and Otto Pöggler. Frankfurt: Suhrkamp, 1988.

Gadamer, Hans-Georg. *Philosophical Apprenticeships.* Translated by Robert R. Sullivan. Cambridge: MIT Press, 1985.

———. *Truth and Method.* Translated by Joel Weinsheimer and Donald G. Marshall. New York: Crossroad, 1989.

Glendinning, Simon. *On Being with Others.* New York: Routledge, 1998.

Granel, Gérard. "Remarques sur le rapport de *Sein und Zeit* et de la phénoménologie Husserlienne." In *Durchblicke, Martin Heidegger zum 80 Geburtstag.* Frankfurt: Vittorio Klostermann, 1970.

Habermas, Jürgen. *The Philosophical Discourse of Modernity.* Translated by F. Lawrence. Cambridge: MIT Press, 1987.

Heidegger, Martin. *The Basic Problems of Phenomenology.* Gesamtausgabe 24. Translated by Albert Hofstadter. Bloomington: Indiana University Press, 1982.

———. *Being and Time.* Gesamtausgabe 2. Translated by John Macquarrie and Edward Robinson. New York: Harper & Row, 1962.

———. *Being and Time.* Gesamtausgabe 2. Translated by Joan Stambaugh. Albany: State University of New York Press, 1996.

———. *Die Grundprobleme der Phänomenologie* (Wintersemester 1919/20). Gesamtausgabe 58. Edited by Hans-Melmuth Gander. Frankfurt: Vittorio Klostermann, 1997.

———. "Drei Briefe Martin Heideggers an Karl Löwith." In *Zur philosophischen Aktualität Heideggers,* edited by Dietrich Papenfuss and Otto Pöggeler. Vol. 2. *Im Gespräch der Zeit.* Frankfurt: Vittorio Klostermann, 1990.

———. *Einführung in die phaenomenologische Forschung.* Gesamtausgabe 17. (Lectures given 1923–24.) Edited by Frederich-Wilhelm von Hermann. Frankfurt: Vittorio Klostermann, 1994.

———. "The End of Philosophy and the Task of Thinking." In *On Time and Being* (*Zur Sache des Denkens*), Gesamtausgabe 14, translated by Joan Stambaugh. New York: Harper & Row, 1972.

———. *Être et temps.* Gesamtausgabe 2. Translated by François Vézin. Paris: Gallimard, 1986.

———. *Frühe Schriften.* Gesamtausgabe 1. Edited by Friedrich Wilhelm von Herrmann. Frankfurt: Vittorio Klostermann, 1978.

———. *The Fundamental Concepts of Metaphysics.* Gesamtausgabe 29/30. Translated by William McNeill and Nicholas Walker. Bloomington: Indiana University Press, 1984.

———. *Hegel's Phenomenology of Spirit.* Gesamtausgabe 32. Translated by Parvis Emad and Kenneth Maly. Bloomington: Indiana University Press, 1988.

———. *History of the Concept of Time: Prolegomena* (*Prolegomena zur Geschichte des Zeitbegriff*). Gesamtausgabe 20. Translated by Theodore Kisiel. Bloomington: Indiana University Press, 1985.

———. *Hölderlins Hymne "Der Ister."* Gesamtausgabe 53. Frankfurt: Vittorio Klostermann, 1989.

———. *Introduction to Metaphysics.* Gesamtausgabe 40. Translated by Ralph Manheim. New Haven: Yale University Press, 1959.

———. *Kant und das Problem der Metaphysik.* Gesamtausgabe 3. Edited by Friedrich-Wilhelm von Herrmann. Frankfurt: Vittorio Klostermann, 1991.

———. "Les séminarires." In *Questions III et IV,* edited by Jean Beaufret. Paris: Gallimard, 1976.

———. "The Letter on Humanism." Translated by Frank A. Capuzzi. In *Martin Heidegger: Basic Writings,* edited by David Farrell Krell. 2d rev. ed. New York: Harper & Row, 1993.

———. *The Metaphysical Foundations of Logic.* Gesamtausgabe 26. Translated by Michael Heim. Bloomington: University of Indiana Press, 1984.

———. "My Way to Phenomenology." In *On Time and Being (Zur Sache des Denkens),* Gesamtausgabe 14, translated by Joan Stambaugh. New York: Harper & Row, 1972.

———. *Nietzsche.* 4 vols. Gesamtausgabe 6. Edited and translated by David Farrell Krell. New York: Harper & Row, 1979–1987.

———. "Only a God Can Save Us." In *The Heidegger Controversy: A Critical Reader,* edited by Richard Wolin. Cambridge: MIT Press, 1933.

———. *On the Way to Language.* Translated by Peter D. Hertz. San Francisco: HarperCollins, 1971.

———. *Ontologie. Hermeneutik der Faktizität.* Gesamtausgabe 63. Edited by Käte Bröcker-Oltmanns. Frankfurt: Vittorio Klostermann, 1988.

———. "The Origin of the Work of Art." In *Poetry, Language, Thought,* translated by Albert Hofstadter. New York: Harper & Row, 1971.

———. *Pathmarks.* Gesamtausgabe 5. Edited by William McNeill. Cambridge: Cambridge University Press, 1998.

———. *Phänomenologie—lebendig oder tot?* Karlsruhe: Badenia Verlag, 1969.

———. *Phänomenologie der Anschauung und des Ausdrucks. Theorie der Philosophischen Begriffsbildung.* Gesamtausgabe 59. Edited by Claudius Strube. Frankfurt: Vittorio Klostermann, 1993.

———. *Phänomenologie des religiösen Lebens.* Gesamtausgabe 60. Edited by Claudius Strube. Frankfurt: Vittorio Klostermann, 1995.

———. *Plato: Sophistes.* Gesamtausgabe 19. Edited by Ingeborg Schuffler. Frankfurt: Vittorio Klostermann, 1992.

———. *Questions III et IV.* Edited by Jean Beaufret. Paris: Gallimard, 1976.

———. *Reden und andere Zeugnisse eines Lebensweges.* Gesamtausgabe 16. Edited by Hermann Heidegger. Frankfurt: Vittorio Klostermann, 2000.

———. *Schelling's Treatise on the Essence of Human Freedom.* Gesamtausgabe 42. Translated by Joan Stambaugh. Athens: Ohio University Press, 1985.

———. "The Self-Assertion of the German University." (Rectoral Address.) In

The Heidegger Controversy: A Critical Reader, edited by Richard Wolin. Cambridge: MIT Press, 1933.

———. *What Is Metaphysics?* Translated by David Farell Krell. In *Martin Heidegger: Basic Writings,* edited by David Farrell Krell. 2d rev. ed. New York: Harper & Row, 1993.

———. *What Is a Thing?* Translated by W. B. Barton, Jr., and Vera Deutsch. Chicago: Henry Regnery, 1967.

———. *What Is Philosophy?* Translated by William Kluback and Jean T. Wilde. New Haven, CT: Twayne, 1958.

———. *Zur Bestimmung der Philosophie.* Gesamtausgabe 56/57. Edited by Bernd Heimbuchel. Frankfurt: Vittorio Klostermann, 1987.

Heidegger, Martin, and Elisabeth Blochmann. *Martin Heidegger, Elisabeth Blochmann: Briefwechsel, 1918–1969.* Marbach: Deutsche Schillergesellschaft: 1989.

Héring, Jean. "La phénoménologie d'Edmund Husserl il y a trente ans." *Revue internationale de philosophie* 2 (January 1939).

———. "Souvenirs et réflexions." In *Edmund Husserl, 1859–1959. Phaenomenologica* 4 (1959).

Herrmann, Friederich-Wilhelm von. *Der Begriff der Phänomenologie bei Heidegger und Husserl.* Frankfurt: Vittorio Klostermann, 1981.

———. *Hermeneutische Phänomenologie des Daseins. Eine Erläuterung von Sein und Zeit.* Vol. 1. Frankfurt: Vittorio Klostermann, 1987.

Hocking, William Ernest. "From the Early Days of the *Logische Untersuchungen.*" In *Edmund Husserl, 1859–1959. Phaenomenologica* 4 (1959).

Hopkins, Burt C. *Intentionality in Husserl and Heidegger.* Dordrecht: Kluwer, 1993.

Husserl, Edmund. *Briefe an Ingarden.* Edited by Roman Ingarden. The Hague: Martinus Nijhoff, 1968.

———. *Briefwechsel.* Edited by Karl Schuhmann. 9 vols. Dordrecht: Kluwer, 1994.

———. *Cartesian Meditations: An Introduction to Phenomenology.* Translated by Dorian Cairns. The Hague: Martinus Nijhoff, 1960.

———. *The Crisis of European Sciences and Transcendental Phenomenology.* Translated by David Carr. Evanston, IL: Northwestern University Press, 1970.

———. *Experience and Judgment.* Translated by James S. Churchill and Karl Ameriks. Evanston, IL: Northwestern University Press, 1973.

———. *Husserl: Shorter Works.* Edited by Peter McCormick and Frederick Elliston. South Bend, IN: University of Notre Dame Press, 1981.

———. [*Ideas I*]. *Ideas Pertaining to a Pure Phenomenology and to a Phenomenological Philosophy. First Book: General Introduction to a Pure Phenomenology.* Translated by Fred Kersten. The Hague: Martinus Nijhoff, 1983.

———. [*Ideas I*]. *Ideas Pertaining to a Pure Phenomenology and to a Phenome-*

nological Philosophy. Translated by W. R. Boyce Gibson. London: Routledge and Kegan Paul, 1931.

——. *[Ideen 3]. Ideen zu einer reinen Phänomenologie und phänomenologischen Philosophie. Drittes Buch.* Husserliana 5. Edited by Marly Biemal. The Hague: Martinus Nijhoff, 1952.

——. *An Introduction to the Logical Investigations* (1913). Edited by Eugen Fink. Translated by Philip Bossert and Curtis Peters. The Hague: Martinus Nijhoff, 1975.

——. Letter to Hugo Munsterberg. In *Husserl: Shorter Works,* edited by Peter McCormick and Frederick Elliston. South Bend, IN: University of Notre Dame Press, 1981.

——. *Logical Investigations.* Translated by J. N. Findlay. 2 vols. London: Routledge & Kegan Paul, 1970.

——. *L'origine de la géométrie.* Translated by Jacques Derrida. Paris: Presses Universitaires, 1974.

——. *Phantasie, Bildbewusstsein, Erinnerung.* Husserliana 23, edited by Eduard Marbach. The Hague: Martinus Nijhoff, 1980.

——. *Phenomenological Psychology.* Translated by John Scanlon. The Hague: Martinus Nijhoff, 1977.

——. "Phenomenology and Anthropology." In *Husserl: Shorter Works,* edited by Peter McCormick and Frederick Elliston. South Bend, IN: University of Notre Dame Press, 1981.

——. *Philosophy as Rigorous Science.* In *Phenomenology and the Crisis of Philosophy,* translated by Quentin Lauer. New York: Harper and Row, 1963.

——. *Psychological and Transcendental Phenomenology and the Confrontation with Heidegger, 1927–1931.* Translated and edited by Thomas Sheehan and Richard E. Palmer. Dordrecht: Kluwer, 1997.

——. "Randbemerkungen Husserls zu Heideggers *Sein und Zeit.*" *Husserl Studies* 11 (1994).

——. *Zur phänomenologie des inneren Zeitbewusstseins.* Husserliana 10. Edited by Rudolph Boehm. The Hague: Martinus Nijhoff, 1966.

Hyppolite, Jean. "Existence et dialectique dans la philosophie de Merleau-Ponty." *Les temps modernes* 184–185 (October 1961).

Ingarden, Roman. "Edith Stein on Her Activity as an Assistant of Edmund Husserl." *Philosophy and Phenomenological Research* 23 (1962).

James, Henry. *The Art of Criticism.* Chicago: University of Chicago Press, 1986.

——. *Letters.* Edited by Leon Edel. Vol. 4. Cambridge: Harvard University Press, 1984.

Jaspers, Karl. *Philosophische Autobiographie.* Munich: Piper, 1977.

Kisiel, Theodore. *The Genesis of Heidegger's "Being and Time."* Berkeley: University of California Press, 1933.

——. "The New Translation of *Sein und Zeit.*" *Man and World* 30 (1997).

———. "On the Way to *Being and Time:* Introduction to the Translation of Heidegger's *Prolegomena zur Geschichte des Zeitbegriffs.*" *Research in Phenomenology* 15 (1985).

Klostermann, Vittorio, ed. *Durchblicke. Martin Heidegger zum 80 Geburtstag.* Frankfurt: Vittorio Klostermann, 1970.

Kusch, Martin. *Language as a Calculus vs. Language as a Medium: A Study of Husserl, Heidegger, and Gadamer.* Dordrecht: Kluwer, 1989.

Lévinas, Emmanuel. "La ruine de la réprésentation." In *Phaenomenologica* 4. The Hague: Martinus Nijhoff, 1959.

———. *The Theory of Intuition in Husserl's Phenomenology.* Translated by André Orianne. Evanston, IL: Northwestern University Press, 1973.

———. *Totalité et infini.* The Hague: Martinus Nijhoff, 1971.

Löwith, Karl. *My Life in Germany before and after 1933.* Translated by Elizabeth King. Urbana: University of Illinois, 1994.

Marion, Jean-Luc. *Réduction et donation: Recherches sur Husserl, Heidegger, et la phénoménologie.* Paris: Presses Universitaires de France, 1989.

Merleau-Ponty, Maurice. "La philosophe et son ombre." In *Signes.* Paris: Gallimard, 1960.

———. *The Phenomenology of Perception.* Translated by Colin Smith. New York: Humanities Press, 1962.

———. *Sense and Non-Sense.* Translated by Hubert L. Dreyfus and Patricia Allen Dreyfus. Evanston, IL: Northwestern University Press, 1973.

———. *Signes.* Paris: Gallimard, 1960.

———. *The Structure of Behavior.* Translated by Alden L. Fischer. Boston: Beacon Press, 1968.

Michelfelder, Diane P., and Richard E. Palmer, eds. *Dialogue and Deconstruction: The Gadamer-Derrida Encounter.* Albany: State University of New York Press, 1989.

Mill, John Stuart. *A System of Logic Ratiocinative and Inductive.* London: Longmans, Green, 1941.

Misch, Georg. *Lebensphilosophie und Phänomenologie.* Stuttgart: Teubener, 1967.

Montaigne, Michel de. *Essais.* Edited by Albert Thibaudet. Paris: Editions de la Nouvelle Revue Française, 1937.

Neske, Gunter, and Emil Kettering, eds. *Antwort.* Pfullingen: Verlag Gunter Neske, 1988.

Petzet, H. W. *Encounters and Dialogues with Martin Heidegger, 1929–1976.* Translated by Parvis Emad and Kenneth Maly. Chicago: University of Chicago Press, 1993.

Philipse, Herman. *Heidegger's Philosophy of Being: A Critical Interpretation.* Princeton, NJ: Princeton University Press, 1998.

Pöggeler, Otto. "Heidegger Heute." In *Heidegger,* edited by Otto Pöggeler. Cologne: Kiepenheuer & Witsch, 1970.

———. *Martin Heidegger's Path of Thinking*. Translated by Daniel Magurschak and Sigmund Barber. Atlantic Highlands, NJ: Humanities Press, 1987.

Prauss, Gerold. *Knowing and Doing in "Being and Time."* Translated by Gary Steiner and Jeffrey S. Turner. Amherst, NY: Humanity Books, 1999.

Richardson, William J. *Heidegger: Through Phenomenology to Thought.* The Hague: Martinus Nijhoff, 1963.

Rorty, Richard. "The Historiography of Philosophy: Four Genres." In *Philosophy in History,* edited by Richard Rorty, J. B. Schneewind, and Quentin Skinner. Cambridge: Cambridge University Press, 1984.

———. *Philosophy and the Mirror of Nature.* Princeton, NJ: Princeton University Press, 1979.

Sallis, John. "Où commence *Être et temps?*" In *"Être et Temps" de Martin Heidegger.* Paris: Sud, 1989.

Sartre, Jean-Paul. *Being and Nothingness.* Translated by Hazel Barnes. New York: Philosophical Library, 1956.

———. "Conscience de soi et connaissance de soi." *Bulletin de la société française de philosophie 3* (April–June 1948).

———. *Les carnets de la drôle de guerre.* 2d ed. Paris: Gallimard, 1995.

———. *Les mots.* Paris: Gallimard, 1964.

———. *L'existentialism est un humanisme.* Paris: Nagel, 1970.

———. *L'imaginarie.* Paris: Gallimard, 1940.

———. *Nausea.* Translated by Lloyd Alexander. New York: New Directions, 1964.

———. *The Philosophy of Jean-Paul Sartre.* Edited and translated by Robert Denoon Cumming. New York: Vintage, 1972.

———. *Sartre: Un film réalisée par Alexandre Astruc et Michel Contat.* Paris: Gallimard, 1977.

———. *Situations.* 10 vols. Paris: Gallimard, 1947–76.

———. "Une idée fondamentale de la phénoménologie de Husserl: Intentionalité." In *Situations,* vol. 1. Paris: Gallimard, 1947.

Schuhmann, Karl, ed. *Husserl-Chronik.* The Hague: Martinus Nijhoff, 1977.

———. "Zu Heideggers Spiegel-Gespräch uber Husserl." *Zeitschrift fur Philosophische Forschung* 32 (1978).

Searle, John R. "Reiterating the Differances: A Reply to Derrida." In *Glyph,* vol. 1. Baltimore: John Hopkins University Press, 1977.

Souche-Dagues, Denise. "La lecture husserlienne de *Sein und Zeit.*" *Philosophie* 21 (1959).

Spiegelberg, Herbert. *The Context of the Phenomenological Movement.* The Hague: Martinus Nijhoff, 1981.

Steiner, George. "Review of Paul Celan: *Marterialien.*" *Times Literary Supplement,* February 10–16, 1989.

Storck, Joachim W. "Martin Heidegger and Elisabeth Blochmann." In *Martin Heidegger: Politics, Art, and Technology.* Edited by Karsten Harries and Christoph Jamme. New York: Holmes & Meier, 1994.

Taminiaux, Jacques. "Heidegger and Husserl's *Logical Investigations.*" In *Dialectic and Difference,* Translated by Robert Crease and James T. Decker. Atlantic Highlands, NJ: Humanities Press, 1989.

Towarnicki, Frédéric de. *À la rencontre de Heidegger.* Paris: Gallimard, 1992.

van Buren, John. *The Young Heidegger.* Bloomington: Indiana University Press, 1944.

Abhebung. See *Weg der Abhebung*
absorption (*Aufgehen in*), 189–95; and ambulatory idiom, 192; and being-by, 189, 191;
Dasein as absorbed in *Das Man,* 236; depsychologization of, 197–200, 279n.9; double
meaning in Heidegger's employment of, 193–
95, 200, 236; Heidegger's introduction of terminology of, 190; Husserl and, 190, 193–94
abstraction, nominalistic analysis of, 112–13
access (*Zugang*): *Destruktion* for gaining, 210;
Heidegger denying immediate accessibility of
knowledge, 81, 83, 90, 91, 191–92, 193; Heidegger on proper method for gaining, 166;
Heidegger on tradition as blocking, 87, 93,
210; Heidegger's mode of investigation for
gaining, 208–9; Husserl on immediate givenness, 58, 81, 82, 83, 89–90, 96, 191–92, 193;
and *Öffentlichkeit,* 244; the reductions for
gaining, 25; as thematic in Heidegger, 244;
translation and access to phenomenology, 11–
12, 94; and *Umgang,* 191; and *zu,* 160
affective meaning, 126
affiliation: as not an issue in *Being and Time,*
285n.19; phenomenology as affiliated with
geometry, 19, 20, 46, 50–51, 59, 70, 155,
228; significant differences in, 97; and style,
177
a-letheia, 252
ambiguity, 109–19; eidetic reduction eliminating,
71, 109–10, 187–88; essential distinctions for
eliminating, 123, 152; Heidegger playing up,
110, 157, 274n.8; in Heidegger's translation of
Plato's *Sophist,* 72–74; in Heidegger's use of
Aufgehen in, 193–95, 200, 236; Husserl on
elimination of, 109–10, 125–26, 158, 186,

ambiguity (continued)
194, 236, 274n.8; of images, 125;
of sign for Husserl, 91–92, 109–
18, 193, 218, 219–20; in translating Heidegger, 157
Anglo-American analytic philosophy:
and Continental philosophy, 6, 28,
31, 259n.1; and Continental
refugees, 9–10
aporia, 75–77, 210
Aristotle, 31, 32, 59, 66, 179, 193,
264n.11
association of ideas, 111, 144
attitude (Einstellung): and "traction"
(Zug) in Heidegger, 212; and style,
178. See also natural attitude
Aufgabe, 83
Aufgehen in. See absorption
Aufhebung, 169, 276n.9
Ausarbeitung: Being and Time on,
24–25, 38; and Heidegger's Auslegung, 82, 83; and Heidegger's stylistic violence, 180; on Husserl's
research manuscripts, 21, 23, 25,
83; and style, 177–78; translation
as, for Husserl, 70; Umarbeitung
distinguished from, 25, 230–31
Ausgang. See starting point
Auslegung, 82–84, 166
Austin, John, 31, 263n.8
authenticity, 73, 269n.9

Basic Problems of Phenomenology,
The (Heidegger): on Destruktion,
87–88, 89, 90, 95; on method of
ontology, 58–59, 268n.16; on primary familiarity, 185, 186; retrieval in, 73–74, 88; on three
components of phenomenology,
56–58, 66
Beaufret, Jean, 49, 231, 237, 241,
243, 248
Beauvoir, Simone de, 61
Becker, Oskar, 60, 63, 131, 142,
268n.16
Begriff. See concept

Being and Nothingness (Sartre): Heidegger and subtitle of, 47; and
Heidegger's break with Sartre,
243; Husserl and Heidegger as reconciled in, 169; translation into
English, 11
Being and Time (Heidegger): Abhebung in, 148, 152; advance announcements in, 60–61, 131,
142–43; ambiguities regarding
Husserl in, 44–46, 266n.6; ambulatory idiom in, 189–93, 200, 208;
on Ausarbeitung, 24–25, 38; as
beginning in middle of Platonic dialogue, 67, 109, 186; blur in, 48–
49, 83–84, 152–53; as breaking
away from Husserl, 37–38; on
breakthrough of Husserl, 44, 89;
concept construction in, 38, 175–
88; "Dasein and Speech. Language," 222–23; dedication of, 68,
238, 249–50; Derrida on starting
point of, 192; Descartes displacing
Husserl in, 217; on Destruktion,
87–92; fame brought to Heidegger
by, 7; first German word of, 67;
first step of, 64–67; on floor idiom, 218–19; Husserl as laying
foundation for, 43, 44–45, 49, 82,
83, 91; Husserl becoming irrelevant in, 219; Husserl not cited in,
43–44, 78, 196, 211; and Husserl
on inner consciousness of time, 23,
262n.16; Husserl on theological-
ethical talk in, 223, 235; and
Husserl's Logical Investigations,
34, 44–46, 91; Husserl's marginal
notes to, 23–24, 32, 44, 45, 48,
53, 153, 212–13, 223, 281n.19;
Husserl's presentation copy of, 68,
80; and intentional analysis, 209;
"Involvement and Meaning: The
Worldliness of the World," 148;
language becoming theme of, 217–
24; "lurch" (Ruck) in, 46–47, 65,
81, 118; method and subject as

overlapping in, 157, 159, 163, 207; method as sequential in, 58–61, 91, 93, 131–33, 143, 147, 149, 268n.15, 273n.1; "The Necessity for an Explicit Retrieval of the Question of Being," 64–65; no passage way from Husserl to, 77–78; on ontology, 50, 52; periods in section titles of, 222, 281n.8; on phenomenological construction, 57; "The Phenomenological Method of Investigation," 46, 47, 56, 60, 80–81, 132, 166, 266n.6, 272n.1, 274n.8; Plato's *Sophist* cited in, 66–69, 72–77, 79–80, 185–86, 210, 223, 244; preamble, 66, 223; "precipice" in, 222–23; preparation in, 209; *Prolegomena* as "draft" of, 37, 38, 196, 197, 200–201, 211; on psychologism, 196–203; publisher of, 249; reductions ignored in, 56; retrieval in, 64–69, 88, 132; second preamble of, 148–49, 150; as shift in method from Husserl, 54–63; as shift in subject from Husserl, 43–53, 110, 128; as startling deviation, 34, 121; on style, 179–80; on theory of knowledge, 204–14; translation of, 94; as translation of Husserl, 49–50, 51, 52, 80, 202; *Versäumnis* in, 118; visual idiom in, 193; way idiom in, 58, 61, 74–75; on *Zeug*, 129

being-by, 189, 190, 191

being-in, 173–214; and being-by, 189, 190; and concern, 280n.5; different relations entailed by, 183–84, 186–87, 188; and Heidegger's defense of his language, 179; Husserl undercut by, 194, 197, 221, 234; the "in" of, 175–76; represented as knowing the world, 204

being-in-the-world, 148–49; and being-in as such, 175–76; as Da-

sein's fundamental structure, 149, 150, 194, 199; directionality of, 201, 209; isolation of sense-perception in Husserl, 206; and reference, 160; relational structure of, 152, 153

Bentham, Jeremy, 269n.21

Bernet, Rudolph, 96, 275n.8

Bewandtnis (involvement), 145, 146, 180, 206

Biemel, Walter, 97, 252

Blanchot, Maurice, 33

Blochmann, Elisabeth, 7–8, 260n.13

blur, the, 48–49, 83–84, 152–53

boundaries, 100–106; Derrida deconstructing, 103–5, 124; Heidegger and disputes over, 203; Husserl defending, 104, 193, 236

Boyce Gibson, William R., 9, 16, 31

breakdown in communication: between Anglo-American and Continental philosophy, 6, 28, 31; as cliché, 27; as confrontation, 30–32; between Heidegger and other philosophers, 283n.17; in Heidegger's "Introduction to the Phenomenology of Religion" course, 29–30; between Husserl and Heidegger, 23, 27–39, 93, 96, 222, 225, 236–42; interruptive transformation as, 115–17; between Sartre and Merleau-Ponty, 27, 34–37

Brentano, Franz, 205

Buchheim, Thomas, 90

Cairns, Dorion, 7, 10, 230

care, 280n.5

caricature, 126

Cartesian Meditations (Husserl), 4, 15, 225, 229, 230

Celan, Paul, 245, 284n.25

clarification: eidetic reduction for, 80, 118, 271n.6; Husserl on Heidegger's transposition of, 50; Husserl's method of, 80–81, 104, 115, 131, 152, 153, 210, 244, 270n.26

closeness (proximity), 97, 158, 191–92, 195, 223, 279n.6
cogito, 90, 229
collaboration: Husserl seeking fellow workers, 17–22, 24; Merleau-Ponty on, 35; phenomenological reduction as stumbling block to, 20
common sense, Heidegger's philosophy contrasted with, 7–8
communication, 215–58; dialogue, 35, 233; difficulties in, 1–39; and Gerede for Heidegger, 235; Heidegger on difficulty of, 186–88; Husserl on, 5, 22, 118–19, 220, 224–33, 235; Husserl relegating to others, 232; indicative signs in, 226; and inside-outside distinction for Heidegger, 217, 221–22, 234, 244; as irrelevant to logic (phenomenology) for Husserl, 115, 229, 232, 235; Öffentlichkeit, 239, 240–45; phenomenological analysis contrasted with, 119; phenomenological reduction for resolving difficulties in, 19–20. See also breakdown in communication
complexity (Umständlichkeit), 38, 179, 180–82
concealment, 81
concept (Begriff): Destruktion accompanied by construction of, 89–91, 93, 140, 161; examples for arriving at, 156, 209; Handlichkeit and, 158; Heidegger's construction of, 175–88; Husserl on objective meaning-content of, 113
concern, 206, 210, 211, 212–13, 280n.5
consciousness: intentionality of, 19, 46, 55, 90, 96, 129, 133; logic as dealing with, 102; Sartre on duplicity of, 125; subjectivity of, 55, 254, 258
construction, 175–88; accompanied by Destruktion, 89–91, 93, 140, 161; eidetic reduction contrasted

with, 156; Heidegger on phenomenological, 57
context, 137–47; circumstances as, 274n.6; eidetic reduction and real, 141; Heidegger giving priority to, 150; Heidegger on real, 139, 141, 157; Heidegger's shift in, 140, 205; Husserl on ideal, 137, 138, 139, 157; shift from Historie to Geschichte of being, 247–48, 251–52. See also Umwelt
Continental philosophy: and Anglo-American philosophy, 6, 28, 31, 259n.1; refugees to England and America, 9–10
Courtine, Jean-François, 264n.8
Crisis of the European Sciences, The (Husserl), 4, 15, 38–39, 98, 225
criteria, 213

Dasein: as absorbed in Das Man, 236; as already outside, 221, 234; and being-by, 189, 191; being-in-the-world as fundamental structure of, 149, 150, 194, 199; as directional, 128, 131, 157, 209; and everyday interpretedness, 235, 244, 245; everydayness of, 223, 234; as exemplary being, 130; Existenz for, 168; falling of, 223, 235; Husserl equating man with, 130; meaning and ontology of Dasein for Heidegger, 218, 219; as "meaning to itself," 146; Öffentlichkeit and disclosure of, 244; seeing primordial structure of, 189, 190, 192–93
deconstruction, 85–106; Derrida's Speech and Phenomena and, 94; and Heidegger's Destruktion, 88, 95; interruptive transformation entailed by, 116; and retrieval, 88
deformalization, 137–38
De la grammatologie (Derrida), 97
Derrida, Jacques: on aporia, 77; boundaries deconstructed by, 103–5, 124; confrontation with

Foucault, 30; confrontation with Searle, 31, 53, 263n.8; *De la grammatologie*, 97; direct confrontation rejected by, 264n.8; on ethics of discussion, 33; on etymological variation in Husserl, 51; *Fug* as interpreted by, 182; and Gadamer, 264n.9; and Habermas, 264n.12; on Heidegger and translation, 70, 72; Husserl and Heidegger treated separately by, 37; on Husserl postponing problem of language, 103, 105, 124, 227; on Husserl's prudent silence, 118; on Husserl's theory of signs, 94, 95, 100–105, 124, 271n.1; on indicative signs, 117; indifference to methodological differences of, 97–98; interruptive transformation of Husserl, 115–16; on metaphysics of presence, 96–97, 192; on oppositional logic, 65, 125, 127, 271n.4; on the other, 33, 265n.19; procedure of this study contrasted with that of, 94; proximity and presence elided by, 192, 279n.6; on regaining the experience of language, 116, 117, 118; shift in subject in, 103, 104, 116; on sign "in general," 101, 120, 132; on starting point of *Being and Time*, 192; on text, 116. See also *Speech and Phenomena*

Descartes, René: *Discourse on Method*, 59; as displacing Husserl in *Being and Time*, 217; Heidegger contrasting himself with, 90, 152, 169, 217; Heidegger's *Destruktion* of geometrical space of, 163; Husserl's *Cartesian Meditations*, 4, 15, 225, 229, 230; *Meditations*, 230; sequence in thinking of, 59; universal doubt of, 88

Destruktion, 87–92; access gained through, 210; access warranting adoption of, 244; and ambulatory

idiom, 191; for arriving at Greek sources, 92; in *Basic Problems of Phenomenology*, 87–88, 89, 90, 95; construction in conjunction with, 89–91, 93, 140, 161; and deconstruction, 88, 95; distinguished from *Zerstörung*, 88; and Heidegger's stylistic violence, 180; and the tradition at large, 88–89, 168, 169, 253

dialectic, 140, 257, 276n.9

dialogue, 35, 233

"Dialogue on Language, A" (Heidegger), 248, 249

Diemer, Alwin, 267n.20

difficulty: *aporia*, 75–77, 210; of communicating results for Husserl, 187–88; in communication, 1–39; Heidegger's difficulties securing understanding, 7–8; for Heidegger with respect to the start, 64; Husserl and Heidegger differing on, 25, 75, 100, 109, 110, 155–56, 251; Husserl encountering, 4–6, 8–9, 263n.29; Husserl on origin of phenomenology's, 189; method shaped by conception of, 109; of ontology, 179; phenomenological reductions disposing of, 19; phenomenology as difficult, 5, 25, 62, 75, 109; philosophies conceiving differently, 208; philosophy as difficult to understand, 5, 25; in Plato's *Sophist*, 66, 67, 68, 72, 75–77, 79; reflexive relatedness as, 59, 61; *Schwierigkeiten*, 4, 79, 155; *Umständlichkeit* (complexity), 38, 179, 180–82. See also *Verlegenheit*

Dilthey, Wilhelm, 282n.9

direction: being-in-the-world's directionality, 201, 209; in comparing philosophies, 164; Dasein as directional, 128, 131, 157, 209; Heidegger as privileging, 131; Heidegger on Husserl's perverted

direction (*continued*)
  direction of interpretation, 166,
    169; and Heidegger's *Destruktion*
    of Descartes, 163; Husserl on Hei-
    degger misunderstanding his, 164;
    of Husserl's reductions, 165; as
    methodological criterion for Hei-
    degger, 163; as not a difficulty for
    Husserl, 133, 141; prefixes and
    prepositions for indicating, 158,
    168–69, 250; as problem for Hei-
    degger, 133, 141, 157; "to" in "to
    the things themselves," 254–55
directional signal. *See* indicator, the
disclosure, 81, 244
Discourse on Method (Descartes), 59
distinctions. *See* essential distinctions
durch, 76, 82
Dussort, Henri, 21, 262n.8

eidetic reduction, 18–19; abstraction
  contrasted with, 113; ambiguity
  eliminated by, 71, 109–10, 187–
  88; and clarity, 80, 118, 271n.6;
  direction of, 165; and *eidos*, 19,
  71; essences intuited by, 19, 46,
  114, 154; for essential distinctions,
  124, 125; examples in, 19, 129,
  130–31, 159, 209; Heidegger as
  ignoring, 46, 50; Heidegger on
  one-sidedness of, 155; Heidegger's
  construction contrasted with, 156;
  in *Ideas I*, 56; and immediate
  givenness, 192; and indicative
  signs, 122–23; intentionality as
  crucial example of, 19, 113, 129;
  in *Logical Investigations*, 55–56,
  98; and Sartre's *l'imaginaire*,
  266n.9; shift in level with, 46, 114,
  154, 155; two kinds of sign distinguished by, 110
eidos, 19, 70–71, 72, 114, 268n.2
Eigentlichkeit, 73, 74
Einrichtung, 163, 201
Einsicht (insight), 19, 139, 140, 143,
  193, 275n.7

Einstellung. *See* attitude
empirical generalization, 113–14
empiricism, 14
Encyclopaedia Britannica, 9, 23, 69,
  231, 232, 262n.16
"End of Philosophy and the Task of
  Thought, The" (Heidegger), 248,
  252, 253, 258
epochē: Heidegger's *Destruktion* undertaken in opposition to, 95,
  280n.12; and Husserl's commitment to "the things themselves,"
  44, 88–89, 90, 209
ēporēkamen, 75–77, 79, 110, 140,
  208
equipment, 159–60; as conspicuous
  when unutilizable, 169, 170; as
  etwas-um-zu, 160, 201; examples
  in Husserl's analysis of intentionality, 161, 162; hammer as, 129,
  158, 167; the indicator as, 130,
  158, 159, 160; as nearest, 191;
  readiness-to-hand of, 142, 156,
  158; and reference, 142, 156, 160,
  161, 205; a room as equipment for
  dwelling, 162–63, 201
Erinnerung (historical recollection),
  74, 88
essences: eidetic reduction for intuitions into, 19, 46, 114, 154; *eidos*,
  19, 70–71, 72, 114, 268n.2; examples in emergence of, 19, 129;
  facts distinguished from, 127, 129,
  154, 165; Heidegger on essence-
  fact distinction, 154–55; in
  Husserl's oppositional structure,
  127; immediacy of intuition of, 55,
  89, 143, 193; insight (*Einsicht*)
  into, 19, 139, 140, 143, 193,
  275n.7; *Wesen*, 19, 71, 72
essentia, 72
essential distinctions: and clarification, 152; for delimitation of logic,
  114, 142, 145; disorganizing,
  117–18; eidetic reduction for arriving at, 124, 125; Heidegger's de-

construction of Husserl's, 123–24, 145; Husserl's as one-sided, 123, 125, 126, 127, 154, 183, 226; between phenomenological analysis and communication of results, 226
everydayness, 223, 234, 235, 241, 281n.10
examples: in eidetic reduction, 19, 129, 130–31, 159, 209; in Heidegger, 129–31, 143–44, 159–60; in Husserl, 129, 143, 156, 159, 161–62; in Sartre, 129, 156
existentia, 167, 168
Existentialism Is a Humanism (Sartre), 242, 243, 283n.17
Existenz, 168
experimental psychology, 18
expressive sign (expression): eidetic reduction abstracting, 221; facial expressions distinguished from, 115, 127, 158; Heidegger and, 122, 145, 219–21; Husserl as privileging, 124, 126, 127; Husserl's restrictive use of, 126, 142; indicative sign contrasted with, 102, 111, 114, 115, 228; and meaning, 111, 115–16, 145–47, 220; outspokenness replacing in Heidegger, 220, 234

facial expressions, 115, 126, 127, 158
familiarity (*Vertrautheit*): as familiar and colloquial term, 146; and Heidegger's defense of his language, 179; Husserl on familiar objects, 188; as mode of conduct, 183–85; primary familiarity, 185–86; of referential whole, 200; with relations, 146–47
Fichte, Johann Gottlieb, 31
Findlay, J. N., 9, 194
Fink, Eugen, 231–32
fittingness, 185, 187, 188
formalization, 137–38, 274n.1
Foucault, Michel, 30

Franzen, Wilfred, 180
free variation, 19, 113, 155
Freilegung, 83
Fürsorge, 245, 284n.24

Gadamer, Hans-Georg, 231, 264n.9, 284n.24
garment, 193
geometry: Heidegger's *Destruktion* of Descartes's geometrical space, 163; phenomenology as affiliated with, 19, 20, 46, 50–51, 59, 70, 155, 228
Gerede (talkativeness; loquacity), 222, 235, 241
German language, 72, 77
Glendinning, Simon, 259n.9
Granel, Gérard: on "blur" in *Being and Time*, 48–49, 83, 152–53; on brusqueness in Heidegger, 48, 64; on Heidegger on his relation to Husserl, 43, 53; on question of being for Husserl, 48–49, 186; translation idiom in, 49
Grimm, Jacob, 177, 179, 184, 189, 197

Habermas, Jürgen, 264n.12
hammer, 129, 158, 159, 167, 183, 213
Handlichkeit (manipulability), 158, 159, 167–69, 170, 183
Hegel, Georg Wilhelm Friedrich, 55, 152, 253, 254, 258, 267n.2, 276n.9
Heidegger, Martin: ambiguity played up by, 110, 157, 274n.8; as Aristotle to Husserl's Plato, 31; Blochmann correspondence, 7–8, 260n.13; breakdown in communication with Husserl, 23, 27–39, 93, 96, 222, 225, 236–42; breakdown in personal relations with Husserl, 32, 236–42, 283n.9; breakdowns in communication with other philosophers, 283n.17;

Heidegger, Martin (*continued*)
breaking off in "Introduction to
the Phenomenology of Religion"
course, 29–30; colloquial and conceptual as ambiguous in, 73; common sense contrasted with
philosophy of, 7–8; on concept
construction, 175–88; Derrida on
differences between Husserl and,
94; and Derrida on metaphysics
of presence, 96; "A Dialogue on
Language," 248, 249; dialogue
stressed by, 233; difficulties in securing understanding, 7–8; direction as privileged in, 131; direction
as problem for, 133, 141, 157; as
disciple of Husserl, 23, 38, 69, 89,
196, 204; "The End of Philosophy
and the Task of Thought," 248,
252, 253, 258; on essence-fact distinction, 154–55; examples in,
129–31, 143–44, 156–57, 159–
60; on expression, 122, 145, 219–
21; *Festschrift* for Husserl, 68,
279n.1; on following, 24,
262n.21, 284n.24; as going his
own way, 22–24; holism of, 175,
198, 253, 255, 276n.7; on Husserl
confusing logic and psychology,
102; Husserl criticized in guise of
the tradition, 88, 168, 198, 221,
253; Husserl disappearing from
work of, 38, 219, 247; Husserl in
later work of, 247–51; Husserl on
confusing phenomenology with
empirical science by, 102; and
Husserl on difficulty, 25, 75, 100,
109, 110, 155–56, 251; Husserl
on Heidegger misunderstanding
his direction, 164; and Husserl on
work, 24–26, 62; on Husserl's
analysis of signs, 91–92, 110,
120–25, 132–33, 138, 145–46,
160–61, 218, 252–53; and
Husserl's *The Crisis of the Euro-*
pean Sciences, 38–39; and
Husserl's *Encyclopaedia Britan-*
nica article, 23, 69, 231, 232,
262n.16; on Husserl's intentional
analysis, 139–41, 162, 275n.8;
and Husserl's *Internal Conscious-*
ness of Time manuscripts, 23, 25;
and Husserl's later works, 225,
230; Husserl's public criticism of,
18, 202, 236–42, 261n.3; and
Husserl's "You and I are phenomenology," 14, 32; hyphens used by,
182–83; idiom in, 75; immediate
givenness denied by, 81, 83, 90,
91, 191–92, 193; impasse between
Husserl and, 77–78, 217–19, 225,
235, 251; incomprehensible
opaqueness of, 177; indicative sign
rehabilitated by, 127, 219; indifference to differences in method, 258;
interest in relation of Husserl and,
37; *Introduction to Phenomeno-*
logical Research, 61, 66, 176; on
"isms" in philosophy, 242; and
Jaspers, 7, 24; *Kant and the Prob-*
lem of Metaphysics, 274n.8; "Letter on Humanism," 61, 242–43,
247–48, 268n.18, 283n.17; Lévinas influenced by, 12; Merleau-
Ponty as reconciling Husserl and,
37; method and subject as overlapping in, 157, 159, 163, 207, 209;
as misundersting phenomenology
to Husserl, 5; and Nazism, 180,
239, 242, 243, 263n.21, 265n.35,
283nn. 9, 19; on *Öffentlichkeit*
(publicity), 240–45; "opening up"
in Heidegger opposed to "clarification" in Husserl, 80–81; "The
Origin of the Work of Art,"
278n.12; personal and philosophical issues distinguished by, 32, 36;
personal conduct of, 238–40;
postwar accusations against, 239;
on priority of context, 150; prior-

ity of method denied by, 54–55, 60, 207, 210, 267n.2; on psychologism, 196–203; real context in, 139, 141, 157; rectoral address of, 270n.22; on reference, 137, 141, 142, 143, 144–45, 146; reflexivity of analysis of, 190, 279n.6; relational analysis of, 141–42, 143, 149, 151, 160, 161, 205–8, 222, 244; restriction in analysis of signs of, 141–43, 145–46; Sartre as reconciling Husserl and, 37, 47, 169–70; Sartre attacked by, 242–43, 283n.17; as seducer of the young to Husserl, 23; shift in context in, 140, 205; shift in method in, 54–63, 123–24, 139, 140, 186, 191, 206–7; shift in subject in, 124, 139, 144, 186, 191, 194–95, 196, 204–6; on signs, 78, 132–33, 137, 141–46, 218; on single move for grasping things themselves, 208–9, 280n.12; as slow thinker, 61; *Der Spiegel* interview on break with Husserl, 32, 202, 236, 239, 240, 241, 245; starting point of, 132, 147, 166, 167, 186; style of, 177, 178–80; on theory of knowledge, 185, 186, 204–14; titles for, 34; "to the subject itself," 47, 55, 57, 152, 214, 253; "To the Subject of Thinking," 253, 254; "to the things themselves," 44, 46–47, 57–58, 160, 213–14, 253; on translating Greek into Latin, 71–72, 210; violent style of, 180, 183; *On the Way to Language*, 92; "What Is Metaphysics?" 23, 223–24; "What is Philosophy?" 34; on wholes and parts, 150–51; Zähringen seminar, 37, 49, 120, 248, 253; *Zur Bestimmung der Philosophie* lectures, 202–3. See also *Basic Problems of Phenomenology, The; Being and Time;* "My

Way to Phenomenology"; *Prolegomena*

Héring, Jean, 18, 20, 21

Herrmann, Friedrich-Wilhelm von, 90, 266n.6

historical recollection (*Erinnerung*), 74, 88

historicity, 90

history of philosophy: breakdowns in communication in, 31–32; chronology in, 11; Heidegger dealing with tradition as a whole, 88, 168, 198, 221, 253; Heidegger on *Destruktion* of, 90; Heidegger on *Rückblick* over, 252; kinks in, 93–94

Hobbes, Thomas, 110

Hocking, William Ernest, 6

Hofstadter, Albert, 180

holism, 175, 198, 253, 255, 276n.7

Hopkins, Burt, 275n.8

horizon, 122, 223, 234, 241

Hoy, David, 259n.9

Husserl, Edmund: on absorption (*Aufgehen in*), 190, 193–94; ambiguity eliminated by, 109–10, 125–26, 158, 186, 194, 236, 274n.8; assistants of, 20–22; becoming irrelevant in *Being and Time*, 219; *Being and Time* as shift in method from, 54–63; *Being and Time* as shift in subject from, 43–53, 110; *Being and Time* as translation of, 49–50, 51, 52, 80, 202; *Being and Time* not citing, 43–44, 78, 196, 211; *Being and Time*'s ambiguities regarding, 44–46, 266n.6; *Being and Time*'s dedication to, 68, 238, 249–50; boundaries defended by, 104, 193, 236; breakdown in communication with Heidegger, 23, 27–39, 93, 96, 222, 225, 236–42; breakdown in personal relations with Heidegger, 32, 236–42, 283n.9; *Cartesian*

Husserl, Edmund (*continued*)
Meditations, 4, 15, 225, 229, 230;
on clarification, 80, 115, 131, 152,
153, 210, 244, 270n.26; on communication, 5, 22, 118–19, 220,
224–33, 235; on construction,
89–91; *The Crisis of the European
Sciences,* 4, 15, 38–39, 98, 225;
on criticisms of his phenomenology, 232; Derrida on differences
between Heidegger and, 94; Derrida on theory of signs of, 94, 95,
100–105, 117, 124, 271n.1; Derrida's interruptive transformation
of, 115–16; difficulties encountered by, 4–6, 8–9, 263n.29; diffidence regarding publication, 22,
25; direction as not a difficulty for,
133, 141; as disappearing from
Heidegger's work, 38, 219, 247;
disciples sought by, 14, 18; "the
dream is over," 16; *Encyclopaedia
Britannica* article of, 9, 23, 69,
231, 232, 262n.16; on English philosophy and phenomenology,
260n.15; essential distinctions of,
123–24, 125, 126, 127, 183, 226;
etymological variation in, 51; examples in, 129, 143, 156, 159,
161–62; fellow workers sought by,
17–22, 24; foundation of *Being
and Time* laid by, 43, 44–45, 49,
82, 83, 91; Freiburg lectures of
1923–24, 15; Heidegger and later
works of, 225, 230; Heidegger as
disciple of, 23, 38, 69, 89, 196,
204; and Heidegger as going his
own way, 22–24; on Heidegger
as seducer of the young, 23; on
Heidegger confusing phenomenology with empirical science, 102;
on Heidegger misunderstanding
his direction, 164; Heidegger on
analysis of signs of, 91–92, 110,
120–25, 132–33, 138, 145–46,

160–61, 218, 252–53; Heidegger
on confusion of logic and psychology by, 102; and Heidegger on difficulty, 25, 75, 100, 109, 110,
155–56, 251; Heidegger on intentional analysis of, 139–41, 162,
275n.8; and Heidegger on work,
24–26, 62; Heidegger publicly
criticized by, 18, 202, 236–42,
261n.3; and Heidegger's *Destruktion,* 88–89; Heidegger's *Festschrift* for, 68, 279n.1; in Heidegger's later work, 247–51; and
Heidegger's Nazism, 242, 283n.9;
Heidegger's startling deviation
from, 34, 121; on his students going their own way, 11, 16, 23; on
ideal context, 137, 138, 139, 157;
on immediate givenness, 25, 55,
57, 81, 82, 83, 89–90, 96, 133,
191–92, 193; impasse between
Heidegger and, 77–78, 217–19,
225, 235, 251; inability to collaborate of, 231–33; inability to finish
of, 4, 15, 16; intentional analysis
of, 60, 80, 139–41, 162, 175, 182,
254–55, 275n.8; interest in relation of Heidegger and, 37; *Internal
Consciousness of Time* manuscripts of, 21, 23, 25; interruptive
transformation of Mill, 117; introductions as characteristic genre of,
4; on invariance, 20; invitation
from University of Southern California, 10; Jewishness of, 15–16,
238; lecture style of, 238; London
lectures of, 9, 15, 28; marginal
notes in *Being and Time,* 23–24,
32, 44, 45, 48, 53, 153, 212–13,
223, 281n.19; Merleau-Ponty as
reconciling Heidegger and, 37; and
Merleau-Ponty on interrelation-
ship, 257, 285n.19; as "miserable
beginner, 4, 15, 150; on misinterpretations of phenomenology, 5,

232, 237, 254; as monologist, 231; on no alternative to reading his work, 12; no passage way to *Being and Time* from, 77–78; on the object, 81, 138, 149; one-sided oppositions in, 123, 125, 126, 127, 183, 226; personal and philosophical issues distinguished by, 32, 36; on phenomenological movement, 20, 45, 165; phenomenology as interruption for, 4, 261n.7; "Philosophy and Anthropology" lecture, 230, 238; *Philosophy as Rigorous Science,* 22–23, 223–24, 237, 282n.12; on philosophy as rigorous science, 58; on "picture-book phenomenology," 20, 82, 261n.6; as Plato to Heidegger's Aristotle, 31; presentation copy of *Being and Time,* 68, 80; "principle of principles" of, 55, 89, 96, 191; on priority of method, 54–56, 60, 91, 95, 207, 210; psychologism opposed by, 102–3, 112, 114, 205, 226; *Randbemerkungen,* 267n.20; on reactivating the original experience, 22, 25; references to Heidegger disappearing in, 38–39; reflective character of analysis of, 190; research manuscripts of, 21–22, 231; on *Rückgang* in Heidegger, 66; Sartre and Merleau-Ponty differing on, 27, 34; Sartre approaching via Lévinas, 12, 33; Sartre as reconciling Heidegger and, 37, 47, 169–70; and Sartre on meaning, 125–27; Sartre translating, 43, 78, 269n.20; shift in level in, 46, 51–52, 98, 112, 114, 154, 155, 165; shift in method in, 113–15; shift in subject in, 102, 105, 110, 112, 114, 140, 271n.4; and *Sophist* citation in *Being and Time,* 68–69; as starting over again, 21–22, 25–26, 99; starting

point of, 101; and style, 177–78; "Supplement to My Ideas," 237; on theological-ethical talk in *Being and Time,* 223, 235; "to the things themselves," 44, 46–47, 55, 62, 89, 90, 133, 209, 213, 232, 235, 236, 253; and tradition at large for Heidegger, 88, 168, 198, 221, 253; translation into English of, 8–9; *Tua res agitur,* 13–14, 20, 228; on uniqueness of his thought, 13; "You and I are phenomenology," 14, 32; zigzag procedure of, 59–60, 62, 149, 165. See also *Ideas I; Logical Investigations*
hyphens, 146, 182–83
Hyppolite, Jean, 35

Ideas I (Husserl): on act and object, 278n.1; on ambiguity of words, 118; on clarification, 153; Derrida downplaying differences between *Logical Investigations* and, 98–99; eidetic reduction in first part of, 56; *eidos* in, 71; English translation of, 9, 16; examples in Husserl's analysis of intentionality in, 161; on expression and meaning, 145, 220; first published formulation of phenomenological reduction in, 20; as foundational for Husserl, 45; Husserl as dissatisfied with, 25; Husserl's inability to follow up on, 4; *Logical Investigations* as superseded by, 24, 25, 45, 89; on natural attitude, 165, 188, 229; ontology in, 47; period of struggle culminating in, 15; phenomenological reduction in second part of, 56, 165, 176, 229; on phenomenology as methodologically foundational, 46; on possibility and actuality, 46; on presupposing nothing, 88–89; priority of method in, 55–56, 267n.2; Sartre's

Ideas I (Husserl) *(continued)*
interruptive transformation of,
117; shift in level in, 154; on simple meditations in first person singular, 229
*"idée fondamentale de la philosophie
de Husserl, Une—Intentionnalité"*
(Sartre), 256, 285n.16
images, ambiguity of, 125
imaginaire, L' (Sartre): on caricature,
126; Husserl translated in, 43; on
interplay, 125; and relation between Husserl and Sartre, 181;
shift in subject in, 47, 266n.9; as
written while Sartre was disciple of
Husserl, 12, 261n.6
imagination, L' (Sartre), 161
imagination, Sartre on, 125
impersonation, 125, 126
indicative sign, 120–27; communication relying on, 226; defined, 112;
Derrida on Husserl's notion of,
117; Derrida privileging, 124; expressive sign contrasted with, 102,
110–11, 114, 115, 228; Heidegger
as rehabilitating, 127, 219; Heidegger on Husserl's examples of,
121–23; Heidegger's indicator as,
128, 139, 219; in Husserl's oppositional structure, 127; as irrelevant
to logic for Husserl, 139, 140; as
meaningless, 111; psychological
origin of, 144; and reference,
144
indicator, the (directional signal),
128–33; as equipment, 130, 158,
159, 160; as indicative sign, 128,
139, 219; ontological conclusion
drawn from, 131, 183; overlap in
Heidegger's analysis of, 157; readiness-to-hand of, 156, 158, 159,
168; relational context indicated
by, 139, 143–44; and *Umwelt,*
139, 140, 142
Ingarden, Roman, 21, 22, 262n.8

insight (*Einsicht*), 19, 139, 140, 143,
193, 275n.7
intentional analysis: *Being and Time*
as no longer, 209; in Heidegger's
Prolegomena, 207–8; Heidegger's
shift from Husserl's, 139–41, 162,
275n.8; of Husserl, 60, 80, 139–
41, 162, 175, 182, 254–55,
275n.8; and relational analysis recurring in phenomenology, 255–57
intentionality: Brentano on significance of, 205; and care, 280n.5; of
consciousness, 19, 46, 55, 90, 96,
129, 133; as crucial example of
eidetic reduction, 19, 113, 129;
examples in Husserl's analysis of,
161–62, 205, 206, 229; Husserl
reformulating concept of, 60; Merleau-Ponty and Sartre differing on,
256–57, 285n.16; as objectivating
for Husserl, 166; as obstruction to
phenomenology, 208–9. *See also*
intentional analysis
Internal Consciousness of Time
(Husserl), 21, 23, 25
interplay, 125–27
interpretative tendencies, 209–10
intimating, 227–28
*Introduction to Phenomenological
Research* (Heidegger), 61, 66, 176
intuition: in eidetic reduction, 19;
Heidegger's criticism of Husserl's
intuitive method, 82; Husserl on
immediacy of objects of, 55, 81,
82, 89–90, 191–92, 193; insight
(*Einsicht*), 19, 139, 140, 143, 193,
275n.7
involvement (*Bewandtnis*), 145, 146,
180, 206

James, Henry, 11–12, 27, 29, 263n.2
James, William, 8, 28, 29
Jaspers, Karl: communication difficulties with Heidegger, 7; on contemplation and laziness, 24, 263n.26;

Heidegger asking about work, 24; and Heidegger's Nazism, 243, 265n.35; *Psychology of World Views*, 24

Kant, Immanuel, 31, 104, 124, 274n.8
Kant and the Problem of Metaphysics (Heidegger), 274n.8
Kennzeichen, 122
Kisiel, Theodore: *Aufgehten in* translation of, 199; on Dasein as going about, 190; on formal indication in *Being and Time*, 274n.1; on Heidegger as wanting to communicate, 177; on Heidegger's advance announcements, 142–43, 268n.16; *Umgang* translation of, 157; *Umständlichkeit* translation of, 180
knowledge: Heidegger and Husserl differing on, 213; Husserl on immediate givenness of, 25, 55, 57, 81, 82, 83, 89–90, 96, 133, 191–92, 193. *See also* theory of knowledge

language: becoming theme of *Being and Time*, 217–24; Derrida on Husserl and, 103, 105, 124, 227; Derrida on regaining the experience of, 116, 117, 118; *Gerede*, 222, 235, 241; Husserl postponing problem of, 103, 105, 226–27; Husserl's analysis not depending on, 103, 141; and meaning, 103; Mill's instrumentalist conception of, 106; outspokenness, 220, 234–35. *See also* meaning; translation
Lessing, Gotthold Ephraim, 80
"Letter on Humanism" (Heidegger), 61, 242–43, 247–48, 268n.18, 283n.17
level: eidetic reduction as shift in, 46, 114, 154, 155; flexibility of Hei-

degger's, 159, 169; Hegel's shift in, 276n.8; Heidegger's shift from ontic to ontological, 182–83; *Logical Investigations'* shift in, 112; phenomenological reduction as shift in, 51–52, 98, 165; significant differences in, 97
Lévinas, Emmanuel: Heidegger's influence on, 12; and Husserl's Jewishness, 15–16; on the other, 33, 264n.19; Sartre coming to Husserl via, 12, 33
linguistic turn, 227
logic: communication as irrelevant to, 115; Derrida on oppositional logic, 65, 125, 127, 271n.4; as eidetic science for Husserl, 102, 114; Husserl's *Logical Investigations* on definition of, 101–5; meaning as domain of, 114–15; and psychology, 102–3, 113, 115, 138, 140, 145, 205; unity of, 114
Logic (Mill), 101–5, 111–12, 260n.21
Logical Investigations (Husserl): on ambiguity in term "sign," 91–92, 100, 109–18, 187, 193–94, 218, 219–20; Anglo-American philosophers ignoring, 6; as breakthrough work, 44–45, 89; on communication, 225–29; Derrida downplaying differences between *Ideas I* and, 98–99; Derrida's *Speech and Phenomena* on, 93, 94, 95, 98, 100–105; "The Difficulties of Pure Phenomenological Analysis," 5, 17; "Expression and Meaning," 122, 145, 219, 221; on fellow workers, 17–18; Heidegger on analysis of signs in, 91–92, 120–25; Heidegger on subtitle of, 204; and Heidegger's *Being and Time*, 34, 44–46, 91; Husserl as dissatisfied with, 25, 55; Husserl on a *historisch und sachlich* introduction

Logical Investigations (*continued*)
for, 254; *Ideas I* as superseding, 24, 25, 45, 89; on intentional experience as objectivating, 166; on intentionality, 60; introductions and forewords to, 4, 101, 259n.1; on Mill's logic, 101–5; on phenomenology as descriptive, 82; phenomenology as founded by, 3; on philosophy as work, 24; and priority of method, 55–56; publisher of, 249; question of being in, 49; on language, 103, 141; reviews of, 3; starting point of, 101–2, 105; translation into English, 8–9, 11, 94, 260n.21; volume two as psychological for Heidegger, 201–2; on wholes and parts, 149–51
logical positivism, 9
logocentrism, 102, 105, 127
logos, 146
loquacity (*Gerede*; talkativeness), 222, 235, 241
Löwith, Karl, 270n.22, 284n.24
lurch, the (*Ruck*): as absent in *Being and Nothingness*, 65; in *Being and Time*, 46–47, 65, 81, 118

Macquarrie, John, and Robinson, Edward: and ambiguities in Heidegger's *Sophist* translation, 72, 73, 79; *Aufgehen in* translation of, 190; *der Weg der Abhebung* translation of, 152; *die Hinausgesprochenheit der Rede ist die Sprache* translation of, 220; indentation after *Sophist* citation, 67; *Öffentlichkeit* translation of, 241; and period in section 34 title, 222; *Umgang* translation of, 157; *Umständlichkeit* translation of, 180; *vertraut mit* translation of, 185
Man, Das, 236
manipulability (*Handlichkeit*), 158, 159, 167–69, 170, 183

Marburg school, 202, 208
meaning: affective meaning, 126; as domain of logic for Husserl, 114–15; and expression, 111, 115–16, 145–47, 220; Husserl and Sartre on, 125–27; Husserl postponing problem of, 103; indicative signs not expressing, 111; and language, 103; objective meaning-content, 113; and ontology of Dasein for Heidegger, 218, 219; univocal, 119, 226. *See also* ambiguity; clarification
measurement, 159
Meditations (Descartes), 230
Merkzeichen, 122
Merleau-Ponty, Maurice: analysis repudiated by, 257; breakdown in communication with Sartre, 27, 34–37, 264nn. 8, 19, 265nn. 20, 24; on fabric (*tissu*) of a text, 272n.13; interrelatedness as preoccupation of, 257; as not confrontational, 264n.8; on phenomenology as style, 278n.7; *Phenomenology of Perception*, 11, 257–58; as reconciling Husserl and Heidegger, 37; and Sartre differing on intentionality, 256–57, 285n.16; Sartre on caution of, 258; on work of the other, 35, 245, 256
metaphysics: Derrida on metaphysics of presence, 96–97, 192; Heidegger on fundamental question of, 224; Heidegger on scientific rigor and, 224, 237. *See also* ontology
method: *Being and Time* as shift in, 54–63; conception of difficulty as shaping, 109; Heidegger's indifference to differences in, 258; Heidegger's presented in its applications, 151–52; Heidegger's shift in, 54–63, 123–24, 139, 140, 186, 191, 206–7; Husserl on priority of, 54–

56, 60, 91, 95, 207, 210, 267n.2; phenomenology as concept of method for Heidegger, 46; proximity and Heidegger's, 192; relational versus intentional analysis, 255–56; Sartre's shift in, 125, 126; as sequential in Heidegger, 58–61, 91, 93, 131–33, 143, 147, 149, 268n.15, 273n.1; significant differences in, 97; a single philosophical method, 177; and style, 177; and subject as overlapping in Heidegger, 157, 159, 163, 207, 209; and way in Heidegger, 58, 74, 75, 76
Mill, John Stuart: Husserl on *Logic* of, 101–5, 111–12, 260n.21; instrumentalist conception of language of, 106; nominalistic analysis of abstraction of, 112
Misch, Georg, 266n.13
Mithebung, 151, 187, 188, 222
modes of conduct, 131, 183–85
Momente, 151
monologue, 227–28, 231
Montaigne, Michel de, 265n.20
Mühsam, Erich, 237, 238
Mühsam, Heinrich, 238
"My Way to Phenomenology" (Heidegger): and Husserl, 248–51; only beginning and end of phenomenology in, 255; on second volume of *Logical Investigations*, 201–2, 203; "to" in title of, 250; way idiom in title of, 58, 191

Natorp, Paul, 202, 204, 267n.2
natural attitude: as factual level, 165; familiar natural objects belonging to, 188; Heidegger's everydayness replacing, 223; in phenomenological reduction, 165; as starting point, 165, 212; things as "on hand" for, 165, 167; as unnatural for Heidegger, 212

Nausea (Sartre), 170
neo-Kantianism, 20, 57, 89, 202, 281n.16
Niemeyer, Max, 249, 250
Nietzsche, Friedrich, 156, 276n.7
nominalism, 112–13

object: Husserl and direction toward, 133, 141; Husserl on objects of use, 166; Husserl's clarification of term, 81; in Husserl's intentional analysis, 175, 182; in Husserl's ontology, 138; priority over relation in Husserl, 138, 139, 149; relations in Heidegger's analysis of, 139, 151
objective meaning-content, 113
offenbar, 79–80, 210, 244
Öffentlichkeit (publicity), 239, 240–45
On the Way to Language (Heidegger), 92
ontology: Heidegger as transforming phenomenology into, 47; Heidegger on ancient, 64, 66; Heidegger on difficulty of, 179; Heidegger on sequential method of, 58–59; Heidegger on traditional categories of, 50, 52, 176; Husserl on concept of an object, 138; meaning and ontology of Dasein for Heidegger, 218, 219
opening the door example, 209, 211
oppositional logic, 65, 125, 127, 271n.4
"Origin of the Work of Art, The" (Heidegger), 278n.12
other, the: Derrida on, 33, 265n.19; and differences between Husserl and Heidegger, 36; Heidegger's *Fürsorge* for, 245; Lévinas on, 33, 264n.19; Merleau-Ponty on, 35, 245, 256; Sartre on, 35, 245, 256
outspokenness, 220, 234–35
Oxford philosophy, 8

Palmer, Richard E., 262n.16
Parmenides (Plato), 179
parts, and wholes, 149–51
Petzet, Heinrich, 239
phenomenological reduction, 19–20;
  and clarity, 80; direction of, 165;
  Heidegger on, 56–57, 165; in
  Ideas I, 56, 165, 176, 229; in Logical Investigations for Derrida, 98;
  shift in level in, 51–52, 98, 165; as
  stumbling block to collaboration,
  20; as transcendental reduction,
  261n.5; transcendental solitude
  resulting from, 230
phenomenology: as blending into
  modern thinking for Merleau-
  Ponty, 257–58; chronology of
  Anglo-American understanding of,
  11; communication as irrelevant to
  Husserl's, 229, 232, 235; as "concept of method" for Heidegger, 46;
  Continental philosophy as dominated by, 3, 5–6; demarcated from
  psychology in Heidegger's Prolegomena, 205; as description for
  Husserl, 82; as difficult, 5, 25, 62,
  75, 109; disappearing as a title for
  Heidegger, 249, 250, 251–52; discussion as having no place in
  Husserl's, 231; as eidetic science,
  19, 46, 50–51, 228; fellow workers for settling most important
  questions of, 17–18; as first personal for Husserl, 230; geometry
  as affiliate of, 19, 20, 46, 50–51,
  59, 70, 155, 228; Heidegger depsy-
  chologizing, 196; Heidegger on
  theme determined by mode of
  analysis, 204, 206–7, 210, 213;
  Heidegger on three basic components of, 56–58; Husserl on Heidegger confusing with empirical
  science, 102; Husserl on origin of
  difficulty of, 189; Husserl on unassailable claim to truth of, 232;

Logical Investigations as founding,
  3; as methodologically foundational for Husserl, 46; phenomenologist refugees in England and
  America, 9–10, 11; as possibility
  for Heidegger, 45, 46; relational
  and intentional analysis recurring
  in, 255–57; Sartre translating into
  empirical psychology, 78; transcendental ego in, 20; translation
  and access to, 11–12, 94; as Umarbeitung for Husserl, 25, 26, 60
Phenomenology of Perception (Merleau-Ponty), 11, 257–58
phenomenon, 81, 132
Philipse, Herman, 272n.1
philosophy: conceptions of difficulty
  in, 208; as difficult to understand,
  5, 25; direction in comparing
  philosophies, 164; exposition of
  relations between philosophers,
  62–63; as giving things back their
  weight for Heidegger, 110, 155;
  Heidegger on "isms" in, 242; interruptive transformation between
  philosophers, 115–17; Merleau-
  Ponty on work of the philosopher,
  257; methodological differences
  in, 97; no one begins thinking
  philosophically on his own, 13–
  14; the personal versus the philosophical, 32, 240; a single philosophical method, 177; translation
  in, 49–50, 219; two traditions in,
  3–10. See also Anglo-American
  analytic philosophy; Continental
  philosophy; history of philosophy;
  metaphysics; phenomenology; theory of knowledge
"Philosophy and Anthropology" lecture (Husserl), 230, 238
Philosophy as Rigorous Science
  (Husserl), 22–23, 223–24, 237,
  282n.12
physis, 279n.9

Pitkin, Walter, 8
Plato: Aristotle interpreting, 31, 32; Heidegger's deconstruction of dialectic of, 140; *Parmenides,* 179; "to the subject itself," 253. See also *Sophist*
Pöggeler, Otto, 129
pragmatism, 14
prefixes, 82
presence, 96–97, 192, 279n.6
Presocratics, 97
Prolegomena (Heidegger): on absorption (*Aufgehen in*), 197–99; ambulatory idiom in, 208; on breakthrough of Husserl, 89; as "draft" of *Being and Time,* 37, 38, 196, 197, 200–201, 211; on eidetic reduction, 155; on Heidegger as disciple of Husserl, 37–38, 69, 89, 196, 204; Heidegger's undertaking blurred with Husserl's in, 83–84; on Husserl's analysis of signs, 120–21; on Husserl's intentional analysis, 275n.8; on Husserl's perverted direction of interpretation, 166, 169; intentional analysis in, 207–8; "opening up" attributed to Husserl by, 83; phenomenology demarcated from psychology in, 205; preparation in, 209; on referential totality, 200, 206; on starting point of the reductions, 165, 212; straightforwardness called for, 210–12; on style, 178–80; as too psychological, 201; visual idiom in, 198–200
proximity (closeness), 97, 158, 191–92, 195, 223, 279n.6
psychological conduct (*seelischen Verhaltung*), 197, 207–8
psychologism: Heidegger's opposition to, 196–203; Husserl's opposition to, 102–3, 112, 114, 205, 226
psychology: demarcated from phenomenology in Heidegger's *Prole-*

gomena, 205; experimental psychology, 18; Husserl on Sartre transposing phenomenology into, 78; and indicative relation, 111; and logic, 102–3, 113, 115, 138, 140, 145, 205. *See also* psychologism
Psychology of World Views (Jaspers), 24
publicity (*Öffentlichkeit*), 239, 240–45

quaestio, 77

Randbemerkungen (Husserl), 267n.20
rationalism, 14
readiness-to-hand (*Zuhandenheit*): and familiarity, 185; of a hammer, 158, 213; and *Handlichkeit* (manipulability), 158, 159, 167; Husserl on, 213; Sartre and, 170; *Vorhandenheit* contrasted with, 167–68, 169, 183, 277n.10
reductions: *Being and Time* ignoring, 56; Heidegger on starting point of, 165, 212; in Husserl, 18–20. *See also* eidetic reduction; phenomenological reduction
reference: and equipment, 142, 156, 160, 161, 205; examples in Heidegger's construction of, 159, 160–61; Heidegger's use of *Verweisung* for, 144–45; Husserl's use of *Hinweis* for, 144, 145; and involvement, 146; referential totality, 200, 206; and restriction on Heidegger's analysis of signs, 141, 142, 143; and *um-zu,* 160, 168; *Zeigen* as kind of referring, 137
reflection, 189, 190
reflexive relatedness (*Rückbezogenheit*), 59, 61
relation: being-in-the-world's relational structure, 152, 153; in Hei-

relation (*continued*)
   degger's analysis of an object, 139,
   151; and *logos* for Heidegger, 146;
   objects' priority over for Husserl,
   138, 139, 149; and reference for
   Heidegger, 142. *See also* relational
   analysis
relational analysis, 135–71; of Heidegger, 141–42, 143, 149, 151,
   160, 161, 182, 205–8, 222, 244;
   restriction pro tem as trait of,
   141–42; a room as a relational
   totality, 162–63, 200–201
res, 162, 210
Robinson, Edward. *See* Macquarrie,
   John, and Robinson, Edward
Rorty, Richard, 6, 49–50, 157
Ruck. See lurch, the
Rückbezogenheit (reflexive relatedness), 59, 61
Rückblick, 252–54
Rückzeichen, 121, 122, 123

Sallis, John, 66–67, 186
Salmon, Christopher Verney, 9
Sartre, Jean-Paul: bookishness of,
   181; breakdown in communication with Merleau-Ponty, 27, 34–
   37, 264nn. 8, 19, 265nn. 20, 24;
   coming to Husserl via Lévinas, 12,
   33; and essentiality of history of
   being for Heidegger, 248; examples in, 129, 156; *Existentialism Is
   a Humanism*, 242, 243, 283n.17;
   Handlichkeit literalized by, 170;
   Heidegger's attack on, 242–43,
   283n.17; on Heidegger's style,
   177–78; Husserl and Heidegger
   as reconciled by, 37, 47, 169–70;
   and Husserl on meaning, 125–27;
   Husserl translated by, 43, 78,
   269n.20; Husserl understood in
   terms of, 12; "*Une idée fondamentale de la philosophie de Husserl—
   Intentionnalité*," 256, 285n.16;
   L'imagination, 161; interruptive

transformation of Husserl, 117;
   and Merleau-Ponty differing on intentionality, 256–57, 285n.16; on
   Merleau-Ponty's caution, 258; and
   Montaigne, 265n.20; *Nausea*,
   170; rapid pace of work of, 61;
   shift in method in, 125, 126; shift
   in subject in, 115, 125, 126; two-
   sided oppositions in, 125, 127; on
   work of the other, 35, 245, 256.
   See also *Being and Nothingness*;
   imaginaire, L'
Scheler, Max, 12, 18, 91, 237, 239
Schuhmann, Karl, 238
Schwierigkeiten, 4, 79, 155
Searle, John, 31, 53, 263n.8
seeing: of primordial structure of
   Dasein, 189, 190, 192–93; visual
   idiom in Heidegger, 193, 198–200
seelischen Verhaltung (psychological
   conduct), 197, 207–8
sēmainein, 132
sense-perception, 206–7
Sheehan, Thomas, 262n.16
shift. *See* context; lurch, the; level;
   method; subject
sign, 107–33; Derrida's deconstruction of Husserl's treatment of, 94,
   95, 100–105, 271n.1; in general,
   101, 120, 127, 132, 139; Heidegger on Husserl's concept of, 91–
   92, 110, 120–25, 132–33, 138,
   145–46, 160–61, 218, 252–53;
   Heidegger on *Zeigen* and *Zeichen*,
   273n.3; Heidegger's analysis of,
   78, 132–33, 137, 141–46, 218;
   Hobbes's definition of, 110;
   Husserl on ambiguity of, 91–92,
   100, 109–18, 187, 193–94, 218,
   219–20. *See also* expressive sign;
   indicative sign; indicator; language
Smith, Adam, 269n.21
Socrates, 129
soliloquy, 227–28
solipsism, 230
solitude, 230

Sophist (Plato): authenticity as central in, 269n.9; Heidegger's citation of, 66–69, 223; Heidegger's translation of, 72–77, 79–80, 132, 185–86, 210, 244
Sophocles, 76
Souche-Dagues, Denise: on Heidegger's philological acrobatics, 177, 178, 278n.5; on Husserl's misinterpretation of Heidegger, 48, 52, 53, 152, 267n.27
Speech and Phenomena (Derrida): as founding work of deconstruction, 94; on Husserl's *Logical Investigations,* 93, 94, 95, 98, 100–105; on metaphysics of presence, 96; starting point of, 100, 101
Spinoza, 59
Stambaugh, Joan: *die Hinausgesprochenheit der Rede ist die Sprache* translation of, 220; *Öffentlichkeit* translation of, 241; and period in section 34 title, 222; and *Sophist* citation, 67, 79, 185; "to" in "My Way to Phenomenology," 250
starting point (*Ausgang*), 164–71; Derrida on *Being and Time*'s, 192; Derrida on Husserl's, 101; of Derrida's *Speech and Phenomena,* 100, 101; of Heidegger, 132, 147, 166, 167, 186; Heidegger citing Plato on, 34; Heidegger's *Basic Problems* on, 57; of Husserl's *Logical Investigations,* 101–2, 105; of the reductions for Heidegger, 165, 212; as retrieval for Heidegger, 66; in traditional theory of knowledge, 204
startling deviations, of Heidegger from Husserl, 34, 121
Stein, Edith, 21, 22, 23, 150, 262n.12
Steiner, George, 245–46, 284n.25
Storck, Joachim W., 260n.13
Stumpf, Carl, 8
style, 177–80

subject: *Being and Time* as shift in, 43–53, 110, 128; Derrida's analysis of Husserl as shift in, 103, 104, 116; Heidegger's shift in, 124, 139, 144, 186, 191, 194–95, 196, 204–6; Husserl on priority of method over, 54–56, 60, 91, 95, 207, 210; Husserl's logic as shift in, 102, 105, 110, 112, 114, 140, 271n.4; and method as overlapping in Heidegger, 157, 159, 163, 207, 209; Sartre's shift in, 115, 125, 126; "to the subject itself," 47, 55, 57, 152, 214, 253
subjectivism, 205, 258
subject-object relationship, 204–5, 221
"Supplement to My Ideas" (Husserl), 237

talkativeness (*Gerede;* loquacity), 222, 235, 241
text, 116, 272n.13
theory of knowledge, 204–14; Heidegger on traditional, 185, 186, 213; and psychology, 203
things: as objects *vor mir,* 162; *res,* 162, 210; "to the things themselves," 44, 46–47, 55, 62, 89, 90, 133, 209, 213–14, 232, 235, 236, 253–55
threshold, 106, 110
time, 23, 122, 223
"To the Subject of Thinking" (Heidegger), 253, 254
traffic, 140, 157
transcendental ego, 20, 176, 230
transcendental reduction. *See* phenomenological reduction
translation: and access to phenomenology, 11–12, 94; ambiguities in translating Heidegger, 157; as *Ausarbeitung* for Husserl, 70; *Being and Time* as, 49–50, 51, 52, 80, 202; of Greek into Latin, 71–72, 210; in Heidegger, 70–84;

translation (*continued*)
of Husserl by Sartre, 78; Husserl
having no philosophical problems
with, 103; philosophical, 49–50,
219; of Plato by Heidegger, 72–
77, 79–80, 132, 185–86, 210, 244

Übersicht, 139, 140
Umarbeitung: Ausarbeitung distinguished from, 25, 230–31; for
communication of univocal meaning, 119, 226; in Husserl, 99, 101;
phenomenology as, 25, 26, 60
Umgang, 154–63; and absorption,
190–91; as colloquial term becoming concept for Heidegger, 73;
and concern, 213; as "going
about," 75, 157–58, 199; as Heidegger's starting point, 166, 167;
perception and, 208; philosophical
commitment associated with,
158–59; and *pragmata,* 210; and
psychologism, 197
Umsicht, 139, 140
Umständlichkeit (complexity), 38,
179, 180–82
Umwelt: Heidegger on Husserl's
analysis of, 176; Heidegger on
philosophical tradition on, 198–
99; and Husserl's analysis of intentionality, 162; and Husserl's
essence-fact distinction, 154; and
the indicator, 139, 140, 142;
methodological implications of
Heidegger's analysis of, 156–57
universal doubt, 88

Verlegenheit: and *Auslegung,* 82; Heidegger on dialectic as an obstruction, 140; in Heidegger's
translation of *ēporēkamen,* 75, 79–
80, 117, 132, 140, 208, 210, 244
Versäumnis, 49, 118
Vertrautheit. See familiarity
Vézin, François, 180, 186
violence, 180, 183

visual field, 200
Vorhandenheit: in Husserl's analysis
of intentionality, 162, 165–66;
Zuhandenheit contrasted with,
167–68, 169, 183, 277n.10
Vorzeichen, 121, 122, 123, 128

way: and *Abhebung,* 151; and ambulatory idiom, 191; in *Being and
Time,* 58, 61, 74–75; direction for,
141, 157; *Feldweg,* 58, 75, 191;
Heidegger as *weglos,* 202, 206;
and method, 58, 74, 75, 76. See
also *Weg der Abhebung*
Weg der Abhebung, 148–53; and ambulatory idiom, 193; and Hegel's
Aufhebung, 276n.9; and *Mithebung,* 151, 187, 188, 222; and
modes of conduct, 183; and proximity, 192; and relational structure
of being-in-the-world, 151, 153
Welch, E. Parl, 12, 18
Wesen, 19, 71, 72
"What Is Metaphysics?" (Heidegger),
23, 223–24
"What is Philosophy?" (Heidegger),
34
wholes, and parts, 149–51
work: Husserl and Heidegger differing regarding, 24–26, 62; Merleau-Ponty on work of the
philosopher, 257; Sartre and Merleau-Ponty on work of the other,
35, 245, 256. See also *Ausarbeitung;* collaboration; *Umarbeitung*
Wundt, Wilhelm, 18

Zähringen seminar, 37, 49, 120, 248,
253
Zeug, 129
Zugang. See access
Zugehörigkeit, 161
Zuhandenheit. See readiness-to-hand
Zur Bestimmung der Philosophie lec-
tures (Heidegger), 202–3